INTERNATIONAL LAW AND CANNABIS

INTERNATIONAL LAW AND CANNABIS

Regulation of Cannabis Cultivation and Trade for Recreational Use: Positive Human Rights Obligations versus UN Narcotic Drugs Conventions

Volume II

Piet Hein van Kempen
Masha Fedorova

intersentia
Cambridge – Antwerp – Chicago

Intersentia Ltd
8 Wellington Street | Cambridge
CB1 1HW | United Kingdom
Tel.: +44 1223 736 170
Email: mail@intersentia.co.uk
www.intersentia.com | www.intersentia.co.uk

Distribution for the UK and Ireland:
NBN International
Airport Business Centre, 10 Thornbury Road
Plymouth, PL6 7PP
United Kingdom
Tel.: +44 1752 202 301 | Fax: +44 1752 202 331
Email: orders@nbninternational.com

Distribution for Europe and all other countries:
Intersentia Publishing nv
Groenstraat 31
2640 Mortsel
Belgium
Tel.: +32 3 680 15 50 | Fax: +32 3 658 71 21
Email: mail@intersentia.be

Distribution for the USA and Canada:
Independent Publishers Group
Order Department
814 North Franklin Street
Chicago, IL 60610
USA
Tel.: +1 800 888 4741 (toll free) | Fax: +1 312 337 5985
Email: orders@ipgbook.com

International Law and Cannabis. Regulation of Cannabis Cultivation and Trade for Recreational Use: Positive Human Rights Obligations versus UN Narcotic Drugs Conventions

ISBN 978-1-78068-871-8
D/2019/7849/106
NUR 828

GPRC Guaranteed Peer Reviewed Content

British Library Cataloguing in Publication Data. A catalogue record for this book is available from the British Library.

PREFACE

What legal avenues are there to regulate cannabis cultivation and trade for recreational use? This question has generated heated discussions in various societies, in political and academic discourses. Several states are considering or have adjusted their legal and policy approaches towards a more lenient regulation of cannabis cultivation and trade for the recreational user market. These discussions have been the overture for two academic studies that we have conducted recently.

The first study focused on the question to what extent are domestic initiatives involving regulation of cannabis cultivation for recreational use compatible with the relevant UN narcotic drugs conventions and European Union law. It was this question that took centre stage in the political discussion in the Netherlands at that time. The results of this study were presented to the Minister of Justice and Security in the Netherlands in 2014.[1] Because of the limitation of this first study to the framework of UN and EU law regulating drugs only, we decided to complement our research by involving international law more broadly and by looking more specifically at the positive human rights obligations.

The second study covered two questions. First, to what extent can regulation of cannabis for recreational use, for the sake of health, safety and crime control, be considered a positive human rights obligation resulting from the right to health, the right to life, the right to physical and psychological integrity and the right to privacy. In the event this obligation can be established, the second question concerned the hierarchical relationship between these positive human rights obligations and the obligations arising from the UN drugs conventions and EU anti-drugs laws. This second study was presented to politicians in the Netherlands in 2016.[2] Since that time, the developments in the Netherlands have progressed to the extent that the government has decided to set up an experiment for legal supply of cannabis to point-of-sale for recreational use. The legislation concerning this experiment is being prepared as we speak.

---

1 Piet Hein P.H.M.C. van Kempen & Masha I. Fedorova, *Internationaal recht en cannabis. Een beoordeling op basis van VN-drugsverdragen en EU-regelgeving van gemeentelijke en buitenlandse opvattingen pro regulering van cannabisteelt foor recreatief gebruik*, Deventer: Wolters Kluwer, 2014.

2 Piet Hein P.H.M.C. van Kempen & Masha I. Fedorova, *Internationaal recht en cannabis II. Regulering van cannabisteelt en –handel voor recreatief gebruik: positieve mensenrechtenverplichtingen versus VN-drugsverdragen*, Deventer: Wolters Kluwer, 2016.

Due to the topical nature of the issue and the ongoing discussions on national and international levels, we decided to make our both studies available to a broader academic forum to which end these books have been translated and updated:

- Piet Hein. P.H.M.C. van Kempen & Masha I. Fedorova, *International Law and Cannabis I. Regulation of Cannabis Cultivation for Recreational Use under the UN Narcotic Drugs Conventions and the EU Legal Instruments in Anti-Drugs Policy*, Cambridge: Intersentia, 2019.
- Piet Hein P.H.M.C. van Kempen & Masha I. Fedorova, *International Law and Cannabis II. Regulation of Cannabis Cultivation and Trade for Recreational Use: Positive Human Rights Obligations versus UN Narcotic Drugs Conventions*, Cambridge: Intersentia, 2019.

For the fine translation work we are indebted to Mr. Paul de Wit, *Dutch Translations*, London. We are also grateful to the publishing house Intersentia for their patience and support in publishing the two books.

All errors are our own. The sources have been updated and all the websites were accessible on 1 January 2019.

Piet Hein van Kempen and Masha Fedorova

CONTENTS

LIST OF CASES AND DECISIONS

INTERNATIONAL COURT OF JUSTICE

INTERNATIONAL CRIMINAL TRIBUNAL FOR THE FORMER YUGOSLAVIA

HUMAN RIGHTS COMMITTEE

COMMITTEE ON ECONOMIC, SOCIAL AND CULTURAL RIGHTS

COMMITTEE ON THE RIGHTS OF THE CHILD

EUROPEAN COURT OF HUMAN RIGHTS

EUROPEAN COMMISSION OF HUMAN RIGHTS

COURT OF JUSTICE OF THE EUROPEAN UNION

EUROPEAN COMMITTEE OF SOCIAL RIGHTS

INTER-AMERICAN COMMISSION ON HUMAN RIGHTS

ARBITRAL TRIBUNAL

LIST OF ABBREVIATIONS

CESCR	Committee on Economic, Social and Cultural Rights
CJEU	Court of Justice of the European Union
CND	Commission on Narcotic Drugs
CSC	Cannabis Social Clubs
ECommHR	European Commission of Human Rights
ECOSOC	Economic and Social Council
ESC	European Social Charter
ECSR	European Committee of Social Rights
ECtHR	European Court of Human Rights
EU	European Union
ECHR	European Convention on Human Rights
GA	General Assembly
GC	Grand Chamber
I-ACionHR	Inter-American Commission on Human Rights
I-ACtHR	Inter-American Court of Human Rights
ICJ	International Court of Justice
ICTY	International Criminal Tribunal for the former Yugoslavia
ILC	International Law Commission
INCB	International Narcotics Control Board
ICCPR	International Covenant on Civil and Political Rights
ICESCR	International Covenant on Economic, Social and Cultural Rights
HRC	Human Rights Committee
OJ	Official Journal (of EU)
CoE	Council of Europa
SC	Security Council
Trb.	Tractatenblad
UN	United Nations
UNODC	United Nations Office on Drugs and Crime
UDHR	Universal Declaration of Human Rights
UN	United Nations
WHO	World Health Organization
WTO	World Trade Organization

CHAPTER 1
INTRODUCTION

1.1. RATIONALE AND PURPOSE OF THE RESEARCH

In our first book on *International Law and Cannabis I*, a legal analysis leads us to the conclusion that the UN narcotic drugs conventions and the EU laws on drugs leave no room for legalization, decriminalization, policy-based tolerance and/or other forms of regulation of cannabis cultivation for the recreational user market.[1] Because of the obligations for states arising from these international instruments with respect to fighting drugs, there is no room for regulating the cultivation of cannabis for supplying points-of-sale (wholesale, retail shops), in the context of so-called Cannabis Social Clubs or via other modalities involving recreational use of cannabis by third parties. This conclusion about the international drug regulations still stands as far as we are concerned.

This does not alter the fact that the above-mentioned book is limited in scope. It concerns itself only with the international drug regulations, not with the way these relate to other legal norms. At the time, there was a lot to be said for that focus and that is still the case even now, for reasons of substance and research methodology. In that respect, a perspective that had been much wider from the outset would have made it considerably more difficult to get a grip on the detailed and multi-layered subject matter of those drug regulations. However, this does not in any way imply that the wider perspective is of no relevance. In the aforementioned book, we have therefore explicitly pointed out that international human rights may be germane to the discussion about the cannabis issue – that is to say: the question whether it is legally permissible under international law to regulate cannabis cultivation and trade for the recreational use of cannabis.

That potential relevance of international human rights depends, among other things, on arguments that are presented in favour of the regulated permission of cannabis cultivation and trade. After all, opinions to that effect are often based on considerations that individual and public health, the safety of individuals, preventing nuisances and fighting crime would be achieved

---

1 Piet Hein P.H.M.C. van Kempen & Masha I. Fedorova, *International Law and Cannabis I. Regulation of Cannabis Cultivation for Recreational Use under the UN Narcotic Drugs Conventions and the EU Legal Instruments in Anti-Drugs Policy*, Cambridge: Intersentia, 2019 (further referred to without subtitle).

better with such tolerance than with a more prohibitive and repressive policy on drugs and/or cannabis. That is interesting from the point of view of human rights, since human rights conventions give rise to, among other things, positive obligations to protect individual and public health, the safety of citizens and to control crime. The preceding constitutes the justification for the research in this book, which effectively forms a diptych together with the first book on *International Law and Cannabis I*. Where the first book offers a strictly internal legal perspective on the drugs conventions, this book adds to it an external legal perspective, to wit from the point of view of human rights.

1.2. CENTRAL QUESTION AND DESIGN OF THE RESEARCH

Given the potential relevance of international human rights for the cannabis issue outlined above, the following two questions are paramount in this research:

> To what extent can regulation of cannabis cultivation and trade for recreational use, for the sake of public health, safety and crime control, be married to positive human rights obligations that ensue from international human rights conventions?

Only to the extent that this is possible, does the second key question arise:

> To what extent can positive human rights obligations that justify or necessitate the regulated permission of cannabis cultivation and trade leave the national governments room under international law to interpret their obligations under the international drug control system differently or set these aside?

These questions therefore also determine the subsequent design of this book. The questions are approached from the perspective of international law and from the perspective of the state in general.

1.2.1. POSITIVE HUMAN RIGHTS OBLIGATIONS: CHAPTER 2

To arrive at a substantiated answer to the first question, Chapter 2 deals in detail with the *right to health* and subsequently the *right to life*, the *right not to be subjected to inhumane treatment* and the *right to a private life*. The emphasis will be on the positive obligations that states have to protect these rights, in other words: obligations that require states to provide actively for the protection of those rights. We will look at both general obligations under conventions that apply to all rights under the conventions and the positive obligations specific to some of those rights.

As far as the right to health is concerned, the analysis is primarily based on the International Covenant on Economic, Social and Cultural Rights

(UN, 1966) (ICESCR) and the (Revised) European Social Charter (CoE, 1961/1996) (ESC), as well as the considerations about it of the Committee on Economic, Social and Cultural Rights (ICESCR Committee or CESCR) and the European Committee of Social Rights (European CSR or ECSR). The discussion of the rights regarding life, inhumane treatment and a private life relates first and foremost to the International Covenant on Civil and Political Rights (UN, 1966) (ICCPR) and the European Convention on Human Rights (ECHR), as well as the considerations about it of the Human Rights Committee (HRC) and the European Court of Human Rights (ECtHR), respectively. Secondly, when we discuss the various rights, we sometimes dwell on the opinions of other relevant human rights bodies, notably those of the United Nations Special Rapporteur on the right of everyone to the enjoyment of the highest attainable standard of physical and mental health. For each of the four rights, the analysis of these legal sources and subsequently the process by which we arrive at an answer to the first question is carried out by looking at subsidiary questions that have been formulated in more detail in Chapter 2.[2]

1.2.2. HUMAN RIGHTS CONVENTIONS VERSUS UN NARCOTIC DRUGS CONVENTIONS: CHAPTER 3

This chapter aims to answer the second key question formulated above. In fact, the results of Chapter 2 and those of our first book, *International Law and Cannabis I*, regarding the international anti-drug regulations come together here, at least to the extent that Chapter 2 shows that regulating cannabis cultivation and trade for recreational use is supported by positive human rights obligations. In essence, the third chapter deals with the question how the interference between the positive human rights obligations and the obligations under narcotic drugs conventions must be resolved.

In order to answer that question, we will look at, among other things, the so-called priority clauses in the conventions and the rules with respect to determining priority (*lex specialis*, *lex posterior* and *lex prior* and *lex superior*). Essentially, this is about determining whether human rights obligations take priority over the obligations under the drugs conventions or rather the other way round. Subsequently, the conflict approach (one norm unconditionally takes precedence over the other) and the harmony approach (where the norms are reconciled as much as possible through interpretation) respectively are applied to the interference. The latter approach in particular will prove to be important. This involves, among other things, looking at the possibility that there are sufficient objectives and values common to human rights and the drug control systems that they can be integrated systematically through harmonizing interpretation.

---

2 See sections 2.3, 2.4, 2.4.8.i, 2.4.9.i and 2.4.10.i.

The analyses and reflections regarding positive law in this chapter are primarily based on the *Vienna Convention on the Law of Treaties* (VCLT), the *Charter of the United Nations* (UN Charter), the case law of the International Court of Justice (ICJ), the work of the International Law Commission (ILC) and the pertinent literature about this. Of course, in addition to the legal sources from Chapter 2, the UN narcotic drugs conventions that are relevant to the cannabis issue also play a part. These are the *Single Convention on Narcotic Drugs* as amended by the Protocol amending the Single Convention on Narcotic Drugs (Single Convention), and the *United Nations Convention Against Illicit Traffic in Narcotic Drugs and Psychotropic Substances* (Illicit Traffic Convention).

1.2.3. SYNTHESIS AND CONCLUSIONS: CHAPTER 4

Answering the two key questions in this book will therefore take place in Chapter 2 and Chapter 3 respectively. Each of these chapters ends with an overview of the conclusions. They will not be repeated again in Chapter 4. Instead, this final chapter will discuss the steps, assumptions and conditions that may be important if a state were to consider regulated permission of cannabis cultivation and trade for the recreational user market. The topical and exact situation in a certain country is not relevant as such, so it will be disregarded in principle.

1.2.4. SCHEMATIC REPRESENTATION OF THE RESEARCH

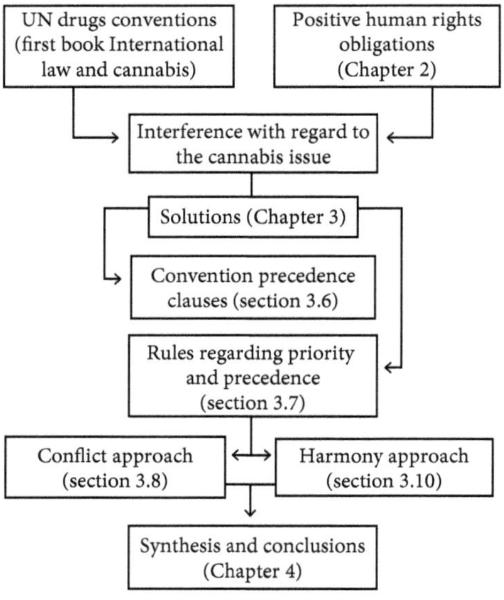

Source: Produced by the authors.

1.3. RELEVANT DEFINITIONS

In some places in this book, terms are used the meaning of which it is expedient to explain in more detail already at this stage.[3]

- *Cannabis issue.* To avoid long sentences, this research sometimes refers to the cannabis issue. What is meant by this is the question whether it is legally permissible under international law to regulate cannabis cultivations and trade for recreational use. The medical use of cannabis therefore falls outside the scope of this issue and as it happens also outside the scope of this book.
- *Permission.* The cannabis issue therefore focuses on regulated permission. Permission is also the term which is used in this book. Permission implies active approval, licensing, enabling. Regulated permission is more far-reaching than regulated tolerance. Tolerance also covers not hindering or thwarting and can therefore be passive.
- *Cannabis cultivation and trade.* In this book, these terms are used in a wide sense to cover the entire chain from cultivation of cannabis to delivery to the consumer for recreational purposes. This includes, among other things: growing, cultivation, extraction, production, manufacture, preparation, offering, offering for sale, possession for sale, distribution, transport, dispatch in transit, dealing, sale and delivery.
- *Negative obligations.* These involve obligations from state authorities to refrain from unlawful infringements of human rights, in other words the obligation to respect the fundamental rights of individuals. According to these obligations, states must therefore refrain from affecting the health of individuals negatively, taking their lives, torturing them and interfering with their private lives unlawfully.[4]
- *Positive obligations.* These involve obligations arising from human rights conventions for states and authorities to safeguard and protect rights under the convention actively against the conduct of other private persons, among other things. Because of these obligations, the authorities are required to act rather than refrain from acting. For example, obligations to provide for legislation, measures, policies or operational action.[5]
- *Legalization.* This is the case if prohibited conduct (an act or omission to act) is declared legal. The conduct then no longer contravenes the law, from that moment on it is legally allowed and permitted. This is without prejudice to

[3] Part of the following is – for the sake of consistency– borrowed from Chapter 1 of Piet Hein P.H.M.C. van Kempen & Masha I. Fedorova, *International Law and Cannabis I*, Cambridge: Intersentia, 2019.

[4] See for more information section 2.2.

[5] See for more information section 2.2.

the government's option to impose conditions for that conduct. In that case, the legalization can be said to be regulated. For example, the use of alcohol in many countries is legal in itself, but that does not alter the fact that legal restrictions apply to both the supply and the demand side of the market, where the authorities have the power to act in case these restrictions are violated.

- *Decriminalization*. This is less far-reaching than legalization. In this book, decriminalization means that conduct which is prohibited under criminal law is removed from the criminal code. The conduct as such is no longer subject to criminalization, but is still prohibited by virtue of legislation not related to criminal law. In other words, decriminalization does not yet mean that the decriminalized conduct is legal and/or permissible from now on. The conduct is still deemed undesirable and it can be subject to action other than under criminal law, for example through administrative law or civil law. One example of decriminalization is that a provision from the Highway Code is no longer enforced under criminal law but only via administrative law.
- *Policy-based tolerance*. This concept in this book refers to the situation that a form of conduct which has been criminalized is explicitly tolerated by the Public Prosecution Service and the administrative authorities, on the basis of documented policy. That tolerance is therefore subject to explicitly formulated rules, assumptions and criteria. Policy-based tolerance can involve tolerance on a criminal and administrative level. *Policy-based penal tolerance* means that the Public Prosecution Service refrains in general from prosecution for conduct covered by the formulated rules, assumptions and criteria on the basis of documented policy. The possibility for such tolerance has its origin in the expediency principle (Article 167(2) of the Netherlands Code of Criminal Procedure, CCP). *Policy-based administrative tolerance* is the situation where the administrative authorities in general refrain from acting against situations and conduct that comply with the formulated rules, assumptions and criteria, on the basis of a documented policy. For example, if the municipality issues a licence to a coffee shop, this would be a case of administrative tolerance.
- *Harm reduction*. This concept refers to policies, programmes and practices aiming to reduce the damage as a result of the use of psychoactive drugs by people who are unable or unwilling to stop. The emphasis here lies on preventing harm rather than preventing drug use itself.[6]
- *Interference between conventions and convention norms*. We use the term interference in a non-legal sense, to describe the situation in which there is tension, friction, conflict or something similar between conventions or the norms of various conventions. This book then deals with the interference between human rights conventions and drugs conventions and/or between

6 Borrowed from Harm Reduction International, 'What is harm reduction?', at: http://www.ihra.net/what-is-harm-reduction.

positive human rights obligations and obligations arising from the pertinent UN Narcotic Drugs Conventions. The term was chosen so as to have a concept that is distinct from the more legally defined 'conflict between conventions'.[7]

1.4. RELEVANCE OF HUMAN RIGHTS IN OTHER RESPECTS

As far as we know, no attention has been paid in the national and international academic literature to the question that is the reason for this research: is it possible to base regulated permission of cannabis cultivation and trade on positive obligations (arising from international human rights) to protect individual and public health, the safety of individuals and against crime? There is a good deal of literature, particularly foreign and international literature, about the meaning of human rights for drugs and/or cannabis policies in various other respects. The most important ones of these are the following:

1.4.1. THE FIGHT AGAINST DRUGS LEADS TO INFRINGEMENTS AND VIOLATIONS OF HUMAN RIGHTS

First, much has been written about how fighting the production, trade and use of drugs leads to infringements and violations of the individual rights of persons this fight is directed at.[8] This includes infringement and violations

---

7 See section 3.3.

8 See among other sources Richard Lines, *Drug Control and Human Rights in International Law*, Cambridge: Cambridge University Press, 2017; Joanne Csete et al., 'Public health and international drug policy', *The Lancet* 2016, vol. 387, pp. 1427–1480; Juan Carlos Garzón & Luciana Pol, 'The Elephant in the Room: Drugs and Human Rights in Latin America', *SUR International Journal on Human Rights* 2015, vol. 12, no. 21, pp. 1–7; United Nations Development Programme, *Perspectives on the Development Dimensions of Drug Control Policy*, UNDP 2015; M. McFarland Sánchez-Moreno, 'The Human Rights Case for Drug Reform. How Drug Criminalization Destroys Lives, Feeds Abuses, and Subverts the Rule of Law', in: *Human Rights Watch World Report* 2014, New York: HRW, 2014, pp. 19–28; Steve Rolles et al., *The Alternative World Drug Report. Counting the Costs of the War on Drugs*, United Kingdom: Count the Costs, 2012, pp. 71–83; Daniel Heilmann, 'The International Control of Illegal Drugs and the U.N. Treaty Regime: Preventing or Causing Human Rights Violations?', *Cardozo Journal of International & Comparative Law* 2011, vol. 19, pp. 237–290; Damon Barrett & Manfred Nowak, 'The United Nations and Drug Policy: Towards a Human Rights-Based Approach', in: Aristotle Constantinides & Nikos Zaikos (eds.), *The Diversity of International Law: Essays in Honour of Professor Kalliopi K. Koufa*, Amsterdam: Brill & Martinus Nijhoff, 2009, pp. 449–477; Damon Barrett et.al, *Recalibrating the Regime. The Need for a Human Rights-Based Approach to International Drug Policy*, The Beckley Foundation Drug Policy Programme, Report Thirteen, March 2008. See also Report of the Special Rapporteur on the right of everyone to the enjoyment of the highest attainable standard of physical and mental health, Anand Grover, *UN Doc.* A/65/255, 6 August 2010, Summary and among other places, para. 8, 17–18, 29, 30–31, 48 and 70.

arising from upholding the enforcement of drug-related (criminal) law, the operational activities with regard to dealing with crops, as well as discriminatory and inhumane treatment of drug addicts. It also covers the restriction of access to medicinal use of drugs.[9] Although these topics are not separate subjects for the research in this book, they do have some bearing on it, as we will see in Chapter 2.[10]

1.4.2. HUMAN RIGHTS NECESSITATE THE APPLICATION OF HARM REDUCTION MEASURES

All sorts of publications also look at the question to what extent certain human rights necessitate or give rise to the application of harm reduction measures.[11] These measures can include programmes for (providing) needles and syringes, users' rooms, interventions to promote non-injection methods for drug use, overdose prevention as well as outreach work and educational programmes. Admittedly, harm reduction is not a subject in its own right within this book, but indirectly it has some relevance. Where relevant, we will briefly deal with it in Chapter 2.[12]

1.4.3. A HUMAN RIGHT TO CANNABIS CULTIVATION, TRADE AND/OR USE?

Finally, pleas can be found in the literature as to why production, trade and/or use of certain drugs has or should have protection under certain human rights.[13]

---

9 See also for example Melissa Bone & Toby Seddon, 'Human rights, public health and medicinal cannabis use', *Critical Public Health* 2016, vol. 26, no. 1, pp. 51–61; Marie Elske C. Gispen, 'A human rights view on access to controlled substances for medical purposes under the international drug control framework', *European Journal of Pharmacology* 2013, pp. 16–24; Robin Room & Peter Reuter, 'How well do international drug conventions protect public health?', 379 *The Lancet* 2012 (January 7), pp. 84–91.

10 In particular, see section 2.4.12.ii.

11 See for example Damon Barrett, 'Drug Use and the Right of Everyone to the Highest Attainable Standard of Health', in: Sven Hessle (ed.), *Human Rights and Social Equality: Challenges for Social Work*, Farnham, UK/Burlington, USA: Ashgate, 2014, pp. 158–166; Saul Takahashi, 'Drug Control, Human Rights, and the Right to the Highest Attainable Standard of Health: by no means straightforward issues', *Human Rights Quarterly* 2009, vol. 31, no. 3, pp. 748–776; Rick Lines, *International Human Rights Jurisprudence on Issues relating to Drug Use and Harm Reduction*, New York : Open Society Institute, 2007. See also Report of the Special Rapporteur on the right of everyone to the enjoyment of the highest attainable standard of physical and mental health, Anand Grover, *UN Doc.* A/65/255, 6 August 2010, para. 50–55.

12 See in particular sections 2.3.10.i, 2.3.11, 2.3.12.ii, 2.4.11 and 2.4.12.ii.

13 See for example All Party Parliamentary Group for Drug Policy Reform (APPG), *Guidance on Drug Policy. Interpreting the UN Drug Conventions*, 2015, p. 7. See also Erik van Ree, 'Drugs as a human right', International Journal of Drug Policy 1999, vol. 10, pp. 89–98.

One can think of the protection of or even the right to drug use under fundamental rights, such as the right to a private life, the right to freedom of opinion and expression, the right of freedom of religion or belief, the right to equal treatment, the right to participate in cultural life, the right to self-determination and the right to enjoy the benefits of scientific progress. The idea here is that because of those rights, the state must abstain from prohibiting cannabis and acting against behaviours related to cannabis. This raises the question whether the regulated permission of cannabis cultivation and trade for recreational use would be protected under these rights. Yet, we will not include this question in this book, the reason being that the current positive law of international human rights leaves very little or no room to arrive at a positive answer to that question, as will become evident from the following.

The question whether non-medicinal use of drugs – cannabis in particular – can find protection under human rights conventions is addressed in various cases in international human rights bodies.[14] In the case of *M.A.B., W.A.T. and J.-A.Y.T.*, the Human Rights Committee is of the opinion that the worship and distribution of cannabis does not fall within the scope of the right to religion in Article 18 ICCPR.[15] Neither does the right not to be subjected to arbitrary deprivation of liberty in Article 9 ICCPR preclude arrest on the grounds of possession or distribution of drugs. In the *Prince* case – revolving around the use of marihuana by Rastafarians – the Committee makes clear that if cannabis possession and use is part of a religion that is also recognized as such under Article 18 ICCPR, the state is entitled to prohibit such possession and use subject to the condition of the third paragraph of this provision.[16] While it is true that cannabis use can be subsumed under this right, the government may subsequently restrict this right by prohibiting cannabis. Such a prohibition is also allowed with respect to the equality principle and the non-discrimination principle in Article 26 ICCPR and the right to enjoy one's own culture and profess and practise one's religion in Article 27 ICCPR.[17] The Human Rights Committee recognizes that a state has the right to prohibit cannabis if that state deems this to be necessary in order to protect public safety, public order, public health, public decency or the fundamental rights and freedoms of other people in the light of the harmful effects of cannabis.

A similar approach is used by the ECtHR. In the *Marlow* case, the plaintiff had been prosecuted and convicted for inciting cannabis cultivation because he had published a book on cultivation and production of cannabis.[18] Marlow was

14 The topics mentioned here will be discussed in a little more detail in section 2.4.11.
15 HRC 8 April 1994, *M.A.B., W.A.T. and J.-A.Y.T./Canada*, no. 570/93, para. 4.2.
16 HRC 31 October 2007, *Prince/South Africa*, no. 1474/06, para. 7.2–7.3.
17 Ibid, para. 7.5 and 7.4 respectively.
18 ECtHR 5 December 2000, *Marlow/The UK*, No. 42015/98, para. 1.

of the opinion that among other things, his conviction breached his right to freedom of expression in Article 10 ECHR. The ECtHR ruled that the decision of the authorities to maintain the criminalization of instigating cannabis production and to punish the authors of books that serve such production falls within the state's margin of appreciation.[19] This approach is corroborated by the case centring on *De Bruin*, in which the authorities had revoked the licence for the applicant's coffee shop and had closed down his coffee shop.[20] The applicant had taken his case to the Court and appealed to the right of a fair trial in Article 6 ECHR as well as the right to an effective remedy in Article 13 ECHR and the prohibition of discrimination in Article 14 ECHR and Article 1 Twelfth Protocol ECHR.[21] The ECtHR explains that states are free to criminalize dealing in soft drugs. According to the Court, if states choose to conduct a policy of tolerance, this does not mean that states are not allowed to prosecute people for offences.[22] Not only are states at liberty to decide which policy they may adopt with regard to criminalization and prosecution regarding cannabis, but this policy may also deviate from the policy concerning alcohol, for example.[23]

Finally, we point out that the ICESCR Committee and the European CSR never assumed that non-medicinal use of drugs and/or cannabis can find protection under human rights conventions. As far as we have been able to ascertain, this also applies to UN Special Rapporteur on the right to health. Incidentally, the International Narcotics Control Board (INCB), which is relevant for this book (although it is not human rights body), takes the view 'that drug control must be, and is, fully reconcilable with respect for human rights. However, the international drug control conventions do not accept the existence of a "right" to possess narcotic drugs or psychotropic substances unless they are to be used for medical or scientific purposes.'[24]

On the strength of these cases (or to be more precise, on the basis of the provisions of the conventions mentioned as they are interpreted by the relevant human rights supervisory bodies), we conclude that prohibition of cannabis cultivation, trade and use is permissible under administrative and criminal law. In principle, no protection against this is actually provided by the right to freedom of religion and belief, the right to equal treatment and the right of

---

19 With regard to the ECHR, see 2.4.7.ix.

20 Sales outlets licensed by the municipality in the Netherlands where the sale of alcohol is prohibited but the sale of cannabis in small amounts to adults for personal use is permitted. All the references in this book are meant in this way. Other possible retail locations will be referred to more generally as retail shop or points-of-sale.

21 ECtHR 17 September 2013, *De Bruin/The Netherlands*, No. 9765/09.

22 Ibid, para. 56–58.

23 Ibid, para. 71.

24 INCB, *Report of the International Narcotics Control Board for 2008*, New York: United Nations, 2009, p. 7 (no. 31).

non-discrimination, and the right to enjoy one's own culture and profess and practise one's religion and the right to freedom of expression. With all these rights, states can in principle opt for prohibition and/or criminalization and enforcing administrative and criminal legislation aimed at cannabis. In view of the fact that states can already choose this approach when fundamental freedoms such as the right to freedom of religion and the right to freedom of expression are involved, we consider it hardly realistic to suppose that the international human rights bodies will want to protect cannabis cultivation, trade and/or use under other human rights. However, this is not to say we rule out the possibility that this may be different in the future.

1.5. THE RESEARCH: CHOICES AND LIMITATIONS

It is evident that choices had to be made for this research too and that certain restrictions apply. The most important ones of these are the following:

1.5.1. FOUR HUMAN RIGHTS

The research is aimed primarily at positive obligations arising from the right to health, the right to life, the right not to be subjected to inhumane treatment and the right to a private life. The reason for choosing to discuss these rights is that the associated positive obligations are most relevant from the point of view of individual health and public health, the safety of individuals, preventing nuisances and fighting crime. The added value of discussing the positive obligations pertaining to other human rights would in our view be marginal at best, whereas it would significantly increase the scope of the research.

1.5.2. EMPHASIS ON POSITIVE OBLIGATIONS

Furthermore, the emphasis will be on positive obligations. These obligations force the state and/or the authorities to act and actively provide protection against (imminent) violations rather than refraining from acting – as is the case with negative obligations. Consequently, positive obligations are potentially the most relevant for arguments that regulated permission of cannabis cultivation and trade would provide better protection of individual health and public health, the safety of individuals and would better prevent nuisances and tackle crime than a more prohibitive and repressive policy on drugs and/or cannabis. In addition to this, as we saw just now in section 1.4.3, the negative obligations do not offer protection against the state prohibiting cannabis cultivation and trade.

1.5.3. FOUR HUMAN RIGHTS CONVENTIONS

Another choice was related to the human rights conventions we studied. Across the world, there is a huge number of human rights conventions, many of which also lay down the rights discussed in this book.[25] This fact forces us to make a selection. We settled on conventions (which are legally binding) to which most European countries are a party, which are generally applicable to the relationship between those countries' authorities and individuals, and which are the most relevant for the rights that this book refers to in relation to protecting individual health and public health, the safety of individuals, preventing nuisances and fighting crime. These criteria account for our discussion of the International Covenant on Economic, Social and Cultural Rights (ICESCR), the European Social Charter (ESC), the International Covenant on Civil and Political Rights (ICCPR) and the European Convention on Human Rights (ECHR). In the first instance, our attention will be focused on the two UN human rights conventions: the ICESCR and the ICCPR. The reason for that is that in the case of a conflict between human rights obligations and obligations to combat drugs, the latter primarily involves the narcotic drugs conventions of the United Nations as well. However, the fact that we also take into consideration other conventions is because different human right regimes sometimes interpret one and the same human right slightly differently. In the event of such discrepancies, this usually shows most clearly in the jurisprudence of the international Committees and Courts that supervise those conventions. By including two human rights conventions in our analysis for each of the four selected human rights, there will be more clarity as to which obligations exactly states have with respect to each of these four human rights.

The Charter of Fundamental Rights of the European Union is not included in this research. A practical reason for this is that discussing this Charter would increase the already extensive analysis in this book by approximately 50%. Given the selection criteria mentioned above, there are also content-related reasons to exclude the Charter. First, it is important that according to Article 51(1) of the Charter, states must adhere exclusively to the Charter insofar as they implement European Union law. The Charter's objective is merely to guarantee an implementation of European Union law in conformity with fundamental rights. Nor is it possible to derive from Union law – including the Charter – an obligation to honour fundamental rights that does not originate from the fact that

[25] For example, see the collection in Piet Hein P.H.M.C. van Kempen (ed.), *International and Regional Human Rights Documents* (with a foreword by ECtHR Judge E. Myjer), Nijmegen: Wolf Legal Publishers, 2010.

the Union itself is bound by fundamental rights.[26] This means that the Charter is not directly relevant for even the member states of the European Union in the implementation and application of all their obligations under the UN narcotics drugs conventions. Admittedly, the European Union is a party to the UN Illicit Traffic Convention, but only to the extent that it concerns the aspects that fall under the Union's competence.[27] Even if this means that the UN Illicit Traffic Convention is a component part of the legal order of the Union to which the Charter applies,[28] this does not hold true for the Illicit Traffic Convention in its entirety and not at all for the UN Single Convention.

It is also important that in particular the positive obligations concerning the protection of the safety of individuals and preventing nuisance and fighting crime have not yet fully developed from the Charter or have not even developed at all.[29] To the extent that positive obligations regarding these matters are currently in force pursuant to the Charter, this is mostly the case because Article 53(3) of the Charter states that Charter rights corresponding to rights under the ECHR have the same content and scope as those which have been assigned to them by the latter convention.[30] This obligation of equalization

---

26 For more information on this see Mirjam de Mol, *De directe werking van de grondrechten van de Europese Unie* (diss. Maastricht), Oisterwijk: Wolf Legal Publishers, 2014, p. 80 (i.e., Mirjam de Mol, *The direct effect of fundamental rights of the European Union*, Oisterwijk: Wolf Legal Publishers, 2014, p. 80).

27 90/611/EEC: Council Decision of 22 October 1990 concerning the conclusion, on behalf of the European Economic Community, of the United Nations Convention against Illicit Traffic in Narcotic Drugs and Psychotropic Substances, *OJ* 1990 L 326/56.

28 Cf. Mirjam de Mol, *De directe werking van de grondrechten van de Europese Unie*, Oisterwijk: Wolf Legal Publishers, 2014, pp. 89, 90, who remarks that the fundamental rights under Union law have to be observed in the implementation of external conventions as well ('*de Unierechtelijke grondrechten ook bij de uitvoering van externe verdragen in acht* [dienen] *te worden genomen*'). She bases her view on the fact that the European Court of Justice considers Article 7 of Decision no. 1/80 of the Association Council of 19 September 1980 on the development of the Association (which Association Council was set up by Agreement establishing and Association between the European Economic Community and Turkey, concluded, approved and confirmed on behalf of the Community by Council Decision 64/732/EEC of 23 December 1963, *OJ* 1964, 217, p. 3685)) as 'an integral part of European Union law'. See CJEU 29 March 2012, *Staatssecretaris van Justitie Nederland/Kahveci en Inan*, Joint cases C-7/10 and C-9/10, ECLI:EU:C:2012:180, para. 23). Nor can it be ruled out that multilateral conventions to which the European Union is party become part of the Union law following the same line of reasoning, but that is not certain, since such conventions are of a somewhat different order than an Association Agreement for which the EU itself is also directly partly responsible.

29 Cf. Malu Beijer, 'Active Guidance of Fundamental Rights Protection by the Court of Justice of the European Union: Exploring the Possibilities of a Positive Obligations Doctrine', *Review of European Administrative Law* 2015, vol. 8, no. 2, pp. 127–150 on pp. 132–135.

30 Piet Hein P.H.M.C. van Kempen & Joeri Bemelmans, 'EU protection of the substantive criminal law principles of guilt and ne bis in idem under the Charter of Fundamental Rights: Underdevelopment and overdevelopment in an incomplete criminal justice framework', *New Journal of European Criminal Law* 2018, vol. 9(2) pp. 247–264 on pp. 251–252.

as a minimum requirement also applies to the protocols and the case law of the ECtHR.[31] Incidentally, this is also an important point because in this way, discussion of the ECHR it is also relevant with regard to the European Union.

1.5.4. RECREATIONAL CANNABIS, EXCLUDING MEDICINAL CANNABIS

The research question concerns regulation of cannabis cultivation and trade for recreational use. Therefore, the book does not look at the cultivation and trade of cannabis for medicinal use, which is also called medicinal cannabis occasionally.[32] The reason for this is that the discussion about cannabis cultivation and trade for recreational use is fundamentally different from the discussion about medicinal cannabis from a social and legal point of view. Also in the context of international drug conventions (which has an exception for medicines but not for recreational drugs[33]) and that of international human rights (in which access to medicines falls under the right to health, whereas access to recreational drugs does not[34]), any permissibility of the cultivation of and trade in medicinal cannabis does not say much about the issue at the heart of this book.

1.5.5. RESEARCH INTO POSITIVE LAW AND HYPOTHESIS OF ACTUAL VALIDITY

The book is as strictly legal in nature as possible. It focuses on positive law of the international human rights and it aims, through description and a multi-faceted analysis of that law, to determine how it works and how it applies, on the basis of the central questions in this research. We will refrain from normative or idealistic approaches of human rights and from using human rights as a social

---

31 See the official explanations relating to the Charter of Fundamental Rights, *OJ* 303/17, 14.12.2007, p. 33 (Explanation on Article 52). See also Steve Peers & Sacha Prechal, 'Article 52 – Scope and Interpretation of Rights and Principles', in: Steve Peers et al. (eds.), *The EU Charter of fundamental rights: a commentary*, Oxford: Hart Publishing 2014, pp. 1455–1522, in particular pp. 1456, 1492–1495.

32 See also for example Melissa Bone & Toby Seddon, 'Human rights, public health and medicinal cannabis use', *Critical Public Health* 2016, vol. 26, no. 1, pp. 51–61; Tony Bogdanoski, 'A dose of human rights: An antidote to the criminal prohibition of cannabis for medical use?', *Criminal Law Journal* 2009, vol. 33, pp. 251–262.

33 Piet Hein P.H.M.C. van Kempen & Masha I. Fedorova, *International Law and Cannabis I*, Cambridge: Intersentia 2019, section 2.2.3.

34 See for example Report of the Special Rapporteur on the right of everyone to the enjoyment of the highest attainable standard of physical and mental health, Anand Grover, on access to medicines, *UN Doc.* A/HRC/23/42, 1 May 2013, para. 3–6; INCB, *Availability of Internationally Controlled Drugs: Ensuring Adequate Access for Medical and Scientific Purposes*, New York: United Nations, 2016, pp. 2–4.

concept, in order to arrive at legal findings and conclusions in the most neutral and objective way possible.

Moreover, this research is not about assessing whether the arguments used to support pleas for a regulated permission of cannabis cultivation and trade for recreational use are sound or not. We will only describe these arguments briefly[35] and for this book we will work from the assumption that each of these arguments is valid. This hypothesis is the starting point for answering the central questions in section 1.2. It is therefore from this starting point that we assess whether the arguments can be supported by the human rights and positive obligations that have been discussed. For example, we will not assess whether it is true that individual health and public health can be more easily guaranteed by regulating cannabis cultivation and trade or by separating the soft drugs market from the hard drugs market.

Although we have already observed this in our first book on *International Law and Cannabis I*, we emphasize here once again that we do not let personal opinions about the alleged desirability of regulated permission of cannabis cultivation and trade for recreational use play any part in this research, at any rate not consciously.[36] In aiming to arrive at an assessment that is as purely legal as possible, we will avoid the angles that would be taken by advocates or opponents of such regulation and the arguments and claims fashioned for that purpose. Here, this means that we will not pass judgment on the question of legal policy whether any country should play a pioneering role internationally with regard to permitting cannabis cultivation if this research showed that permitting such cultivation (other than under international anti-drug regulations) can or cannot (pursuant to these regulations) be justified pursuant to human rights conventions.

1.6. METHODOLOGY

This book constitutes desk research and as we have seen before concerns positive law. This involves legal descriptions, analyses and assessments. For the legal analysis of provisions of conventions, we will follow the generally accepted concepts of public international law for the interpretation of conventions as they are expressed in Article 31 of the Vienna Convention on the Law of Treaties, Article 38 of the ICJ Statute and Guideline 3.1.5.1 of the Guide to Practice on Reservations to Treaties of the International Law Commission.[37]

---

35 See sections 2.3.1 and 2.4.1.

36 See Chapter 1 in Piet Hein P.H.M.C. van Kempen & Masha I. Fedorova, *International Law and Cannabis I*, Cambridge: Intersentia, 2019.

37 Included in Report of the ILC on the Work of its 63rd session, General Assembly, Official Records, 66th Session, Supplement n° 10, Addendum 1, *UN Doc.* A/66/10/ Add.1. (2011); see also the comments there on Guideline 3.1.5.1 on pp. 359 ff.

That interpretation is thus based primarily on the text of the relevant provisions in the conventions (linguistic and grammatical methods) and also the international jurisprudence about it. The system of the conventions (systematic method) and the rationale for the conventions (teleological method) also play a part, as well as the academic literature about the relevant human rights provisions.[38] As the preparatory history very rarely is of any importance in the interpretation of the selected human rights conventions,[39] we will not pay any attention to this in principle. Attention will be paid to the preparatory history of the UN drugs conventions as a supplementary means of interpretation.[40]

1.7. LEGAL SOURCES

Several sources of international law are pertinent to this research. The most important ones of these are the following:

1.7.1. THE CONVENTIONS

First, there are the four selected human rights conventions. We saw earlier that the provisions in the ICESCR, ESC, ICCPR and the ECHR are legally binding for states that are party to these conventions. The same is true for the relevant UN Narcotic Drugs Conventions (the Single Convention and the Illicit Traffic Convention), for the Charter of the United Nations and for the Vienna Convention on the Law of Treaties.[41]

1.7.2. JURISPRUDENCE AND REPORTS

As the wording of the provisions in these conventions is usually fairly open and general in nature, so that it is easy to include a good deal under it, it is

---

38 Cf. Article 38(1)(d) ICJ Statute, which provision acknowledges 'the teachings of the most highly qualified publicists of the various nations, as subsidiary means for the determination of rules of law'.

39 See for example Dinah L. Shelton, *Advanced Introduction to International Human Rights Law*, Cheltenham, UK/Northampton, USA: Edward Elgar, 2014, p. 109; David J. Harris, Michael O'Boyle, Ed P. Bates & C.M. Buckley (ed.), *Harris, O'Boyle & Warbrick, Law of the European Convention on Human Rights*, Oxford: Oxford University Press, 2014, pp. 19–20; Magdalena Sepúlveda, Theo van Banning, Gudrún D. Gudmundsdóttir, Christine Chamoun & Willem J.M. van Genugten, *Human Rights Reference Handbook*, Ciudad Colon, Costa Rica: University for Peace, 2004, pp. 47–48.

40 Cf. Article 32 of the Vienna Convention on the Law of Treaties.

41 See section 3.1 for the various dates of entry into force and the relevant numbers of the Treaty Series.

important to exercise caution with conclusions that are based exclusively on the text of the convention. That is why the jurisprudence on these conventions of the ICESCR Committee/CESCR, the European CSR/ECSR, the Human Rights Committee/HRC and the ECtHR plays an important part in both national and international legal practice and case law. That is also the case in this book. Although description, analysis and assessment of human rights provisions with respect to legal issues – such as the cannabis issue – are therefore of little value if it does not take the jurisprudence of these bodies into consideration as well, it is still appropriate to say a little more about its authority and force. Hereafter, we will also do this for some other important sources of information for this book: the case law of the International Court of Justice (ICJ), the reports of the UN Special Rapporteur on the right to health and the work of the International Law Commission (ILC). As will become evident immediately hereafter and in Chapter 2, in certain aspects there are relevant differences between the methods of these bodies and sometimes also between their interpretations of the four human rights that will be discussed, insofar as they actually express an opinion about them. Moreover, below we will provide a brief explanation of the most important supervisory body with regard to the UN narcotic drugs conventions: the International Narcotics Control Board (INCB). Finally, a comment will be made about the Commission on Narcotic Drugs (CND).

1.7.3. HUMAN RIGHTS COMMITTEES AT ICESCR, ESCR AND ICCPR

To begin with, a few comments about the ICESCR Committee, the European Committee of Social Rights (ECSR) and the Human Rights Committee (HRC).[42] These are quasi-judicial bodies. Formally, judgments and interpretation of conventions based on case law by these Committees have no binding force from a legal point of view, whether they are expressed in 'General Comments', 'Concluding observations' about country reports or 'Views' with respect to complaints from countries or individuals (at the UN Committees) or 'Conclusions' about country reports or 'Decisions' regarding collective complaints (at the ECSR). That does not diminish the fact that the ICESCR Committee, the ECSR and the Human Rights Committee act as the highest and independent expert bodies that were specifically established for the supervision

[42] For more information about these Committees (in addition to the literature mentioned in Chapter 2), see among other items Malcolm Langford (ed.), *Social Rights Jurisprudence: Emerging Trends in International and Comparative Law*, Cambridge: Cambridge University Press, 2008; Dinah Shelton, *Remedies in International Human Rights Law*, Oxford: Oxford University Press, 2015; Olivier De Schutter, *International Human Rights Law: Cases, Materials, Commentary*, Cambridge: Cambridge University Press, 2014.

of compliance with the ICESCR, the ESCR and the ICCPR. In other words, we are dealing with judgments and interpretations of authoritative international bodies. Thus, it can be argued that these judgments and interpretations eventually contribute to the legally binding force of the provisions in the conventions that they refer to. Even if one would not go as far as that, it is still true that these judgments are authoritative to such a degree that for that reason alone they need to be treated as a starting point in determining the meaning of the rights under the conventions.[43]

1.7.4. EUROPEAN COURT OF HUMAN RIGHTS (ECtHR)

The case law of the ECtHR commands a stronger position. The Court rules as a strictly judicial authority primarily in specific cases with regard to complaints from individuals and sometimes also from states, but it does not assess country reports. The rulings of this Court are typically casuistic in nature and typically do not constitute general judgments about national legislation, measures and policies *in abstracto*. Consequently, the jurisprudence of the ECtHR is less focused on general practice than the judgments of the above-mentioned Committees.

Pursuant to Article 46 ECHR, the decisions of the Court are at any rate legally binding in the cases in which they were given for the states that are parties to those cases. By virtue of this provision, states may also be required to take general measures to prevent the violation or redress it, so that in that sense the decision already can have a general effect for the state to which it applies.[44] Furthermore, the case law of the Court carries great general authority. Moreover, it is usually assumed that the decisions of the ECtHR – indirectly or de facto – also have

---

[43] For further references see also, for example, Dinah L. Shelton, *Advanced Introduction to International Human Rights Law*, Cheltenham, UK/Northampton, USA: Edward Elgar, 2014, p. 256; Renate Kicker & Markus Möstl, *Standard-setting through monitoring? The role of Council of Europe expert bodies in the development of human rights*, Strasbourg: Council of Europe Publishing, 2012, para. I.1.1, IV.2 and V.I. We also like to point what can be read on the website for the Council of Europe on the page of The European Committee of Social Rights: 'Insofar as they refer to binding legal provisions and are adopted by a monitoring body established by the Charter and the relevant protocols, decisions and conclusions of the European Committee of Social Rights must be respected by the States concerned; even if they are not directly enforceable in the domestic legal systems, they set out the law and can provide the basis for positive developments in social rights through legislation and case-law at national level.'; see: http://www.coe.int/en/web/turin-european-social-charter/european-committee-of-social-rights.

[44] David J. Harris, Michal O'Boyle, Ed. Bates & C.M. Buckley (ed.), *Harris, O'Boyle & Warbrick, Law of the European Convention on Human Rights*, Oxford: Oxford University Press, 2014, pp. 162–164.

an *erga omnes* effect, or generally binding force.[45] In this respect, it is important that the state acting in breach of a decision given against another state (incidentally, it is not always easy to determine whether that is the case, on account of the casuistic approach of the Court) could, upon assessment by the Court, also be convicted by a binding decision because of violation of the convention.[46] Consequently, it is not possible to act against a decision of the Court without violating the convention at the same time. Therefore, the decision (as a source of insight into the convention) shares the binding force bestowed on the convention (the source) pursuant to Article 1 ECHR.[47]

It is interesting that a general effect of the case law of the ECtHR is indirectly generated by Article 53 of the Charter. As we have discussed before, it follows from this provision that the fundamental rights in the Charter of Fundamental Rights of the European Union have the same content and scope as those which have been assigned to corresponding rights in the ECHR or the case law of the ECtHR. To that extent, the case law has de facto general binding force for issues within the scope of the Charter.

1.7.5. INTERNATIONAL COURT OF JUSTICE (ICJ)

The International Court of Justice (ICJ) is an independent judicial authority too. This Court, which is also called 'The World Court', rules on disputes between states and gives legal advice (Advisory Opinions) on legal issues it receives from the competent bodies of the United Nations, among other sources. In respect of states that have recognized its competence versus every other state that accepts the same obligation, the Court has compulsory jurisdiction with regard to all legal disputes involving, among other things, the interpretation of a treaty and

45 See also, with many references, Kanstantsin Dzehtsiarou, *European Consensus and the Legitimacy of the European Court of Human Rights*, Cambridge: Cambridge University Press, 2015, pp. 90–91, 102–103, and also Marie-Louise Bemelmans-Videc, 'Guaranteeing the authority and effectiveness of the European Convention on Human Rights. Explanatory memorandum', Council of Europe Parliamentary Assembly, 4 November 2011, *AS/Jur* (2011) 44, para. 35; Judge Pinto de Albuquerque, Concurring Opinion, on: ECtHR (Grand Chamber) 7 February 2013, *Fabris/France*, no. 16574/08.

46 See, for example, ECtHR 9 June 2009, *Opuz/Turkey*, Appl. 33401/02, para. 163, 'In carrying out this scrutiny, and bearing in mind that the Court provides final authoritative interpretation of the rights and freedoms defined in Section I of the Convention, the Court will consider whether the national authorities have sufficiently taken into account the principles flowing from its judgments on similar issues, even when they concern other States'.

47 For more information on the source of insight effect of the Strasbourg case law, see Piet Hein P.H.M.C. van Kempen, *Heropening van procedures na veroordelingen door het EHRM* (diss. Tilburg), Nijmegen: Wolf Legal Publishers, 2003, pp. 40–46 (i.e., Piet Hein P.H.M.C. van Kempen, *Re-opening of procedures after convictions by the ECtHR* (dissertation Tilburg), Nijmegen: Wolf Legal Publishers, 2003, pp. 40–46).

any question of international law.[48] The ICJ settles the dispute submitted to them on the basis of international law, relying on international conventions, customary international law, the general principles of law recognized by civilized nations, and as subsidiary means for the determination of rules of law, judicial decisions as well as the most authoritative literature.[49] Consequently, the decisions by the Court provide a significant degree of insight into the contents, scope and functioning of international law. According to Article 59 ICJ Statute, the decision by the Court is only binding for the parties and only with regard to the case it dealt with. Nonetheless, great general authority is vested in the decisions. They play an important part in establishing what international law covers – including customary law – and in developing new international legal concepts.[50]

1.7.6. UN SPECIAL RAPPORTEUR ON THE RIGHT TO HEALTH

We will also make a few comments regarding a non-(quasi) judicial institute: the UN Special Rapporteur on the right of everyone to the enjoyment of the highest attainable standard of physical and mental health. He has been appointed to examine the specific human rights theme of the right to health.[51] The Special Rapporteur, however, has not been formally designated as a body charged with supervising compliance with the ICESCR or another convention, nor with the interpretation of its provisions. The advice, reports and judgments of Special Rapporteurs are not legally binding for states either. Having said that, Special Rapporteurs are independent, possess a high degree of autonomy in their work and wield great influence on the development, interpretation and implementation of human rights.[52] They act as an important part of the human rights supervisory system of the United Nations. Moreover, reports of Special Rapporteurs are deemed authoritative sources of law, which supervisory human

---

48 Article 36 ICJ Statute.

49 Article 38 ICJ Statute.

50 Antonio Cassese, *International Law*, Oxford: Oxford University Press, 2005, pp. 194–196. See also, among other sources, Jan Klabbers, *International Law*, Cambridge: Cambridge University Press, 2013, pp. 160–161; Gideon Boas, *Public International Law: Contemporary Principles and Perspectives*, Cheltenham, UK/Northampton, USA: Edward Elgar, 2012, p. 112–114; Marc Jacob, 'Precedents: Lawmaking Through International Adjudication', in: Armin von Bogdandy & Ingo Venzke (eds.), *International Judicial Lawmaking*, Heidelberg: Springer, 2012, pp. 35–68 in particular on pp. 47–59; James Crawford, *Brownlie's Principles of Public International Law*, Oxford: Oxford University Press, 2012, pp. 37–39.

51 For his mandate, see: Commission on Human Rights resolution 2002/31, 22 April 2002; Human Rights Council resolution 6/29, 14 December 2007; Human Rights Council resolution 24/6, 20 September 2013.

52 For a detailed discussion see Surya P. Subedi, 'Protection of Human Rights through the Mechanism of UN Special Rapporteurs', *Human Rights Quarterly* 2011, vol. 33, pp. 201–228.

rights bodies rely on in their work. In view of the authority of the work of Special Rapporteurs, we will also pay attention – largely separately – to the insights of the Special Rapporteur on the right to health. In a more marginal way, this is also true for the Special Rapporteurs on globalization and its impact on the full enjoyment of all human rights.

1.7.7. INTERNATIONAL LAW COMMISSION (ILC)

Where more specific doctrines of public international law play an important part, we rely on both relevant literature and the work of this Commission. This is particularly the case in Chapter 3. The ICL was set up by the United Nations in 1948 to promote the development and codification of international law.[53] The work of the ILC is generally seen as the authoritative representation of the content of international law as reflected in the generally recognized sources of public international law. In addition to the Vienna Convention on the Law of Treaties, we will therefore also refer to the work of the ILC.

1.7.8. INTERNATIONAL NARCOTICS CONTROL BOARD (INCB)

The INCB is the international body responsible for monitoring the implementation of the Single Convention and to a lesser extent also the Illicit Traffic Convention by the states parties.[54] It acts as an independent and quasi-judicial control and regulatory authority, which is comparable to the human rights committees with the ICESCR, ICCPR and the ESCR.[55] The INCB is therefore the internationally designated body to monitor compliance with the anti-drugs conventions. To this end, the Board publishes a report each year on the functioning of the international drug control system (the three UN narcotic drugs conventions) and developments in the international fight against drugs. The states parties acknowledged this authority by their accession to the convention. A difference between the INCB and the human rights committees is that the former does not assess complaints in concrete cases and that it rarely specifically looks into the

53 See Articles 1, 15 and 16–24 Statute of the International Law Commission (1947). See also the ICL website, http://legal.un.org/ilc/, and for example Jeffrey S. Morton, *The International Law Commission of the United Nations*, Columbia, South Carolina: University of South Carolina Press, 2000, pp. 1–18.

54 See in more detail Piet Hein P.H.M.C. van Kempen & Masha I. Fedorova, *International Law and Cannabis I*, Cambridge: Intersentia, 2019, sections 2.2.5, 2.3.5 and 2.4 on which the following description is based.

55 See Damon Barrett, *'Unique in International Relations'? A Comparison of the International Narcotics Control Board and the UN Human Rights Treaty Bodies*, London: International Harm Reduction Association, 2008.

meaning of concrete provisions of the conventions. The assessments by the INCB about compliance by states with the UN narcotic drugs conventions are not legally binding either. Nevertheless, as with the human rights committees, there is a case to be made that the INCB's assessments and interpretations eventually contribute to the legally binding force of the provisions of the conventions that they relate to and that at any rate they have to be the starting point for determining the obligations of the parties to the convention.

1.7.9. COMMISSION ON NARCOTIC DRUGS (CND)

The CND exists in the annual meeting of ministers and government representatives of all UN member states during which they debate, make decisions and adopt resolutions about all sort of issues regarding the United Nations drug control system, the working programme of the United Nations Office on Drugs and Crime (UNODC) and the INCB.[56] This, in other words, is a political body.

1.8. CONCLUSION

The main research was concluded on 1 April 2016, but developments and information after that date and until 1 January 2019 have been taken into account as much as possible in the course of updating the research for the English version of the book.

[56] See in more detail Piet Hein P.H.M.C. van Kempen & Masha I. Fedorova, *International Law and Cannabis I*, Cambridge: Intersentia, 2019, sections 2.2.5, 2.3.5 and 2.4.

CHAPTER 2

CANNABIS REGULATION ON THE BASIS OF POSITIVE HUMAN RIGHTS OBLIGATIONS?

2.1. INTRODUCTION

Pleas for regulating cannabis cultivation and trade for recreational use are often based on arguments that relate to the interests of (individual and public) health, the safety of citizens, preventing nuisances and fighting crime.[1] Therefore, the key question in this chapter is:

> To what extent can regulation of cannabis cultivation and trade for recreational use, for the sake of public health, safety and crime control, be married up to positive human rights obligations that ensue from international human rights conventions?

In order to answer that question, we will first look more specifically at the *right to health*. This particularly concerns the positive obligations for states to promote public health on the basis of this right. Subsequently, the *rights to life, physical and psychological integrity and a private life* and the way they interrelate will be covered, in particular the ensuing positive obligations for states to guarantee the safety of its citizens and to fight crime. Our examination is grounded in positive law: we will analyse which rights and obligations arise from international human rights conventions and international case law on them.[2] It most certainly is not a prescriptive assessment: we are not arguing which rights and obligations should be derived from the conventions.

The analysis of the right to health is primarily based on the International Covenant on Economic, Social and Cultural Rights (UN, 1966) (ICESCR)[3] and the jurisprudence, commentaries and observations of the Committee on

---

1 See Piet Hein P.H.M.C. van Kempen & Masha I. Fedorova, *International Law and Cannabis I*, Cambridge: Intersentia, 2019, Chapter 4.

2 For more information on the conventions and supervisory human rights bodies to be mentioned below see section 1.7.

3 *International Covenant on Economic, Social and Cultural Rights* (ICESCR), New York, 19 December 1966 (*Trb.* 1969/100, *Trb.* 1975/61).

Economic, Social and Cultural Rights (ICESCR Committee or CESCR). We will also pay attention in particular to the (Revised) European Social Charter (CoE, 1961/1996) (ESC),[4] as well as the considerations about it of the European Committee of Social Rights (European CSR or ECSR).

The most important basis for the discussion of the rights to life, physical and psychological integrity and a private life is the International Covenant on Civil and Political Rights (UN, 1966) (ICCPR)[5] and the jurisprudence, commentaries and observations of the Human Rights Committee (HRC). Obviously, we will also dwell on the European Convention on Human Rights (CoE, 1950) (ECHR)[6] and the corresponding jurisprudence of the European Court of Human Rights (ECtHR).

Both for the right to health and the rights to life, physical and psychological integrity and the right to a private life, there will be more attention for opinions and commentaries of other specialized UN authorities, such as the UN Special Rapporteur on the right to health.

In this chapter, therefore, human rights take pride of place. In discussing and explaining those rights, we will not take into account the obligations that states have under the UN narcotic drugs conventions as regards cannabis in particular: the Single Convention on Narcotic Drugs (1961) as amended by the Protocol of 1972 amending the Single Convention on Narcotic Drugs, and the United Nations Convention Against Illicit Traffic in Narcotic Drugs and Psychotropic Substances (1988). The synthesis regarding the relation between the human rights instruments that we will discuss here on the one hand and drugs conventions on the other will be discussed in Chapter 3 of this book.

2.2. POSITIVE OBLIGATIONS AS A LEGAL CONCEPT

It becomes clear from the case law of the ICESCR Committee,[7] the Human Rights Committee[8] and the ECtHR[9] that states not only have negative obligations to

4 *European Social Charter* (ESC); see for the original ESC: Turin, 18 October 1961 (*Trb.* 1962/3, *Trb.* 1963/90). *(Revised) European Social Charter*; see for the revised ESC: Strasbourg, 3 May 1996 (*Trb.* 2004/13).

5 *International Covenant on Civil and Political Rights* (ICCPR), New York, 19 December 1966 (*Trb.* 1969/99, *Trb.* 1975/60).

6 *Convention for the Protection of Human Rights and Fundamental Freedoms* (ECHR), Rome, 4 November 1950 (*Trb.* 1951/154, *Trb.* 1961/8).

7 See for example CESCR, General Comment No. 14, 'The right to the highest attainable standard of health', 11 May 2000, *UN Doc.* E/C.12/2000/4, para. 33–37.

8 See for example HRC, General Comment No. 31, 'The Nature of the General Legal Obligation Imposed on States Parties to the Covenant', 26 May 2004, *UN Doc.* CCPR/C/21/Rev.1/Add.13 (2004), para. 6–8.

9 See among other sources ECtHR 26 March 1985, *X and Y/The Netherlands*, no. 8978/80, para. 23.

ensure human rights, but also positive ones. The European CSR focuses almost exclusively on the latter category.[10] In essence, *negative obligations* entail that states must refrain from unlawful violations of the convention rights. The emphasis with negative obligations therefore is on the state abstaining from action and respecting the right(s). On the other hand, *positive obligations* force the state to intervene actively so as to guarantee that citizens can fully enjoy their fundamental rights. Because of these obligations, the authorities are required to act rather than refrain from acting. This concerns obligations such as providing legislation, taking measures, conducting policies, making financial and other resources available and operationalizing the effective protection of individuals against unlawful breaches of their human rights.

Nearly all human rights involve both negative and positive obligations. This is also true for the fundamental rights which are in the spotlight in this chapter. For example, if we look at the right to health, one example of a negative obligation is that the authorities are not allowed to poison water as a result of which people could fall ill or die. An example of a positive obligation with this right is that the state has to provide a system of health care. In respect of the right to life, the right not to be subjected to inhuman treatment and the right to a private life, the state should not shoot and kill people, assault people or enter into homes unlawfully. These are all negative obligations. Positive obligations in this respect are, for example, that the state must protect individuals from such conduct by other private persons.

Although there may also be situations in which the distinction between negative and positive obligations is not particularly clear-cut, in most cases it is fairly easy to determine which is which. We note that there are all sorts of positive obligations from a conceptual point of view, but as the differences between them are not relevant for the following, we will not look into this. This also applies to the question to what extent positive obligations are more problematic than negative ones.[11] What is important for this chapter, though, is keeping the general distinction between negative and positive obligations in mind at all times.[12]

---

10 Therefore, negative obligations hardly feature in the huge number of judgments mentioned in Council of Europe, *Digest of the Case Law of the European Committee of Social Rights*, 1 September 2008.

11 For more information on these various issues, see Piet Hein P.H.M.C. van Kempen, 'Four Concepts of Security – A Human Rights Perspective', *Human Rights Law Review* 2013, vol. 13, no. 1, pp. 1–23.

12 For an elaborate discussion see also Laurens Lavrysen, *Human rights in a positive state: rethinking the relationship between positive and negative obligations under the European Convention on Human Rights*, Cambridge/Antwerp/Portland: Intersentia, 2016.

2.3. OBLIGATIONS OF STATES ENSUING FROM THE RIGHT TO HEALTH

In answering the ultimate question in this chapter, various sub-questions will be dealt with in connection with the right to health. The most important ones of these are the following three:

> Does the human right to health resist the introduction of a drug policy that permits the cultivation of and trade in cannabis for recreational use, even if and insofar as that drug policy de facto guaranteed individual and public health better than a more prohibitive drug policy?

Related to this question is the following, although the approach is command-based:

> Is a drug policy that permits the cultivation of and trade in cannabis for recreational use an acceptable and possibly even required tool for implementing the human right to health, if and insofar as that drug policy de facto guaranteed individual and public health better than a more prohibitive drug policy?

And finally:

> Does the human right to health require a drug and/or cannabis policy that is also aimed at implementing this right and if yes, what should it constitute?

Below, the emphasis will be on the second question, as the answer to it is crucial in arriving at an answer to the main question of this chapter. Having said that, all the above questions – and others – will, of course, be examined below. Answering the questions will not be possible until the end of this section, as all the various obligations and their aspects that will be discussed below have a bearing on it.

We will now discuss the right to health in a more general sense first. In particular, we will focus our attention on the background, rationale, scope and level of protection of the right to health as well as the definition of health; see sections 2.3.2–2.3.6. Subsequently, the general obligations in connection with the protection of human rights from a good deal of angles will be discussed in section 2.3.7. Each time, this will also include more in particular an examination of the meaning of the various general obligations in relation to the right to health and the cannabis issue. After the detailed discussion of these topics, in section 2.3.8 we will look at the positive obligations arising specifically from the right to health, obviously again in the light of the cannabis issue. Section 2.3.9 then deals with the relevance of democratic decision-making, social consensus and participation of citizens in defining the particulars of the right to health, while section 2.3.10 constitutes an explanation of the possibilities, restrictions and conditions regarding the right to health and alcohol, tobacco and drugs from the point of view of specifically the ICESCR Committee and the European CSR. Building on this, we turn our attention in section 2.3.11 to the UN Special Rapporteur on the right to health and his insights regarding drugs and the right to health. We round our analysis off with a conclusion in section 2.3.12, in which the above-mentioned questions are answered.

First of all, in section 2.3.1 we will provide a brief overview of arguments related to individual and public health that are put forward to back up proposals for regulated permission of cannabis cultivation and trade for recreational consumption. This will also shed more light on how the right to health could be relevant in relation to the cannabis issue.

2.3.1. ARGUMENTS FOR REGULATION BASED ON INDIVIDUAL AND PUBLIC HEALTH

As we have seen earlier, pleas for regulated permission of cannabis cultivation and trade for recreational consumption often refer to the interests of individual and public health. This book is not about providing a full overview of arguments based on individual and public health that could substantiate pleas for regulation. What follows is restricted to arguments that have been used in the Netherlands and in several other countries in this respect.[13,14] Essentially, the various (and sometimes interconnected) arguments that have been proposed amount to the following.

- *Cannabis quality control.* Through regulation, the government creates an opportunity to control the quality of cannabis. This will benefit the consumer's health. In the Netherlands, for example, cannabis growers feel a constant pressure because of the possibility of a police raid, so they feel they have to harvest rather sooner than later. This may result in drugs of poorer quality.

---

13 The following is based on the inventory as presented in Piet Hein P.H.M.C. van Kempen & Masha I. Fedorova, *Internationaal recht en cannabis. Een beoordeling op basis van VN-drugsverdragen en EU-drugsregelgeving van gemeentelijke en buitenlandse opvattingen pro regulering van cannabisteelt voor recreatief gebruik*, Deventer: Kluwer, 2014, pp. 140–141 and 181–186 (see also pp. 6 and 8) – of letters, notes and reports from 25 Dutch municipalities, the literature to which these municipalities refer and the initiatives deployed in countries other than the Netherlands as described in particular in Beau Kilmer, Kristy Kruithof, Mafalda Pardal, Jonathan P. Caulkins & Jennifer Rubin, *Multinational overview of cannabis production regimes*, RAND Europe/WODC, 2013.

14 For another illustration of how more liberal approaches can match the interests of individual and public health see the recent Report of the United Nations High Commissioner for Human Rights, Study on the impact of the world drug problem on the enjoyment of human rights, *UN Doc.* A/HRC/30/65, 4 September 2015, para. 24–30; see also the extensive overview in Joanne Csete et al., 'Public health and international drug policy', *The Lancet* 2016 (online).

- *Cannabis chain control.* Through regulation of cannabis cultivation, clearly defined requirements can be imposed on the entire business process of cultivation. This will benefit the health of the consumer, producer and stakeholders. Requirements could relate to fire risks, the technical installations, the packaging of cannabis, the security of the nursery, the quantity and quality of the pesticides, the THC content, the THC/CBD ratio, the HSE requirements for employees, the integrity of the entrepreneur and education for users. A system of regulated cultivation would also mean that adherence to the above-mentioned requirements can be checked.
- *Protection of health and lives of local residents.* As illegal hemp nurseries are currently often located in residential areas, they cause dangerous situations there. There would be a direct risk of seriously harmful infections, such as legionella, for local residents as a result of the high humidity in combination with high temperatures. Moreover, the theft of power and the unsafe wiring of the electrical installations increase the risk of fire, which could cause severe burns or death.
- *Protection of health of juveniles.* If cannabis cultivation and trade were regulated, the consumption by juveniles could also be under stricter control.
- *Distinction between soft drugs and hard drugs markets.* Regulating cannabis cultivation and trade contributes to a clear differentiation between the markets for soft drugs and hard drugs. The argument goes that if the entire cannabis chain is regulated, there will be no more hard drugs available from soft drugs dealers/growers and the soft drugs user would be less likely to slide down the slippery slope towards hard drugs. This argument is also at the heart of the current soft drugs policy in The Netherlands.
- *Cannabis as a less risky, alternative, stimulant.* Furthermore, regulation of cannabis would contribute to the individual freedom of choice for intoxication; cannabis, according to some, is significantly less risky than legal substances such as alcohol and tobacco.

It must be emphasized once again that this research is not about assessing the validity or correctness of these health-related arguments. So we will not do anything of the kind. We are acting from the hypothesis that each of these arguments is valid and subsequently assess whether that argument with that state of affairs could find a basis in the right to health.

2.3.2. ARTICLE 25 UNIVERSAL DECLARATION OF HUMAN RIGHTS AS THE BASIS

The codification of the right to health in international human rights provisions is based on Article 25 of the Universal Declaration of Human Rights (UDHR), which while it is not legally binding, is authoritative. This provision guarantees that everyone has the right to 'a standard of living *adequate* for the health and well-being of himself and of his family' (emphasis added), and the first paragraph of that article goes on to state:

> including food, clothing, housing and *medical care* and necessary social services, and the right to security in the event of unemployment, *sickness*, disability, widowhood, old age or other lack of livelihood *in circumstances beyond his control* (emphasis added).

Owing to the extent and complexity of the two rights that effectively come to the fore here, namely the right to an adequate standard of living and the right to health, these have been included in binding instruments in separate provisions, such as Article 11 and Article 12 ICESCR, respectively.[15] In the European Social Charter, the purpose of which is the implementation of the Universal Declaration,[16] the rights have also been separated; for the right to health see Article 11 ESC.[17] Nonetheless, for a good understanding and interpretation of the right to health it is important to realize that this right is conceptually linked to the right to an adequate standard of living and that the realization of this right also depends on the realization of other rights. The ICESCR Committee explicitly acknowledges this relation and dependency.[18]

2.3.3. RATIONALE FOR THE RIGHT TO HEALTH

The right to health is a fundamental human right and is of crucial importance to achieve peace and security.[19] We have hereby also embedded the interests to be protected within a broader framework: the conceptual basis of international human rights is not only informed by individual interests, they also serve the wider, more instrumental interest of social order.[20] Good health is essential

---

15 Ben Saul, David Kinley & Jacqueline Mowbray, *The International Covenant on Economic, Social and Cultural Rights*, Oxford: Oxford University Press, 2014, p. 978.

16 Council of Europe, *Digest of the Case Law of the European Committee of Social Rights*, 1 September 2008, p. 13.

17 Incidentally, also see the right to benefit from any measures [...] to enjoy the highest possible standard of health attainable in Part I point 11 and the right to social and medical assistance in Part I point 13 and in Article 13 ESC; these rights are not directly relevant though for the question to which this research relates, so they will therefore be disregarded in principle.

18 CESCR, General Comment No. 14, 'The right to the highest attainable standard of health', 11 May 2000, *UN Doc.* E/C.12/2000/4 (also: CESCR, General Comment No. 14 (2000) 'Right to Health'), para. 3.

19 Preamble of the Constitution of the World Health Organization.

20 Annotations on the Text of the Draft International Covenants on Human Rights, *UN Doc.* A/2929, 1 July 1955, p. 25 (para. 51): "[t]here was, it was said, an absolute necessity for harmonising the rights of the individual on the one hand and the requirements of the community on the other". See also Piet Hein P.H.M.C. van Kempen, 'Four Concepts of Security – A Human Rights Perspective', *Human Rights Law Review* 2013, vol. 13, no. 1, pp. 1–23.

for a life in keeping with human dignity,[21] and healthy individuals are valuable and even indispensable for society in general. In this way, when the right to health has been fully realized, this does not serve only a fundamental individual interest, but also a substantial public interest.[22]

2.3.4. WHAT IS UNDERSTOOD BY HEALTH?

The Preamble in the Constitution of the World Health Organization (WHO) contains a definition of health:

> Health is a state of complete physical, mental and social well-being and not merely the absence of disease or infirmity.

This definition, or any other, has not been included explicitly in the ICESCR nor in the ESC. As far as the ICESCR is concerned, the reason for that is that including such definitions was unusual in this convention and because the reference to social well-being would be out of place in the article of the convention.[23] The meaning of the term 'social well-being' was considered unclear. It was also pointed out that the addition of this term would give the right to health too wide a scope and would lead to an unclear and unworkable definition of health.[24]

Nevertheless, the European CSR explicitly relies on the definition by the WHO.[25] The ICESCR Committee now uses an even broader definition than the one manifested in the Constitution of the WHO.[26] The ICESCR Committee emphasizes that the term 'the highest attainable standard of physical and mental health' is not limited to healthcare:

---

21 See in particular European CSR; see Council of Europe, *Digest of the Case Law of the European Committee of Social Rights*, 1 September 2008, p. 81; ECSR 3 November 2004, *International Federation of Human Rights Leagues (FIDH)/France*, no. 14/2003, para. 31.

22 See also section 2.3.8.iii.

23 Annotations on the Text of the Draft International Covenants on Human Rights, *UN Doc.* A/2929, 1 July 1955, p. 111 (para. 34).

24 See among others John Tobin, *The Right to Health in International Law*, Oxford: Oxford University Press, 2012, p. 125; Richard Baker & Vanessa Taylor, 'The Right to Health: A Right On The Rise?', *The Journal Jurisprudence* 2013, pp. 275–303 on pp. 276–280. Toebes is of the opinion that the definition of 'health' does not necessarily contribute to a better understanding of the 'right to health', which right can best be explained by practical application of rulings of international and national (judicial) authorities; see Brigit Toebes, *The Right to Health as a Human Right in International Law*, Antwerp: Intersentia, 1999, p. 24.

25 See Council of Europe, *Digest of the Case Law of the European Committee of Social Rights*, 1 September 2008, p. 81.

26 Maša Marochini, Council of Europe and the Right to Healthcare – Is the European Convention on Human Rights Appropriate Instrument for Protecting the Right to Healthcare?, *Zbornik Pravnog fakulteta Sveučilista u Rijeci* 2013, pp. 729–760 on pp. 730–731.

> On the contrary, the drafting history and the express wording of article 12.2 acknowledge that *the right to health embraces a wide range of socio-economic factors* that promote conditions in which people can lead a healthy life [...] (emphasis added).[27]

This is also expressed by the UN Special Rapporteur on the right to health, who opts for an even wider angle by also including protection against violence as well as environments that are safe and offer opportunities for health and well-being:

> Importantly, the right to health includes more than access to health services; it is also the right to the underlying determinants of health, including equality and non-discrimination, protection against violence, participation, and safe and enabling environments for health and well-being.[28]

One objection raised against too wide a definition of health is that the right to health would then be a catch-all for everything that influences the health of individuals.[29] Almost anything could then eventually be subsumed under this right. At the same time, too narrow a definition of health would mean that factors that genuinely have or can have a significant influence on the health of individuals would be excluded from the sphere of influence of the right.

This book is not the place to deal at length with the discussion about the definition of health and the problems surrounding it. A few observations will suffice. First, the notion of 'health' in international law is a multi-dimensional construction containing both biophysical and psychosocial elements.[30] Moreover, it is important that the right to health has no hard or natural boundary. On the contrary: the ICESCR Committee acknowledges that the meaning of health has changed substantially and has increased in scope since the ICESCR was established in 1966. This is why the ICESCR Committee decides to interpret the term 'health' broadly:

> The Committee interprets the right to health, as defined in article 12.1, as an inclusive right extending not only to timely and appropriate health care but also to *the underlying determinants of health*, such as access to safe and potable water and adequate sanitation, an adequate supply of safe food, nutrition and housing, healthy occupational and environmental conditions, and access to health-related education and information, including on sexual and reproductive health.[31]

---

27 CESCR, General Comment No. 14 (2000) 'Right to Health', para. 4; see also para. 9 and 10.

28 Open Letter by the Special Rapporteur on the right of everyone to the highest attainable standard of mental and physical health, Dainius Pūras, in the context of the preparations for the UN General Assembly Special Session on the Drug Problem (UNGASS), which will take place in New York in April 2016, 7 December 2015.

29 John Tobin, *The Right to Health in International Law*, Oxford: Oxford University Press, 2012, p. 132.

30 See also CESCR, General Comment No. 14 (2000) 'Right to Health', para. 4 and 9.

31 Ibid, para. 11; see also para. 4, 9 and 10.

The right to health and the obligations that arise from it for the state are therefore not limited to health care, but also have a clear bearing on factors that affect the health of individuals and the public at large. The European CSR also does not limit the right to health to healthcare, and pursuant to the text of Article 11 ESC it treats health in a much wider context in which the emphasis is on prevention and general public health.[32] A drug and/or cannabis policy can therefore be important to the concept of 'health' in the sense of the right to health. Below, we will see repeatedly – more in particular in sections 2.3.6, 2.3.10, 2.3.11 and 2.3.12 – that this is indeed the case and that drugs are not a marginal but a core subject in the context of the right to health.

2.3.5. LEVEL OF GUARANTEE FOR RIGHT TO HEALTH ('HIGHEST ATTAINABLE STANDARD')

Article 12 ICESCR contains the most elaborate general provision in international law regarding the right to health.[33] The first paragraph of Article 12 ICESCR guarantees 'the right of everyone to the enjoyment of the *highest attainable standard* of physical and mental health' (emphasis added).[34]

The '*highest attainable standard*' in Article 12 ICESCR reveals an approach that differs from that of the '*adequate standard*' in Article 25 UDHR. The standard in the UDHR has been couched in more specific (absolute) terms: individuals have the right to 'a standard of living adequate for the health [...] of himself and of his family', but no more than that, even if the state could achieve a higher standard of living. The level of health has not been qualified any further here, but it seems plausible that health too must be adequate. This is different in Article 12 ICESCR. After all, this provision requires 'the *highest attainable standard* of physical and mental health'. The obligation has been couched in relative terms, but it also implies that it will not do to achieve a merely adequate level of health if a higher level is achievable, taking into account the resources that the state has at its disposal, among other things.[35] Consequently, the obligation

---

32 See Council of Europe, *Digest of the Case Law of the European Committee of Social Rights*, 1 September 2008, pp. 81–88.

33 The right to health and healthcare is also recognized in Article 25 UDHR, Article 5(e)(iv) International Convention on the Elimination of All Forms of Racial Discrimination; Art. 11 and Article 12 Convention on the Elimination of All Forms of Discrimination against Women; Art. 24 Convention on the Rights of the Child; Article 35 Charter of Fundamental Rights of the European Union, Article 11 European Social Charter, Article 16 African Charter on Human and Peoples' Rights, and Article 10 Additional Protocol to the American Convention on Human Rights in the area of Economic, Social, and Cultural Rights. ('Protocol of San Salvador').

34 See also Annotations on the Text of the Draft International Covenants on Human Rights, *UN Doc.* A/2929, 1 July 1955, p. 20 (para. 25).

35 CESCR, General Comment No. 14 (2000) 'Right to Health', para. 47.

to realize the right to health therefore has no upper limit and is boundless in this respect. This more ambitious and result-oriented wording is founded in the Constitution of the World Health Organization,[36] which served as a model in formulating Article 12 ICESCR.[37,38] In itself, the text of this provision implies that states must choose policies and other measures that they are genuinely able to effect and which best guarantee the health of individuals and society. This is also true for the right to health in Article 11 ESC. While this provision requires states merely to take 'appropriate measures' to ensure 'the effective exercise of the right to protection of health', the European CSR uses the result-driven norm of 'the highest possible standard of health'.[39] Insofar as the right to health extends to recreational use of cannabis, policies and measures regarding cannabis must therefore also contribute to the highest possible standard of health.

2.3.6. SCOPE OF OBLIGATIONS REGARDING THE RIGHT TO HEALTH

The scope of the individual right to health is limited to an important degree by the very nature of this right itself. The right to health after all does not imply the right to be healthy.[40] In this respect, the government is not tasked with providing individuals with 'health'. However, the government has all sorts of obligations in connection with that health. These include so-called negative obligations (respect for the individual's control over his own body and health, refraining from torture and non-consensual medical treatment and experiments; there is a clear overlap here with the right to privacy and the right not to be subjected

---

36 The Constitution of the WHO was signed by 61 states on 22 July 1946 and came into force on 7 April 1948. Currently, the WHO has 194 member states. This definition of health, however, was not used in formulating Article 12 of the International Covenant on Economic, Social and Cultural Rights (ICESCR), see CESCR, General Comment No. 14 (2000) 'Right to Health', para. 4.

37 For the historical background, see Ben Saul, David Kinley and Jacqueline Mowbray, *The International Covenant on Economic, Social and Cultural Rights*, Oxford: Oxford University Press, 2014, pp. 978–979; John Tobin, *The Right to Health in International Law*, Oxford: Oxford University Press, 2012, Chapter 2.

38 See the preamble to the Constitution of the World Health Organisation: 'The enjoyment of the highest attainable standard of health is one of the fundamental rights of every human being without distinction of race, religion, political belief, economic or social condition.' See also Article 1 of the Constitution: 'The objective of the World Health Organization (hereinafter called the Organization) shall be the attainment by all peoples of the highest possible level of health'.

39 See also, among other sources, ECSR, Conclusions 2013 on the European Social Charter (The Netherlands), January 2014, under: Article 11. See also Council of Europe, *Digest of the Case Law of the European Committee of Social Rights*, 1 September 2008, p. 81.

40 CESCR, General Comment No. 14 (2000) 'Right to Health', para. 8 and 9. See also Brigit Toebes, 'Het recht op gezondheid: geen recht om gezond te zijn', *Ars Aequi* 1999, pp. 912–915 (i.e., 'The right to health: not a right to be healthy', *Ars Aequi* 1999, pp. 912–915).

to torture or inhuman/humiliating treatment), as well as so-called positive obligations (as expressed for example by subparagraphs a to d of the second paragraph).[41] These obligations will be reviewed in more concrete terms later.[42]

More generally, it can the observed already at this stage that the ICESCR Committee takes a broad view on what states are required to do to realize the right of health:

> The realization of the right to health may be pursued through numerous, complementary approaches, such as the formulation of health policies, or the implementation of health programmes developed by the World Health Organization (WHO), or the adoption of specific legal instruments. Moreover, the right to health includes certain components which are legally enforceable.[43]

Article 11 ESC and the European CSR also demonstrate a similarly broad interpretation, partly because the Committee under Article 11 ESC explicitly dwells on all sorts of avoidable health risks, the promotion of a healthy lifestyle, preventing diseases and accidents and using certain resources.[44] The European CSR stresses:

> under Article 11 para. 1 of the Charter, health systems must respond appropriately to avoidable health risks, i.e. ones that can be controlled by human action, and *states must guarantee the best possible results* in line with *the available knowledge* (emphasis added).[45]

The broad view of obligations under the right to health taken by the ICESCR Committee and the European CSR is a key component of this research. It is exactly because drugs constitute a potential health risk that this raises the question to what extent the right to health forces states to adopt a drug policy with public health in mind. Both the ICESCR Committee[46] and the European CSR[47] demand a policy that is aimed at discouragement of recreational use of tobacco, alcohol and drugs, and at measures against such use.[48] If we assume,

---

41 Opposing these various obligations are the individual's freedoms and entitlements; see CESCR, General Comment No. 14 (2000) 'Right to Health', para. 8.

42 See section 2.3.8.

43 CESCR, General Comment No. 14 (2000) 'Right to Health', para. 1.

44 See Council of Europe, *Digest of the Case Law of the European Committee of Social Rights*, 1 September 2008, pp. 81–88.

45 See for example ECSR 23 January 2013, *International Federation of Human Rights Leagues (FIDH)/Greece*, No. 72/2011, para. 144; Council of Europe, *Digest of the Case Law of the European Committee of Social Rights*, 1 September 2008, p. 81.

46 CESCR, General Comment No. 14 (2000) 'Right to Health', para. 9, 36.

47 Council of Europe, *Digest of the Case Law of the European Committee of Social Rights*, 1 September 2008, p. 84.

48 For more information on this, see section 2.3.10.

as the UN narcotic drugs conventions do,[49] that recreational cannabis use in general entails health risks, it follows that a policy concerning cannabis for recreational use in principle also falls under the sphere of influence of the right to health in Article 12 ICESCR and Article 11 ESC.

Both the ICESCR Committee and a little more frequently the European CSR pay attention to cannabis with respect to the right to health.[50] However, it is crucial that neither the ICESCR and the ICESCR Committee nor the ESC and the European CSR demand policies or measures aimed at an absolute prohibition and/or eradication of drugs (use) where adults are involved.[51] The reason for this is that individual and public health are key instead of the drugs as such. Consequently, this still raises the question whether a drug policy that permits the cultivation of and trade in cannabis for recreational use up to a point is an acceptable and possibly even required vehicle for implementing the human right to health, if and insofar as that drug policy de facto guaranteed individual and public health better than a more prohibitive drug policy. Of course, we will return to this question, in the conclusion about the right to health for example.

Upon further examination of the obligations the state has pursuant to the right to health, it is also important to keep in mind that there are all sorts of health aspects that involve more than just the relation between the state and the individual. These include individual genetic factors and risky lifestyles. The right to health must therefore be understood as the right to enjoy various facilities, goods, services and conditions that are necessary for an individual to strive for the highest possible level of health.[52] This is not to say though that the state could not assume any responsibility at all for unhealthy lifestyles. Later in this chapter, especially in sections 2.3.10 and 2.3.11, it will become clear that states are explicitly required to discourage drug use, on the grounds of the right to health.

In this context, it is also interesting that the rationale of the UN narcotic drugs conventions[53] is partly based on public health interests and that they

49 Piet Hein P.H.M.C. van Kempen & Masha I. Fedorova, *International Law and Cannabis I*, Cambridge: Intersentia, 2019.

50 See CESCR, Summary record of the 14th meeting (The Netherlands), *UN Doc.* E/C.12/1998/SR.14, 15 September 1998, para. 55–56, and ECSR, Conclusions 2013 on the European Social Charter (The Netherlands) respectively, among other sources, under: Article 11(3); Conclusions 2013 on the European Social Charter (Sweden), under: Article 11(3).

51 Cf. Council of Europe, *Digest of the Case Law of the European Committee of Social Rights*, 1 September 2008, p. 87. For more information on this, see section 2.3.10.

52 CESCR, General Comment No. 14 (2000) 'Right to Health', para. 9.

53 Single Convention on Narcotic Drugs (1961) as amended by the Protocol amending the Single Convention on Narcotic Drugs (1972), the Convention on Psychotropic Substances (1971) and United Nations Convention Against Illicit Traffic in Narcotic Drugs and Psychotropic Substances (1988).

aim to ensure the following in a certain way: 1. Availability of narcotic drugs as meaningful and/or effective medicine or research into this; 2. Treatment of and care for drug users so as to wean them off these narcotic drugs; 3. Protecting society against narcotic drugs by fighting and eliminating the production, trade and possession of these drugs for recreational purposes by means of criminal law and many other kinds of prohibitions and measures.[54] While it is true that public health in the general sense is not an interest recognized or pursued under the drugs conventions, the conventions force states to fight drug use, particularly with the obligations regarding care for drug users and fighting drugs. Incidentally, this does not imply, as follows from the above, that the way in which the drugs conventions aim to contribute to public health is aligned with the way in which the right to health from the human rights point of view aims to ensure public health.

Additionally, a few broader subjects play a prominent part in realizing the rights to health. For example, access to health care and the underlying health determinants must be equal and non-discriminatory. The ICESCR Committee recommends that states integrate a gender-based approach in their public health policy).[55] Women, children and adolescents, the elderly, people with a handicap and indigenous peoples require special attention with regard to the right to health.[56] The European CSR points out that effective healthcare for everyone without discrimination is a 'basic human right'.[57]

2.3.7. GENERAL OBLIGATIONS TO ENSURE THE RIGHT TO HEALTH

Human rights conventions cover various general obligations for states that they are required to fulfil in relation to the individual human rights enshrined in those conventions. The general obligations in the ICESCR and the ESC therefore also apply to the right of health. Before we turn our attention in the next section to the specific positive obligations for states that ensue from this right, we will discuss those general obligations. Incidentally, the general starting point in this respect is always that rights and obligations must be implemented effectively. The ICESCR Committee emphasizes this repeatedly, for example in General

54 See Piet Hein P.H.M.C. van Kempen & Masha I. Fedorova, *International Law and Cannabis I*, Cambridge: Intersentia, 2019, Chapter 2.

55 CESCR, General Comment No. 14 (2000) 'Right to Health', para. 18–20.

56 Ibid, para. 21–27.

57 Council of Europe, *Digest of the Case Law of the European Committee of Social Rights*, 1 September 2008, p. 82.

Comment No. 14 as regards the right to health.[58] Furthermore, the European CSR states with respect to the nature of the obligations for the state that the rights must be 'concrete and effective' and must be protected not 'merely theoretically' but also 'in fact'.[59] In addition to this, the European Social Charter must also be regarded as a 'living instrument'.[60] This also entails that current knowledge or available knowledge may be important or the meaning to be assigned to the right to health.[61] In this sense, the developing knowledge about the effects and risks of cannabis could play a part.

i. General Provisions: Article 2 ICESCR and Part I Preamble ESC

First of all, what is relevant here is Article 2 ICESCR. The history of the creation of the convention shows that there were three options as regards the wording of the general obligation in the ICESCR. One option was that each individual provision in the ICESCR would mention in detail the specific steps that states should have to take.[62] This idea was abandoned. This also applies to the second option. The second option was based on the view that as all human rights are equally important, states would have equal obligations under the ICCPR and the ICESCR, and that the more binding obligations as laid down in Article 2 ICCPR would also have to be included in the ICESCR.[63] Eventually, a third option was adopted, namely 'that it would be realistic to limit the terms of each individual article to a recognition of the particular right by the State and to add an "umbrella" article imposing a general obligation on states which would be applicable to all the rights recognized in the covenant.'[64] So in addition to the general obligations, the provisions of the convention specifying the individual rights, including the right to health,

58 CESCR, General Comment No. 14 (2000) 'Right to Health', see also para.31: 'States parties have a specific and continuing obligation to move as expeditiously and effectively as possible towards the full realization of article 12.'; see also CESCR, General Comment No. 3 (1990) 'Obligations', para. 9.

59 Council of Europe, *Digest of the Case Law of the European Committee of Social Rights*, 1 September 2008, p. 15; see also ECSR 9 September 2015, *Matica Unione Italiana del Lavoro U.I.L. Scuola – Sicilia/Italy*, no.113/2014, para. 14, 'the aim and purpose of the Charter, being a human rights protection instrument, is to protect rights not merely theoretically, but also in fact'; in the same vein: ECSR 2 July 2014, *European Federation of National Organisations working with the Homeless (FEANTSA)/The Netherlands*, no. 86/2012, para. 224.

60 See also, among other sources, ECSR, Conclusions 2014 on the European Social Charter (Georgia), under: Article 5: 'The Committee recalls that "the Charter is a living instrument, whose purpose is to protect rights not merely theoretically but also in fact"'.

61 ECSR 6 December 2006, *Marangopoulos Foundation for Human Rights (MFHR)/Greece*, no. 30/2005, para. 194 and 202. See for information on this also section 2.3.6.

62 Annotations on the Text of the Draft International Covenants on Human Rights, *UN Doc.* A/2929, 1 July 1955, p. 19 (para. 19).

63 Ibid, p. 20 (para. 20).

64 Ibid, p. 20 (para. 21).

now indicate which obligations (be they more stringent or less so) states have under the relevant specific rights.[65] In the European Social Charter there is a somewhat different approach in the sense that it contains a general provision about the objectives, which applies to certain rights (see Part I ESC) and subsequently a general obligation that in turn applies to different other rights again (Part II).

The general provision in the ICESCR contains 'what was felt to be the firmest commitment which could reasonably be undertaken in relation to all the rights treated in the covenant'.[66] Article 2 ICESCR therefore requires, among other things, that the states parties:

- take steps 'to the maximum of its available resources' and 'by all appropriate means, including particularly the adoption of legislative measures', 'with a view to achieving progressively the full realization of the rights recognized' in the convention.
- This concerns measures to be taken individually as well as measures through international assistance and cooperation.

Part I Preamble ESC is a little more limited in this respect. According to its provisions, among other things, the states parties accept:

- as the aim of their policy, to be pursued by all appropriate means, the attainment of conditions in which certain rights and principles – such as the right to benefit from any measures enabling people to enjoy the highest possible standard of health attainable – may be effectively realized.
- This concerns appropriate means, both national and international.

This general objective therefore only refers to the right to health care facilities rather than the right to health in Article 11 ESC. There is another general obligation for that, according to which the states parties:

- consider themselves bound by the obligations set out in the provisions specified.

This general obligation is therefore also applicable to the right to health in Article 11 ESC. This provision contains obligations that go even further, which we will look into later. What matters here is that the right to health in article 11 ESC is subject to a more binding obligation than the right to health facilities in Part I ESC.

---

65 Ibid, p. 20 (para. 22).
66 Ibid, p. 20 (para. 22).

ii. Tripartite Typology: Obligations to Respect, Protect and Fulfil

The obligations in Article 2 ICESCR are intrinsically hybrid[67] and they cover – according to the ICESCR Committee – both obligations of conduct and obligations of result.[68] These obligations are also characterized by three distinct dimensions (types or levels): to respect, protect and fulfil the human rights. This tripartite typology has been developed in the literature.[69] Subsequently, this typology has been recognized by the international human rights organizations and is applied by them.[70] That is the case for the ICESCR Committee too, also in relation to the right to health.[71] On the other hand, as far as we know, the European CSR has never referred explicitly to the tripartite typology, but it is clear that the obligations under the ESC also add substance to the three dimensions of respect, protection and fulfilment.

- *The obligation to respect.* Within the tripartite typology, this obligation most clearly refers to that negative freedom of individuals in the sense that the state is required to not intervene (or in some cases: not without a legal basis, not without a legitimate purpose, not without necessity and not disproportionately) in individuals exercising their rights as recognized in the ICESCR.

---

67 Philip Alston and Gerard Quinn, 'The Nature and Scope of States Parties' Obligations under the International Covenant on Economic, Social and Cultural Rights, *Human Rights Quarterly* 1987, vol. 9, pp. 156–229 on p. 185.

68 CESCR, General Comment No. 3, The Nature of States Parties' Obligations (Art. 2, Para. 1, of the Covenant), 14 December 1990, *UN Doc.* E/1991/23 (also: CESCR, General Comment No. 3 (1990) 'Obligations'), para. 1.

69 Shue introduced a 'tripartite typology' of obligations that corresponds to each fundamental human right: 'to avoid depriving', 'to protect from deprivation' and 'to aid the deprived'; see Henry Shue, *Basic Rights: subsistence, affluence and U.S. foreign policy*, New Jersey: Princeton University Press, 1996, p. 52. Eide proposed a slightly modified classification: 'obligations to respect, to protect, to facilitate and to fulfil'; see AsbjØrn. Eide, *Food as a Human Right*, AsbjØrn Eide et al. (eds.), Tokyo: United Nations University, 1984, p. 154. Van Hoof introduced the obligations 'to respect, to protect, to ensure and to promote'; see G.J.H. Van Hoof, Legal nature of economic, social and cultural rights: a rebuttal of some traditional views, in: Philip Alston & Katarina Tomaševski (eds.), *The Right to Food*, Utrecht: Martinus Nijhoff Publishers, 1984, pp. 106–108. Steiner & Alston apply a fivefold distinction: obligation 'to respect', 'to create institutional machinery essential to the realisation of rights', 'to protect rights/prevent violations,' 'provide goods and services to satisfy rights' and 'to promote rights'; see Henry J. Steiner & Philip Alston, *International Human Rights in Context: Law, Politics, Morals*, Oxford: Oxford University Press, 2000, 180–185.

70 See also (with additional references) Piet Hein P.H.M.C. van Kempen, *Repressie door mensenrechten. Over positieve verplichtingen tot aanwending van strafrecht ter bescherming van fundamentele rechten* (oratie Nijmegen), Nijmegen: Wolf Legal Publishers, 2008, p. 22 (i.e., *Repression because of human rights. About positive obligations for applying criminal law to protect fundamental rights* (inaugral lecture Nijmegen)).

71 CESCR, General Comment No. 14 (2000) 'Right to Health', para. 33 ff.: 'The right to health, like all human rights, imposes three types or levels of obligations on States parties: the obligations to *respect, protect* and *fulfil.*' See also for example CESCR, General Comment No. 12, Right to Adequate Food, *UN Doc.* E/C.12/1999/5, 12 May 1999, para. 15.

Specifically with regard to the right to health, the obligation to respect means, according to the ICESCR Committee, that states must refrain from intervening directly or indirectly in the enjoyment of this right.[72] According to the UN Special Rapporteur on the right to health, it comprises the right and the autonomy of individuals to make well-informed decisions about their health.[73] In contrast with the European CSR, which focuses primarily on positive obligations, the ICESCR Committee also fleshes out the obligation 'to respect' in a concrete way by formulating all sorts of prohibitions of interfering with health. For example, states must refrain from prohibiting or obstructing traditional preventative care, healing practices and medicines and from marketing unsafe drugs.[74] States are not allowed to engage in activities, policies and regulations either if these lead to a conflict with the norms embedded in Article 12 ICESCR and if these activities etc. are likely to cause physical harm, unnecessary illness or death. It also means that intentionally withholding or twisting information which is of vital importance to the protection of health or treatment is unacceptable.[75]

In this study, the obligation to respect is therefore relevant to the extent that the state must refrain from acting in a way that adversely affects the health of individuals, directly or indirectly. In itself, this does not mean that states may not regulate the cannabis market for recreational use with an appeal to the right to health and under certain conditions and within certain limits permit – or actively take it upon themselves to ensure – the availability of recreational cannabis to consumers. After all, the question still remains whether a drug policy that permits the cultivation of and trade in cannabis for recreational use up to a point is an acceptable and possibly even required vehicle for implementing the human right to health, insofar as that drug policy de facto guaranteed individual and public health better than a more prohibitive drug policy.

- *The obligation to protect.* This belongs primarily to the domain of the positive obligations. The obligation implies a high degree of state action with regard to guaranteeing the rights in horizontal relationships. The obligation to protect means that states need to take measures, in order to ensure that non-state actors (such as individuals and enterprises) do not engage in unwarranted infringements of the enjoyment of the rights by others.

As regards the right to health and to the extent that this is relevant here, in the opinion of the ICESCR Committee this means among other things

72 CESCR, General Comment No. 14 (2000) 'Right to Health', para. 33. See also CESCR, An Evaluation of the Obligation to Take Steps to the 'Maximum of Available Resources' under an Optional Protocol to the Covenant, *UN Doc.* E/C.12/2007/1, 10 May 2007, para. 7.

73 See also: Report of the Special Rapporteur on the right of everyone to the enjoyment of the highest attainable standard of physical and mental health, Anand Grover, *UN Doc.* A/HRC/26/31, 01 April 2014, para. 14.

74 CESCR, General Comment No. 14 (2000) 'Right to Health', para. 34.

75 Ibid, para. 50.

that states also must control the sale of medical devices and medicines by third parties.[76] More generally, the obligation to protect entails that states must regulate the activities of individuals, groups or companies in such a way that violations of the right to health are prevented. This obligation illustrates that states can be responsible for products of private parties that are available on the consumer market if these can negatively affect individual or public health. This raises the question whether permitting the sale of cannabis for recreational use without a quality control system is not at odds with the obligations to protect under the right to health. In this respect, the arguments about quality control for cannabis and the control of the cannabis chain as mentioned in section 2.3.1[77] are relevant. This is also the case for the arguments in that same section concerning the protection of health of residents, juveniles and protection against the use of hard drugs by separating the soft drugs market from the hard drugs market.

A state can also fail in its obligation to protect if it does not sufficiently discourage the production, sale and consumption of tobacco, drugs and other harmful substances. As we have observed several times before, this does not automatically mean that states would not be allowed to regulate the cannabis market for recreational use with an appeal to the right to health. What it does mean (if it were permitted; that is still the question) that such policies would at any rate have to be accompanied by serious and genuine measures of discouragement.[78]

- *The obligation to fulfil.* This means that states need to take positive measures to realize the right to health. In the case of the right to health, this must take place by providing appropriate measures. These include, among other things, regulation, policies, available budget, promotional activities, monitoring of the measures to implement the right, identifying the health indicators and criteria, all this with a view to realize the right to health fully.[79] The state is required to:

> give sufficient recognition to the right to health in the national political and legal systems, preferably by way of legislative implementation, and to adopt a national health policy with a detailed plan for realizing the right to health (emphasis added).[80]

---

76 Ibid, para. 35.

77 Section 2.3.1 contains an enumeration of arguments based on individual health and public health in favour of regulation that have been used in Dutch municipalities and by the authorities of several other countries and in the literature.

78 See by comparison, regarding tobacco, Virginia A. Leary, 'The Right to Health in International Human Rights Law', *Health and Human Rights* 1994, vol. 1, no. 1, pp. 24–56 on p. 45: 'The obligation to *protect* – preventing others from violating the right – might be considered as obligating the state to control tobacco companies' promotion of tobacco use'.

79 CESCR, General Comment No. 14 (2000) 'Right to Health', para. 33 and 52. See also, for example, Ben Saul, David Kinley & Jacqueline Mowbray, *The International Covenant on Economic, Social and Cultural Rights*, Oxford: Oxford University Press, 2014, pp. 1041–1049.

80 CESCR, General Comment No. 14 (2000) 'Right to Health', para. 36.

As we have seen before – and see also section 2.3.10 and 2.3.11 below in particular – a policy regarding cannabis for recreational use also falls within the sphere of influence of the right to health in Article 12 ICESCR and Article 11 ESC.[81] Given the obligation to fulfil, such a policy is required even if cannabis must be seen as a serious matter of public health. According to the ICESCR Committee, this also covers the obligation to promote medical research and health education and to organize information campaigns with regard to, among other things, the abuse of alcohol and the use of cigarettes, drugs and other harmful substances (quite apart from the question whether such a policy should or can be liberal or rather prohibitive.).[82]

So the obligation to fulfil covers a wide range of obligations, involving positive measures that enable individuals and communities to realize their right to health ('facilitate'), the assignment of rights when individuals or a group are not able to realize the right to health, for reasons beyond their control ('provide'), and promotion of a healthy lifestyle ('promote').[83] It also entails regulating the right to health in national legislation ('regulate'), to monitor its implementation ('monitor') and to intervene in the event of non-compliance with the regulation ('adjudicate').[84]

As we observed before, it is clear that the obligations under the ESC also give further effect to the three dimensions of respect, protection and fulfilment. Among other things, the case law of the European CSR[85] shows, that states must take both legal and concrete action so as to implement the rights in the Charter fully,[86] and that they must also make available means and provide for the operational procedure which is necessary for that implementation.[87]

The foregoing shows that in principle, all instruments at the disposal of the authorities fall within the scope of the general obligations to guarantee the right to health, among other things. In this way, there may be an obligation with regard to these instruments to deploy them if that may contribute to that guarantee. Naturally, then that also applies insofar as cannabis for

81 See section 2.3.6; in particular see also section 2.3.10 below.

82 CESCR, General Comment No. 14 (2000) 'Right to Health', para. 36.

83 Ibid, para. 37; CESCR, An Evaluation of the Obligation to Take Steps to the 'Maximum of Available Resources' under an Optional Protocol to the Covenant, *UN Doc.* E/C.12/2007/1, 10 May 2007, para. 3.

84 Stefaan Smis, Christine Janssens, Sophie Mirgaux & Karen Van Laethem, *Handboek mensenrechten. De internationale bescherming van de rechten van de mens*, Antwerpen: Intersentia, 2011, p. 576 (i.e., *Handbook of human rights. The international protection of human rights*).

85 See also Council of Europe, *Digest of the Case Law of the European Committee of Social Rights*, 1 September 2008, p. 15.

86 ECSR 4 November 2003, *Autism Europe/France*, no. 13/2002, para. 53.

87 ECSR 5 December 2007, *International Movement ATD Fourth world/France*, no. 33/2006, para. 61.

recreational use is considered an issue related to the right to health. Below, we will explore the level, scope and content of the general obligations to deploy the instruments that are available to states. We shall also see that some of the obligations mentioned above are deemed to be the so-called 'minimum core obligations'.

The total scope of the obligations to respect, protect and fulfil is so vast that the arguments related to individual and public health used for the regulated permission of cannabis cultivation and trade – assuming that they are valid – are all in principle relevant for these obligations under the right to health. In short, it is about the following arguments mentioned in section 2.3.1: safeguarding the quality of cannabis, monitoring the cannabis chain, protection of the health of residents and juveniles, separating the soft drugs and hard drugs markets and cannabis as a less risky alternative stimulant. Below, we will see (especially in section 2.3.8) that these arguments also tie in with the specific positive obligations resulting from the right to health.

iii. Obligation for Progressively Achieving Full Realization

The obligation for states, pursuant to Article 2 ICESCR, to achieve 'progressively the full realization of the rights recognized in the present Covenant', is an expression of the central objective to be achieved through the efforts of the states parties.[88] This obligation applies in the context of the scarcity of resources and funds at the disposal of states, which scarcity may make it impossible to give full effect to the rights.[89] This is expressed in Article 2 in the phrase: 'to the maximum of its available resources'. The obligation of progressively achieving 'full realization' does not feature in a general sense in the ESC,[90] but the European CSR assumes there is an obligation to ensure 'steady progress towards achieving the goals laid down by the Charter'.[91] Reasonable time limits should be set here as well.[92]

The concept of further, progressive or increasing realization is intrinsically dynamic and it clearly contains obligations of conduct and result. The concept implies the recognition that the full realization of all economic, social and

88 CESCR, General Comment No. 3 (1990) 'Obligations', para. 9.

89 Ibid, para. 9; CESCR, General Comment No. 14 (2000) 'Right to Health', para. 30. See also Philip Alston & Gerard Quinn, 'The Nature and Scope of States Parties' Obligations under the International Covenant on Economic, Social and Cultural Rights', *Human Rights Quarterly* 1987, vol. 9, pp. 156–229.

90 By the way, this is the case in some specific provisions: see Article 2(1) ESC ('the working week to be progressively reduced') and Article 3(4) ESC ('progressive development of occupational health services for all workers') and Article 12(3) ESC ('raise progressively the system of social security to a higher level').

91 ECSR 5 December 2007, *International Movement ATD Fourth world/France*, no. 33/2006, para. 61.

92 Ibid, para. 65–66.

cultural rights in general is not feasible in the short term.[93] However, this does not mean that states can remain passive or can delay acting. On the contrary: for the right to health too, the obligation of progressively achieving full realization implies a specific and permanent obligation to move as quickly and effectively as possible towards full realization of the highest attainable standard of this right.[94] Thus, the obligation to realize the right to health has no upper limit and in this respect is unlimited, as Article 12(1) and (2) ICCPR also show, actually.[95] Still, no unreasonable demands should be placed on states, or as the UN Special Rapporteur on the right to health puts it: 'States' policies to progressively realize the right to health should be reasonable [...] and fulfil, at a minimum, States' core obligations.'[96]

iv. Ban on Retrogressive Measures

States are not allowed to take retrogressive measures, which means measures which lead to a reduction in the protection of a convention right. This at least is the strong presumption: if the state does take such measures, the state party 'has the burden of proving' that these measures were introduced after the most careful evaluation of all alternatives and that they are appropriately justified in the light of the convention rights in the context of the full use by the state of all the available resources.[97] This also applies to the right of health in Article 12 ICESCR, provided that the deterioration does not relate to the core obligations ensuing from this right.[98,99]

This is a relevant point if a state with regard to the cultivation of cannabis for the recreational consumer market were to consider legalization, regulation or application of a more liberal policy than is currently the case. If such a change led

93 CESCR, General Comment No. 3 (1990) 'Obligations', para. 9.

94 CESCR, General Comment No. 14 (2000) 'Right to Health', para. 31 and also 2, 5, 30, 33, 38, 49. See also, among other sources, Office of the United Nations High Commissioner for Human Rights, *Economic, Social and Cultural Rights. Handbook for National Human Rights Institutions*, U.N./OHCHR: New York/Geneva, 2005, pp. 10–12, with a reference to the Limburg Principles on the Implementation of the International Covenant on Economic, Social and Cultural Rights.

95 In respect of the ESC, this follows from the case law of the European CSR; see section 2.3.5.

96 Report of the Special Rapporteur on the right of everyone to the enjoyment of the highest attainable standard of physical and mental health, Anand Grover, *UN Doc.* A/69/299, 11 August 2014, para. 3.

97 CESCR, General Comment No. 3 (1990) 'Obligations', para. 9; CESCR, An Evaluation of the Obligation to Take Steps to the 'Maximum of Available Resources' under an Optional Protocol to the Covenant, *UN Doc.* E/C.12/2007/1, 10 May 2007, para. 8. See also Report of the United Nations High Commissioner for Human Rights, *UN Doc.* E/2007/82, 25 June 2007, para. 19.

98 For more information on this, see section 2.3.7.viii.

99 CESCR, General Comment No. 14 (2000) 'Right to Health', para. 32 and 48.

to a reduced protection of the right to health, this is not permissible in principle. In view of the room provided by the ICESCR Committee, it would appear that legalization, regulation or application of a more liberal policy need not founder on this ban, if it is neither certain that the change constitutes a deterioration nor that it is an amelioration, but the state has reason to assume that the latter applies. This is even more pertinent if the government were to limit itself in first instance to a pilot scheme, so as to examine the effects of the measures.

Additionally, there might even be room for the aforementioned legalization, regulation or policy if it did lead to a deterioration in the right to health, but that it is urgently required or even necessary in order to guarantee other rights – such as the right to life, physical and psychological integrity, and the right to a private life. In that scenario too, a step-by-step approach through a pilot scheme could reduce potential tension because of the ban on retrogressive measures.

v. *Obligation to Take Steps*

The obligation under Article 2 ICESCR to take steps, which obligation in this provision is not qualified or limited, generates an obligation with an immediate effect, according to the ICESCR Committee.[100] States are required to take action, which in principle reflects the general obligation to comply with the obligations under the conventions in good faith ('pacta sunt servanda').[101]

The obligation 'to take steps' is different from an obligation to guarantee or to ensure,[102] in the sense that the first obligation imposes less strict demands on states. Nevertheless, the obligation to take steps also entails an identifiable

---

100 CESCR, General Comment No. 3 (1990) 'Obligations', para. 1–2. The English wording of 'to take steps' has been translated into French as 's'engage à agir' and in Spanish as 'a adoptar medidas'. The original proposal to use the term 'to promote' was almost immediately brushed aside and terms such as 'to guarantee', 'to ensure' and 'to pledge themselves' were also deemed unacceptable. For more information see Philip Alston & Gerard Quinn, 'The Nature and Scope of States Parties' Obligations under the International Covenant on Economic, Social and Cultural Rights', *Human Rights Quarterly* 1987, vol. 9, pp. 156–229 on pp. 165–166. The other important obligation with an immediate effect is the obligation contained in Article 2(2) ICESCR, which says that states 'undertake to guarantee that the rights [...] will be exercised without discrimination of any kind'.

101 Article 26 of the Vienna Convention on the Law of Treaties.

102 Already during the creation of the ICESCR, it was noted that the wording of Article 2(1) contained too many loop-holes allowing states to wriggle out of the obligations: (1) taking steps for the realization of the right is not the same as guaranteeing these rights; (2) the phrase 'to the maximum of its available resources' could lead to a situation where state always rely on the absence of resources, and moreover (3) the progressively achieving the full realization of rights leaves the door wide open for unlimited delays. This was countered by the observation that the realization of economic, social and cultural rights depends on the available means and national and international economic and social conditions 'over which the State exercised only incomplete control and which not only varied from country to country but were also liable to sudden change.' Annotations on the Text of the Draft International Covenants on Human Rights, *UN Doc.* A/2929, 1 July 1955, p. 20 (paras. 23–24).

and immediate legal obligation.[103] The steps to be taken towards progressively achieving the full realization of the convention rights must be well-informed, concrete and goal-oriented.[104] Taking into account the available resources, states must therefore do as much as possible to realize the rights, but they must at least make progress, which also has to be demonstrated.[105]

In the context of the general obligations, the obligation to take steps is de facto thus not lighter than an obligation to guarantee or give full effect to these rights. It is exactly with respect to the latter that steps need to be taken. To that extent, adhering to policies and measures that produce insufficient results would run counter to this obligation. This could also be of importance for the cannabis issue: if a certain approach of this issue by the authorities results in the situation where individual health and public health are not protected as much as possible, there is an obligation to introduce policies and measures that lead to a better result. Also, new information, increased knowledge and developing insights could give rise to the conclusion that the policy can be improved.[106]

vi. Obligation to Deploy All Appropriate Means

Pursuant to Article 2 ICESCR, states must take steps to achieve the full realization of the rights recognized in the Covenant 'by all appropriate means, including particularly the adoption of legislative measures'. Slightly less demanding is Article 11 ESC, which says that states 'either directly or in cooperation with public or private organizations' will take 'appropriate measures' designed to ensure 'the effective exercise of the right to protection of health'. As can already be seen from the text of these provisions, appropriate measures are not limited to regulations for implementation of the rights under the covenant.[107] We saw earlier with

---

[103] Philip Alston & Gerard Quinn, 'The Nature and Scope of States Parties' Obligations under the International Covenant on Economic, Social and Cultural Rights, *Human Rights Quarterly* 1987, vol. 9, pp. 156–229, op 166.

[104] CESCR, General Comment No. 3 (1990) 'Obligations', para. 2; CESCR, An Evaluation of the Obligation to Take Steps to the 'Maximum of Available Resources' under an Optional Protocol to the Covenant, *UN Doc.* E/C.12/2007/1, 10 May 2007, para. 3.

[105] Stefaan Smis, Christine Janssens, Sophie Mirgaux & Karen Van Laethem, *Handboek mensenrechten. De internationale bescherming van de rechten van de mens*, Antwerpen: Intersentia, 2011, p. 572 (i.e., *Handbook of human rights. The international protection of human rights*).

[106] See section 2.3.7.ix below, among other sources.

[107] CESCR, General Comment No. 3 (1990) 'Obligations', para. 4. See also (about the preference for formal adoption or incorporation of the covenant rights in national law) CESCR, General Comment 9: The domestic application of the Covenant, *UN Doc.* E/C.12/1998/24 (1998) and *UN Doc.* HRI/GEN/1/Rev.6 at 54 (2003) (also: CESCR, General Comment 9 (1998) 'The domestic application of the Covenant'), para. 8. For the ESC, see: Council of Europe, *Digest of the Case Law of the European Committee of Social Rights*, 1 September 2008, pp. 81–88 and 265–274.

regard to the ICESCR that in principle, all instruments at the disposal of the authorities fall within the scope of the general obligations to guarantee the right to health, among other things. This concerns for example: regulation, policies, finances and budgetary measures, promotional activities, information provision and education, enforcement, control an otherwise operational action.[108] Consequently, the wording 'all appropriate measures' must be taken literally. According to the ICCPR Committee, the ICCPR shows a broad and flexible approach here that makes it possible to take into consideration the specifics of the legal and administrative system of each state as well as other relevant factors.[109] However, this flexibility is accompanied by the obligation to use 'all the means at its disposal' to give full effect to the right under the Covenant.[110] In brief: everything that contributes to realizing the rights under the Covenant must be deployed if that is actually possible for the state. The obligation to take appropriate measures is unlimited in that sense. That is an important point here. Seen in this light, the regulated permission of cannabis cultivation and trade for recreational use could be an obligation insofar as that drug policy de facto guaranteed the right to health better than a more prohibitive drug policy.

vii. Obligation to Use Maximum Available Resources

Pursuant to Article 2 ICESCR, the state must achieve full realization of the covenant rights using 'the maximum of its available resources'. There is no similar provision in the ESC. Nevertheless, as we saw in the previous subsection, the European CSR also requires taking measures with 'the maximum use of available resources'.[111]

Already at the time of creation of the ICESCR, it was not considered realistic to demand more from states than an obligation to take steps in the context of maximum available resources to arrive at full realization of the right to health in a progressive way.[112] The inherent tension between realizing the economic, social and cultural rights and the scarcity of resources available to a state took and still takes centre stage in the discussion about the implementation of these rights.[113] In the context of economic, social and cultural rights, this tension is at the heart

---

108 See section 2.3.7.ii.

109 CESCR, General comment No. 9 (1998) 'Domestic application Covenant', para. 1.

110 Ibid, para. 2.

111 ECSR 4 November 2003, *Autism Europe/France*, no. 13/2002, para. 53; ECSR 18 October 2006, *European Roma Rights Centre (ERRC)/Bulgaria*, no. 31/2005, para. 37; ECSR 6 December 2006, *Marangopoulos Foundation for Human Rights (MFHR)/Greece*, no. 30/2005, para. 203 and 205.

112 Annotations on the Text of the Draft International Covenants on Human Rights, *UN Doc.* A/2929, 1 July 1955, p. 20 (para. 21).

113 Audrey R. Chapman, 'A "Violations Approach" for Monitoring the International Covenant on Economic, Social and Cultural Rights', *Human Rights Quarterly* 1996, vol. 18, no. 1, pp. 23–66 on p. 31.

of the necessary evaluation of the conflicting interests. States are given an ample margin of appreciation so as to achieve adequate allocation and/or distribution of resources for the protection of the right to health.[114] 'Maximum available resources' are understood to include both national resources and resources received by the state in the context of international cooperation and assistance.[115]

The obligation to use 'the maximum of its available resources' is not directly relevant to the question in this book whether a drug policy which to some extent permits the cultivation of and trade in cannabis for recreational use can qualify as an acceptable and possibly even necessary realization of the right to health. Consequently, we will not address the obligation to use financial means and other resources further.

viii. Minimum Core Obligations

It is exactly because the scope of the obligations under the ICESCR is inherently dynamic that the ICESCR Committee designates certain obligations as 'minimum core obligations' that are absolute and non-derogable.[116] These obligations must ensure that at least the essential level of each right is guaranteed, because the ICESCR would otherwise be deprived of its raison d'être.[117] According to the Committee, a state in which a significant number of people has no access to primary health care for example, does not meet its obligations under the ICESCR prima facie.[118] When assessing whether a state has fulfilled its minimum core obligations, the limitations with respect to the resources available to that state must by necessity be taken into account.[119] Even if the resources available can be shown to be insufficient, the state retains the obligation to strive for as full a protection of a human right as possible under the specific conditions.[120]

The ICESCR Committee also designates all sorts of obligations as minimum core obligations in relation to the right to health. The most relevant ones for the cannabis issue are:[121]

- 'To ensure the right of access to health facilities, goods and services on a non-discriminatory basis, especially for vulnerable or marginalized groups;'

---

114 John Tobin, *The Right to Health in International Law*, Oxford: Oxford University Press, 2012, p. 228.

115 CESCR, An Evaluation of the Obligation to Take Steps to the 'Maximum of Available Resources' under an Optional Protocol to the Covenant, *UN Doc.* E/C.12/2007/1, 10 May 2007, para. 5.

116 See for more information about the concept of minimum core obligations Katharine G. Young, 'The Minimum Core of Economic and Social Rights: A Concept in Search of Content', *The Yale Journal of International Law* 2008, pp. 113–175; Ingrid A.E.M. Leijten, *Core Rights and the Protection of Socio-Economic Interests by the European Court of Human Rights* (PhD Leiden University), Leiden, 2015, pp. 183–222 (about the ICESCR).

117 CESCR, General Comment No. 3 (1990) 'Obligations', para. 10.

118 Ibid, para. 10.

119 Ibid, para. 10.

120 Ibid, para. 11. See also CESCR, General Comment No. 14 (2000) 'Right to Health', para. 43.

121 See the full listing in CESCR, General Comment No. 14 (2000) 'Right to Health', para. 43–44.

- 'To adopt and implement a national public health strategy and plan of action, on the basis of epidemiological evidence, addressing the health concerns of the whole population.' The strategy and plan of action must be devised, and periodically reviewed, on the basis of a participatory and transparent process. In doing so, methods must be used such as right to health indicators and benchmarks, by which progress can be closely monitored. The process by which the strategy and plan of action are devised, as well as their content, shall give particular attention to all vulnerable or marginalized groups;
- To provide education and access to information concerning the main health problems in the community, including methods of preventing and controlling them.

In particular the obligation regarding adopting and implementing a national public health strategy and plan of action is remarkably broad and detailed for a *minimum* core obligation. This obligation appears to contain all ingredients for a developed system to protect public health, something which even the richest states always struggle with in practice.[122] Given the wide range of this obligation, it is hard to see that it would not also cover the obligation to devise a policy with regard to cannabis for recreational use. Also in view of the fact that alcohol, tobacco and drugs are important topics from the point of view of the right to health (see for more information sections 2.3.10 and 2.3.11 below), we take the position that the above-mentioned obligations for a strategy and plan also require states to conduct a drug and/or cannabis policy and that these explicitly pay attention to the right of health.

The European CSR does not explicitly make use of a system of minimum core obligations. It does, however, apply a so-called decency threshold, and also applies various other thresholds, which imply de facto minimum obligations.[123] However, such thresholds are not (yet) applied in relation to the right to health. Moreover, the European CSR repeatedly reminds the reader of the human dignity, the fundamental values and the core of the European human rights law.[124]

The concept of minimum core obligations and the recognition and interpretation of this concept by the ICESCR Committee is not undisputed in the

---

122 John Tobin, *The Right to Health in International Law*, Oxford: Oxford University Press, 2012, p. 246.

123 Council of Europe, *Digest of the Case Law of the European Committee of Social Rights*, 1 September 2008, p. 217 and passim. See also Evelyne Schmid, *Taking Economic, Social and Cultural Rights Seriously in International Criminal Law*, Cambridge: Cambridge University Press, 2015, p. 53 fn 51.

124 See for example ECSR 23 January 2013, *International Federation of Human Rights Leagues (FIDH)/Greece*, No. 72/2011, para. 50; ECSR 3 November 2004, *International Federation of Human Rights Leagues (FIDH)/France*, no. 14/2003, para. 31; ECSR 26 June 2007, *Mental Disability Advocacy Center (MDAC)/Bulgaria*, no. 41/2007, para. 9.

literature.[125] The Committee bases these minimum obligations on 'the extensive experience gained by the Committee, as well as by the body that preceded it, over a period of more than a decade of examining States parties' reports'.[126] The Committee does not explain why its experience necessitates such a recognition of the concept of minimum core obligations, nor why this recognition (which incidentally does not rely on a grammatical interpretation or interpretation based on the history of the convention) is essential for achieving the objective of the ICESCR.[127]

For the interpretation of the concept of minimum core obligations, Tobin makes a case for a more restrained and more practical approach than the one adopted by the ICESCR Committee.[128] He proposes a few obligations, both with regard to conduct and result, which provide a *minimum* rather than an *optimum* interpretation of the concept. As far as the obligations of conduct are concerned, he suggests two types:

> First, there is an obligation to ensure that when taking steps to secure the right to health, states remain cognisant of the interdependence of this right with other rights. [...] The second type of conduct obligation concerns the processes required for the direct realization of the right to health. As a minimum states must undertake reasonable efforts to develop an appropriate health strategy or plan to achieve this end.[129]

Where the Committee requires that adopting and implementing a national public health strategy and plan of action takes place 'on the basis of epidemiological evidence', Tobin is of the opinion that this should indeed be the ambition, but that this cannot qualify as a minimum core obligation, in

---

125 See for a critical discussion with references to other literature Katharine G. Young, 'The Minimum Core of Economic and Social Rights: A Concept in Search of Content', *The Yale Journal of International Law* 2008, pp. 113–175 on pp. 114–116. Among the advocates is Philip Alston, 'Out of the Abyss: The Challenges Confronting the New U.N. Committee on Economic, Social and Cultural Rights', *Human Rights Quarterly* 1987, vol. 9, no. 3, pp. 332–381 on pp. 352–353. Incidentally, the concept is also recognized in the Maastricht Guidelines on Violations of Economic, Social and Cultural Rights, Maastricht, January 22–26, 1997 (in Guideline 9). See also John Tobin, *The Right to Health in International Law*, Oxford: Oxford University Press, 2012, pp. 241–246.

126 CESCR, General Comment No. 3 (1990) 'Obligations', para. 10.

127 See also David Bilchitz, *Poverty and Fundamental Rights: The Justification and Enforcement of Socio-Economic Rights*, Oxford: Oxford University Press, 2007, p. 185.

128 John Tobin, *The Right to Health in International Law*, Oxford: Oxford University Press, 2012, pp. 243–246. See also Katharine G. Young, 'The Minimum Core of Economic and Social Rights: A Concept in Search of Content', *The Yale Journal of International Law* 2008, pp. 113–175.

129 John Tobin, *The Right to Health in International Law*, Oxford: Oxford University Press, 2012, p. 245.

view of the fact that even developed countries are struggling to create such an advanced system. In his view, the starting point for states should instead be that they can show reasonable and genuine efforts to develop at least a suitable health policy.[130]

Tobin's approach is interesting, because it emphasizes the actual good intentions of states and their concrete reasonable efforts to arrive at a suitable public health policy. This way, states would be able to implement the right to health in such a manner that they believe to be genuinely beneficial to the right, without having to prove this with epidemiological data. It would also allow room for a more liberal drug policy based on the assertion that this would de facto guarantee individual health and public health better than a more prohibitive drug policy. After all, that assertion would not have to be substantiated with hard evidence, but it must be possible to make it in good faith. Although there is certainly something to be said for this approach,[131] also in the light of the primarity principle which will be discussed in the following section, the ICESCR Committee uses a stricter interpretation for the time being. Consequently, in conformity with this interpretation we will assume below that a state must substantiate and/or make plausible the adequacy of the adopted policies.

ix. Primarity: National Authorities are Primarily Responsible for Realizing the Right to Health

Pursuant to international law, it is first and foremost the state that is responsible for ensuring the individual rights and for fulfilling the obligations under conventions to which the state is a signatory. This obvious observation is essential for the analysis in this chapter. The fact that the aforementioned primary responsibility rests with the state – the principle of primarity can be said to apply here[132] – is the basis of, and at the same time follows from, among other things, the general obligations pursuant to Article 2(1) ICESCR. Pursuant to these obligations, the states must take steps with all 'appropriate means', alone or through international assistance and cooperation, to achieve progressively the full realization of the convention rights and implementation of the obligations under it in a way that is most suitable within the context

130 Ibid, p. 246.

131 See also by way of comparison the analysis by Katharine G. Young, 'The Minimum Core of Economic and Social Rights: A Concept in Search of Content', *The Yale Journal of International Law* 2008, pp. 113–175.

132 This term was coined by Jonas Christoffersen, *Fair Balance: Proportionality, Subsidiarity and Primarity in the European Convention on Human Rights*, Leiden/Boston: Martinus Nijhoff Publishers, 2009, pp. 5–6.

of the pertinent state.[133] Taking measures that best match the specific circumstances of the relevant state does not only involve a possibility, which we will look at in the next subsection, but also an obligation for each state. This responsibility of the states parties, to take measures that best achieve the full realization of the convention rights, taking into account the specific situation of the country, also applies to the right to health. The aforementioned also applies in relation to the ESC. The European CSR repeatedly confirmed that 'the primary responsibility for implementing the European Social Charter rests with national authorities'.[134] The observation that the primary responsibility for realizing the right to health also rests with the states parties is endorsed in various respects in international law.

- *The 'pacta sunt servanda' requirement.* The principle of international law 'in good faith' ('pacta sunt servanda') is relevant here. It was codified in Article 26 of the Vienna Convention on the Law of Treaties (VCLT), among other places: 'Every treaty in force is *binding upon the parties* to it and must be performed by them *in good faith*' (emphasis added). The positively worded 'pacta sunt servanda' requirement therefore applies in two respects: with regard to the binding nature of the rights and obligations under the conventions itself and also with respect to the obligation to realize these rights and fulfil these obligations in good faith.[135] The requirement is aimed primarily at states, as also becomes clear from the text of Article 26 of the Vienna Convention on the Law of Treaties that we quoted just now.

  This means that a state party must refrain from acts which would undermine the object and purpose of the obligation under the convention. It also means – as illustrated by Article 31(1) of the VCLT, that a 'treaty shall

---

133 CESCR General Comment No. 14 (2000) 'Right to Health', para. 53, 'The most appropriate feasible measures to implement the right to health will vary significantly from one State to another. Every State has a margin of discretion in assessing which measures are most suitable to meet its specific circumstances. The Covenant, however, clearly imposes a duty on each State to take whatever steps are necessary to ensure that everyone has access to health facilities, goods and services so that they can enjoy, as soon as possible, the highest attainable standard of physical and mental health. This requires the adoption of a national strategy to ensure to all the enjoyment of the right to health [...]. The national health strategy should also identify the resources available to attain defined objectives, as well as the most cost-effective way of using those resources.' See also CESCR, General Comment No. 9 (1998) 'Domestic application Covenant', para. 1.

134 ECSR, Conclusions XX-3 (2014) on the European Social Charter (Denmark), under: Article 6; ECSR 18 March 2013, *International Federation of Human Rights (FIDH)/Belgium*, no. 75/2011, para. 54; Council of Europe, *Digest of the Case Law of the European Committee of Social Rights*, 1 September 2008, p. 14.

135 See International Court of Justice, Judgment of 25 September 1997, *I.C.J. Reports* 1997, p. 7 on pp. 78–79 (para. 142) (*Gabčíkovo-Nagymaros Project (Hungary v. Slovakia)*). See also, with a reference to this judgment, Daniel Davison-Vecchione, 'Beyond the Forms of Faith: Pacta Sunt Servanda and Loyalty', *German Law Journal* 2015, vol. 16, no. 5, pp. 1163–1190 on p. 1166.

be interpreted in good faith in accordance with the ordinary meaning to be given to the terms of the treaty in their context and in the light of its object and purpose'. This provision, too, which is also worded positively, is aimed in any event at states (or to be more precise: at the parties to the VCLT).[136] This also shows from the fact that interpreting treaties in good faith is essential for and the consequence of the general requirement of 'pacta sunt servanda' as expressed in Article 26 of the VCLT.[137] This implies that the interpretation of treaties is also the domain of the state, which also follows from the following consideration by the International Court of Justice: 'The principle of good faith obliges the Parties to apply it [that is to say, the treaty, PHvK & MF] in a reasonable way and in such a manner that its purpose can be realized.'[138]

In view of this and the above-mentioned primary responsibility of states, such interpretation and application (both in practice and according to the system of international law) will need to be undertaken by states in first instance – and in good faith. In relation to the right to health, it is of special importance that the 'pacta sunt servanda' requirement also applies to the duty to fulfil[139] and in particular to the duty to use all appropriate means to achieve progressively 'the full realization' of the right to health with a view to ensuring health of 'the highest attainable standard'.[140] If a state in accordance with these obligations establishes that a certain approach yields the best results in fulfilling an obligation under the convention (such as ensuring the right to health), then in principle that state is required to deploy that approach.[141]

- *Jurisdiction and territoriality of states.* Another important aspect is that the obligation to guarantee human rights is in principle tied up with the territorial jurisdiction of states: it is primarily within these confines that the rights and obligations under the conventions must be effectuated.[142] As the power

136 See also Markus Kotzur, 'Good Faith (Bona fide)', in: *Max Planck Encyclopedia of Public International Law*, Oxford: Oxford University Press (online; last updated: Jan. 2009, para. 19–21; Anthony D'Amato, 'Good Faith', in: Rudolf Bernhardt (ed.), *Encyclopedia of Public International Law*, 1992, p. 600.

137 See also ILC, Draft Articles on the Law of Treaties with commentaries 1966, *Yearbook of the International Law Commission* 1966, vol. II, p. 219 (para. 5) and p. 221 (para. 12).

138 International Court of Justice, Judgment of 25 September 1997, *I.C.J. Reports* 1997, p. 7 on pp. 78–79 (para. 142) (*Gabčíkovo-Nagymaros Project (Hungary v. Slovakia)*).

139 See section 2.3.7.ii.

140 *Cf.* Lorand Bartels, 'Human rights and sustainable development through regional trade agreements', in: Jan Wouters, Axel Marx, Dylan Geraets & Bregt Natens (eds.), *Global Governance through Trade: EU Policies and Approaches*, Cheltenham, UK/Northampton, USA: Edward Elgar, 2015, p. 77.

141 *Cf.* Steven Reinhold, 'Good Faith in International Law', UCL *Journal of Law and Jurisprudence* 2013, vol. 2, pp. 40–63 on p. 58: 'the principle of good faith […] can guide a State's behaviour as to how the inherent rights and obligations are exercised.'

142 John Tobin, *The Right to Health in International Law*, Oxford: Oxford University Press, 2012, p. 325, 'In international law a state has the primary responsibility for securing the realization

over the national territory rests with the sovereign states, it is also states only that can actually be responsible for giving full effect to the human rights treaties within their own territorial borders.[143] Even where the ICESCR – in Article 2 – lays down an explicit obligation regarding international cooperation, the responsibility for discharging that duty lies first and foremost with the states parties themselves. In brief: both the general obligations and the specific human rights and the obligations arising from them of fruit, are aimed primarily at states and these are primarily responsible for the realisation of the rights and the fulfilment of the obligations. This is also clearly reflected in the following consideration by the ICESCR Committee:

> While only *States are* parties to the Covenant and thus *ultimately accountable for compliance* with it, all members of society – individuals, including health professionals, families, local communities, intergovernmental and non-governmental organizations, civil society organizations, as well as the private business sector – have responsibilities regarding the realization of the right to health. *State parties should therefore provide an environment which facilitates the discharge of these responsibilities* (emphasis added).[144]

So even where the ICESCR Committee extends the responsibility for realizing a right to health to the community and its individuals in general, in the final analysis it is still the state that is responsible for achieving this. The same approach can be seen with the European CSR.[145]

– *Principle of subsidiarity.* We also like to point out the principle of subsidiarity, which is relevant for the relation between national and international. The principle states that measures have to be taken on a national level as much as possible and that only if this is not sufficiently feasible or effective, measures may be imposed on an international level as well.[146] According to this principle, the international level is therefore subsidiary to the national level. The subsidiarity principle is partly founded on the premise of the central

of the right to health for the individuals within its jurisdiction.' See also International Court of Justice, Advisory Opinion of 9 July 2004, Legal Consequences of the Construction of a Wall in the Occupied Palestinian Territory, para. 112, 'The International Covenant on Economic, Social and Cultural Rights contains no provision on its scope of application. This may be explicable by the fact that this Covenant guarantees rights which are essentially territorial'.

143 See also Article 29 of the Vienna Convention on the Law of Treaties, entitled 'Territorial Scope of Treaties': 'Unless a different intention appears from the treaty or is otherwise established, a treaty is binding upon each party in respect of its entire territory'.

144 CESCR, General Comment No. 14 (2000) 'Right to Health', para. 42.

145 ECSR, Conclusions 2013 on the European Social Charter (Montenegro), under: Article 11: 'These measures should be introduced [by the state] [...] to develop a sense of individual Responsibility'. See also ECSR 11 September 2012, *Médecins du Monde – International/France*, no. 67/2011, para. 150; Council of Europe, *Digest of the Case Law of the European Committee of Social Rights*, 1 September 2008, p. 84.

146 *Cf.* Andreas Follesdal, 'The Principle of Subsidiarity as a Constitutional Principle in International law', *Global Constitutionalism* 2013, vol. 2, pp. 37–62 on p. 37.

position of sovereign states. This position covers multiple assumptions, including the notion that public international law must complement the national legal systems; that the core of international obligations lies within the notion of mutual consent of states; and that on the level of adjudication of concrete cases, national remedies must be exhausted first before access to an international authority is available. The principle of subsidiarity is also expressed in the concept of 'margin of appreciation' which is used in case law,[147] and also in the generally weak international enforcement mechanisms regarding compliance with international obligations.[148]

With respect to the latter, it is important that the principle of subsidiarity limits the possibilities for international bodies to establish and implement the measures for adequate realization of the covenant rights in all respects. It is exactly there where the monitoring mechanism can only guarantee the realization of convention rights in a limited way that it is necessary that states determine where their attempts to guarantee covenant rights in their territory fall short and which measures are needed to remedy this and then go on to implement those measures.[149] Another approach would substantially undermine the effectivity of the convention. If an international supervisory body has not explicitly established that states must take certain measures so as to ensure compliance with the convention, that does not mean that the state has no obligation to take those measures. The position that this is in fact the case, would be problematic in another respect as a matter of fact. After all, it would mean that for conventions without a monitoring mechanism there will be no obligations to take measures which have not been included explicitly in the convention, but which are nevertheless necessary to comply with the provisions in the convention. In the event that the authorities have to conclude that a certain situation in their own territory is unacceptable in view of human rights and that it requires certain measures to be taken, the state in principle is therefore required to take those measures. It can be different yet again, if the international supervisory body has established that there is no obligation to take those measures or that these are not even allowed.

Thus, the fact that states are first and foremost responsible for realizing the rights and fulfilling the obligations with respect to, among other things, the right to health, in a manner that is most appropriate given the specific circumstances of the relevant state, does not mean that the state is completely at liberty to decide what is the best manner and/or that it has

---

147 For more information about this see the following paragraph.

148 Andreas Follesdal, 'The Principle of Subsidiarity as a Constitutional Principle in International law', *Global Constitutionalism* 2013, vol. 2, pp. 37–62 on p. 38.

149 For more information see Jonas Christoffersen, *Fair Balance: Proportionality, Subsidiarity and Primarity in the European Convention on Human Rights*, Leiden/Boston: Martinus Nijhoff Publishers, 2009, in particular pp. 544–577.

the final say in the matter. After all, states must take primary responsibility within the limits of the individual rights and obligations that arise from the convention to which they are bound. Those rights and obligations are to all intents and purposes the factors that determine the responsibility of states. Additionally, the states parties (as we saw above) are bound by the 'in good faith' principle of international law ('pacta sunt servanda'). Within these frameworks, the principle of subsidiarity contributes to the effectiveness of human rights norms. Firstly, because the principle makes a broader platform for consensus between states possible and thereby furthers the object and purpose of the human rights conventions (universal protection of individuals).[150] Secondly, because states (as we noted before) are best placed to consider the relevant insights, make the evaluations and choices in order to fulfil the obligations adequately.[151] To that extent, the principle of subsidiarity is already embedded in the nature of human rights norms as well as the human rights instruments. The relatively open norms as enshrined in the human rights treaties offer the states a wide margin of interpretation,[152] and in that sense increase the responsibility of states to apply these norms in an appropriate and adequate manner. The room for discretion in interpreting human rights norms in the light of the national context is also increased by the internal system of limitations, the possibility to suspend rights under certain conditions as well as the system of potential reservations.[153]

- *Responsibility for finding more effective fulfilment of the obligation.* The aforementioned is of paramount importance in the case of realizing the right to health in relation to cannabis for recreational purposes. After all, the primary responsibility of the state entails that it is first and foremost up to the national authorities to consider which steps, given the specific circumstances in the state, are the most appropriate so as to achieve progressively the full realization of the right to health in relation to cannabis consumption. In that sense, states are also obliged to keep looking for better solutions themselves for reining in illegal cannabis cultivation and trade and the health risks caused by them if and as long as the current policy with at least adequate or reasonable steps (see the next section) does not give full effect to this right. This does not exclude

150 Paolo G. Carozza, 'Subsidiarity as a Structural Principle of International Human Rights Law', *American Journal of International Law* 2003, vol. 97, pp. 38–79 on p. 60.

151 See also Article 1 Protocol 15 ECHR: 'At the end of the preamble to the Convention, a new recital shall be added, which shall read as follows: "Affirming that the High Contracting Parties, in accordance with the principle of subsidiarity, have the primary responsibility to secure the rights and freedoms defined in this Convention and the Protocols thereto, and that in doing so they enjoy a margin of appreciation, subject to the supervisory jurisdiction of the European Court of Human Rights established by this Convention …"'.

152 Paolo G. Carozza, 'Subsidiarity as a Structural Principle of International Human Rights Law', *American Journal of International Law* 2003, vol. 97, pp. 38–79 on p. 60.

153 Ibid, pp. 38–79 on p. 61.

the possibility that the above-mentioned restriction takes place by organizing the cultivation and trade in such a way that health risks are avoided the most. Eventually, it is all about avoiding health risks as much as possible. If relevant new knowledge becomes available, it will have to be taken into consideration.[154] The ICESCR Committee even considers this a core obligation.[155] Progressive insight can be important too. In this respect, the following comment from the UN Special Rapporteur on the right to health is interesting:

> The current international system of drug control has focused on creating a drug free world, almost exclusively through use of law enforcement policies and criminal sanctions. Mounting evidence, however, suggests this approach has failed, primarily because it does not acknowledge the realities of drug use and dependence. While drugs may have a pernicious effect on individual lives and society, this excessively punitive regime has not achieved its stated public health goals, and has resulted in countless human rights violations.[156]

According to the Special Rapporteur, it is appropriate that states are responsible for development, innovation and/or modification of policies and measures with a view to the full realization of the right to health in respect of individual and public health in relation to drugs.

x. Discretion about Appropriate Means and Stricter Obligation to State Reasons

The foregoing does not yet answer the question which means are appropriate in a concrete case. The ICESCR Committee takes the view that:

> While each State party must decide for itself which means are the most appropriate under the circumstances with respect to each of the rights, the 'appropriateness' of the means chosen will not always be self-evident. It is therefore desirable that States parties' reports should *indicate not only the measures that have been taken but also the basis on which they are considered to be the most 'appropriate' under the circumstances* (emphasis added).[157]

The final assessment, however, is made by the Committee:

> However, the ultimate determination as to *whether all appropriate measures* have been taken remains one for the Committee to make' (emphasis added).[158]

---

154 See the introductory part of section 2.3.7 for this.

155 See section 2.3.7.viii for this, where it says: The strategy and plan of action must be devised, and periodically reviewed, on the basis of a participatory and transparent process.

156 Report of the Special Rapporteur on the right of everyone to the enjoyment of the highest attainable standard of physical and mental health, Anand Grover, *UN Doc.* A/65/255, 6 August 2010, p. 2 (Summary) and also para. 14–16.

157 CESCR, General Comment No. 3 (1990) 'Obligations', para. 4.

158 Ibid, para. 4.

The criterion applied in this consideration is whether 'all appropriate measures' have been taken. According to a document of a later date in which the ICESCR Committee sets out general principles, this is actually about an 'assessment of whether a State party has taken reasonable steps', or whether the measures taken are 'adequate' or 'reasonable'.[159] This seems to be a less strict requirement than 'all appropriate measures' and it would appear to imply a more marginal assessment than the one originally envisaged by the Committee. The ICESCR Committee adds the following:

> To this end, and in accordance with the practice of judicial and other quasi-judicial human rights treaty bodies, the Committee *always respects the margin of appreciation* of States to take steps and adopt measures *most suited to their specific circumstances* (emphasis added).[160]

In assessing which measures are appropriate or necessary, states therefore have a fair degree of discretion.[161] Taking into account the national legal and social economic structures, states can determine which measures are 'appropriate' to realize the right to health. Consequently, there may be significant differences between states as to the measures to be taken: what is appropriate for one state may not necessarily be so for another state. The foregoing does not imply a carte blanche for the state though. The considerations quoted above show that the discretion is not aimed at ensuring freedom for the state as such, nor at allowing states to implement the positive obligations in anything but an optimum manner. The freedom granted to states is primarily a means to arrive at the measures that do actually meet the obligation to ensure the right to health under the convention ('most appropriate steps', 'measures most suited'), since this is possible only if the social peculiarities and the constellation of the state are sufficiently taken into account.[162] According to the Committee, the state is uniquely positioned to

---

159 CESCR, An Evaluation of the Obligation to Take Steps to the 'Maximum of Available Resources' under an Optional Protocol to the Covenant, *UN Doc.* E/C.12/2007/1, 10 May 2007, para. 11 and also para. 8 and 12.

160 CESCR, An Evaluation of the Obligation to Take Steps to the 'Maximum of Available Resources' under an Optional Protocol to the Covenant, *UN Doc.* E/C.12/2007/1, 10 May 2007, para. 11.

161 See also CESCR, General Comment No. 14 (2000) 'Right to Health', para. 53; Article 8(4) Optional Protocol ICESCR: '4. When examining communications under the present Protocol, the Committee shall consider the reasonableness of the steps taken by the State Party in accordance with part II of the Covenant. In doing so, the Committee shall bear in mind that the State Party may adopt a range of possible policy measures for the implementation of the rights set forth in the Covenant.' See also for example John Tobin, *The Right to Health in International Law*, Oxford: Oxford University Press, 2012, p. 200, who speaks of 'a reasonable margin of appreciation to states [...]. The margin afforded to states is not, however, without boundaries.'

162 Cf. Yutaka Arai-Takahashi, *The Margin of Appreciation Doctrine and the Principle of Proportionality in the Jurisprudence of the ECHR*, Antwerp/Oxford/New York: Intersentia, 2001, pp. 84–85.

determine what is needed to this end. None of this alters the fact that the final decision whether states have indeed taken all possible appropriate or at any rate reasonably required measures is the prerogative of the ICESCR Committee.

Although it is not clear what the ICESCR Committee allows or does not allow, it does give some indications about the criteria to be applied whether the measures actually taken by the state are 'adequate' or 'reasonable'. The following factors are the most relevant in this context:[163]

- the extent to which the measures taken are well-informed, concrete and aimed at realizing the right;[164]
- whether the discretion has been used non-arbitrarily;
- in the event that various policy options are available, whether the state chose the option which restricts the rights in the ICESCR the least;
- the period during which the measures were taken;
- whether the measures give priority to serious or risky situations;
- whether specific attention was paid to the impact the choices made would have on vulnerable groups as well as other persons affected by the measures.[165]

The foregoing and in particular the first quote of this subsection also illustrate that much can depend on the way in which a state party states its reasons for its decisions for taking certain measures or alternatively for not taking these measures, in other words: substantiates the decisions with data, arguments and considerations that are relevant for the right to health.[166] The less obvious the decision is, or the more controversial, the more convincing and coherent the substantiation will have to be.[167]

We also like to include a few comments about the ESC and the European CSR. This committee also frequently uses the concept of the 'margin of appreciation'.[168] It recognizes that national authorities are in the best position to evaluate the needs of their own state. Consequently, states have a margin in assessing the positive steps that must be taken in order to ensure compliance with the Charter, in particular regarding the balance that must be struck between the public interest

163 These criteria and other ones that are not relevant here are mentioned in: CESCR, An Evaluation of the Obligation to Take Steps to the 'Maximum of Available Resources' under an Optional Protocol to the Covenant, *UN Doc.* E/C.12/2007/1, 10 May 2007, para. 8.

164 See also section 2.3.7.v.

165 This latter criterion is presented in ECSR 4 November 2003, *Autism Europe/France*, no. 13/2002, para. 53.

166 See John Tobin, *The Right to Health in International Law*, Oxford: Oxford University Press, 2012, p. 179.

167 As a matter of fact, democratic decision-making, social support and citizen participation may also play a part in the measures taken; see section 2.3.9 below.

168 See also (with additional references) Holly Cullen, 'The Collective Complaints System of the European Social Charter: Interpretative Methods of the European Committee of Social Rights', *Human Rights Law Review* 2009, vol. 9, no. 1, pp. 61–93 on p. 89.

and the interest of a specific group and the choices that must be made in terms of priorities and resources.[169] It is not part of the Committee's mandate to put itself in the position of the state in assessing the policy that best suits the concrete situation. However, the choices made by the state are most certainly subject to evaluation by the European CSR. In doing so, it applies the following criteria:[170]

- whether measures are taken within a reasonable period of time;
- whether there is measurable progress;
- whether there is funding in accordance with the maximum use of the available resources.

This does not alter the fact that the European CSR in many cases rejects appeals to discretion by states. Even if the assessment by a state is in principle within the 'margin', the Committee will still check if it is reasonable. This also applies in the case of taking measures to meet positive obligations.[171]

This can result in the limitation being deemed in conflict with the Charter, although there are also instances where the Committee concludes that there is no violation of a charter right because of the 'margin of appreciation'.[172] Since the judgment of the European CSR will also depend on the data, arguments and considerations provided by the state, it can ultimately boil down to a question of the strength of the justification provided by the state for the measures taken. The foregoing illustrates that the 'margin of appreciation' does not give the state 'carte blanche' with the ESC either, and that it is primarily a means to arrive at appropriate measures.

In our opinion, the stricter obligation to state reasons – which is particularly prominent in the case of the ICESCR Committee – is applicable in any event if a state were to proceed to the legalization, regulation or application of a more liberal policy regarding cannabis cultivation and trade for the recreational consumer market. After all, such measures are not explicitly recognized in the right to health or in opinions about it held by the ICESCR Committee and the European CSR, while the adequacy of such measures to some extent is counter-intuitive, since cannabis also carries health risks. In applying such measures, that state (assuming that such an interpretation of the right to health is possible) will have

---

169 ECSR 18 October 2006, *European Roma Rights Centre (ERRC)/Bulgaria*, no. 31/2005, para. 37 and 35. See also ECSR 11 September 2012, *Médecins du Monde – International/France*, no. 67/2011, para. 54; ECSR 23 May 2012, *Confederation of Greek Civil Servants Trade Unions (ADEDY)/Greece*, no. 66/2011, para. 20 and 12–13.

170 ECSR 18 October 2006, *European Roma Rights Centre (ERRC)/Bulgaria*, no. 31/2005, para. 37; ECSR 4 November 2003, *Autism Europe/France*, no. 13/2002, para. 53.

171 ECSR 18 October 2006, *European Roma Rights Centre (ERRC)/Bulgaria*, no. 31/2005, para. 35–37.

172 See also Holly Cullen, 'The Collective Complaints System of the European Social Charter: Interpretative Methods of the European Committee of Social Rights', *Human Rights Law Review* 2009, vol. 9, no. 1, pp. 61–93 on pp. 88–90.

to make a convincing case, supported by data, arguments and considerations, why and in which respect a drug policy permitting the cultivation of and trade in cannabis for recreational use to a certain extent, would de facto guarantee the right to health better than a more prohibitive drug policy.

The foregoing, however, does not yet imply an answer to the question whether a drug policy that permits the cultivation of and trade in cannabis for recreational use up to a point is an acceptable and possibly even required vehicle for implementing the right to health, insofar as that drug policy de facto guaranteed individual and public health better than a more prohibitive drug policy. Still, the conclusion can be drawn that the room for a state to decide which measures it considers appropriate or necessary in view of the specific situation in that state is so large that in that sense there is no obstacle to answering that particular question in the affirmative. It would have been different, for example, if states were bound to a limited number of measures to be implemented.

xi. The Right to Health in Relation to Other International Instruments

Human rights conventions in which the right to health is enshrined and other international instruments are relevant to each other in at least two ways. Firstly, it is relevant that according to Article 2 ICESCR, states are not only individually obliged to take measures, but also 'through international assistance and co-operation, especially economic and technical'. By the way, the ESC does not contain such a general obligation which applies in respect of the right to health in Article 11 ESC.[173] According to the ICESCR Committee, the general obligation for international cooperation in Article 2 ICESCR means, among other things, that:

> States parties have to respect the enjoyment of the right to health in other countries, and to prevent third parties from violating the right in other countries, if they are able to influence these third parties by way of legal or political means, in accordance with the Charter of the United Nations and applicable international law.[174]

This is an important point in connection with the cannabis issue. The drug policy conducted by a country is not allowed to be detrimental to the protection of individual and public health in other countries, and one might even read this as an obligation to act against threats to health in countries other than, for example, the Netherlands caused by cannabis cultivation and trade in the Netherlands.

---

173 However, see Part I preamble of the ESC, which requires the states parties to create such conditions for realizing the rights mentioned in Part I 'both national and international in character', including the right for everyone to use the healthcare facilities in Part I point 11. The European CSR sometimes also recognizes the relevance of international strategies; see Council of Europe, *Digest of the Case Law of the European Committee of Social Rights*, 1 September 2008, p. 87.

174 CESCR, General Comment No. 14 (2000) 'Right to Health', para. 39.

The obligation for international cooperation can also cover the duty to offer help to other countries so as to realize the right to health.[175]

Secondly, states must take the right to health into consideration in international agreements they enter into.[176] On account of the obligation to respect,[177] they must ensure that international instruments (such as conventions) have due consideration for the right to health and that those instruments do not have an adverse impact on effectuating the right to health. They must even take steps to that end.[178] These obligations are also an important point in connection with the cannabis issue. Insofar as obligations arising from the UN narcotic drugs conventions and other international drug regulations would be an obstacle to optimizing the right to health, there would therefore be an obligation to remove those obstacles in this respect. One can then be faced with the question of how this conflict between obligations should be resolved; this will be the subject of Chapter 3.

2.3.8. SPECIFIC POSITIVE OBLIGATIONS FLOWING FROM THE RIGHT TO HEALTH

The previous section contains an elaborate explanation of the applicable general obligations emanating from the ICESCR in particular and also the ESC and their meaning for the right to health. Now we will briefly but more explicitly discuss the obligations of states that have been included in those provisions in which the right to health is embedded and which are relevant for the cannabis issue. These are Article 12 ICESCR and Article 11 ESC and of course also the case law about these articles of the ICESCR Committee and the European CSR respectively. Incidentally, the obligations flowing from these articles partly overlap with what has been discussed before.

i. The Specific Obligations in Article 12(2) of the ICESCR

The second paragraph of Article 12 of the ICESCR contains an enumeration of steps to be taken by states with a view to the right to health.[179] This list most

175 Ibid, para. 39–41 and 45; CESCR, General Comment No. 3 'Obligations', para. 14.

176 CESCR, General Comment No. 14 (2000) 'Right to Health', para. 39.

177 Ibid, para. 50.

178 Ibid, para. 39, 'In relation to the conclusion of other international agreements, States parties should take steps to ensure that these instruments do not adversely impact upon the right to health.' See also para. 50.

179 Article 12(2) ICESCR reads: 'The steps to be taken by the States Parties to the present Covenant to achieve the full realization of this right shall include those necessary for: a. The provision for the reduction of the stillbirth-rate and of infant mortality and for the healthy development of the child; b. The improvement of all aspects of environmental and industrial hygiene; c. The prevention, treatment and control of epidemic, endemic, occupational and other diseases; d. The creation of conditions which would assure to all medical service and medical attention in the event of sickness'.

definitely is not restricted witness the use of the phrase 'shall include those'. None of these obligations explicitly bears relation to the key question of this research about regulation of cannabis cultivation and trade aimed at recreational use. However, this is not to say that they are without relevance to this question.

Regarding item a. (which after all requires steps to ensure the healthy development of the child, among other things), the necessity to protect children against drugs can be based on it. Section 2.3.1 refers to the public health argument that in the event of regulating cannabis cultivation and trade, the ban on its use by juveniles could be maintained more effectively. Insofar as this argument is correct, it fits in with item a.

The ICESCR Committee infers the obligation to discourage the use of alcohol, tobacco, drugs and other harmful substances from item b (albeit not the obligation to implement a ban on these substances for adults).[180] The obligations connected with these means will be reviewed in section 2.3.10. Nevertheless, we already note at this point that the arguments in section 2.3.1 concerning the division between the soft drugs market and the hard drugs market and of cannabis as a less risky alternative stimulant can be seen in this light.

Item c has no bearing on the cannabis issue in principle, but it is another matter for item d. Among other things, it covers the obligation for states to provide equal and timely access to preventive, curative and rehabilitative health care and health education. According to the ICESCR Committee, another important aspect of item d is the improvement and promotion of the participation of the population in providing preventive and curative health care. A significant point here is participation by the population in the political decision-making regarding the right to health at a local, national and international level.[181] We will come back to this in more detail in section 2.3.9. After all, it raises the question how important it is when after direct participation of citizens, a democratic and widely endorsed choice is made to permit cannabis cultivation and trade in a regulated manner in the interest of public health, among other reasons.

ii. The Specific Obligations in Article 11 ESC

In comparison to Article 12 ICESCR, the emphasis in Article 11 ESC is much more on the obligations for the state than on the right of an individual.[182] Moreover, the central issue is ensuring public health in general rather than

180 CESCR, General Comment No. 14 (2000) 'Right to Health', para. 15.

181 Ibid, para. 17.

182 See also Lorenza Mola, 'The margin of appreciation accorded to States in times of economic crisis. An analysis of the decision by the European Committee on Social Rights and by the European Court of Human Rights on national austerity measures', *Lex Social* 2015, vol. 5, no. 1, pp. 174–194 on p. 190.

individual health. Admittedly, the title of Article 11 ESC is 'The right to protection of health', but the text reads as follows:

> With a view to ensuring the effective exercise of the right to protection of health, the Parties undertake, either directly or in cooperation with public or private organisations, to take appropriate measures designed *inter alia*:
>
> 1. to remove as far as possible the causes of ill-health;
> 2. to provide advisory and educational facilities for the promotion of health and the encouragement of individual responsibility in matters of health;
> 3. to prevent as far as possible epidemic, endemic and other diseases, as well as accidents.

Here too, none of the obligations listed is explicitly related to the key question in this research regarding the regulation of cannabis cultivation and trade for recreational user market, but some of these obligations are pertinent to it.

According to the case law of the European CSR, Part 1 entails the obligation for states to respond adequately to avoidable health risks, that is to say risks that can be brought under control by human intervention.[183] Since health risks attach to cannabis use as well, these could be within the scope of the obligation. In principle, all the arguments listed in section 2.3.1 may be relevant insofar as these arguments are valid.

The obligation formulated in Part 2 to make arrangements in the area of information and education is relevant here at any rate. This is because the obligation covers the duty to take steps to prevent activities that are harmful to health, such as smoking, alcohol consumption and drug use, and to develop a sense of individual responsibility.[184] This duty therefore applies in relation to the recreational use of cannabis also – or perhaps: particularly – if the cultivation of and trade in cannabis were to be permitted.

Lastly, the European CSR is of the opinion that the duties of prevention in Part 3 also demand that the supply of tobacco is restricted by means of checks on production, distribution, advertising and pricing. The committee even demands bans on smoking in public indoor spaces and on advertising on posters and in the press. This approach is also required, mutatis mutandis, for measures against alcoholism and drug addiction. In section 2.3.10 below, we will pay more attention to the obligations regarding harmful substances. We already note at

---

183 See for example ECSR 23 January 2013, *International Federation of Human Rights Leagues (FIDH)/Greece*, No. 72/2011, para. 144; Council of Europe, *Digest of the Case Law of the European Committee of Social Rights*, 1 September 2008, p. 81.

184 See also, among other sources, ECSR, Conclusions 2013 on the European Social Charter (Montenegro), under: Article 11; Council of Europe, *Digest of the Case Law of the European Committee of Social Rights*, 1 September 2008, p. 81.

this point that the most significant of the arguments in section 2.3.1 in relation to Part 3 is the argument regarding controlling the cannabis chain.

The list of 'appropriate measures' in Article 11 ESC is clearly not restricted either, as the use of the words 'inter alia' shows. Consequently, arguments as mentioned in section 2.3.1 that are not directly connected to one of the measures mentioned explicitly in Article 11 ESC may actually well be relevant under that provision.

iii. Public Health versus Individual Health

Much more so than in Article 11 ESC, one can see a tension in Article 12 ICESCR that is inherent in the nature of economic, social and cultural rights in general. On the one hand, the latter provision is aimed specifically at the protection of the individual right to a certain level of health and health care (see primarily the first paragraph quoted earlier)[185] and on the other hand, it contains obligations for the state to guarantee public health in general (the second paragraph). The ICESCR Committee emphasizes that states parties are bound by both the collective and the individual aspects of Article 12 ICESCR.[186] Nonetheless, the two objections are not necessarily or always compatible.[187] A balance must then be struck between the protection of individual rights of citizens and public health in general.[188]

The question is how that balance needs to be achieved or which approach (positive protection of individual health or positive protection of public health) should take priority if striking such a balance is not possible. This is a poignant question for the cannabis issue. If regulated permission of the cultivation of and trade in cannabis for recreational use de facto and on balance guaranteed public health better than a more prohibitive drug policy, then this could also mean that certain individuals have access to cannabis, whereas they would be protected against that under a more prohibitive drug policy. Would there be room after all for such a more liberal cannabis policy aimed at public health, or does the interest of individual health pose an obstacle?

We think that the latter need not necessarily be the case in principle. The general interest with public health in itself is after all a legitimate ground in human rights conventions to infringe on individual rights. For example, Article 8 ECHR recognizes 'the protection of health' as a legitimate objective

185 See section 2.3.5.
186 CESCR, General Comment No. 14 (2000) 'Right to Health', fn. 30.
187 See also Aart Hendriks, 'Het recht op gezondheid en het IVESCR-Comité', *NJCM-bul.* 1994, pp. 171–180 on pp. 171–172 (i.e., 'The right to health and the ICESCR Committee').
188 Ben Saul, David Kinley & Jacqueline Mowbray, *The International Covenant on Economic, Social and Cultural Rights*, Oxford: Oxford University Press, 2014, p. 979.

to limit the right to a private life.[189] In that case, there is an infringement on the negative right to a private life in order to arrive at the positive protection of health. There is a much less far-reaching situation in the case to which the key question of this research relates. After all, we are not dealing with the infringement of and/or limitation of the negative right to individual health, but only with the limitation of the positive protection of that right. Against the background of the meaning of the general interest within the system of human rights, it is not remarkable if one chooses a more limited positive protection of an individual against access to recreational cannabis in favour of the positive protection of many others against harmful consequences of illegal cannabis cultivation and trade. Fundamentally, this is also about the opposing interests of various individuals. Whether one opts for regulated permission or an absolute ban on cannabis cultivation and trade, the choice will always satisfy to a certain extent a general interest of public health and the protection of individuals and equally be detrimental to other individuals at the same time. If the choice is reasonable, it will be bound to fall in the 'margin of appreciation' for limitation of convention rights, and this is probably the case even more so if the choice is supported by society at large (see section 2.3.9 below). Moreover, Article 12 ICESCR also clearly aims to protect public health, and the ICESCR Committee considers the adoption and implementation of a 'national public health strategy' to be a minimum core obligation.

Therefore, we are of the opinion that a state does not need to shy away from the choice for a policy that best ensures public health on the sole ground that this policy entails a limitation of the positive protection to the right of individual health. However, in doing so, there can be no discrimination against certain individuals or groups. Nor may there be a disproportionate impact on certain vulnerable groups.[190] The ICESCR Committee also explicitly requires that special attention is paid to all vulnerable and marginalized groups.[191] That is why we think it is obvious that the limitation of the protection in question must be compensated as much as possible.

As we have seen before, the emphasis in Article 11 ESC is clearly on the obligations for the state (rather than the right of individuals) and on guaranteeing public health in general (instead of individual health). This perspective of public interest also comes to the fore in the European CSR, which requires among other

189 For more references and examples see Benjamin Mason Meier & Larisa M. Mori, 'The Highest Attainable Standard: Advancing a Collective Human Right to Public Health', *Columbia Human Rights Law Review* 2005, pp. 101–147 on pp. 136–137; Ronald Bayer, 'The continuing tensions between individual rights and public health. Talking Point on public health versus civil liberties', *EMBO reports* 2007, vol. 8, no. 12, pp. 1099–1103.

190 See also Report of the Special Rapporteur on the right of everyone to the enjoyment of the highest attainable standard of physical and mental health, Anand Grover, *UN Doc.* A/69/299, 11 August 2014, para. 27.

191 See section 2.3.7.viii.

things a 'public health education policy in favour of the general population and population groups affected by specific problems'.[192] The conclusion drawn in the previous section therefore applies here *a fortiori*. However, it is also true that specific attention must be paid to the impact the choices made would have on vulnerable groups as well as other persons affected by the measures.[193]

2.3.9. RELEVANCE OF DEMOCRATIC PREFERENCES AND 'PRESUMPTION OF APPROPRIATENESS'

In view of the discussion about regulating cannabis cultivation and trade for recreational use, it is also interesting that the ICESCR Committee stresses the importance of participation by the public in the decision-making process concerning health related issues at the local, national and international level in the context of the meaning of the right to health.[194] The European CSR also holds the view that the national legal framework must provide possibilities for participation in the decision-making process about issues that pertain to the right to health, such as the environment,[195] but this point is not particularly emphasized.[196] Additionally, as far as the ICESCR Committee is concerned, the right of individuals and groups to participate in decision-making that touches on their development must be an integral part of each policy, programme and strategy to discharge the obligations of the authorities under Article 12 ICESCR.[197] This obligation also comes to the fore with the UN Special Rapporteur on the right to health: 'States' policies to progressively realize the right to health should be reasonable [...] [and] be formulated with the participation of affected communities and fulfil, at a minimum, States' core obligations.'[198] Information and education to promote public health is also explicitly required

192 Council of Europe, *Digest of the Case Law of the European Committee of Social Rights*, 1 September 2008, p. 84.

193 ECSR 4 November 2003, *Autism Europe/France*, no. 13/2002, para. 53.

194 CESCR, General Comment No. 14 (2000) 'Right to Health', para. 11, 17 and 54.

195 ECSR 6 December 2006, *Marangopoulos Foundation for Human Rights (MFHR)/Greece*, no. 30/2005, para. 205 and 216 (this case centred on environment policy and regulations).

196 That is different in relation to Article 22 ESC in particular (the right to take part in the determination and improvement of the working conditions and working environment): 'The Committee recalls that workers and/or their representatives (trade unions, workers' delegates, health and safety representatives, works councils) must be granted an effective right to participate in the decision-making process', according to, for example, ECSR, Conclusions 2014 on the European Social Charter (Armenia), under: Article 22.

197 CESCR, General Comment No. 14 (2000) 'Right to Health', para. 54.

198 Report of the Special Rapporteur on the right of everyone to the enjoyment of the highest attainable standard of physical and mental health, Anand Grover, *UN Doc.* A/69/299, 11 August 2014, para. 3.

by Article 11 Preamble and Part 2 ESC.[199] Moreover, as we noted before, the ICESCR Committee points out that all members of society (including medical practitioners, families, local communities, governments, NGOs, civil society and the corporate sector) are responsible for the realization of the right to health.[200] The authorities must therefore ensure that the prerequisites are met for the involved parties to be able to realize their social responsibilities.

It is especially the requirement of social participation in decision-making regarding health issues that raises the question to what extent democratic choices for a certain policy can shape or even direct the obligations under the right to health. What does it mean if, after direct participation of citizens (for example via interest groups),[201] a democratic decision with a broad platform of support in society is made to permit the regulated cultivation and trade of cannabis, partly on the ground of public health interests? The question is particularly important if the democratic choice made with the direct involvement of the population flies in the face of the obligations under the human rights convention. Does such a choice then by definition qualify as a choice required by the right to health? Is it a choice that is not required by the right to health but which does have to be recognized as a legitimate way to realize this right? Or even less far-reaching again: is it a choice that can neither qualify as a way to exercise the right to health nor be designated as impermissible by this right? In our view, none of these variants can be accepted. According to international law (see Article 27 of the Vienna Convention on the Law of Treaties[202]), national law – even if it has a democratic foundation – cannot derogate from obligations under a convention, unless the convention explicitly allows for that possibility, for example through safeguard clauses.[203] Such clauses do not exist in either the ICESCR or the ESC, though. Also choices about policy and steps regarding the right to health and cannabis that come about in a democratic fashion involving the direct participation of the population, will therefore have to comply with the obligations under these human rights conventions.

In determining policies and measures regarding public health, it is important to take into consideration the special health needs of individuals, groups and the

---

199 The European CSR adds various other requirements; see Council of Europe, *Digest of the Case Law of the European Committee of Social Rights*, 1 September 2008, pp. 84–85.

200 CESCR, General Comment No. 14 (2000) 'Right to Health', para. 42.

201 See for example Mashood Baderin & Robert McCorquodale, *Economic, Social, and Cultural Rights in Action*, Oxford: Oxford University Press, 2007, p. 323 (see matrix Participation).

202 Article 27 of the Vienna Convention on the Law of Treaties states, among other things, that: 'A party may not invoke the provisions of its internal law as justification for its failure to perform a treaty'.

203 For example, the obligation in Article 3(2) of the Convention Against Illicit Traffic in Narcotic Drugs and Psychotropic Substances (1988) is tied to the clause regarding compliance with 'constitutional principles' of the state party and 'the basic concepts of its legal system; see Piet Hein P.H.M.C. van Kempen & Masha I. Fedorova, *International Law and Cannabis I*, Cambridge: Intersentia, 2019.

population as a whole. Without that, it would not be possible to realize this right fully with at least adequate or reasonable steps. Tobin argues that the requirement of participation 'mandates that the implementation of a rights-based approach must be sensitive to, informed by, and reflect the needs and interests of local populations.'[204] In fact, this is also reflected in the Concluding Observations of the ICESCR Committee, in which this body brings up the topic of participation particularly with a view to effectuating the right to health among other things, in relation to specific groups, such as Roma and indigenous populations.[205] To that extent, the obligation about the participation appears to be mainly formal and instrumental to the ability to realize the right to health.

However, this does not mean that the obligation does not have a more independent substantive meaning too. Earlier, we observed that the national authorities are primarily responsible for realizing the right to health, that they are best placed to gain the relevant insights, weigh the pros and cons and make choices so as to fulfil the obligations in an adequate manner in their own territory and that they are therefore also obliged to consider how they can ensure the full realization of the right (principle of primarity).[206] Suppose the state genuinely works towards meeting its obligations and creates a policy and adopts measures that meet with the support of a large part of society after democratic decision-making with direct participation of citizens. Then there is a lot to be said for working from the assumption that this policy and those measures are indeed the best way to bring about the realization of the right to health in full and that they are therefore required. Only if there are compelling reasons to assume that these are not at least reasonable adequate steps ('appropriate measures') to achieve full realization of the right, or if these steps must actually and genuinely be held to be at odds with the obligations under the conventions, would one be allowed, in our opinion, to assume that the steps are not appropriate and therefore are not required for the realization of the convention right.

Democratic decision-making, public support and citizen participation in measures taken to realize the right to health do not yet make these measures mandatory under the law of the convention per se. However, in our opinion such legitimization of measures taken forces one to *presume* that the measures are appropriate for the full realization of the right and are therefore required. Such a 'presumption of appropriateness' also reduces the onus of showing convincingly

---

204 John Tobin, *The Right to Health in International Law*, Oxford: Oxford University Press, 2012, p. 111. See also Mashood Baderin & Robert McCorquodale, *Economic, Social, and Cultural Rights in Action*, Oxford: Oxford University Press, 2007, p. 314; Lawrence O. Gostin, *Global Health Law*, Cambridge, Massachusetts: Harvard University Press, 2014, p. 245.

205 See for example CESCR, Concluding Observations (Serbia and Montenegro), *UN Doc.* E/2006/22 (2005) 41, para. 301; CESCR, Concluding Observations (Ecuador), *UN Doc.* E/2005/22 (2004) 39, para. 301.

206 See section 2.3.7.ix.

that the measures taken are necessary for a full realization of the right. This would also have to be true in the case of regulated permission of cannabis cultivation and trade for recreational use, unless this were not permissible as such under the right to health – for more information on this see section 2.3.10 below.

By the way, we note that if regulated permission of cannabis cultivation and trade for recreational use can qualify as a suitable and required realization of the right to health, this does not in itself mean that then all states would have to proceed with taking this step. If after all such a step in these other states is not backed by democratic decision-making, public support and citizen participation, it can less easily be called an appropriate step. Not only do policies and measures then fail to meet an important condition, but it will also be less easy for these policies and those measures to be effective. Additionally, in our opinion the 'margin of appreciation' entails that the state often can escape from taking the appropriate step of regulated permission by taking other appropriate steps that the state in question deems preferable.

2.3.10. DRUGS, ALCOHOL AND TOBACCO AND THE RIGHT TO HEALTH IN THE ICESCR AND ESC

In the previous sections, tobacco, alcohol and drugs were mentioned as important areas in relation to the right to health. In the following section, we will be looking more specifically at the obligations imposed on states by the ICESCR Committee and the European CSR regarding these three substances that are potentially harmful to health. To what degree do the Committees require limits to the production, trade and use of tobacco, alcohol and drugs? What are the requirements by which they assess policies and measures with regard to these substances? What does this mean in the case of cannabis for recreational use? Incidentally, none of these substances are mentioned explicitly in the ICESCR and the ESC. Cannabis does not feature in them either. This does not diminish the fact that both the ICESCR Committee and the European CSR regard drugs – including cannabis – as subjects that fall within the scope of the right to health.[207]

i. The Approach by the ICESCR Committee

The ICESCR Committee does not require states to ban alcohol, tobacco, recreational drugs or other harmful stimulants, not with respect to adults

---

207 Cannabis is dealt with explicitly in CESCR, Summary record of the 14th meeting (The Netherlands), *UN Doc.* E/C.12/1998/SR.14, 15 September 1998, para. 55–56, and, amongst others, in ECSR, Conclusions 2013 on the European Social Charter (The Netherlands) respectively, under: Article 11(3); Conclusions 2013 on the European Social Charter (Sweden), under: Article 11(3).

anyway.[208] So within the ICESCR, there is room for legalization, decriminalization as well as a policy of tolerance. However, the Committee holds the view that states are required to discourage the use of alcohol, tobacco, drugs and other stimulants.[209] Pursuant to the obligation to protect, this also entails, among other things, that states must discourage the production and marketing of these harmful substances. It is also relevant here that states, pursuant to the obligation to fulfil, are required to promote health education and the organization of information campaigns, particularly regarding the said stimulants.[210] It must also include raising awareness of their harmful effects.[211] In the framework of the periodic monitoring of compliance with the ICESCR, states must provide information in their reports to the ICESCR Committee about their efforts to discourage (recreational) use of alcohol, tobacco, drugs and other stimulants.[212] States must specify which measures they have taken to prevent such recreational use, specifically with regard to children and adolescents, and to ensure an adequate treatment and rehabilitation of drug users as well as providing support to their families.[213] The ICESCR Committee also urges some states to provide

---

208 Regarding the right to health of children and juveniles, the ICESCR Committee refers to the convention on the Rights of the Child, even though this is not done explicitly in connection with drugs. Nevertheless, Article 33 of this convention merits to be mentioned for this reason: 'The States Parties shall take all appropriate measures, including legislative, administrative, social and educational measures, to protect children from the illicit use of narcotic drugs and psychotropic substances as defined in the relevant international treaties, and to prevent the use of children in the illicit production and trafficking of such substances.' Although this provision does not explicitly contain the obligation to ban the supply of recreational drugs to children, it would appear that the UN Committee on the Rights of the Child does indeed interpret this provision in this way; see Committee on the Rights of the Child, General Comment No. 15 on the right of the child to the enjoyment of the highest attainable standard of health (Article 24), 17 April 2013, *UN Doc.* CRC/C/GC/15, para. 66, 'The Committee encourages States parties that have not yet done so to ratify the international drug control conventions and the World Health Organization Framework Convention on Tobacco Control. The Committee underscores the importance of adopting a rights-based approach to substance use and recommends that, where appropriate, harm reduction strategies should be employed to minimize the negative health impacts of substance abuse.' See also, with references to these judgments of the Committee, Rachel Hodgkin & Peter Newell, *Implementation Handbook for the Convention on the Rights of the Child*, Geneva: UNICEF, 2007, pp. 504, 508, 507, 510.

209 CESCR, General Comment No. 14 (2000) 'Right to Health', para. 15.

210 Ibid, para. 36. See also CESCR, Concluding Observations (Finland), *UN Doc.* E/C.12/FIN/CO/6 (2014), para. 25; CESCR, Concluding Observations (Poland), *UN Doc.* E/C.12/POL/CO/05 (2009), para. 25.

211 CESCR, Concluding Observations (Uzbekistan), *UN Doc.* E/C.12/UZB/CO/2 (2014), para. 24, 'Focus should be on preventive care, in particular raising awareness of harmful effects of [...] alcohol and tobacco consumption, the monitoring of those practices, [...] and the promotion of healthy lifestyles'.

212 Report of the Secretary-General, Compilation of Guidelines on the Form and Content of reports to be submitted by State Parties to the International Human Rights Treaties, 3 June 2009, *UN Doc.* HRI/GEN/2/Rev.6, para. 57(d).

213 As far the latter is concerned, the report mentioned in the previous footnote refers to CESCR, General Comment No. 14 (2000) 'Right to Health', para. 16.

an all-encompassing strategy for the fight against the illegal drugs trade. The Committee emphasizes that the efforts to combat drugs should not have negative consequences for the enjoyment of economic, social and cultural rights[214] (it goes without saying that violations of other human rights, such as civil rights and political rights are also unacceptable[215]). In the final analysis, according to the ICESCR Committee, states have:

- the obligation to discourage the production, marketing and consumption of alcohol, tobacco, recreational drugs and other harmful substances in particular, but not exclusively, among children and adolescents;
- the obligation to inform the public effectively about the risks posed by these substances;
- the obligation to combat illicit drugs trade without this having negative consequences for the enjoyment of economic, social and cultural rights.
- The obligation to ensure an adequate treatment and rehabilitation of drug users as well as providing support to their families.

Furthermore, there are all sorts of specific obligations in connection with alcohol and tobacco. Many of these are closely linked to the obligation to discourage harmful substances and may be useful in the case of cannabis.[216] That is why we will list these obligations where it is logical to assume that they might be linked to recreational cannabis if its cultivation and trade were permitted under regulation. This involves:

- the obligation to levy high taxes (excise duties) on the stimulant;[217]
- the obligation to ban advertising for stimulants;[218]

---

214 CESCR Concluding Observations (Afghanistan), *UN Doc.* E/C.12/AFG/CO/2-4, 7 June 2010, para. 33; CESCR Concluding Observations (Mauritius), *UN Doc.* E/C.12/MUS/CO/4, 21 May 2010, para. 27–28.

215 This was recently confirmed by the UN in U.N. General Assembly resolution 69/201, 18 December 2014, para. 2, 11, 24(a), and by the elaborate analysis in Report of the United Nations High Commissioner for Human Rights, Study on the impact of the world drug problem on the enjoyment of human rights, *UN Doc.* A/HRC/30/65, 4 September 2015.

216 Cf. Mark Haden & Brian Emerson, 'A vision for cannabis regulation: a public health approach based on lessons learned from the regulation of alcohol and tobacco', *Open Medicine* 2014, vol. 8(2)e, pp. 73–80.

217 CESCR, Concluding Observations (Finland), *UN Doc.* E/C.12/FIN/CO/6 (2014), para. 25, 'high taxes [...] to counter alcohol abuse and drug use'. See also Report of the Special Rapporteur on the right of everyone to the enjoyment of the highest attainable standard of physical and mental health, Anand Grover, on access to medicines, *UN Doc.* A/HRC/23/42, 01 May 2013, para. 34 and 71(d).

218 CESCR, Concluding Observations (Finland), *UN Doc.* E/C.12/FIN/CO/6 (2014), para. 25, 'prohibition of advertisements, to counter alcohol abuse and drug use'. See also CESCR, Concluding Observations (Brazil), *UN Doc.* E/C.12/BRA/CO/2 (2009), para. 30.

- the obligation to ban the use of the stimulant (tobacco) in public indoor spaces;[219]
- the obligation to prohibit the sale to children.[220]

Incidentally, these sub-obligations are mostly discussed in broader assessments of policy in respect of addictive stimulants. Eventually, the result of the policy as a whole is key and that is also what the state should focus on. For example, in our opinion a state would not have to decide to increase excise duties if that were to result in certain stimulants becoming more available illegally and its use would actually increase consequently. After all, that would run counter to the obligation to strive for 'the highest attainable standard'.

At the same time, judgments by the ICESCR Committee illustrate that states will not reach the 'ceiling' soon with respect to the obligation pursuant to Article 12 ICESCR for states to take the necessary steps to progressively achieve 'the full realization' of the right to health. For example, the Committee placed considerable emphasis on the fact that Slovakia, in spite of its many legal initiatives and awareness raising campaigns aimed at combating the use of tobacco, must 'step up its efforts' to counter the use of tobacco, seeing that this use in Slovakia remains alarmingly high.[221] The Committee is unmistakably result-driven.

Here, the Committee uses the statistical data about the use of substances carrying a risk to health as an important yardstick for the extent to which states meet their obligations under Article 12 ICESCR.[222] This is why a package of policies and measures regarding cannabis cultivation and trade that is based on arguments related to individual and public health – see section 2.3.1 about this – will therefore at least require facts to justify this package. The foregoing also implies that if a state were to permit regulated cannabis cultivation and trade, that state would in the course of time have to present genuine data

219 CESCR, Concluding Observations (Brazil), *UN Doc.* E/C.12/BRA/CO/2 (2009), para. 30, on tobacco use.

220 CESCR, Concluding Observations (Uzbekistan), *UN Doc.* E/C.12/UZB/CO/2 (2014), para. 24, 'Focus should be on [...] the prohibition of the sale of alcohol and tobacco to children and the promotion of healthy lifestyles'.

221 CESCR, Concluding Observations (Slovakia), *UN Doc.* E/C.12/SVK/CO/2, 8 June 2012, para. 23 '[...] despite the State party's many legislative initiatives and awareness-raising campaigns aimed at combating tobacco use (art. 12) [...] [the] Committee strongly recommends that the State party step up its efforts to combat tobacco use and to address the implications thereof, especially for young people. The Committee urges the State party to ensure the effective application of its anti-tobacco legislation and to intensify its awareness-raising campaigns in that respect. The Committee also recommends that the State party adopt a comprehensive national plan or strategy to combat tobacco use and that these include health-care provisions'.

222 See also section 2.3.7.viii.

showing that it led to a decrease and at any rate did not lead to an increase of adverse effects from the use of substances or did not lead to other health risks.

The focus on results in reaching the highest attainable standard of health in the sense of Article 12(1) of the ICESCR is also expressed by the ICESCR Committee. It berates countries that fail to provide (sufficient) 'harm reduction' measures such as the medical use of methadone and buprenorphine for drugs users and programmes for (providing) needles and syringes.[223] Although such measures are seen by some as condoning and facilitating drug use and sidestepping the objective to combat drugs,[224] the Committee sees it as an approach which eventually de facto yields the best results in realizing the right to health.[225] This even applies to such an extent that states can be obliged to implement these measures. This is interesting and ironic, because regulated permission of cannabis cultivation and trade as such leaves room for (increased and individual) use of cannabis, a harmful stimulant after all, but this permission is advocated in the general interest of individual and public health, as we saw before in section 2.3.1. At the same time, it is also clear that such permission may be a mandatory means but can never be an end in itself from the perspective of the right to health.

On the strength of the foregoing, the ICESCR Committee places the emphasis on regulation through legislation and policy with a heavy slant towards prevention, discouragement and raising awareness.[226] States must be able to demonstrate that their endeavours in that area are genuinely effective. Eventually, what matters is that states apply policies and measures which yield the best possible health results.

---

223 CESCR, Concluding Observations (Ukraine), *UN Doc.* E/C.12/UKR/CO/6 (2014), para. 24; CESCR, Concluding Observations (Russian Federation), *UN Doc.* E/C.12/RUS/CO/5 (2011), para. 29; CESCR, Concluding Observations (Mauritius), *UN Doc.* E/C.12/MUS/CO/4 (2010), para. 27–28; CESCR, Concluding Observations (Tajikistan), *UN Doc.* E/2007/22 (2006), para. 510.

224 See Saul Takahashi, 'Drug Control, Human Rights, and the Right to the Highest Attainable Standard of Health: by no means straightforward issues', *Human Rights Quarterly* 2009, vol. 31, no. 3, pp. 748–776 on p. 767.

225 More generally, Saul Takahashi draws the conclusion: 'Drug Control, Human Rights, and the Right to the Highest Attainable Standard of Health: by no means straightforward issues', *Human Rights Quarterly* 2009, vol. 31, no. 3, pp. 748–776 on p. 770: 'The human right to the highest attainable standard of health, therefore, appears to be used as one of the pillars of harm reduction.' See also Damon Barrett, 'Drug Use and the Right of Everyone to the Highest Attainable Standard of Health', in: Sven Hessle (ed.), *Human Rights and Social Equality: Challenges for Social Work*, Farnham, UK/Burlington, USA: Ashgate, 2014, pp. 158–166 on p. 159, concludes, referring to documents of various UN bodies: 'Indeed, in recent years, harm reduction has increasingly been seen as a component of the right to the highest attainable standard of health in the context of drug policies'.

226 See also CESCR, Concluding Observations (Poland), *UN Doc.* E/C.12/POL/CO/05, 2 December 2009, para. 25; CESCR, Concluding Observations (Mauritius), *UN Doc.* E/C.12/MUS/CO/4, 21 May 2010, para. 27–28.

ii. The Approach by the European CSR

The European CSR does not require states to prohibit alcohol, tobacco, recreational drugs and other stimulants either in relation to the use of these substances, at any rate not the consumption by adults.[227] So within the ESC too, there is room for legalization, decriminalization or policy of tolerance. Yet, states will need to pay special attention for tobacco, alcohol and drugs in taking measures to promote health.[228] The policy of protection against these harmful substances must in any case 'place effective restrictions on the supply of tobacco, alcohol and drugs, particularly through controls on production, distribution, advertising and prices.'[229] This requires sufficiently precise regulation.[230] If necessary, states must also initiate education and launch campaigns aimed at raising awareness of the risks of drug use.[231] Also if there is no prohibition on these stimulants, their use must still be countered effectively and consequently be discouraged. It follows from Conclusions on the Netherlands that these obligations apply in relation to cannabis too.[232] In brief, the European CSR provided as follows:

- the obligation to provide effective restrictions on and checks of production, distribution, advertising and pricing of alcohol, tobacco and recreational drugs;
- the obligation to inform the public effectively about the risks posed by these substances.

In its Conclusions about the national reports on the implementation of the ESC, the European CSR invariably pays attention to the measures taken to prevent

---

227 Such a prohibition is required for sales to juveniles, as illustrated by Council of Europe, *Digest of the Case Law of the European Committee of Social Rights*, 1 September 2008, p. 97. In any case, the European CSR requires a ban on the sale of tobacco and alcohol to juveniles; see among other sources ECSR, Conclusions XIX-2 (2009) on the European Social Charter (Hungary), under: Article 11(3) (on tobacco); ECSR, Conclusions 2013 on the European Social Charter (Cyprus), under: Article 11(3) (on alcohol).

228 Council of Europe, *Digest of the Case Law of the European Committee of Social Rights*, 1 September 2008, p. 97. 'Tobacco, alcohol and drugs' are also an integral part of the checks by the European CSR on the measures adopted by the member states with regard to the right to health.

229 ECSR, Conclusions XVII-2 (2005) on the European Social Charter (Malta), under: Article 11(3).

230 See for example ECSR, Conclusions 2009 on the European Social Charter (Cyprus), under: Article 11(3).

231 See among other sources ECSR, Conclusions 2013 on the European Social Charter (Cyprus), under: Article 11(2); ECSR, Conclusions 2009 on the European Social Charter (Cyprus), under: Article 11(2) and (3).

232 ECSR, Conclusions 2013 on the European Social Charter (The Netherlands), under: Article 11(3).

the use of 'Tobacco, alcohol and drugs' in the context of Article 11 ESC. Because tobacco and alcohol are usually not prohibited, it is also interesting here to see which obligations the European CSR imposes in connection with these substances, as this is a further implementation of the requirement to prevent and discourage the use of these stimulants. The following may be relevant if the regulated cultivation and trade of cannabis for recreational use were to be permitted:

- the obligation to prohibit the sale of tobacco and alcohol to juveniles[233] (this can also apply to cannabis);
- the obligation to ban smoking in public spaces, including public transport[234] (in the case of cannabis, this could involve a ban on smoking in public indoor spaces);
- the obligation to ban advertising for tobacco (including on posters, in the press, magazines, on television and radio)[235] (this can also apply to cannabis);
- the desirability (but possibly an obligation) of including health warnings on packs of cigarettes[236] (this can also apply to cannabis);
- the desirability (but possibly an obligation) to limit the amount of tar allowed in cigarettes[237] (in the same way, it could be the maximum THC content in the case of cannabis).

The European CSR assesses the effectivity of the adopted policy and the measures taken more explicitly, than the CESCR, on the basis of statistical data of the consumption of tobacco, alcohol and drugs.[238] In the absence of 'up-to-date statistics or information on trends in the consumption of alcohol, tobacco and drugs', the Committee deems itself insufficiently able to assess whether the

233 As we observed before in one of the previous footnotes, see among other sources ECSR, Conclusions XIX-2 (2009) on the European Social Charter (Hungary), under: Article 11(3) (on tobacco); ECSR, Conclusions 2013 on the European Social Charter (Cyprus), under: Article 11(3) (on alcohol).

234 ECSR, Conclusions XV-2 (2001) on the European Social Charter (Greece), under: Article 11(3); ECSR, Conclusions 2013 on the European Social Charter (Andorra), under: Article 11(3).

235 ECSR, Conclusions XV-2 (2001) on the European Social Charter (Greece), under: Article 11(3); ECSR, Conclusions 2013 on the European Social Charter (Andorra), under: Article 11(3).

236 ECSR, Addendum to Conclusions XV-2 (2001) on the European Social Charter (Cyprus), under: Article 11(3).

237 Ibid.

238 See for example ECSR, Conclusions XVII-2 (2005) on the European Social Charter (Malta), under: Article 11; ECSR, Conclusions 2013 on the European Social Charter (Andorra), under: Article 11(3).

situation in a state complies with its obligations arising from the ESC.[239] This can result in the European CSR delaying its Conclusions so as to wait for the necessary information[240] or to conclude that it cannot be established whether the state has met its obligations emanating from the right to health under Article 11 ESC.[241] The focus on figures illustrating a reduction in the use of alcohol, tobacco and drugs also shows that this Committee is clearly results-oriented.

iii. Conclusions about the Committees' Approach

Neither the ICESCR Committee nor the European CSR demands from states that they ban alcohol, tobacco and recreational drugs or other harmful substances for adults. This approach is in line with Article 12 ICESCR and Article 11 ESC, in the sense that these provisions do not require or assume such a ban either. Nor does it show from the Committees' approach that regulated permission of the production, trade and use of stimulants (and that includes cannabis) would not be a sensible or meaningful implementation of the right to health. In the end, the approach of these bodies is informed by the need for results: to achieve 'the highest attainable standard' of health.[242]

To that extent, a drug policy that permits regulated cannabis cultivation and trade for recreational use via legalization, decriminalization or a policy of tolerance can qualify as a required implementation of the right to health. This is the case insofar as that drug policy de facto guaranteed individual and public health better than a more prohibitive drug policy. At the same time, such permission may be a mandatory means, but it can never be an end in itself based on the obligation to realize the right to health.

It also means (and that is what the Committees emphasized, regardless of whether a state opts for the permission or the prohibition of cannabis) that policies and measures regarding drugs, or cannabis as the case may, must be squarely aimed at preventing its use. Key to this approach must be a policy of discouragement of production, trade and use), a limited regulation (of the possibilities for production, trade and use) and education and information campaigns (to raise awareness of the risks of substance abuse). A state that proceeds to permitting the cultivation and trade of cannabis for recreational use in a regulated system so as to realize the right to health will therefore also have to make concerted efforts to raise awareness of the risks related to the use of cannabis for recreational purposes and to discourage and limit that use, by virtue of the very same right.

---

239 ECSR, Conclusions 2005 on the European Social Charter (Cyprus), under: Article 11(3).

240 Ibid; ECSR, Conclusions 2013 on the European Social Charter (Belgium), under: Article 11(3).

241 ECSR, Conclusions 2013 on the European Social Charter (Andorra), under: Article 11(3).

242 See also section 2.3.5.

2.3.11. DRUGS AND THE RIGHT TO HEALTH ACCORDING TO THE UN SPECIAL RAPPORTEUR

Finally, the insights of the UN Special Rapporteur on the right of everyone to the enjoyment of the highest attainable standard of physical and mental health (hereinafter to be referred to as: UN Special Rapporteur on the right to health) merit our attention here. As we noted before, as an independent expert, the Special Rapporteur has not been formally designated as a body charged with supervising compliance with the ICESCR nor with the interpretation of its provisions, but while his insights, points of view, conclusions and recommendations are not legally binding, they are deemed authoritative sources of law. For that reason, it is appropriate to discuss them here.

Of particular relevance here is the report by the Special Rapporteur of 2010, in which he dwells at length on 'The right to health and international drug control'.[243] In this report, the Special Rapporteur presents all sorts of findings and recommendations, several of which are relevant to our purpose as well. We will mention the most important ones.

- The Special Rapporteur recommends the integration of human rights in the international response to drug control.[244]
- The Special Rapporteur is of the opinion that states must reform national legislation in order to arrive at decriminalization or de-penalization of possession and use of drugs, while emphasizing that this does not mean that legalization is required.[245]
- The Special Rapporteur notes that it is clear that human rights obligations must prevail if the goals and approaches of the international drug control

[243] Report of the Special Rapporteur on the right of everyone to the enjoyment of the highest attainable standard of physical and mental health, Anand Grover, *UN Doc.* A/65/255, 6 August 2010 (to be referred to in the footnotes hereafter as: Special Rapporteur Health, A/65/255, 2010).

[244] Special Rapporteur Health, A/65/255, 2010, para. 6 and 77. See also Open Letter by the Special Rapporteur on the right of everyone to the highest attainable standard of mental and physical health, Dainius Pūras, in the context of the preparations for the UN General Assembly Special Session on the Drug Problem (UNGASS), which will take place in New York in April 2016, 7 December 2015. Cf. U.N. Secretary-General, Ban Ki-Moon, 'Message on International Day Against Drug Abuse and Illicit Trafficking', *UN Doc.* UNIS/SGSM/645, 26 June 2015.

[245] Special Rapporteur Health, A/65/255, 2010, para. 6, 62–69 and 76. See also Open Letter by the Special Rapporteur on the right of everyone to the highest attainable standard of mental and physical health, Dainius Pūras, in the context of the preparations for the UN General Assembly Special Session on the Drug Problem (UNGASS), which will take place in New York in April 2016, 7 December 2015, where the emphasis is on education and treatment, inter alia.

regime (that is to say, the three UN narcotic drugs conventions) conflict with those of the international human rights regime.[246]

- The Special Rapporteur calls it unfortunate that in the current approach of global drug control, drugs are considered 'an undisputable "evil"' that the international community has a 'duty to combat'. This approach does not realize its stated primary objective (to prevent health-related damage caused by drug use), nor does it succeed in actually controlling drugs either, according to the Special Rapporteur. The 'war on drugs' approach also ignores the reality of drug use and drug dependency, and that is the reason why the approach is not successful and the objectives are not met. In this respect, the rapporteur points out that 'people invariably continue using drugs irrespective criminal laws.' He also points out that punitive actions actually increase the damage by drug use, because inappropriate methods and misguided solutions are chosen, while 'evidence-based' approaches are neglected. The Special Rapporteur also notes that the current approach to drugs control (where he apparently refers to the approach under the UN narcotic drugs conventions) causes more damage than it prevents.[247]
- The Special Rapporteur argues that a humane drug control system must be created that does meet its own objectives and that therefore the current international drug control system has to be overhauled. That should be done at all levels of policy, including national levels. The WHO Framework Convention on Tobacco Control (2003) could be the model for such an alternative drug control system, according to the rapporteur.[248]
- The Special Rapporteur holds the view that national authorities need to implement 'harm reduction' programmes and policies. In this context, he mentions, among other things, programmes for (providing) needles and syringes, drug-consumption rooms, interventions to promote non-injection methods for drug administration, overdose prevention as well as outreach work and educational programmes.[249]

---

246 Special Rapporteur Health, A/65/255, 2010, para. 10; see for more information on that section 3.7.9.

247 Special Rapporteur Health, A/65/255, 2010, para. 14–16. See also Report of the Special Rapporteur on the right of everyone to the enjoyment of the highest attainable standard of physical and mental health, Dainius Pūras, *UN Doc.* A/HRC/29/33, 02 April 2015, para. 27.

248 Special Rapporteur Health, A/65/255, 2010, para. 48–49 and 73–74 and 77.

249 Special Rapporteur Health, A/65/255, 2010, para. 49–55. See also Report of the Special Rapporteur on the right of everyone to the enjoyment of the highest attainable standard of physical and mental health, Paul Hunt, Addendum (mission to Sweden), *UN Doc.* A/HRC/4/28/Add.2, 28 February 2007, para. 35, 60–62; Special Rapporteur on the right of everyone to the enjoyment of the highest attainable standard of physical and mental health, Anand Grover, Submission to the Committee against Torture regarding drug control laws, 19 October 2012, pp. 3–5.

- The Special Rapporteur points out that policies and measures 'must be developed in an inclusive, participatory and transparent consultation process with affected communities.'[250]

The above illustrates that the UN Special Rapporteur on the right to health, on the grounds of that same right, rejects the overtly prohibitive and repressive approach of the drugs problem prescribed by the UN narcotic drugs conventions. According to him, instead of this approach, a human rights-based approach to drug control is called for.

The WHO Framework Convention on Tobacco Control (2003)[251] could be the model for such an alternative drug control system, according to the Rapporteur.[252] It is interesting that this convention does not contain an obligation to prohibit the production, trade and use of tobacco, but it does constitute a detailed package of measures aimed at limiting and discouraging production, trade and use. This includes pricing and taxation measures, protection of third parties against tobacco smoke, regulation of the contents of the product, obligations with regard to packaging and labelling of the product in the sense of warnings and information on the relevant ingredients and emissions, promoting public awareness about the health risks among other things, introduction of an all-encompassing ban of advertising, promoting and sponsoring of the product, measures to drive down demand, combating illicit traffic, the obligation to prohibit the sale of tobacco to juveniles and the promotion of national research focusing on the determinants and consequences of consumption for third parties. This model (which can be summarized as 'permit, but limit and discourage') apparently offers an approach that can be useful for drugs as well, according to the Special Rapporteur. Moreover, according to the Special Rapporteur states have a responsibility to implement 'harm reduction' programmes and policies, by providing users' rooms for example. In doing so, the state would facilitate drug use in a sense, but it does not diminish the fact that this would be required by the right to health.

We conclude that the Special Rapporteur also takes the view that states by virtue of the right to health are obliged to take those measures that eventually will lead to 'the highest attainable standard' of health. We detect a strong drive

---

250 Special Rapporteur Health, A/65/255, 2010, para. 70. See also, for example, Report of the Special Rapporteur on the right of everyone to the enjoyment of the highest attainable standard of physical and mental health, Anand Grover, *UN Doc.* A/69/299, 11 August 2014, para. 3 and also 27, 30, 33, 50, 73(c), 75(e), 78.

251 WHO Framework Convention on Tobacco Control, Geneva, 21 May 2003: Trb. 2003, 127.

252 See also Mark Haden & Brian Emerson, 'A vision for cannabis regulation: a public health approach based on lessons learned from the regulation of alcohol and tobacco', *Open Medicine* 2014, vol. 8(2)e, pp. 73–80; Cyrille Fijnaut & Brice De Ruyver, *De derde weg. Een pleidooi voor een evenwichtig cannabisbeleid*, Antwerpen/Cambridge: Intersentia, 2014, pp. 229–240 (i.e., *The third way. A plea for a balanced cannabis policy*).

for results with the rapporteur as well, just like the one expressed in the text of the convention. Having said that, the rapporteur never argued or implied that states have (or a certain state has) the obligation to adopt, or conversely, not adopt a system in which cannabis cultivation and trade is permitted in a regulated way. Nevertheless, it follows from the foregoing that the introduction of such regulated permission on the basis of the right to health may be appropriate if this guarantees individual and public health in the best possible way. Whether this is really appropriate eventually, will also depend on the degree to which the measures arise from a process with participation of citizens, are backed up by democratic decision-making and enjoy wide public support.

2.3.12. CONCLUSION AS REGARDS THE RIGHT TO HEALTH

The right to health in Article 12 ICESCR and Article 11 ESC does not explicitly refer to drugs or cannabis. Nevertheless, there is frequent and considerable attention for the risks attached to these substances and the related policies and measures from the ICESCR Committee and the European CSR and otherwise also from other bodies inside the UN, such as the Special Rapporteur and the Council of Europe.[253] This is consistent with the broad definition of the concept of 'health' in the sense of the aforementioned provisions and the extensive scope of the right to health. Drugs are not just a marginal topic in relation to this right, it is a key element. While it is true that less serious individual health and public health related risks adhere to cannabis than to heroin, cocaine and methamphetamine for example, there is no reason to suppose that policies and measures regarding cannabis as a recreational drug do not also constitute an important health subject in the context of the aforementioned conventions. Although the aforementioned bodies usually talk about drugs in general, the European CSR also pays attention to cannabis specifically in assessing country reports.

i. First Question: Does the Right to Health Preclude Regulated Permission?

We formulated three key questions in the introductory part to section 2.3. In view of this, a first conclusion that is important to this discussion is that the

253 See for example the recent Committee on Social Affairs, Health and Sustainable Development of the Parliamentary Assembly of the Council of Europe, Statement: Committee calls for a public-health-oriented drug policy, 23 November 2015: 'the committee strongly supports the call for a change in approach to drug policy and calls on member States to adopt and promote a public-health-oriented drug policy based on prevention, treatment and harm reduction.' See also Council of Europe Parliamentary Assembly, Resolution 1576 (2007) For a European convention on promoting public health policy in drug control, 3 October 2007.

right to health does not resist the introduction of a drug policy that permits the cultivation of and trade in cannabis for recreational use by adults, if and insofar as that drug policy de facto guaranteed individual and public health better than a more prohibitive drug policy. Whether that permission takes the form of legalization, decriminalization or a policy of tolerance is not pertinent as such. Cultivation, trade and availability of cannabis for minors however, are at odds with the right to health and must therefore be prohibited. The fact that the right to health with regard to adults is not necessarily an impediment to regulated permission of cannabis does not mean that such permission may qualify as a possible implementation of the right or is even required by it. This brings us to the following.

ii. Second Question: Is Regulated Permission Required under the Right to Health?

Is a drug policy that permits the cultivation of and trade in cannabis for recreational use an acceptable and possibly even required vehicle for implementing the right to health, if and insofar as that drug policy de facto guaranteed individual and public health better than a more prohibitive drug policy? Given the answer to the previous question, there is room for approximately one of the three alternative scenarios to be mentioned below. With each of these scenarios, the hypothesis is that regulated permission of the cultivation of and trade in cannabis for recreational use (via legalization, decriminalization or a policy of tolerance) leads to a better protection of individual and public health than a more prohibitive drug policy. The first variant is that the state not only may proceed to regulated permission but must do so, pursuant to the right to health (may and must). The second variant is that the state then may and can implement the right to health by permitting regulated cannabis cultivation and trade, but is not obliged to do so (may, can, not obliged). The third variant is that the right to health does not resist regulated permission, but that this cannot qualify as an implementation of the right (may, without relevance). Also because cannabis is a serious issue from the point of view of health (and incidentally, this is the presupposition of the UN narcotic drugs conventions), this last variant is a non-starter at any rate: policies and measures that relate to cannabis for recreational use are within the sphere of influence of the right to health in Article 12 ICESCR and Article 11 ESC.

In light of the foregoing, the first variant (may and must) is in principle the option that can be defended best. To that end, it is crucial that under the right to health, states are obliged to use 'all appropriate means' with which they can fully realize 'the highest attainable standard of health'. The obligation to implement the right to health is unlimited in the sense that 1. it has no ceiling (full realization of the highest attainable standard) and 2. that all measures that contribute to realizing the convention rights must be deployed if that is actually possible for the state (all appropriate means). This obligation to achieve results follows explicitly from Article 12 ICESCR as well as the case law of the ICESCR Committee and the

European CSR. To that extent, it is simple: if regulated permission of cannabis cultivation and trade best guarantees individual and public health in a country, there is a priori an obligation to initiate such regulation (may and must). From a less simple point of view, the following is important as well.

To achieve the highest attainable standard, states must take almost all conceivable effective measures that are at their disposal. Insofar as the authorities can discharge their obligations to respect, protect and fulfil the highest possible standard of health through regulation and policies with respect to cannabis, they will have to provide for this. Relevant new knowledge and progressive insights may play a role in this. A relevant consideration is that states are also primarily responsible for considering which measures or steps, given the specific circumstances in the state, are the most appropriate so as to achieve progressively the full realization of the right to health (principle of primarity). If a state in accordance with the requirement of 'pacta sunt servanda' genuinely decides and demonstrates that regulated permission of the cultivation of and trade in cannabis for recreational use best protects individual and public health, that state therefore primarily meets its obligation under the convention to achieve 'the highest attainable standard' of health by introducing such regulation. If such regulation has the support of a large part of society and comes about after democratic decision-making and direct participation of citizens, it reinforces the assumption that this policy and those measures are indeed the appropriate steps that can best bring about the general realization of the right to health and that they are therefore required. We conclude that if regulated permission of cannabis cultivation and trade best safeguards individual and public health in a country, also according to the position of that country taken in good faith, it can be seen as an obligation arising from the right to health to adopt such regulation, provided a number of criteria that we will discuss later are met (may and must).

Or are there still any arguments that decisively prevent this conclusion, in the sense that it must be assumed that while states may adopt the aforementioned regulation under the right to health, they are not required to do so under this right (may, can, not obliged)? That is not the case in our opinion.

The first possible argument against the 'may and must' conclusion that merits attention is that regulated permission of cannabis cultivation and trade creates room for and in a certain sense even facilitates cannabis use. Even if one were to see this as cooperation (facilitating cannabis use), this argument does not constitute an obstacle to regulated permission. The problem with this argument after all is that it isolates a single adverse effect of such regulation (access to recreational cannabis), instead of looking at the greater picture, the overall effect (on balance, a better implementation of the right to health). And the latter is what matters. After all, states are required to use all appropriate means to achieve progressively 'the full realization' of the right to health with a view to ensuring physical and mental health of 'the highest attainable standard'. If one had to look at certain effects in isolation, then even the use of many medicines would become problematic: many medicines are known to carry risks for one's health (side-effects), but in many cases the administration of such medicines on balance leads to better health for the patient. More directly in relation to recreational drugs, the isolated approach is not accepted either from the point of view of the right to health. For example, states are required (e.g., by the ICESCR Committee and more emphatically by the UN Special Rapporteur on the right to health) to provide needles and syringes, drug-consumption rooms with a view to harm reduction so as to realize the right to health. The fact that the Special Rapporteur urges states to decriminalize or de-penalize possession and use of drugs also illustrates that a result-oriented approach must be used to decide which measures enable the state to achieve the highest attainable standard. In principle, the state is then required to take those measures. Once again, we point out here that the Special Rapporteur, because of the right to health, declares himself to be in favour of introducing an international drug control system for which the WHO Framework Convention on Tobacco Control (2003) could be the model. What is interesting here is that this convention does not contain an obligation to prohibit the production, trade and use of tobacco, but it does constitute a detailed package of measures aimed at limiting and discouraging production, trade and use.

Another argument one might want to use against the 'may and must' conclusion is that regulated permission of cannabis cultivation and trade does not feature as an obligation in the provisions of the conventions nor in the case law about the right to health. This argument is bound to fail. First of all, recognition of this argument would mean that nothing that a state could do in concrete terms to arrive at the highest attainable standard will qualify as an obligation, unless the measure taken was explicitly mentioned in the provisions of the conventions. That is an approach that does not work well in human rights, as these need to be protected effectively in concrete and practical terms, and it would narrow the scope of the right to health dramatically. This approach also ignores the fact that both Article 12(2) ICESCR and Article 11 ESC clearly do not contain a limited list of measures that must be taken. In other words: these provisions also assume all sorts of obligations that are not mentioned explicitly, as becomes clear from the case law of the ICESCR Committee and the European CSR. Moreover, various health arguments put forward for regulated permission are actually quite clearly based on some measures that are mentioned explicitly in these provisions.

Furthermore, as a more political objection, one could argue that if regulated permission of cannabis cultivation and trade for the Netherlands would qualify as an obligation under the right to health, that other countries too would then have to take the same steps. We believe that such an obligation could well be on the cards in other countries, but it is not true that this would automatically apply to all or even most other countries. First of all, it is important that states, as we observed before, are primarily responsible for considering which measures or steps, given the specific circumstances in the state, are the most appropriate so as to achieve progressively the full realization of the right to health (principle of primarity).

If the state concludes in accordance with that right that a certain approach is the most effective, then in principle that state is required to adopt that approach. This also means that a state which does not draw such a conclusion, would not have two go down that route, unless this particular obligation would be established by an official supervisory body. Secondly, it is important whether regulated permission of cannabis cultivation and trade in a state is the result of democratic decision-making, citizen participation and reflects the views of society at large. If this is not the case, then it could less easily be considered an appropriate step. Not only do policies and measures then fail to meet an important condition, but it will also be less easy for these policies and those measures to be effective. Thirdly, in our opinion the 'margin of appreciation' often entails that the state can escape the required appropriate step of regulated permission by taking other appropriate steps that the state in question deems preferable.

Finally, the three arguments mentioned just now (principle of primarity, democratic support, margin of appreciation) are also important for the question whether lower authorities in a state will be able to keep the national government and the national legislator beholden to implementing regulated permission under the law of the convention if the national government refuses to do that. We are of the opinion that the three arguments imply that this is not possible in principle. While it is true that lower state bodies (such as federal states, provinces, municipalities) are also bound by the rights and obligations under the conventions insofar as they are relevant for them,[254] they cannot force the national government to take measures that these authorities are entitled to abstain from by virtue of the provisions of the convention. It is for the same reasons that individuals or private organizations are also unable to do this.

iii. Third Question: Which Requirements does the Right to Health Impose on Cannabis Policy?

Pursuant to the right to health, states are required to provide for adequate health policies. The ICESCR Committee even treats the adoption and implementation of a national public health strategy and plan of action regarding addressing the health problems of the entire population as a core obligation. This policy will at

254 See Article 27 of the Vienna Convention on the Law of Treaties. See HRC, General Comment No. 31, 'The Nature of the General Legal Obligation Imposed on States Parties to the Covenant', 26 May 2004, *UN Doc.* CCPR/C/21/Rev.1/Add.13 (2004) (also: HRC, General Comment No. 31 (2004) 'General Legal Obligation'), para. 4, respectively ECtHR 26 October 1988, *Martins Moreira/Portugal*, no. 11371/85, para. 60; Tom Barkhuysen, 'Het EVRM als integraal onderdeel van het Nederlandse materiële bestuursrecht' (i.e., 'The ECHR as an integral part of Dutch substantive administrative law'), in: T. Barkhuysen, A.B. Blomberg, M.K. Bulterman & J.M. Verschuuren, *De betekenis van het EVRM voor het materiële bestuursrecht* (Preadviezen VAR), Den Haag: Boom Juridische uitgeverij, 2004, pp. 7–113 on p. 36 (i.e., *The meaning of the ECHR for substantive administrative law (considerations of the VAR, the Dutch association for administrative law)*).

any rate need to meet both the general requirements to respect, protect and fulfil the right to health and the specific positive obligations arising from this right.

In the light of these general and special obligations, it must be noted that all arguments related to individual and public health which are propounded in favour of regulated permission of cannabis cultivation and trade, always assuming that they are valid, are in principle relevant under the right to health. In short, it is about the following arguments: safeguarding the quality of cannabis, monitoring the cannabis chain, protection of the health of residents and juveniles, separating the soft drugs and hard drugs markets and cannabis as a less risky alternative stimulant. However, the content of these arguments does not yet provide sufficient substance to the required policy. The question is what exactly this policy should address if a state were to adopt regulated permission of cannabis cultivation and trade.

First, production, marketing and consumption of cannabis will really have to be discouraged effectively. This applies particularly to regulated permission too. Such permission may be an appropriate means, but can never be an end in itself with respect to the obligation to realize the right to health. This also means that policies and measures regarding cannabis must focus heavily on preventing its use. This is true for cannabis use among adults and even more so with regard to minors and children. The obligation to discourage use covers a huge number of sub-obligations. In the case of cannabis, the most important ones are the obligation to provide for effective restrictions on and control of production, distribution and trade of or in cannabis; the obligation to inform the public effectively about and making them aware of the risks associated with cannabis; the obligation to combat illegal cannabis trade with due regard for human rights; the obligation to levy high taxes (excise duties) on cannabis; the obligation to ban advertising and promoting cannabis; the obligation to ban smoking cannabis in public indoor spaces. While the following may not qualify as obligations then at any rate they must be treated as urgent desirabilities: inclusion of health warnings on packets/units of cannabis and putting a legal limit on the THC content of cannabis for example. In setting out these sub-obligations, the state will also have to assess what is most effective in the long run. The focus on results which is manifest in the convention (witness the obligation to aim for the highest attainable standard) entails that obligations must not be discharged in a manner that actually has the opposite effect.

Secondly, the drug policy and/or regulated permission of cannabis must not discriminate against certain individuals or groups in the state. Nor may there be a disproportionate impact on certain vulnerable groups. Insofar as regulated permission would increase the risks of cannabis for certain groups, sufficient compensatory protective measures will have to be taken.

Thirdly, the policy must be based on statistical data. A package of policies and measures regarding cannabis cultivation and trade that is based on arguments related to individual and public health will therefore at least require some substantiation with numerical data. Of course, in general the principle applies that when policy is changed in a direction for which there are as yet no empirical data, this is like venturing into uncharted territory, and it will usually be difficult to back up the effects of the new course with hard evidence. However, this should not be allowed to block a change in policy, since the requirement of data could then become an obstacle to fulfilling the main obligation, i.e. progressively achieving the full realization of the right to health. Having said that, the authorities will then have to argue persuasively why they expect that the new policy will lead to better protection of individual and public health. Moreover, they will need to present genuine evidence in due course that the change in policy has led to a reduction and at any rate, on balance, not to an increase in health risks.

Fourthly, a drug policy conducted by a country is not allowed to diminish the protection of individual and public health in other countries. This could be seen as an obligation to take action against health threats in other countries caused by cannabis cultivation and trade in the Netherlands. It goes without saying that these obligations require even more attention if cannabis cultivation and trade were permitted under regulation.

iv. Summary

In our opinion, the conclusion must be that the position which can be best defended is that a state is required to permit cannabis cultivation and trade under regulation (via legalization, decriminalization or a policy of tolerance) if that provides the best safeguards for individual and public health in the country and if the conclusion that this is the case is supported by that state itself on the basis of democratic decision-making, wide societal support and citizen participation. This follows from the duty to use all appropriate means to achieve progressively 'the full realization' of the right to health with a view to ensuring health of the highest attainable standard. This duty also implies that the regulation package seriously limits the cultivation of, the trade in and the use of cannabis, subjects these activities to effective conditions and discourages them as much as possible.

2.4. STATES' OBLIGATIONS REGARDING RIGHTS TO LIFE, AGAINST INHUMAN TREATMENT AND A PRIVATE LIFE

The right to life, the right not to be subjected to inhuman treatment and the right to a private life protect an individual against being deprived of his life, against inhuman treatment and unlawful violations of his private life both by the state and government bodies and to some extent by now also by private entities.

The latter category comprises individuals as well as for example companies and other private organizations. This is the background against which the right to life, the right not to be subjected to inhuman treatment and the right to a private life are potentially relevant for the cannabis issue. After all, the question presents itself whether in general terms these rights entail that states are also required to protect the lives, the physical and psychological integrity and the private lives of citizens against a lack of safety, nuisance and criminality caused by persons and organizations involved in the cultivation and trade of cannabis.

Against that background and with a view to answering eventually the key question of this chapter (see section 2.1), several subquestions related to the right to life, the right not to be subjected to inhuman treatment and the right to a private life will be discussed which correspond with the subquestions in section 2.3. The most important ones of these are the following three:

> Do the right to life, the right not to be subjected to inhuman treatment and the right to a private life resist the introduction of a drug policy which permits the cultivation of and trade in cannabis for recreational use, even if and insofar as such a drug policy would de facto prevent serious nuisance, help to combat crime and protect the safety and health of citizens better than a more prohibitive drug policy?

And subsequently, but now using a requirement-based approach:

> Is a drug policy that permits the cultivation of and trade in cannabis for recreational use an acceptable and possibly even required vehicle for implementing the right to life, the right not to be subjected to inhuman treatment and the right to a private life, and insofar as such a drug policy de facto prevents serious nuisance, helps to combat crime and protects the safety and health of citizens better than a more prohibitive drug policy?

And thirdly:

> Do the right to life, the right not to be subjected to inhuman treatment and the right to a private life require a drug and/or cannabis policy that is also aimed at implementing this right and if yes, what should it constitute?

Here too, the emphasis will be on the second question, as the answer to it is crucial in arriving at an answer to the main question of this chapter. Still, all the above questions – and others – will of course be looked at below. Again, answering the questions will not be possible until the end of the section, as all the various obligations and their aspects that will be discussed below have a bearing on it.

Below, it will become clear that the right to life, the right not to be subjected to inhuman treatment and the right to a private life are fundamentally different in content and nature from the right to health, whereas the positive obligations with the first category of rights are based almost exclusively on case law. For the sake of comparison between the previous and following discussions, we have nevertheless attempted to retain the structure of the previous section as much as possible. First, we will discuss the rights in a more general sense. We will review the text of the Articles of the conventions, the rationale of the rights, the meaning of the concepts life, inhuman treatment and a private life, the level of protection and the general scope of the obligations regarding protection flowing from the rights; see sections 2.4.2–2.4.6. We will then discuss in section 2.4.7 the general obligations arising from the ICCPR and the ECtHR concerning the protection of human rights, from various angles. This will be done in relation to the cannabis issue, as much as possible. Following the detailed explanation, in sections 2.4.8–2.4.10 we will look at positive obligations for protection that apply specifically to the right to life, the right not to be subjected to inhuman treatment and the right to a private life, of course again in the context of the cannabis issue. Section 2.4.11 then offers a more detailed explanation of the perspective of the Human Rights Committee and the ECtHR on alcohol, tobacco and drugs. We round our analysis off with a conclusion in section 2.4.12, in which the above-mentioned questions are answered.

First of all, in section 2.4.1 we will provide a brief overview of arguments related to the safety of citizens and combating crime that are put forward to back up proposals for regulated permission of cannabis cultivation and trade for recreational consumption. At the same time, this provides some concrete examples of how the right to life, the right not to be subjected to inhuman treatment and the right to a private life could be relevant in relation to the cannabis issue.

2.4.1. ARGUMENTS IN FAVOUR OF REGULATION, BASED ON THE SAFETY OF CITIZENS AND CRIME CONTROL

In addition to the above-mentioned arguments of health, the interests of the safety of citizens, protection against nuisance and combating (organized) crime often come into play in pleas for regulated permission of cannabis cultivation and trade for recreational consumption. Again, rather than providing a full inventory of all the arguments that have ever been propounded, we will limit ourselves to giving an overview of arguments used in particular in Dutch municipalities and by the authorities of several other countries in this respect.[255]

[255] The following is based on the inventory as presented in Piet Hein P.H.M.C. van Kempen & Masha I. Fedorova, *Internationaal recht en cannabis. Een beoordeling op basis van VN-drugsverdragen en EU-drugsregelgeving van gemeentelijke en buitenlandse opvattingen pro regulering van cannabisteelt voor recreatief gebruik*, Deventer: Kluwer, 2014, pp. 186–193 (see also pp. 6 and 8) – of letters, notes and reports from 25 Dutch municipalities, the literature to which these municipalities refer and the initiatives deployed in countries other than the Netherlands as described in particular in Beau Kilmer, Kristy Kruithof, Mafalda Pardal, Jonathan P. Caulkins & Jennifer Rubin, *Multinational overview of cannabis production regimes*, RAND Europe/WODC, 2013.

Roughly speaking, the various (and sometimes interconnected) arguments that have been proposed amount to the following:

- *A reduction of organized crime.* It is sometimes claimed that ever-increasing amounts of money circulating in the criminal circuit are earned from cannabis cultivation. Regulation of cannabis cultivation will help tackle crime. By regulating cultivation it will be taken out of the illegal sector. The argument is that this market will become less interesting for organized crime. In the Netherlands, for example, the supply of cannabis to the so-called coffee-shops will no longer be dependent on criminal activity. The cannabis market would also be less attractive for criminal networks, because the tax authorities could check regulated purchase and sale.
- *Decreased export of cannabis.* It is also argued that the consequence of regulated permission of cannabis cultivation will be that the export of soft drugs will fall. The export of soft drugs will also decrease by matching demand (by cannabis outlets) with supply (by cannabis growers), so no products will be left over (closed system). Since the quality, continuity and diversity of the supply-side can better be managed if cannabis cultivation is regulated, this can prevent cannabis consumers from switching to an underground circuit.
- *A reduction of peripheral crime.* Regulation would also lead to a reduction of indirect crime such as the theft of electrical power, corruption, money laundering, criminal involvement of sectors such as real estate, the violent settling of scores between drug gangs and the use of drug money for illicit arms trafficking. The problem of bribery and threats is also pointed out: socially weak citizens in deprived neighbourhoods are roped in by criminals for the production of soft drugs.
- *Countering the corruption of the 'upper world' (undermining legitimate society[256]).* The foregoing could also lead to another problem: by engaging socially weaker citizens in deprived neighbourhoods for the cultivation of cannabis, individuals who are not involved in criminal activities and entire districts end up in the clutches of organized crime.
- *Reduction of nuisance and damage.* Because illegal cultivation sites are poorly set up, they lead to stench, noise, and flooding. Then there is also the illegal dumping of cultivation-related waste. All these problems would be reduced by regulating cannabis cultivation. It is also argued that regulation will reduce a number of recurring costs, such as irrecoverable damage to rented property and losses to energy companies, which are now recovered by higher charges for all energy users.

---

256 For the phenomenon of 'undermining' see among other sources, *Kamerstukken II* 2013–2014, 29 911, no. 92 (Brief minister van Veiligheid en Justitie over Bestrijding georganiseerde criminaliteit) (i.e., *Dutch Parliamentary Documents* 2013–2014, 29 911, no. 92, (Letter of the Minister of Security and Justice about fighting organized crime).

- *Protection of health and lives of local residents.* This argument, which we already mentioned in section 2.3.1 in connection with the right to health, is potentially relevant here insofar as it concerns the risk of seriously harmful infections and fire because of unsafe installations.
- *Distinction between soft drugs and hard drugs markets.* This argument, which we already mentioned in section 2.3.1 in connection with the right to health, also plays a certain role here, in particular insofar as this distinction would lead to fewer deaths as a result of the use of hard drugs.

Here too, a disclaimer is called for: we emphasize that this book is not about assessing the validity or correctness of the arguments regarding the safety of citizens, preventing nuisances and fighting crime. We are acting from the hypothesis that each of these arguments is valid and subsequently assess later whether that argument with that state of affairs could find a basis in the right to life, the right not to be subjected to inhuman treatment and the right to a private life.

2.4.2. TREATY PROVISIONS ON LIFE, INHUMAN TREATMENT AND A PRIVATE LIFE

The International Covenant on Civil and Political Rights (ICCPR) and the European Convention on Human Rights (ECHR) do not contain provisions that require states explicitly and positively to protect the safety of individuals, prevent nuisances and/or combat crime.[257] Likewise, there is no reference at all to any obligation to deal with the risks of and objections to drugs and/or cannabis in a specific way. This does not mean that these conventions are without meaning in this respect. The human rights regarding life, inhuman treatment and a private life in particular are the source of positive obligations for states to guarantee the safety and health of citizens and to combat crime.

The right to life entails:

According to Article 6(1) ICCPR:

> Every human being has the inherent right to life. This right shall be protected by law. No one shall be arbitrarily deprived of his life.

---

257 However, Article 9 ICCPR states: 'Everyone has the right to liberty and security of person.' This provision, which we will not consider any further, is primarily aimed at arrest and detention. Nevertheless, under special circumstances it may entail an obligation for the state to protect persons against death threats from third parties; see also Sarah Joseph & Melissa Castan, *The International Covenant on Civil and Political Rights*, Oxford: Oxford University Press, 2014, para. 11.03–11.07.

According to Article 2(1) ECHR:

> Everyone's right to life shall be protected by law. No one shall be deprived of his life intentionally [...].

The right to protection against inhuman treatment is defined as follows:

According to Article 7 ICCPR:

> No one shall be subjected to torture or to cruel, inhuman or degrading treatment or punishment. In particular, no one shall be subjected without his free consent to medical or scientific experimentation.[258]

According to Article 3 ECHR:

> No one shall be subjected to torture or to inhuman or degrading treatment or punishment.

Finally, the right to a private life is formulated as follows:

According to Article 17 ICCPR:

> 1. No one shall be subjected to arbitrary or unlawful interference with his privacy, family, home or correspondence, nor to unlawful attacks on his honour and reputation.
> 2. Everyone has the right to the protection of the law against such interference or attacks.

According to Article 8(1) ECHR:

> Everyone has the right to respect for his private and family life, his home and his correspondence.

In many respects, these provisions differ significantly from provisions about the right to health, as discussed earlier in this chapter. Although several of the Articles just quoted require 'protection of the law', they primarily focus on what the states parties – whom the conventions address, after all – are not allowed to do, in short: no deprivation of life, no torture and inhuman treatment and no unjustified interference with one's private life. Insofar as the Articles explicitly impose requirements in a positive sense, this is limited to the aforementioned

258 Compare this with the otherwise irrelevant Article 10 ICCPR: 'All persons deprived of their liberty shall be treated with humanity and with respect for the inherent dignity of the human person'.

requirement to provide 'protection of the law'. The articles do not explicitly indicate that further measures must also be taken, let alone that the measures to be taken to that end are mentioned specifically. It is therefore the case law of the supervisory bodies for the ICCPR and the ECHR, to wit the Human Rights Committee and the ECtHR, where such further measures and/or positive action on the grounds of the above-mentioned provisions are required. This is why that case law will be central to our discussions below.

2.4.3. RATIONALE FOR RIGHTS ABOUT LIFE, INHUMAN TREATMENT AND A PRIVATE LIFE

Broad objectives are assigned to the rights about life, inhuman treatment and a private life. Whereas these rights traditionally aim to protect against deprivation of life, inhuman treatment and unlawful violations of one's privacy by the state, these days a far wider objective underpins these rights.[259] These rights also aim to protect against threats that do not emanate from the state. This may involve threats from private entities, but also for example from nature, unsafe situations or the state of affairs in society. Therefore, risks for life, the physical and mental integrity and the private life of citizens arising from a lack of safety, nuisance and criminality caused by persons and organizations involved with cannabis cultivation and trade could also be relevant for these rights.

The foregoing shows that the rationale of the human right to life has become more general in nature. This right currently aims to have the state respect life as such and have the state protect it from intentional deprivation of life and in certain cases also from the unintentional killing of a person.[260] The rationale

259 For more information about this with additional references see Piet Hein P.H.M.C. van Kempen, *Repressie door mensenrechten. Over positieve verplichtingen tot aanwending van strafrecht ter bescherming van fundamentele rechten* (oratie Nijmegen), Nijmegen: Wolf Legal Publishers, 2008, pp. 12–25 (i.e., *Repression because of human rights. About positive obligations for applying criminal law to protect fundamental rights* (lecture Nijmegen)). See also HRC, General Comment No. 31 (2004) 'General Legal Obligation', para. 6–8.

260 For the ICCPR, see HRC, General Comment No. 6, 'Article 6 (Right to life)', 30 April 1982, *UN Doc.* HRI/GEN/1/Rev.9, Vol. I (2008) (additionally: HRC, General Comment No. 6 (1982) 'Right to Life'), p. 176, para 2–4, also in connection with HRC, General Comment No. 31 (2004) 'General Legal Obligation', para. 8, and also: Sarah Joseph & Melissa Castan, *The International Covenant on Civil and Political Rights*, Oxford: Oxford University Press, 2014, para. 8.41–8.54. For the ECHR, see for example ECtHR 9 June 1998, *L.C.B./The UK*, no. 23413/94, para. 36 (about consequences of exposure to radiation); ECtHR (Grand Chamber) 28 October 1998, *Osman/The UK*, no. 23452/94, para. 115 (homicide by private person), with confirmation in ECtHR (Grand Chamber) among other sources, 30 November 2004, *Öneryildiz/Turkey*, no. 48939/99, para. 92–94 (deaths after explosion municipal landfill site) and ECtHR 9 May 2006, *Pereira Henriques/Luxembourg*, no. 60255/00, para. 54–57 (fatal accident employee of construction company); see also David J. Harris, M. O'Boyle, Ed. P. Bates & Carla M. Buckley (eds.), *Harris, O'Boyle & Warbrick, Law of the European Convention on Human Rights*, Oxford: Oxford University Press, 2014, p. 203 and pp. 207–212.

of the right not to be subjected to inhuman treatment is to have an individual's dignity and both his physical and mental integrity respected and protected by the state.[261] The right to a private life aims to offer protection of the individual against arbitrary or unlawful interference with his privacy by the state.[262]

2.4.4. WHAT IS COVERED BY LIFE, INHUMAN TREATMENT AND A PRIVATE LIFE?

Neither the ICCPR nor the ECHR provides definitions of the concepts used in the conventions such as life, inhuman treatment and private life. Nor does the case law of the Human Rights Committee and the ECtHR provide clear-cut descriptions of these concepts, although they do contain some clarification.

i. Life

With regard to the concept of 'life' in the right to life in Article 6(1) ICCPR and Article 2 ECtHR, it is important to realize that this refers to human life, not the lives of animals, plants or organizational bodies. It is also about life in the sense of 'being alive'. The right to life therefore does not include the right to die or the right to prefer one's own death to life.[263] Finally, it is about life as such and longevity, and in principle[264] not about a certain quality of life.

The Human Rights Committee considers the obligations in connection with the right to life to be applicable to the deprivation of life committed or caused by private persons (including murder, manslaughter or death caused otherwise)[265]

---

261 For the ICCPR, see HRC, General Comment No. 20, 'Article 7 (Prohibition of torture, or other cruel, inhuman or degrading treatment or punishment)', 30 September 1992, *UN Doc.* HRI/GEN/1/Rev.9, Vol. I (2008), p. 200 (also: HRC, General Comment No. 20 (1992) 'Prohibition of torture and inhuman treatment', para. 2. For the ECHR and further references see for example David J. Harris, Michael O'Boyle, Ed P. Bates & Carla M. Buckley (eds.), *Harris, O'Boyle & Warbrick, Law of the European Convention on Human Rights*, Oxford: Oxford University Press, 2014, pp. 235–248.

262 HRC, General Comment No. 16, 'Article 17 (Right to privacy)', 28 September 1988, *UN Doc.* HRI/GEN/1/Rev.9, Vol. I (2008), p. 193 (also: HRC, General Comment No. 16 (1988) 'Right to privacy'), para. 1. For the ECHR see for example DavidJ. Harris, Michael O'Boyle, Ed P. Bates & Carla M. Buckley (eds.), *Harris, O'Boyle & Warbrick, Law of the European Convention on Human Rights*, Oxford: Oxford University Press, 2014, pp. 522–524.

263 ECtHR 29 April 2002, *Pretty/The UK*, No. 2346/02, para. 38–40.

264 Cf. HRC, Draft general comment No. 36, Article 6: Right to life. Draft prepared by Yuval Shany and Nigel Rodley, Rapporteurs, *UN Doc.* CCPR/C/GC/R.36/Rev.2, 2 September 2015, para. 28, 'States parties should aim to facilitate and promote adequate conditions for a dignified existence for all individuals'.

265 HRC, General Comment No. 6 (1982) 'Right to Life', para. 3, 8; and for example HRC 26 March 2012, *Krasovskaya and Krasovskaya/Belarus*, no. 1820/2008, para. 8.3; HRC 21 October 2010, *Novaković/Serbia*, no. 1556/2007, para. 7.2–9; HRC 13 November 1995, *Bautista/Colombia*, no. 563/1993, para. 8.6, 10; HRC 29 March 1982, *Bleier/Uruguay*, no. 30/1978, para. 11–15.

as well as to general life-threatening individual and public health issues.[266,267] The ECtHR also applies the positive obligations with the right to life to deprivation of life or death by non-natural causes, including crime[268] as well as threats to life on account of dangerous situations and activities in industry and nature,[269] dangerous substances such as asbestos,[270] poisonous emissions,[271] exposure to radiation,[272] insufficient protection against the transmission of infectious diseases such as hepatitis C.[273] Also the contraction of HIV and hepatitis C as a consequence of using previously used needles for injecting drugs may (in the case of serious risks) fall within the scope of the positive protection obligation pursuant to Article 2 ECHR.[274] The scope of that obligation is certainly not limited to these examples. According to the ECtHR, 'the Article 2 positive obligation must be construed as applying in the context of any activity, whether public or not, in which the right to life may be at stake.'[275]

In respect of the cannabis issue, this leads us to the conclusion that in the event of murder and manslaughter (if those acts were committed in the context of illegal cannabis cultivation and trade) or an overdose or contracting fatal diseases through the use of hard drugs (if this happens because they are available too easily), this in principle is relevant in the context of the concept of 'life' in the sense of the above-mentioned provisions. The same is true for people killed in a fire as a result of the theft of power and the unsafe wiring of the electrical installations for illegal cannabis cultivation, or when life-threatening infections are caused by cannabis cultivation.

ii. Inhuman Treatment

We use this concept as an umbrella term for everything that is covered by Article 7 ICCPR and Article 3 ECHR.[276] These provisions cover both the

266 HRC, General Comment No. 6 (1982) 'Right to Life', para. 5.
267 For more examples, see section 2.4.8.ii.
268 See for example ECtHR (Grand Chamber) 28 October 1998, *Osman/The UK*, no. 23452/94, para. 115; ECtHR 15 September 2015, *Lari/The Republic of Moldova*, no. 37847/13, para. 33–35; ECtHR 9 June 2009, *Opuz/Turkey*, no. 33401/02, para. 150; ECtHR (Grand Chamber) 30 November 2004, *Öneryildiz/Turkey*, no. 48939/99, para. 94.
269 See the elaborate overview of case law in ECtHR 2 February 2016, *Cavit Tinarlioğlu/Turquie*, no. 3648/04, para. 62–78.
270 ECtHR 24 July 2014, *Brincat/Malta*, no. 60908/11, para. 103–117.
271 ECtHR (Grand Chamber) 19 February 1998, *Guerra/Italy*, no. 14967/89, para. 60, 62.
272 ECtHR 9 June 1998, *L.C.B./The UK*, no. 23413/94, para. 36.
273 ECtHR 1 December 2009, *G.N./Italy*, no. 43134/05, para. 69; for references to cases about all sorts of other diseases, see ECtHR 24 July 2014, *Brincat/Malta*, no. 60908/11, para. 82.
274 This is evident from ECtHR 4 January 2008, *Shelley/The UK*, no. 23800/06, para. 1, in which the risk was insufficiently 'severe', incidentally.
275 See also for example ECtHR 16 June 2011, *Ciechońska/Poland*, no. 19776/04, para. 63, with reference to ECtHR (Grand Chamber) 30 November 2004, *Öneryildiz/Turkey*, no. 48939/99, para. 71.
276 For the text of the provisions see section 2.4.2.

prohibition of torture and the prohibition of inhuman or degrading treatment or punishment at any rate. The Human Rights Committee gives no definition of the behaviours proscribed in this provision.[277] Nevertheless, the Committee makes it clear that Article 7 ICCPR aims to protect both the dignity and the physical and mental integrity of the individual.[278] The scope of the provision covers both physical pain and mental suffering.[279] It appears that there must be 'severe pain or suffering' or 'adverse physical or mental effects'.[280] Whether something is inhuman treatment in the sense of Article 7 ICCPR, eventually depends on the circumstances of the case, such as the duration and the manner of the treatment, the physical or mental effects, and also on the gender, age and the state of health of the victim.[281] There is a heavy emphasis on the violations of the victim's physical and mental integrity caused by others. Examples of behaviours within the domain of the right to be protected from inhuman treatment are corporal punishment, including excessive chastisement and solitary confinement.[282] Also grievous bodily harm and the intentional burning down and demolishing of houses can qualify as inhuman treatment.[283]

There is a slightly clearer general framework for Article 3 ECHR. It covers no suffering, pain or humiliation if it does not involve 'a minimum level of severity'.[284] Whether this criterion is met, depends on all circumstances of the case, including the factors mentioned just now, as well as the purpose and motive of the mistreatment. An important, though not necessarily decisive factor, is that treatment that meets the required minimum level usually concerns physical injury or intense physical or mental suffering. It therefore includes grievous bodily harm[285] and that can also apply for example to death threats,[286] rape[287] and severe sexual abuse.[288] Also the contraction of HIV and hepatitis C through

277 HRC, General Comment No. 20 (1992) 'Prohibition of torture and inhuman treatment', para. 2.
278 Ibid, para. 2.
279 Ibid, para. 5.
280 HRC 2 May 1989, *Vuolanne/Finland*, no. 265/1987, para. 9.2.
281 Ibid.
282 HRC, General Comment No. 20 (1992) 'Prohibition of torture and inhuman treatment', para. 5, 6.
283 See the examples in Sarah Joseph & Melissa Castan, *The International Covenant on Civil and Political Rights*, Oxford: Oxford University Press, 2014, para. 9.28–9.39, in which some examples were incidentally taken from case law of the UN Committee Against Torture (CAT), which is also considered relevant for the scope of Article 7 ICCPR; for more information on that see also para. 9.02.
284 See the recent case, with further references, ECtHR (Grand Chamber) 28 September 2015, *Bouyid/Belgium*, no. 23380/09, para. 86–87.
285 See also for example ECtHR 16 June 2015, *Vasil Hristov/Bulgaria*, no. 81260/12, para. 39; ECtHR 9 June 2009, *Opuz/Turkey*, no. 33401/02, para. 160–161; ECtHR 23 September 1998, *A./The UK*, no. 25599/94, para. 22–24.
286 ECtHR 9 June 2009, *Opuz/Turkey*, no. 33401/02, para. 160–161.
287 ECtHR 4 December 2003, *M.C./ Bulgaria*, no. 39272/98, para. 148.
288 ECtHR 4 January 2007, *Szual/The UK*, no. 18727/06, para. 1 (sexual abuse).

the use of used needles can in case of serious risks fall within the scope of the positive obligation of protection pursuant to Article 3 ECHR.[289] The right not to be subjected to inhuman treatment substantially overlaps the right to a private life, in the sense that certain behaviours such as rape[290] violate both rights.[291] In addition to this, in cases where the 'minimum level of severity' is not attained, there may still be a violation of a person's private life (see below). For example, this may apply in certain cases of domestic violence.[292] The foregoing once more confirms that inhuman treatment by private persons also falls within the scope of the prohibitions of Article 7 ICCPR and Article 3 ECHR. There is a heavy emphasis in Article 3 ECHR as well on the violations of the victim's physical and mental integrity caused by others.

In the light of the foregoing, we conclude that any crime related to illegal cannabis cultivation and trade – such as grievous bodily harm and causing severe burns and seriously harmful infections – is covered in principle by the concept of 'inhuman treatment'. On the other hand, this is not the case for nuisance caused by cannabis, unless this actually caused intense psychological suffering. Likewise, no protection seems to be required here against health problems caused by the use of hard drugs, insofar as these problems are not directly caused by others as would be the case with involuntary administration of hard drugs, but they are the result of a social reality in which hard drugs are available. In principle, the argument of the distinction between the soft drugs and hard drugs markets is therefore not relevant in the context of the right not to be subjected to inhuman treatment.

iii. Private Life

The concept of a 'private life' in the sense of Article 17 ICCPR and Article 8(1) ECHR is a very broad one, the meaning of which cannot be defined exactly.[293] According to the Human Rights Committee, the concept 'refers to the sphere of a person's life in which he or she can freely express his or her identity, be it by entering into relationships with others, or alone'.[294] With respect to behaviours of

---

289 This is evident from ECtHR 4 January 2008, *Shelley/The UK*, no. 23800/06, para. 1, in which the risk was insufficiently 'severe', incidentally.

290 That does not mean that complaints about insufficient protection against rape are actually investigated under both rights by the ECtHR; see David J. Harris, Michael O'Boyle, Ed P. Bates & Carla M. Buckley (eds.), *Harris, O'Boyle & Warbrick, Law of the European Convention on Human Rights*, Oxford: Oxford University Press, 2014, p. 541.

291 Ibid, p. 238.

292 Ibid, pp. 541–542.

293 See Sarah Joseph & Melissa Castan, *The International Covenant on Civil and Political Rights*, Oxford: Oxford University Press, 2014, para. 16.01, or for example ECtHR 2 September 2010, *Uzun/Germany*, no. 35623/05, para. 43.

294 See for example HRC 28 October 2010, *Raihman/Latvia*, no. 1621/2007, para. 8.2.

private persons, the Committee (pursuant to the right to a private life) requires protection against these behaviours if they unlawfully violate somebody else's private life (including his or her family life, home and correspondence) or tarnish his or her honour or good name.[295] For example, this would be the case when someone is seriously intimidated in his own home or receives threats in his own home by telephone.[296] Because we are not aware of any case law in which the Committee applies the positive obligations concerning the right to private life specifically with regard to behaviours of private persons, it is difficult to gauge the scope of the obligation of protection as specified in Article 17 ICCPR.[297] Positive protection for citizens against general risks resulting from the social or natural constellation regarding the right to privacy does not receive special attention from the Committee either.[298] With some reservations, we therefore conclude the following with respect to the cannabis issue. If nuisance and damage (such as stench, noise, flooding, fire and seriously harmful infections) and peripheral criminality (such as assault and threats) fundamentally and fairly directly impinge on the enjoyment of a person's private life, this probably falls under the regime of positive obligations of Article 17 ICCPR. In principle, this is the case with unlawful behaviours entering the private sphere, such as one's home, family life or correspondence. However, this probably does not apply if it is a question of protecting citizens against the consequences of their own use of hard drugs. After all, in that case what is at stake is not so much a private life as the psychological and mental integrity, while at the same time the cause in principle is not a specific behaviour of another person but rather the social reality in which hard drugs are available. In principle, the argument of the distinction between the soft drugs and hard drugs markets is therefore probably not relevant for Article 17 ICCPR.

The ECtHR shows a clearly different approach, which provides more concrete detail. For the Court, the physical and psychological integrity of the person is of paramount importance to the concept of a private life. This may involve various

---

295 HRC, General Comment No. 31 (2004) 'General Legal Obligation', para. 8; HRC, General Comment No. 16 (1988) 'Right to privacy', para. 1, 11.

296 HRC 17 October 2011, *Peiris/Sri Lanka*, no. 1862/09, para. 7.6. Although this case involved intimidation by and threats from the police, the obligation to protect should also be applicable if such behaviours were displayed by private persons. According to the Committee, protection needs to be offered against all unlawful violations of Article 17 ICCPR, whether perpetrated by government organizations or private persons; see HRC, General Comment No. 16 (1988) 'Right to privacy', para. 1.

297 To that effect, see also Sarah Joseph & Melissa Castan, *The International Covenant on Civil and Political Rights*, Oxford: Oxford University Press, 2014, para. 16.16.

298 Cf. HRC 30 July 1996, *Bordes and Temeharo/France*, no. 645/1995; HRC 18 October 2006, *Brun/France*, no. 1453/2006. See also United Nations Environment Programme, *UNEP Compendium on Human Rights and the Environment. Selected international legal materials and cases*, UNEP 2014, pp. 121–126, where the right to privacy does not play a part in any of the cases discussed.

aspects of the physical and social identity of the individual. Its scope comprises for example gender, race and ethnicity, name, sexual orientation, a person's right to their images, sexual life personal development, information about health, and the creation and development of relationships with other people and the outside world.[299] The positive obligation of protection of Article 8 ECHR – which partly overlaps with that of Article 3 ECHR[300] – covers among other things assault committed by private persons,[301] domestic violence,[302] rape,[303] slander and libel,[304] unlawful entry into the home,[305] arson and destruction of the home,[306] and child abduction.[307] It is also important that the following can be relevant for a private life in general and for the home in particular: noise, emissions, stench and other forms of nuisance.[308] Pursuant to the right to a private life, under certain conditions protection must also be offered against attacks by stray dogs[309] or the nuisance caused by party goers and revellers.[310] Finally, we point out that contracting HIV and hepatitis C by using used needles can fall within the scope of the positive obligations pursuant to Article 8 ECHR.[311]

The criterion for this is whether the nuisance reaches at least the 'minimum level of severity'. Whether that is the case, depends on 'the intensity and duration of the nuisance, its physical or mental effects, the general context, and whether the detriment complained of was negligible in comparison to the environmental hazards inherent to life in every modern city'.[312] Given the broad interpretation

299 See among other sources ECtHR (Grand Chamber) 4 December 2008, *S. and Marper/The UK*, no. 30562/04 and 30566/04.

300 See among other sources ECtHR 4 December 2003, *M.C./Bulgaria*, no. 39272/98, para. 148–187.

301 ECtHR 8 October 2002, *Benedek/Slovakia*, no. 46115/99, §1.

302 ECtHR 15 September 2009, *E.S./Slovakia*, no. 8227/04, para. 39–44.

303 ECtHR 4 December 2003, *M.C./ Bulgaria*, no. 39272/98, para. 150–166 and 185–187.

304 ECtHR 15 November 2007, *Pfeifer/Austria*, no. 12556/03, para. 37–38 in conjunction with 47–49 in conjunction with 17–22.

305 ECtHR 8 October 2002, *Benedek/Slovakia*, no. 46115/99, §1.

306 ECtHR 12 July 2005, *Moldovan and others/Romania (2)*, no. 41138/98, para. 93–98 and 105–109.

307 ECtHR 25 January 2000, *Ignaccolo-Zenide/Romania*, no. 31679/96, para. 106–110 in conjunction with 113; ECtHR 12 January 2006, *Mihailova/Bulgaria*, no. 35978/02, para. 79–102.

308 See among other sources ECtHR (Grand Chamber) 19 February 1998, *Guerra/Italy*, no. 14967/89, para. 56–60 (about the emission of toxic gases by factory with a risk to the environment and the health of the local residents), and also David J. Harris, Michael O'Boyle, Ed P. Bates & Carla M. Buckley (eds.), *Harris, O'Boyle & Warbrick, Law of the European Convention on Human Rights*, Oxford: Oxford University Press, 2014, pp. 582–585, with many references to case law.

309 ECtHR 26 July 2011, *Georgel and Georgeta Stoicescu/Romania*, no. 9718/03, para. 53–63.

310 ECtHR 22 November 2011, *Zammit Maempel/Malta*, no. 24202/10, para. 34–40.

311 See ECtHR 4 January 2008, *Shelley/The UK*, no. 23800/06, para. 1, 'Article 8, which in its private life aspect protects physical and moral integrity, may require the authorities to take particular preventive measures to counter infection rates in prisons.'

312 ECtHR 22 November 2011, *Zammit Maempel/Malta*, no. 24202/10, para. 37; ECtHR 25 November 2010, *Mileva And Others/Bulgaria*, no. 43449/02, para. 90, 97.

of 'private life' and the wide application of the positive obligations regime in Article 8 ECHR, we conclude that severe nuisance and damage (such as stench, noise, flooding, fire and seriously harmful infections) and peripheral crime (such as aggravated assault and serious threats) are relevant for this provision. In principle, the same applies to the risk posed to the physical and mental integrity of citizens caused by their use of hard drugs. The argument of the distinction between the soft drugs and hard drugs markets may therefore be relevant for Article 8 ECHR.

iv. Concluding Remark

Serious unsafety, nuisance and/or crime aimed at people's physical or mental integrity that finds its cause in illegal cannabis cultivation and trade are in principle within the scope of the concepts of life, inhuman treatment and/or a private life. This is why drug and/or cannabis policy can be relevant in the context of the ICCPR and ECHR. We emphasize, however, that this does not mean that pursuant to the ICCPR and/or ECHR the same level of positive protection must be provided against (all threats of) violation of the rights. In the following sections, we will look at the question to which extent and under which condition positive obligations to safeguard the convention rights apply.

At the same time, it is worth noting that there are no indications that the reduction of organized crime, reduction of cannabis exports and the fight against corruption in the upper world have any relevance as such for the rights concerning life, inhuman treatment and privacy. Only if these phenomena go hand-in-hand with serious unsafety, nuisance and/or crime aimed at people's physical or mental integrity can this be different. In that case, though, what is relevant are the consequences rather than their background in principle.

2.4.5. POSITIVE PROTECTION LEVEL OF RIGHTS REGARDING LIFE, INHUMAN TREATMENT AND A PRIVATE LIFE (NO 'HIGHEST ATTAINABLE STANDARD')

It became clear in earlier sections that the right to health of Article 12 ICESCR and Article 11 ESC entails an unlimited obligation on states to realize this right. After all, states are required to realize this right to the highest attainable standard of health and to take all appropriate measures that are actually feasible for that state. Such a general and unlimited obligation does not enter into the equation in the case of positive achievement and/or protection of the rights regarding life, inhuman treatment and privacy.[313] Pursuant to Article 6(1) ICCPR and

[313] For the provision to be mentioned below, see section 2.4.2.

Article 2(1) ECHR, the right to life must be protected by the law, but states are not required to use all possible measures so as to provide actively for the highest attainable protection of life against all sorts of risks. As we will see below, and in particular in section 2.4.8, such an unlimited obligation does not follow from case law from the Human Rights Committee and/or the ECtHR either. This is the case even more so with regard to the right not to be subjected to inhuman treatment (Article 7 ICCPR and Article 3 ECtHR) and the right to a private life (Article 17 ICCPR and Article 8(1) ECHR). The mere fact that unsafety, nuisance and crime caused by illegal cannabis cultivation and trade may result in risks for life, the physical and psychological integrity and the private lives of citizens does not necessarily mean that the rights regarding life, inhuman treatment and a private life require that protection is provided against those risks. To establish whether such protection is required or not, we will look in more detail at the level and the implementation of positive safeguarding and/or protection which the Human Rights Committee and the ECHR do require for these rights.

2.4.6. SCOPE OF OBLIGATIONS REGARDING THE RIGHTS CONCERNING LIFE, INHUMAN TREATMENT AND A PRIVATE LIFE

The foregoing shows that the scope of the obligations arising from the rights concerning life, inhuman treatment and private life is considerably wider in at least two respects than is shown by the provisions in the conventions in which these rights are embedded.

First, with all these rights there are positive obligations (to ensure the rights actively) in addition to negative obligations (to refrain from violating those rights).

Secondly, the state must not only provide for positive protection measures in view of potential threats to the lives, the physical and psychological integrity and the private lives of individuals by government authorities, but also actively provide protection from the same threats by private actors.[314]

In relation to all three rights, it is also important that the obligations derived from these rights to a certain extent relate to both fighting crime and to the

314 With regard to the ICCPR, see: HRC, General Comment No. 6 (1982) 'Right to Life', para. 2–4, and also HRC, General Comment No. 14, 'Article 6 (Right to life)', 1 January 1985, *UN Doc.* HRI/GEN/1/Rev.9, Vol. I (2008) (additionally: HRC, General Comment No. 14 (1985) 'Right to life'), p. 188; HRC, General Comment No. 20 (1992) 'Prohibition of torture and inhuman treatment', para. 2; HRC, General Comment No. 16 (1988) 'Right to privacy', para. 1. For the ECHR, see: David J. Harris, Michael O'Boyle, Ed P. Bates & Carla M. Buckley (eds.), *Harris, O'Boyle & Warbrick, Law of the European Convention on Human Rights*, Oxford: Oxford University Press, 2014, p. 203 and pp. 207–212, pp. 274–277, and pp. 532–535, always with references to case law.

issues of safety and health. Later, in sections 2.4.8–2.4.10, we will elaborate in more detail on the obligations to protect the lives, physical and psychological integrity and the private lives of individuals against certain forms of crime and against certain health threats. Of course, we will also consider to what extent these obligations could provide a basis for regulating cannabis cultivation and trade if this were to protect the lives, physical and psychological integrity and the private lives of citizens from unsafety, nuisance and criminality better than a more prohibitive drug policy.

2.4.7. GENERAL OBLIGATIONS TO SAFEGUARD THE RIGHTS REGARDING LIFE, INHUMAN TREATMENT AND A PRIVATE LIFE

Both the ICCPR and the ECHR create general obligations for states in relation to all human rights contained in these covenants and convention, therefore also for the rights regarding life, inhuman treatment and a private life. These will be discussed presently and we will find that the general obligations that apply pursuant to these conventions are far less developed and detailed than the general obligations from the ICESCR and the ESC discussed above. This does not change the fact that also in the case of the ICCPR and the ECHR, the general point of departure is that the rights and obligations must be implemented effectively. The Human Rights Committee expresses this principle in, among other things, its General Comments on provisions in the ICCPR.[315] The standard principle used by the ECtHR is that the ECHR aims to guarantee rights that are not 'theoretical or illusory, but practical and effective.'[316] The object and purpose of the convention as an instrument for the protection of individual human rights requires that the provisions of the convention are interpreted and applied so 'as to make its safeguards practical and effective'.[317] This perspective is also used by the ECtHR in establishing positive obligations.[318] Furthermore, the ECHR (like the ESC) is regarded as a 'living instrument', which must be interpreted

315 See for example HRC, General Comment No. 31 (2004) 'General Legal Obligation', para. 6, 14, 15, 20; HRC, General Comment No. 20 (1992) 'Prohibition of torture and inhuman treatment', para. 11, 14; HRC, General Comment No. 16 (1988) 'Right to privacy', para. 8, 10.

316 See among other sources ECtHR (Grand Chamber) 10 December 2007, *Stoll/Switzerland*, no. 69698/01, para. 128.

317 E.g. ECtHR (Grand Chamber) 17 September 2014, *Mocanu/Romania*, no. 10865/09, para. 315; ECtHR (Grand Chamber) 7 July 2011, *Al-Skeini/The UK*, no. 55721/07, para. 162; ECtHR (Grand Chamber) 30 November 2004, *Öneryildiz/Turkey*, no. 48939/99, para. 69.

318 See David J. Harris, Michael O'Boyle, Ed P. Bates & Carla M. Buckley (eds.), *Harris, O'Boyle & Warbrick, Law of the European Convention on Human Rights*, Oxford: Oxford University Press, 2014, pp. 18 and 9.

in the light of 'present-day conditions'.[319] Consequently, as far as the ECHR is concerned, developments in society and the knowledge of the effects and risks of cannabis could play a role in the implementation of positive obligations.

i. General Provisions: Article 2 ICCPR and Article 1 ECHR

Both Article 2 ICCPR and Article 1 ECHR contain obligations in relation with all human rights enshrined in the corresponding convention. These general obligations therefore also apply to the rights regarding life, inhuman treatment and privacy. Article 2 ICCPR has a similar objective as the previously discussed Article 2 ICESCR, but differs from it on essential points. In short, and to the extent that it is relevant here, Article 2 ICCPR requires that the states parties:

- 'respect' the rights in the ICCPR and 'ensure' those rights to everyone; and
- 'adopt such laws or other measures as may be necessary to give effect to the rights' in the ICCPR if they are not already provided for by 'existing legislative or other measures', in accordance with the state's constitutional processes and the provisions of the ICCPR.

Article 1 ECHR requires that the states parties:

- 'secure' to everyone the rights and freedoms in the ECHR.

The striking element of these general obligations in the ICCPR and the ECHR in comparison with the ICESCR and the ESC is that they comprise stronger (absolute) result-oriented obligations, while at the same time they prescribe states less precisely what they must do in order to fulfil these obligations.

ii. Tripartite Typology: Obligations to Respect, Protect and Fulfil

As far as we know, neither the Human Rights Committee nor the ECHR has ever referred explicitly to the tripartite typology of obligations ('the duty to respect, protect and fulfil'). Therefore, the case law of the Human Rights Committee and the ECHR does not contain a specification of obligations for states based on this typology like the one provided by the ICESCR Committee.[320] For that reason, and because the tripartite topology has already been explained in section 2.3.7.ii, we will keep it short. What must be emphasized here is that the obligations arising from the typology are most certainly expressed directly or indirectly to some extent in that case law.[321]

---

319 ECtHR 25 April 1978, *Tyrer/The UK*, no. 5856/72, para. 31, and more recently for example ECtHR (Grand Chamber) 15 March 2012, *Austin/The UK*, no. 39692/09, para. 53.

320 See section 2.3.7.ii.

321 See also Philip Lynch (ed.), *Human Rights Law Resource Manual*, Melbourne: Human Rights Law Resource Centre Ltd, 2006, chapter 3, para. 3; David J. Harris, Michael O'Boyle,

- *The obligation to respect.* This negative obligation is most prominent in the ICCPR and the ECHR. After all, as we have seen these conventions explicitly contain as a general obligation that the states parties must 'respect' the convention rights (Article 2 ICCPR) or – couched in more general terms – to 'secure' them (Article 1 ECHR). Pursuant to the ICCPR and the ECHR, states must refrain from unlawful acts that adversely affect the lives, the physical and psychological integrity and the private lives of citizens directly or indirectly.

  Again, this does not mean that states would not be allowed to regulate the cannabis market for recreational use and to permit that cannabis is available to consumers for recreational purposes under certain conditions and within certain limits, or actively ensure this availability themselves. After all, the question still remains whether a drug policy that permits the cultivation of and trade in cannabis for recreational use up to a point is an acceptable and possibly even required vehicle for implementing the rights regarding life, inhuman treatment and/or privacy, to the extent that such a drug policy de facto would protect the lives, the physical and psychological integrity and/or privacy of citizens better than a more prohibitive drug policy.

  Incidentally, we observe that the obligation to respect is not absolute either, or to be more precise: some human rights may under certain conditions justifiably be restricted. In this respect, the principles of proportionality (in the sense of commensuration between objective and infringement) and subsidiarity (in the sense of necessity) are relevant. The principle of proportionality means that the restriction of the right must not be disproportionate to the goal that is pursued; the weight of the importance in realizing the objective should therefore justify the restriction. The principle of subsidiarity entails that infringements of human rights can only be tolerated if there is not a less onerous means with which the same objective can be achieved.

  This principle of subsidiarity ensues from the 'object and purpose' of the ICCPR and the ECHR, which after all aim to protect individual fundamental rights.[322] Every infringement of a human right is at odds with that. This principle of subsidiarity also shows from the system of the ICCPR and the ECHR respectively as a whole: the conventions offer limited possibilities to infringe human rights, where it is possible at all, it can only happen under certain conditions, and the Human Rights Committee and the ECHR see to it that there are no prohibited and unnecessary restrictions of the convention rights. Finally,

---

Ed Bates & Carla M. Buckley (eds.), *Harris, O'Boyle & Warbrick, Law of the European Convention on Human Rights*, Oxford: Oxford University Press, 2014, pp. 21–24.

322 See the preambles to the ICCPR and the ECHR; see also HRC, General Comment No. 24, 'Issues Relating to Reservations Made upon Ratification or Accession to the Covenant or the Optional Protocols thereto, or in Relation to Declarations under Article 41 of the Covenant', *UN Doc.* CCPR/C/21/Rev.1/Add.6 (1994), para. 7; David J. Harris, Michael O'Boyle, Ed P. Bates & Carla.M. Buckley (eds.), *Harris, O'Boyle & Warbrick, Law of the European Convention on Human Rights*, Oxford: Oxford University Press, 2014, pp. 7–8.

the principle of subsidiarity is also explicitly reflected in these conventions, namely in provisions on human rights that permit restriction of the right (see for example Articles 12, 18, 19, 21 and 22 and Articles 8, 9, 10 and 11 ECHR).

- *The obligation to protect.* This obligation is expressed in various – mainly positive – sub-obligations that states have regarding the rights to life, inhuman treatment and/or a private life so as to protect the lives, physical and psychological integrity and/or the private lives of citizens against private actors (such as individuals and enterprises). This concerns, among other things, obligations to protect citizens against – and therefore also the prevention and combating of – unsafety, nuisance and crime. The obligations 'to protect' are particularly relevant to the cannabis issue insofar as they concern the rights regarding life, inhuman treatment and privacy. For that reason, we will discuss this in detail particularly in sections 2.4.8–2.4.10.
- *The obligation to fulfil.* This would mean that states must take positive measures to implement and realize the rights regarding life, inhuman treatment and privacy. Bear in mind that this is about measures other than those that serve to protect these rights against the pernicious effects of private actors (as these are covered by the typology 'to protect'). In comparison to the ICESCR and the ESC, the obligation to achieve and/or realize rights only plays a minor part in the ICCPR and the ECHR and the case law about this from the Human Rights Committee and the ECtHR respectively. For example, this is the case where the Human Rights Committee points out the importance of raising the level of awareness about the convention among both the authorities and the public at large,[323] and where the Committee, pursuant to the right to life in Article 6 ICCPR, requires from states that they take measures to increase the life expectancy of its population.[324] The importance of the obligation 'to fulfil' is even more limited in the case law of the ECtHR. In respect of the rights regarding life, inhuman treatment and privacy, the obligation of fulfilment is of less importance to the cannabis issue than the obligation 'to protect'.

iii. No Obligation for Progressively Achieving the Full Realization, Instead an Obligation to Respect and Secure

In contrast with the situation pursuant to Article 2 ICESCR and on the grounds of the ESC, there is no obligation by virtue of Article 2 ICCPR and Article 1 ECHR to achieve progressively 'the full realization' of the convention rights. The ICCPR and the ECHR do not impose a requirement of progressive realization of the rights regarding life, inhuman treatment and privacy, nor of full realization of the highest attainable standard of protection of these rights, as

---

323 HRC, General Comment No. 31 (2004) 'General Legal Obligation', para. 7.

324 See Sarah Joseph & Melissa Castan, *The International Covenant on Civil and Political Rights*, Oxford: Oxford University Press, 2014, para. 1.103–1.104.

we saw earlier in section 2.4.5. In that sense, the states parties are not explicitly bound to update policies and other measures every time – including possibly drug policies and measures – if this were to strengthen the safeguards for the convention rights in the ICCPR and the ECHR. However, this does not yet answer the question whether these conventions force states parties to adopt a drug and/or cannabis policy which adequately secures the right to life, the right not to be subjected to inhuman treatment and the right to a private life. After all, it is also important that the ICCPR and the ECHR – unlike the ICESCR and the ESC – contain the stronger (absolute) general obligation of realization: the rights of the conventions must simply be 'respected' and 'secured'.[325] The observation that this does not involve a 'full' guarantee, does not alter the fact that the rights will have to be guaranteed at a certain level and in a certain form, namely the level that is required for each right separately by the provisions in the convention in which that right is embedded and the case law about it from the Human Rights Committee and the ECtHR (for more information about this see sections 2.4.8–2.4.10). In other words, a hard obligation to secure rights instead of a relative obligation to progressively achieve full realization is key here.

iv. No Ban on Retrogressive Measures

In relation to the ICCPR and the ECHR, the general principle is not the ban on retrogressive measures, that is to say, the ban on taking measures that lead to a reduction in the protection of a convention right.[326]

Such a general principle does not apply here, as is evident from the fact that in recent years a great deal of antiterrorism legislation has been deemed permissible by the ICCPR and the ECHR, whereas that legislation in many cases led to a reduction in legal protection of terrorism suspects. Moreover, reinforcement of positive protection in some cases actually leads to a weakening of negative protection. For example, positive obligations to conduct criminal inquiries into a homicide and to prosecute, convict and punish the perpetrator(s) reinforce the protection of the right to life, but at the same time these obligations also lead to infringements of, among other things, the right of respect for freedom and the right of respect for a private life. So such positive obligations do not fit in very well with a ban on retrogressive measures.

---

325 Cf. ibid, para. 1.17, in which the following observation about Article 2 ICCPR is made: 'A state is either fulfilling its obligations or it is not', with which the authors stress that this does not concern a relative obligation, unlike the one in Article 2 ICESCR.

326 In that sense, for the ECHR also see – with references to ECtHR 25 October 2011, *Valkov/Bulgaria*, no. 2033/04 (see para. 91–97) – Judge Pinto de Albuquerque, Partly Concurring, Partly Dissenting Opinion (the sentences before footnote 30 and the footnote itself), in: ECtHR (Grand Chamber) 22 March 2012, *Konstantin Markin/Russia*, no. 30078/06.

The absence of a general ban on retrogressive measures is relevant if a state with regard to the cultivation of cannabis for the recreational consumer market were to consider legalization, regulation or application of a more liberal policy than is currently the case. If such a change entailed a reduction in the protection of life, against inhuman treatment and/or a reduction in privacy, this does not mean per se that implementing the change is not allowed.

v. Obligation to Adopt Necessary Measures

The general Articles 2(1) ICCPR and 1 ECHR put the obligation to 'secure' the rights under these conventions first. This concerns a result-oriented obligation: there must be a system which safeguards the rights effectively at an adequate level. It does not mean that states are required to make sure that no one ever unlawfully infringes any convention right. Among other things, Article 2(2) ICCPR specifies that each state party is required 'to take the necessary steps [...] to adopt such legislative or other measures as may be necessary to give effect to the rights recognized in the present Covenant'. The states parties are therefore required to take all measures that are necessary to effectuate and/or guarantee the right. According to the Human Rights Committee, the obligation arising from Article 2(2) ICCPR to take measures applies without any qualifications and is effective immediately.[327] The Human Rights Committee elaborates on the obligation to take measures when considering:

> Article 2 requires that States Parties adopt legislative, judicial, administrative, educative and other appropriate measures in order to fulfil their legal obligations. [...] In general, the purposes of the Covenant would be defeated without an obligation integral to article 2 to take measures to prevent a recurrence of a violation of the Covenant.[328]

The obligation to take the measures that are needed to effectuate treaty law is interpreted broadly: all sorts of measures that are appropriate for giving effect to the convention rights and to prevent violations of these rights, are deemed necessary if without application of the measure, the right is not given full effect. Potentially, regulated permission of cannabis cultivation and trade for recreational purposes could also qualify as an obligation if and to the extent that such a drug policy were necessary to secure adequately the rights regarding life, inhuman treatment and privacy. Since Article 2 ICCPR – as we have noted repeatedly – relates to both negative obligations (to refrain from violations of the rights) and positive obligations (to safeguard the rights actively and to protect against

327 HRC, General Comment No. 31 (2004) 'General Legal Obligation', para. 14.
328 Ibid, para. 7 and 17.

private entities as well),[329] all the measures that are necessary to fulfil both the negative and positive obligations must be taken. In short: policy can be considered a measure in the sense of Article 2 ICCPR and policy can therefore be required to fulfil positive obligations. Potentially, a progressive drug policy could be required if it offered protection against unsafety, nuisance and/or crime. Whether such a drug policy is actually required, ultimately depends on the level and form of guarantee and/or protection required by the positive obligation specifically associated with the rights concerning life, inhuman treatment and privacy. They will be discussed below in sections 2.4.8–2.4.10.

Article 1 ECHR or another provision in that convention does not contain an interpretation of the general obligation to ensure the rights by taking measures similar to the one in Article 2(2) ICCPR. However, the ECtHR case law offers a few fairly general principles in relation to the measures that must be taken so as to ensure the convention rights. Among other things, the ECtHR considers the following:

> The undertaking given by a Contracting State under Article 1 normally includes two aspects, namely on the one hand a negative duty to refrain from interfering with the enjoyment of the rights and freedoms guaranteed and on the other hand positive obligations *to take appropriate steps to ensure respect* for those rights and freedoms within its territory (emphasis added).[330]

And:

> The general duty imposed on the State by Article 1 of the Convention entails and requires the implementation of *a national system capable of securing compliance* with the Convention throughout the territory of the State for everyone (emphasis added).[331]

The 'appropriate measures' required by the Human Rights Committee are called 'appropriate steps' by the ECtHR. Among other things they mean that states are required to provide a system that guarantees conduct which is in accordance with the convention rights ('ensure respect', 'securing compliance'). This system can therefore not be merely reactive in nature, but will have to be focused first and foremost on preventing unlawful infringement of convention rights.

The quotations above show that the 'appropriate steps' required by the Court must be taken so as to fulfil the positive obligations that apply pursuant to the ECHR. The ECtHR does not formulate these positive obligations in general for all convention rights, but in principle it establishes them individually for

[329] Ibid, see for example para. 6, 'The legal obligation under article 2, paragraph 1, is both negative and positive in nature.' See also Sarah Joseph & Melissa Castan, *The International Covenant on Civil and Political Rights*, Oxford: Oxford University Press, 2014, para. 1.103–1.104.

[330] ECtHR (Grand Chamber) 16 June 2015, *Sargsyan/Azerbaijan*, nor. 40167/06, para. 129.

[331] ECtHR (Grand Chamber) 8 April 2004, *Assanidze/Georgia*, no. 71503/01, para. 147.

an on the grounds of specific convention rights, such as the rights regarding life, inhuman treatment and privacy, with or without a general reference to Article 1 ECHR. In the final analysis, it is about each state party implementing a system that is capable of ensuring that the state acts in accordance with the convention rights. The associated result-oriented obligation here too boils down to the following: there must be a system which effectively safeguards the rights at an adequate level (so this does not mean that states must ensure no one ever unlawfully infringes any convention rights). This implies that pursuant to the ECHR as well, in principle all the steps and/or measures must be taken that are necessary for effecting the convention rights without which the right in question cannot be secured. To that extent, all measures that can be taken can be relevant under this obligation and that could therefore also be for example a drug and/or cannabis policy in which cannabis cultivation and trade for recreational use are permitted. However, the question which measures are actually required specifically and whether or not regulated permission of cannabis cultivation and trade for recreational use is part of that, therefore depends on the level and the form of safeguards and/or protection that are required by the ECtHR for the specific convention right. We refer the reader to the explanation of this in sections 2.4.8–2.4.10.

vi. No Obligation to Use Maximum Available Resources

For the sake of completion, we observe that in contrast with the situation for the ICESCR and the ESC, pursuant to the ICCPR and the ECHR there is no explicit obligation for states parties to effect the convention rights 'to the maximum of its available resources'. Because such an obligation is not directly relevant for the cannabis issue, we will not discuss it any further here.

vii. Core Rights

Unlike the ICESCR Committee, the Human Rights Committee and the ECHR do not use the concept of minimum core obligations. That does not alter the fact that they too deploy mechanisms that must ensure that rights are guaranteed to at least a certain essential level. For rights where restrictions are allowed, for example, the right to a private life, the following applies according to the Human Rights Committee 'In no case may the restrictions be applied or invoked in a manner that would impair *the essence* of a Covenant right' (emphasis added).[332] The ECtHR too sometimes uses as a criterion whether or not a certain issue touches upon the 'core' or 'the essence of the right'. The more that this is the case, the more states parties are allowed a smaller margin of appreciation

332 HRC, General Comment No. 31 (2004) 'General Legal Obligation', para. 6.

regarding the restriction of the right, assuming that the legislation provides for that discretion.[333] Additionally, the ECtHR designates certain human rights as 'core rights'. For example, the Court regards Article 2 ECHR (right to life) and Article 3 ECHR (right not to be subjected to inhuman treatment) as the most fundamental provisions of the convention and as enshrined 'core values' of the democratic societies forming the Council of Europe.[334] The scope of the obligations of states with respect to the effective enjoyment by individuals of these rights is typically very wide.[335] Finally, we point out that the Court has repeatedly reminded its audience of the tenet that respect for human dignity constitutes the essence of the convention.[336]

viii. Primarity: National Authorities are Primarily Responsible for Realizing the Rights Regarding Life, Inhuman Treatment and Privacy

In section 2.3.7.ix, we explained in detail that (and why) the state is primarily responsible, pursuant to international law, for ensuring the individual rights and for fulfilling the obligations under conventions to which the state is a signatory. This obvious observation, which is essential for the analysis in this chapter, also applies in relation to the ICCPR and the ECHR, which is underlined by Article 2 IVCCPR and Article 1 ECHR.[337] The ECtHR also explicitly confirms the existence of the 'primary duty on the State' to secure the convention rights and to take measures to that effect.[338] This is sometimes referred to as the principle of primarity. Because the issues that came to the fore in section 2.3.7.ix applies mutatis mutandis in much the same way to these conventions, we will now suffice with a few findings and refer to the above-mentioned section for background information.

---

333 See for example ECtHR (Grand Chamber) 27 August 2015, *Parrillo/Italy*, no. 46470/11, para. 174–175; ECtHR 6 May 2003, *Appleby/The UK*, no. 44306/98, para. 47–50. See also Judge Pinto de Albuquerque, Dissenting Opinion, on: ECtHR (Grand Chamber) 13 July 2012, *Mouvement Raëlien Suisse/Switzerland*, no. 16354/06.

334 ECtHR (Grand Chamber) 17 September 2014, *Mocanu/Romania*, no. 10865/09, para. 315.

335 According to Judge Hajiyev, Dissenting Opinion, on: ECtHR (Grand Chamber) 16 June 2015, *Sargsyan/Azerbaijan*, no. 40167/06.

336 See for example ECtHR (Grand Chamber) 29 April 2002, *Pretty/The UK*, no. 2346/02, para. 65.

337 See also Sarah Joseph & Melissa Castan, *The International Covenant on Civil and Political Rights*, Oxford: Oxford University Press, 2014, para. 1.25–1.26; David J. Harris, Michael O'Boyle, Ed P. Bates & Carla M. Buckley (eds.), *Harris, O'Boyle & Warbrick, Law of the European Convention on Human Rights*, Oxford: Oxford University Press, 2014, pp. 16–17.

338 See among other sources ECtHR 3 November 2015, *Olszewscy/Poland*, no. 99/12, para. 58; ECtHR (Grand Chamber) 28 October 1998, *Osman/The UK*, no. 23452/94, para. 115. For more information see Jonas Christoffersen, *Fair Balance: Proportionality, Subsidiarity and Primarity in the European Convention on Human Rights*, Leiden/Boston: Martinus Nijhoff Publishers, 2009, in particular. pp. 380–384.

First, it is important that the 'pacta sunt servanda' requirement also applies to the ICCPR and the ECHR of course.[339] For these conventions, that means that if a state determines that a certain approach is required for cannabis in order to fulfil an obligation under the convention (such as a positive guarantee of the rights regarding life, inhuman treatment and privacy), that state is in principle obliged to implement that approach. The principle applies conversely as well: if the state is of the opinion that a certain approach is needed to address a certain human rights problem, the principle is that the state has come to that conclusion in good faith and that the measures applied are the appropriate steps the authorities are required to take.[340]

The conclusion that the general obligations in the ICCPR and the ECHR as well as the specific human rights contained in them and the concomitant obligations are primarily aimed at states and that these are primarily responsible for realizing the rights and meeting the obligations is further supported by, among other things, the jurisdiction and territoriality of states[341] and the subsidiarity principle.[342] As far as this principle is concerned, the following consideration of the ECtHR provides relevant clarification:

> [...] the Court *cannot disregard those legal and factual features which characterise the life of the society in the State* which, as a Contracting Party, has to answer for the measure in dispute. In so doing it cannot assume the rôle of the competent national authorities, for it would thereby lose sight of the subsidiary nature of the international machinery of collective enforcement established by the Convention. The *national authorities remain free to choose the measures which they consider appropriate* in those matters which are

339 See on that point also HRC, General Comment No. 31 (2004) 'General Legal Obligation', para. 3, and among other sources ECtHR (Grand Chamber) 20 October 2013, *Anowiec/Russia*, no. 55508/07, para. 211, 'the Convention is an international treaty which, in accordance with the principle of pacta sunt servanda codified in Article 26 of the Vienna Convention on the Law of Treaties, is binding on the Contracting Parties and must be performed by them in good faith'.

340 Cf. ECtHR 31 May 2011, *Khodorkovskiy/Russia*, no. 5829/04, para. 255, 'The Court reiterates that the whole structure of the Convention rests on the general assumption that public authorities in the member States act in good faith.' However, the following applies in this respect: 'Indeed, any public policy or an individual measure may have a "hidden agenda", and the presumption of good faith is rebuttable.' See for more information about the presumption that the state acts in good faith also Judge Bushev, Partly Dissenting Opinion, Joined in Part by Judge Hajiyev, in ECtHR 20 September 2011, *Oao Neftyanaya Kompaniya Yukos/Russia*, no. 14902/04, para. 2.5.

341 See HRC, General Comment No. 31 (2004) 'General Legal Obligation', para. 3, 10–12; ECtHR (Grand Chamber) 20 November 2014, *Jaloud/The Netherlands*, no. 47708/08, para. 139, 'As provided by [Article 1 of the Convention] the engagement undertaken by a Contracting State is confined to "securing" ("reconnaître" in the French text) the listed rights and freedoms to persons within its own "jurisdiction" [...]'.

342 With regard to the ICCPR, see the analysis with further references in Sarah Joseph & Melissa Castan, *The International Covenant on Civil and Political Rights*, Oxford: Oxford University Press, 2014, para. 1.25 and 6.01.

> governed by the Convention. Review by the Court concerns only the conformity of these measures with the requirements of the Convention (emphasis added).[343]

And also:

> The Court points out that the machinery of protection established by the Convention is subsidiary to the national systems safeguarding human rights [...]. The Convention *leaves to each Contracting State*, in the first place, *the task of securing* the rights and liberties it enshrines (emphasis added).[344]

Here too, it becomes evident that states are primarily responsible for realizing the rights and fulfilling the obligations (including those concerning life, inhuman treatment and privacy) and that the specific circumstances of the state in question may be relevant for the way in which the objective of realization can be achieved. The fact that the Human Rights Committee or the ECHR has not explicitly specified that states must take certain measures to secure the rights under the ICCPR or the ECHR does not mean – as we already discussed in section 2.3.7.ix – that the state is not required to take these measures. If the authorities have to conclude that a certain situation in their own territory is unacceptable in view of human rights and that it requires certain measures to be taken, the state in principle is therefore required to take those measures. It is also important that both the Human Rights Committee and the ECtHR cannot or will not always clarify in every respect what is required to secure the convention rights, because of the design of the control procedures with these bodies. It is interesting for example that the ECtHR only handles individual cases so it does not use general Concluding Observations about general country reports, unlike the Human Rights Committee. Consequently, the ECtHR is less likely to indicate that measures (and which ones) need to be taken by a state if there are general (serious) circumstances where the rights of citizens under the convention are at risk. Of course, the procedural fact that the control mechanism for the ECHR is set up differently and therefore works differently than the one of the ICCPR does not in itself imply that states have substantially different responsibilities under the ECHR from those under the ICCPR. The primary responsibility of the states parties to give effect to the convention entails that it is up to the states to decide which measures they are required to introduce so as to implement both the ICCPR and the ECHR in their legal system. However, this does not imply that the state is completely at liberty to determine what the best course of action is and/or has the final word on it. States must always take primary responsibility within the limits of the individual rights and obligations of states that arise from the convention that they are bound by.

---

343 ECtHR 23 July 1968, *Case Relating to Certain Aspects of the Laws on the Use of Languages in Education in Belgium/Belgium*, no. 1474/62, para. 10.

344 ECtHR 7 December 1976, *Handyside/The UK*, no. 5493/72, para. 48.

The foregoing is potentially of fundamental importance to the cannabis issue. The primary responsibility of the state with respect to the ICPPR and the ECHR entails that it is first and foremost up to the national authorities to consider which measures are necessary to effect the full realization of the convention rights, given the specific circumstances in the state. This involves safeguarding the right to life, the right not to be subjected to inhuman treatment and the right to a private life. However, with respect to these rights there is no obligation to achieve 'full realization' (as with the right to health in the ICESCR and the ESC); instead, there is an obligation to 'secure' these rights on the level and in the form required by the Human Rights Committee and the ECtHR. Unlike the ICESCR and the ESC, under the ICCPR and the ECHR, states are therefore not explicitly responsible to keep searching for measures that will provide an even more effective protection of the rights than of those that currently apply. The level of security of the rights is therefore lower here (not overall), but the obligation is absolute (a cast-iron obligation to achieve a result). It means that only insofar as the obligation to secure the pertinent rights (regarding life, inhuman treatment and a private life) would entail that citizens must be protected against unsafety, nuisance and crime caused by illegal cannabis cultivation and trade, the state has a responsibility to assess how that protection can best be provided nationally. If the state concludes that this protection can be achieved most effectively by regulated permission of cannabis cultivation and trade for the recreational user market, the obligation to secure the rights demands that the state actually implements that solution. However, whether that obligation can really manifest itself, again depends on the crucial question whether rights regarding life, inhuman treatment and a private life require protection from the threats of unsafety, nuisance and crime caused by illegal cannabis cultivation and trade. That is the key question in sections 2.4.8–2.4.10.

ix. Discretion about which Means are Appropriate

The responsibility for states to secure the individual rights that we discussed just now as well as meeting the obligations in the conventions in many cases goes hand in hand with the so-called 'margin of appreciation' for states. Nevertheless, the doctrine of the 'margin of appreciation' – which leaves states the possibility to exercise discretion – hardly ever plays a prominent part in the jurisprudence of the Human Rights Committee, neither in the case of limiting convention rights nor with regard to taking positive protection measures.[345]

345 Sometimes it is implicitly expressed in it regarding a specific convention right. See with further references Sarah Joseph & Melissa Castan, *The International Covenant on Civil and Political Rights*, Oxford: Oxford University Press, 2014, para. 1.77, 18.69, 24.30; Andrew Legg, *The Margin of Appreciation in International Human Rights Law. Deference and*

We will look into this in sections 2.4.8–2.4.10 insofar as this is relevant. In respect of the margin of appreciation regarding positive obligations, it will also become clear that the Human Rights Committee in its Concluding Observations for example formulates fairly general obligations for states to tackle certain problems without specifying which measures need to be taken. Consequently, states have a considerable amount of discretion in practice to assess and determine how the situation that poses a problem in terms of human rights must be ameliorated.

It was the ECtHR that developed the 'margin of appreciation' doctrine. The doctrine means that the national authorities– including at any rate the judiciary, the legislator and the administration – can exercise discretion to determine whether and to which degree it is necessary and proportional to breach convention rights that allow restrictions (such as the right to a private life).[346] With respect to positive obligations, the doctrine means – and that is more important here – that states have discretion in the choice of measures they take to secure the convention rights. The rationale for this is that states are best placed to assess the national social needs, priorities, use of available resources, moral requirements, concrete conditions and interests.[347] The margin does therefore not constitute a carte blanche for the state in the case of positive obligations either. The freedom granted to states is primarily a means to determine what – in the light of the social

---

Proportionality, Oxford: Oxford University Press, 2012, pp. 5–6; Yutaka Arai-Takahashi, *The Margin of Appreciation Doctrine and the Principle of Proportionality in the Jurisprudence of the ECHR*, Antwerp/Oxford/New York: Intersentia, 2001, p. 4; Eyal Benvenisti, 'Margin of Appreciation, Consensus, and Universal Standards', *International Law and Politics* 1999, vol. 31, pp. 843–854 on pp. 844–845.

346 See among other sources ECtHR (Grand Chamber) 10 November 2015, *Couderc and Hachette Filipacchi Associés/France*, no. 40454/07, para. 90; ECtHR (Grand Chamber) 15 October 2015, *Perinçek/Switzerland*, no. 27510/08, para. 196; see also, with further references, David J. Harris, Michael O'Boyle, Ed P. Bates & Carla M. Buckley (eds.), *Harris, O'Boyle & Warbrick, Law of the European Convention on Human Rights*, Oxford: Oxford University Press, 2014, pp. 14–17.

347 See for example ECtHR 4 January 2008, *Shelley/The UK*, no. 23800/06, para. 1, 'best placed to assess priorities, use of resources and social needs' (also quoted later); ECtHR (Grand Chamber) 26 November 2013, *X/Latvia*, no. 27853/09, para. 85; ECtHR 9 March 2010, *R.C./Sweden*, no 41827/07, para. 52; ECtHR (Grand Chamber) 22 April 2013, *Animal Defenders International/The UK*, no 48876/08, para. 111, 'By reason of their direct and continuous contact with the vital forces of their countries, their societies and their needs, the legislative and judicial authorities are best placed to assess the particular difficulties in safeguarding the democratic order in their State.'; see also ECtHR 30 January 2007, *Yumak and Sadak/Turkey*, no 10226/03, para. 76, in which the Court considers that the national legislator, judiciary and political system 'are best placed to assess the choice of an appropriate electoral system'; ECtHR 8 December 2015, *Z.H. and R.H./Switzerland*, no. 60119/12, para. 44 ('sensitive moral choices'); ECtHR 7 December 1976, *Handyside/The UK*, no. 5493/72, para. 47–48 ('requirements of morals') (incidentally, that case dealt with the margin of appreciation in restricting convention rights).

peculiarities and the constellation of the state – the appropriate steps are to fulfil the obligation to secure convention rights.[348] In a positive sense, this is about deciding what is most necessary within the context of the state and what works best there. Factors such as 'social needs' and 'particular difficulties' play a part in this. In a negative sense, the margin is relevant because it sometimes gives states the opportunity to wriggle out of implementing certain measures because they are alleged to be incompatible with the social peculiarities and the constellation of the state. In this context, the use of available resources and moral requirements can play a part. The evaluation of appropriate measures may also be informed by the fact whether or not the measure is supported by democratic decision-making and social consensus. After all, a measure is more likely to be effective if that is the case. However, the margin of appreciation is not about giving states 'carte blanche' within certain limits. Granting this particular freedom is not an end in itself.

If the doctrine applies, this does not mean that the margin of appreciation is unlimited, nor that it is without supervision. To quote the ECtHR:

> However, this margin goes hand in hand with *European supervision*, embracing both the legislation and the decisions applying it, even those delivered by an independent court. In exercising its supervisory function, the Court's task is *not to take the place of the national courts, but rather to review*, in the light of the case as a whole, whether the decisions they have taken pursuant to their power of appreciation *are compatible* with the provisions of the Convention relied on (emphasis added).[349]

Whether national authorities have a 'margin of appreciation' in a concrete case, and if so, how wide that margin is, depends on the human right in question and the purpose of its infringement or alternatively its protection.[350] For that reason, we will devote more attention to it insofar as this is useful, in the discussion in sections 2.4.8–2.4.10 of specific obligations arising from the rights regarding life, inhuman treatment and a private life.

Nevertheless, it is worth mentioning here that as far as positive obligations are concerned that apply to specific human rights, a 'margin of appreciation' is usually assumed – explicitly or implicitly – by the ECtHR and that in principle,

---

348 See also Yutaka Arai-Takahashi, *The Margin of Appreciation Doctrine and the Principle of Proportionality in the Jurisprudence of the ECHR*, Antwerp/Oxford/New York: Intersentia, 2001, pp. 84–85.

349 ECtHR (Grand Chamber) 10 November 2015, *Couderc and Hachette Filipacchi Associés/France*, no. 40454/07, para. 90.

350 See for example ECtHR (Grand Chamber) 27 August 2015, *Parrillo/Italy*, no. 46470/11, para. 169 (on Article 8 ECHR); ECtHR (Grand Chamber) 12 February 2008, *Kafkaris/Cyprus*, no. 21906/04, para. 161 (on Article 14).

it is wider than that for negative obligations for the same right.[351] It is even conceivable that there may be such a margin for positive obligations, but none at all for the negative obligations. That, for example, is the case with inhuman treatment.[352] The above-mentioned wider margin applies in particular to the positive obligations to take measures to prevent risks pertaining to the violation of convention rights:

> As to the choice of particular practical measures, the Court has consistently held that where the State is required to take positive measures, *the choice of means is in principle a matter that falls within the Contracting State's margin of appreciation*. There are different avenues to ensure Convention rights, and even if the State has failed to apply one particular measure provided by domestic law, it may still fulfil its positive duty by other means. In this respect *an impossible or disproportionate burden must not be imposed on the authorities* without consideration being given, in particular, to the *operational choices which they must make in terms of priorities and resources*; this results from the *wide margin of appreciation* States enjoy, as the Court has previously held, in difficult social and technical spheres (emphasis added).[353]

Additionally, the margin for the national authorities – in particular the legislator – in the implementation of social and economic policy is 'a wide one').[354] The same goes for policies on protecting the environment and on healthcare,[355] as well as public health and order.[356] This applies particularly to determining which general preventative measures must be taken, or as the ECtHR puts it:

> While it is not excluded that a *positive obligation might arise to eradicate or prevent the spread of a particular disease or infection*, the Court is not persuaded that any potential threat to health that fell short of the standards of Articles 2 or 3 would necessarily impose a duty on the State to take specific preventive steps. Matters of health care

351 For example, regarding the right to life in Article 2 ECHR, see the considerations in ECtHR (Grand Chamber) 5 June 2015, *Lambert/France*, no. 46043/14, para. 144–148; ECtHR (Grand Chamber) 30 November 2004, *Öneryildiz/Turkey*, no. 48939/99, para. 107. With respect to Article 8 ECHR, see (among other sources) ECtHR 28 May 1985, *Abdulaziz, Cabales and Balkandali/The UK*, no. 9214/80, para. 67.

352 See for example David J. Harris, Michael O'Boyle, Ed P. Bates & Carla M. Buckley (eds.), *Harris, O'Boyle & Warbrick, Law of the European Convention on Human Rights*, Oxford: Oxford University Press, 2014, p. 236 (negative obligation Article 3 ECHR: 'absolute guarantee, there is no room for a margin of appreciation') and p. 15 (regarding positive obligations).

353 ECtHR 24 July 2014, *Brincat/Malta*, no. 60908/11, para. 101, with further references.

354 See among other sources ECtHR (Grand Chamber) 3 April 2012, *Kotov/Russia*, no. 54522/00, para. 131.

355 David J. Harris, Michael O'Boyle, Ed P. Bates & Carla M. Buckley (eds.), *Harris, O'Boyle & Warbrick, Law of the European Convention on Human Rights*, Oxford: Oxford University Press, 2014, pp. 582–583, and p. 546.

356 ECtHR 26 July 2011, *Georgel and Georgeta Stoicescu/Romania*, no. 9718/03, para. 59.

> policy, *in particular as regards general preventive measures, are in principle within the margin of appreciation* of the domestic authorities who are *best placed to assess priorities, use of resources and social needs* (emphasis added).[357]

Taking into account the 'wide margin of appreciation' enjoyed by states in creating preventative measures and policies on social and economic, environmental and public health and public order related issues, it seems obvious that there is also a wide margin for drug policy and the administration of justice. In other words: there is little ground to assume that the ECtHR will prescribe a specific drug policy (see for more information section 2.4.11).

Any motivation by national authorities of their assessment may be important when the ECtHR verifies whether the state acted within the 'margin of appreciation'.[358] This is logical if the question is whether the infringement by the state of a convention right that allows restrictions is truly necessary and proportionate. What is more important for the cannabis issue (which after all is not about states infringing rights under a convention, but rather about the question whether regulated permission of cannabis cultivation and trade could qualify as securing the rights regarding life, inhuman treatment and a private life) is that the justification of measures to meet positive obligations can be pertinent when an assessment is made as to whether the authorities remained within their margin of appreciation.[359] Without such justification, it will be difficult for the ECtHR to determine whether the measures are indeed appropriate, given the social peculiarities and the constellation of the state involved. In certain cases – such as protection of health, care for the environment and economic policy – the Court even requires that the assessment by the national authorities includes adequate research and is based on relevant studies.[360] Even when the policy leads to infringement of convention rights, this categorically does not mean that a state may only go on to implement it if elaborate and measurable date are available with regard to each aspect of the

---

357 ECtHR 4 January 2008, *Shelley/The UK*, no. 23800/06, para. 1; see also ECtHR 13 November 2012, *Hristozov/Bulgaria*, no. 47039/11, para. 119, and with this ruling Dissenting Opinion of Judge De Gaetano joined by Judge Vučinić.

358 See for example ECtHR (Grand Chamber) 16 June 2014, *Hämäläinen/Finland*, no. 37359/09, para. 69–89.

359 See for example ECtHR (Grand Chamber) 12 November 2013, *Söderman/Sweden*, no. 5786/08, para. 78–117 (in which the state's arguments do not convince the Court); ECtHR (Grand Chamber) 3 April 2012, *Kotov/Russia*, no. 54522/00, para. 131 (in which the justification is one of the factors to lead the Court to assume there is no infringement of positive obligations).

360 See with further references ECtHR 24 July 2014, *Brincat/Malta*, no. 60908/11, para. 101; DavidJ. Harris, Michael O'Boyle, Ed P. Bates & Carla M. Buckley (eds.), *Harris, O'Boyle & Warbrick, Law of the European Convention on Human Rights*, Oxford: Oxford University Press, 2014, p. 583.

question on which a decision has to be made.[361] It seems self-evident that this is not the case either if the state actually takes positive measures to achieve the convention rights. The fundamental question is whether the evaluation was carried out with due care and consideration, so that the justification provided will usually be crucial. So it is not a matter of the state proving the effectiveness of measures, but of making that effectiveness plausible and credible. Should a state decide to permit cannabis cultivation and trade for the recreational consumer market (through legalization, decriminalization or policy-based tolerance) so as to effectuate the rights regarding life, inhuman treatment and a private life, that state would be well-advised to argue persuasively why this policy adequately meets the state's positive obligations under these rights.

x. *Rights Regarding Life, Inhuman Treatment and a Private Life in Relation to Other International Instruments*

Unlike Article 2 ICESCR, Article 2 ICCPR, Article 1 ECHR and other provisions in these conventions do not explicitly contain a general obligation to take measures to give effect to convention rights 'through international assistance and co-operation'. However, this is not to say that international cooperation can never be required. For example, according to the Human Rights Committee states are required to assist each other in bringing persons to justice who are suspected of having committed acts in breach of the ICCPR and that are punishable under national or international law.[362] Something similar applies in the framework of the ECHR, for example, if international cooperation is needed to conduct an effective criminal inquiry into acts by private persons that violate the right to life.[363] Insofar as the rights regarding life, inhuman treatment and a private life required that action is undertaken to address unsafety, nuisance and crime caused by illegal cannabis cultivation and trade (see sections 2.4.8–2.4.10 about this), there could consequently also be an obligation to do this in an international context. That could specifically be the case with transnational drug crime.

Moreover, with regard to the ICCPR and the ECHR, the positive measures taken by a country to effectuate rights under a convention are not allowed to have a disproportionate and non-subsidiary impact on the enjoyment of rights secured under these conventions in other countries. This too, is not explicitly stated in the conventions. It is important, however, that this may be at odds with the negative obligation to respect human rights. This can also be relevant for the cannabis issue. It implies that a drug policy implemented by a country will need

---

361 ECtHR 2 November 2006, *Giacomelli/Italy*, no. 59909/00, para. 82.
362 HRC, General Comment No. 31 (2004) 'General Legal Obligation', para. 18.
363 See ECtHR 7 January 2010, *Rantsev/Cyprus and Russia*, no. 25965/04, para. 241.

to respect the convention rights of persons in other countries and that arbitrary infringements of those persons' human rights cannot be allowed.

Finally, Article 2 ICCPR, Article 1 ECHR and other provisions in these conventions do not contain an explicit obligation for states parties to observe the convention rights for international agreements they become party to. This does not change the fact that states do need to take into account their responsibilities pursuant to the ICCPR and the EHCR upon joining conventions in other areas and fulfilling other obligations under international law.[364] As regards the cannabis issue, it is about what these responsibilities entail exactly if the obligations ensuing from the UN narcotic drugs conventions and other international drug regulations were an obstacle to fulfilling positive obligations based on the right to life, the right not to be subjected to inhuman treatment and the right to a private life. For that reason, we will now first discuss in sections 2.4.8–2.4.10 what these positive obligations are about. To the extend they are at odds with the obligations ensuing from the UN narcotic drugs conventions, we will discuss in Chapter 3 how this conflict should be or can be resolved.

2.4.8. SPECIFIC POSITIVE OBLIGATIONS RESULTING FROM THE RIGHT TO LIFE

The elaborate exposition in the previous section concerns the general obligations of states pursuant to the ICCPR and the ECHR with respect to the rights embedded in those conventions. These general obligations therefore also apply to the rights regarding life, inhuman treatment and privacy. The foregoing illustrates, among other things, that states are required to 'respect' and 'secure' these rights, that they have both negative and positive obligations to that end, and that the obligation to protect these rights can also be applicable in the event of threats from private persons. We also saw before that states have no obligation to achieve 'full realization' of these rights (where by contrast this is the case with the right to health in the ICESCR and the ESC); instead, there is an obligation to 'secure' these rights on the level and in the form required by the Human Rights Committee and the ECtHR. This involves an absolute obligation to achieve results instead of a relative obligation to achieve realization progressively. What these obligations entail in concrete terms and which level of security is required ensues from the general obligations discussed above and the specific right involved. Therefore, and to avoid repetition we decided to elaborate on the positive obligations in relation to the relevant convention rights. In this section and the following two, we will look at the relevant positive obligations in relation

---

364 Cf. HRC 22 October 2008, *Sayadi and Vinck/Belgium*, no. 1472/2006, para. 7.2, 10.2–11; ECtHR (Grand Chamber) 12 September 2012, *Nada/Switzerland*, no. 10593/08, para. 196–197.

to the right to life, the right not to be subjected to inhuman treatment and the right to a private life respectively.

i. The Protection Requirement in Article 6 ICCPR and Article 2 ECHR

Both Article 6 ICCPR and Article 2 ECHR state that the right to life is protected by law.[365] Protection, in other words, is paramount. However, these provisions do not specify the nature or extent of that protection or whether the state also has to take non-legal measures in that context. The jurisprudence of the Human Rights Committee and the ECtHR does specify this though. The analysis below of Article 6 ICCPR and Article 2 ECHR respectively and the relevant jurisprudence seeks to provide answers to the following questions in particular:

> Does the positive obligation to protect citizens from life-threatening crime necessitate the prevention and fight against crime that goes with cannabis cultivation and trade, such as lethal violence and the deaths of citizens by fire or seriously harmful infections caused by unsafe and illegal installations for illegal hemp nurseries?
>
> Does the positive obligation to protect citizens from life-threatening health issues necessitate the prevention of deaths caused by the use of hard drugs, and is the argument of the distinction between the soft drugs market and the hard drugs market relevant in this context?

These two questions will now be addressed one by one from various angles. Insofar as the answer turns out to be affirmative, a third question arises:

> Can the positive obligation for protection be fulfilled by a drug and/or cannabis policy that permits regulated cannabis cultivation and trade for recreational user market?

To the extent that such a fulfilment is possible, the question presents itself whether this is merely an acceptable way to honour the obligation (the state is then free to choose whether it adopts that policy or not), or whether in principle a mandatory approach (the state is then required to implement the policy, although there may be ways to get out of this). We will answer this question in the overall conclusion for the rights concerning life, inhuman treatment and privacy, in section 2.4.12.

ii. Positive Obligations Pursuant to Article 6(1) ICCPR

The right to life from Article 6(1) ICCPR concerns itself with the protection of life. The Human Rights Committee shows that states and government

---

365 For the text of the provisions see section 2.4.2.

authorities are bound by both negative obligations (such as the obligations to abstain from arbitrary deprivation of liberty and causing war) and positive obligations (such as the obligation to avoid wars, genocide, other acts of mass violence and arbitrary loss of life).[366] Non-widespread and non-war-related threats to life can also be covered by the right to life in Article 6(1) ICCPR. That applies to both life-threatening violent crime by individuals and life-threatening health issues. We will now discuss the obligations with respect to these items in turn.

- *Protection against crime.* The fact that obligations of protection from life-threatening and deadly violence by private actors also fall within the scope of Article 6(1) ICCPR is manifested prominently in the jurisprudence of the Human Rights Committee.[367] States are required to *protect* citizens from private persons.[368] They are beholden to take 'appropriate measures' and to 'exercise due diligence' so as to *prevent, punish, investigate* or *redress* the taking of life by private persons among other things.[369] In section 2.4.7.v, we already saw that states are required to adopt legislative, judicial, administrative, educative and other appropriate measures to fulfil their obligations under the conventions.[370] Other appropriate measures may include operational measures, for example.[371]

  With regard to the above-mentioned obligation to investigate, it is important that (suspected) violations must be investigated immediately, thoroughly and effectively (under criminal law[372]) by independent and impartial organs.[373]

366 See HRC, General Comment No. 6 (1982) 'Right to Life', para. 2–4; see also HRC, General Comment No. 14 (1985) 'Right to life'.

367 See also HRC, Concluding Observations (Peru), *UN Doc.* CCPR A/52/40 vol. I (1997), para. 167 (requirement of effective protection against rape, sexual abuse and violence against women); HRC, Concluding Observations (Colombia), *UN Doc.* CCPR A/52/40 vol. I (1997), para. 287, 290, 300 (requirement of effective protection against violence against women and children); HRC, Concluding Observations (Venezuela), *UN Doc.* CCPR A/56/40 vol. I (2001), para. 77(17) (requirement of effective protection against kidnapping and murder of women); HRC, Concluding Observations (Russian Federation), *UN Doc.* CCPR A/59/40 vol. I (2003), para. 22 (requirement of criminal investigation and prosecution in the case of threats, violent assaults and murders of journalists). Cf. HRC, Draft general comment No. 36, Article 6: Right to life. Draft prepared by Yuval Shany and Nigel Rodley, Rapporteurs, *UN Doc.* CCPR/C/GC/R.36, 1 April 2015, para. 6.

368 HRC, General Comment No. 6 (1982) 'Right to Life', para. 8.

369 Ibid, para. 3, 8; and for example HRC 26 March 2012, *Krasovskaya and Krasovskaya/Belarus*, no. 1820/2008, para. 8.3; HRC 21 October 2010, *Novaković/Serbia*, no. 1556/2007, para. 7.2–9; HRC 13 November 1995, *Bautista/Colombia*, no. 563/1993, para. 8.6, 10; HRC 29 March 1982, *Bleier/Uruguay*, no. 30/1978, para. 11–15.

370 See also HRC, General Comment No. 6 (1982) 'Right to Life', para. 7.

371 It can also involve operational measures to protect someone's life from concrete threats on account of the right to liberty and security of person as stated in Article 9 ICCPR; see HRC 12 July1990, *Delgado Páez/Colombia*, no. 195/1985, para. 5.6.

372 HRC 26 March 2012, *Krasovskaya and Krasovskaya/Belarus*, no. 1820/2008, para. 8.3; HRC 29 July 1997, *Arhuaco/Colombia*, no. 612/1995, para. 8.2 and also 8.3–11.

373 HRC, General Comment No. 6 (1982) 'Right to Life', para. 15.

If such investigations reveal violations of conventions, states must ensure that the persons responsible are tried in a court.[374] Although victims have no right to prosecution,[375] failure on the part of the authorities to carry out such an investigation or prosecute the suspected perpetrators can qualify as a violation of the convention(s).[376] This is the case, among other things, if according to national or international law the violation of the convention is also an offence, e.g., deprivation of life (manslaughter and murder).[377]

These obligations to take action in criminal matters manifest themselves if there is a material violation of the right to life. This means a situation in which (a serious risk of) deprivation of life or death is not prevented. Insofar as a cannabis policy is conducted where there are no material violations of the right to life, for example because deaths are avoided as a consequence of this policy, the obligations of taking action in criminal proceedings ensuing from the right to life are not relevant for the cannabis issue. It is also important in this respect that the fact that the UN narcotic drugs conventions force states to criminalize cannabis cultivation and trade, among other things, does not give rise to the above-mentioned obligations of investigation and prosecution under the right to life. After all, cannabis cultivation and trade and also the use of this drug as such are not life-threatening. If such cultivation and trade is accompanied by life-threatening crime (such as the settling of scores and rip deals), it is with regard to that crime that the positive obligations of protection, prevention, investigation and prosecution come into play. It could be that these threats to life can be best prevented by combating illegal cannabis cultivation and trade. Whether that fight takes place by initiating criminal proceedings against cannabis cultivation and trade or rather by taking that cultivation and trade out of the criminal circuit through regulation is immaterial from the point of view of the positive obligations pursuant to the right of life. After all, in principle, the approach that best fulfils the obligation to produce results – the protection of life – is the most suitable approach when seen from the positive obligation to protect life.

However, the Human Rights Committee emphasizes first and foremost the importance of preventing violations of convention rights. The obligation of prevention therefore precedes the obligation to take action in criminal matters.

---

374 For an explicit example in that sense see HRC 29 July 1997, *Arhuaco/Colombia*, no. 612/1995, para. 8.8.

375 See HRC 16 August 2007, *Messaouda Grioua/Algeria*, no. 1327/2004, para. 9; HRC 29 July 1997, *José Vicenté/Colombia*, no. 612/1995, para. 8.8; HRC 30 March 1989, *H.C.M.A./The Netherlands*, no. 213/1986, para. 11.6.

376 See for example HRC 26 March 2012, *Khirani/Algeria*, no. 1905/2009, para. 7.10.

377 HRC, General Comment No. 6 (1982) 'Right to Life', para. 18. See also Sarah Joseph & Melissa Castan, *The International Covenant on Civil and Political Rights*, Oxford: Oxford University Press, 2014, para. 8.42.

This applies in particular to cases involving the right to life. Firstly, this is evident from the above-mentioned obligation to protect citizens from private persons, among other actors. As we observed before, protection is also paramount in the text of Article 6 ICCPR. Moreover, the ICCPR's objective would be undermined according to the Committee without an obligation to take measures to prevent repeated violations of the convention.[378] It is also important for the cannabis issue that this obligation to protect and/or to prevent does not apply exclusively to concrete threats to life of a specific person. The Human Rights Committee also requires states to take measures for situations and developments that pose a threat to the lives of people in a general sense. For example, the HRC urged states to take positive measures: to prevent homelessness from leading to death;[379] against child mortality;[380] to increase life expectancy, for example when it is under pressure because of the food situation in the country;[381] against malnutrition and epidemics;[382] against poisoning of the environment.[383] Often, the HRC does not make clear which specific measures the states must take to these ends, unless the general nature of the solution is rather straightforward.[384] To that extent, it usually remains an abstract obligation of protection for states. We have not seen any concrete obligation of protection regarding cannabis cultivation, trade and/or use either, as we will discuss below in section 2.4.11. It is therefore in principle up to the state to determine which measures are best suited to achieve the required result. Nor does the Committee provide criteria or guidance to determine when states are bound by the right to life to adopt positive measures against general threats to life or life expectancy. Nevertheless, it is clear that when such threats manifest themselves, states are required to do something about them according to the Committee. After all, it is exactly these threats where the Committee consistently points out the responsibilities of states to take measures so as to protect life.

---

378 HRC, General Comment No. 6 (1982) 'Right to Life', para. 17.

379 HRC, Concluding Observations (Canada), *UN Doc.* CCPR/C/79/Add.105 (1999), para. 12.

380 See for example HRC, Concluding Observations (Brazil), *UN Doc.* CCPR/C/79/Add.66 (1996), para. 23; HRC, Concluding Observations (Ireland), *UN Doc.* CCPR/A/55/40 (2000), para. 27.

381 HRC, Concluding Observations (Democratic People's Republic of Korea), *UN Doc.* CCPR/CO/72/PRK (2001), para. 12. See also HRC, General Comment No. 6 (1982) 'Right to Life', para. 5 (quoted below).

382 HRC, General Comment No. 6 (1982) 'Right to Life', para. 5 (quoted below).

383 HRC, Concluding Observations (Suriname), *UN Doc.* CCPR/A/59/40 vol. I (2004), para. 69 (21).

384 See also HRC, Concluding Observations (Senegal), *UN Doc.* CCPR/A/53/40 vol. I (1998), para. 61, in which the Committee holds genital mutilation to be incompatible with the right to life, and subsequently declares itself in favour of criminalization of genital mutilation as a protective measure. For a similar stance regarding domestic violence see HRC, Concluding Observations (Suriname), *UN Doc.* CCPR/A/59/40 vol. I (2004), para. 69.

We therefore conclude that pursuant to Article 6 in conjunction with Article 2 ICCPR states must take protective and/or preventive measures when the right to life in a general sense is actually threatened by the consequences of illegal cannabis cultivation and trade. That is the case for example with lethal violence in the circuit and by fires caused by unsafe wiring for (the theft of) power for illegal hemp nurseries. The state can then decide how that protection is best realized. So the obligation of protection does not imply that a criminal prohibition of cannabis cultivation and trade coupled with strict enforcement is the best way forward, or conversely, that regulated permission of such cultivation and trade is the preferred option. The result is what matters: the state can in principle fulfil the positive obligation of protection which ensues from the right to life with those measures that also according to the authorities themselves can best eliminate the actual general threat to life. That is not to say that just anything is permitted. Measures will have to be compatible with other human rights. For example, there is no place for unlimited action under criminal law against cannabis cultivation and trade.

- *Protection of life from health threats.* Under certain circumstances, the right to life requires that states take general public health measures. The obligation to take such measures comes into effect when there are general situations or developments that pose a threat to life or life expectancy, not just when there is already a concrete life-threatening situation for a concrete person. The following consideration of the Human Rights Committee is a clear illustration of this:

> Moreover, the Committee has noted that the right to life has been too often narrowly interpreted. The expression 'inherent right to life' cannot properly be understood in a restrictive manner, and the protection of this right requires that States adopt positive measures. In this connection, the Committee considers that it would be desirable for States parties to take all possible measures to reduce infant mortality and to increase life expectancy, especially in adopting measures to eliminate malnutrition and epidemics.[385]

The right to life should therefore not be interpreted restrictively. It also follows from this consideration that general measures aimed at individual and public health that are necessary to prevent (premature) death can be within the scope of the obligations arising from the right to life in Article 6(1) ICCPR.[386] It is also in the context of the right to life that the Human Rights Committee has asked countries (on account of the duty to report) in general which measures

---

385 HRC, General Comment No. 6 (1982) 'Right to Life', para. 5.

386 See also HRC 21 October 2010, *Novaković/Serbia*, no. 1556/2007, which shows that medical malpractice and serious violations of the right to health may be covered by this provision (the case was about inadequate criminal investigations of the alleged malpractice).

have been taken to improve public health.[387] More specifically, access to health care can also be covered by the sphere of influence of the right to life (as well as the right to a private life in Article 17 ICCPR).[388] The right to life (and the rights regarding inhuman treatment and a private life) can also give rise to the obligation to conduct a policy to prevent unwanted pregnancies and restrictions on or bans of abortion may be unacceptable.[389] Because of the right to life, states are also bound to protect the population against HIV and AIDS according to the Human Rights Committee.[390] As far as we have been able to ascertain, the Human Rights Committee has never explicitly concluded that states are also bound to protect the population against death caused by drugs, on the grounds of the right to life or any other right under a convention. Nevertheless, such protection would be in line with the protection of public health described above that is explicitly required by the Committee, and it also fits the required broad interpretation of the right to life in Article 6 ICCPR.

It is interesting in this context that currently, work is in progress on General Comment No. 36 as regards the right to life.[391] The aim of this new general comment is to review General Comment No. 6 that currently applies to the right of life and General Comment No. 14 and to expand these.[392] The rapporteurs appointed for these issues propose various topics that might be included in the new General Comment No. 36 because questions about them arise under Article 6. For example, they mention regulation of possibly life-threatening practices and circumstances, such as alcohol, tobacco, drugs, violence.[393] The fact that the rapporteurs consider protection from threats to life by drugs and violence a relevant topic under Article 6 ICCPR confirms that

387 HRC, Concluding Observations (Mali), *UN Doc.* CCPR A/36/40 (1981), para. 235, 'In relation to article 6 of the Covenant, it was asked what provisions the Government had enacted to improve public health'; HRC, Concluding observations (Kenya), *UN Doc.* CCPR A/36/40 (1981), para. 188, 'With respect to article 6 of the Covenant, information was requested on the measures that had been taken for the protection of life in its social context such as improvement of the general living conditions of the population and action to eradicate epidemics and provide better health conditions'. See also HRC, Concluding Observations (Mali), *UN Doc.* CCPR A/58/40 (2003), para. 14.

388 HRC, Concluding Observations (Philippines), *UN Doc.* CCPR/C/PHL/CO/4 (2012), para. 13 (sexual and reproductive healthcare); HRC, Concluding Observations (Kenya), *UN Doc.* CCPR/CO/83/KEN (2005), para. 15 (people with HIV).

389 HRC 24 October 2005, *Llantoy Huamán/Peru*, no. 1153/2003; HRC 29 March 2011, *V.D.A./Argentina*, no. 1608/2007; and also, among other sources, HRC, Concluding Observations (Malta), *UN Doc.* CCPR/C/MLT/CO/2 (2014), para. 13; HRC, Concluding Observations (El Salvador), *UN Doc.* CCPR/C/SLV/CO/6 (2010), para. 10.

390 HRC, Concluding Observations (Namibia), *UN Doc.* CCPR/CO/81/NAM (2004), para. 10.

391 See the website of OHCHR (U.N. Office of the High Commissioner on Human Rights): http://www.ohchr.org/EN/HRBodies/CCPR/Pages/GC36-Article6Righttolife.aspx.

392 HRC, Draft general comment No. 36, Article 6: Right to life. Draft prepared by Yuval Shany and Nigel Rodley, Rapporteurs, *UN Doc.* CCPR/C/GC/R.36, 1 April 2015, para. 2.

393 Ibid, para. 6.

these subjects are within the scope of this provision. In principle, that would also apply to a drug policy that aims to limit the number of drug-related deaths. For the right to life, it is therefore also important that within the cannabis debate – see section 2.3.1 – it is argued that by separating the soft drugs and hard drugs markets, soft drug users would less quickly slide into a life-threatening habit of hard drug use.

We conclude that according to the Human Rights Committee a general obligation ensues from Article 6 ICCPR to offer protection to individuals from general threats to life affecting health. If death as a result of using hard drugs is a real possibility in a state, measures will therefore have to be taken against it. A policy in which the soft drugs market and the hard drugs market are separated can serve to fulfil that positive obligation of protection, at any rate to the extent that this policy offers the best protection to the right of life.

iii. Positive Obligations Pursuant to Article 2 ECHR

Many of the positive obligations inferred by the Human Rights Committee from Article 6 ICCPR also apply to Article 2 ECHR, witness the case law of the ECtHR.[394] In the *Osman* case, the ECtHR considers the following:

> The Court notes that the first sentence of Article 2 §1 enjoins the State not only to refrain from the intentional and unlawful taking of life, but also *to take appropriate steps to safeguard the lives of those within its jurisdiction* [...]. It is common ground that the State's obligation in this respect extends beyond its primary duty to secure the right to life by *putting in place effective criminal-law provisions* to deter the commission of offences against the person *backed up by law-enforcement machinery* for the *prevention, suppression and sanctioning of breaches* of such provisions. [...] Article 2 of the Convention may also imply in certain well-defined circumstances a *positive obligation on the authorities to take preventive operational measures* to protect an individual whose life is at risk from the criminal acts of another individual (emphasis added).[395]

394 For more information about this with many additional references see Piet Hein P.H.M.C. van Kempen, *Repressie door mensenrechten. Over positieve verplichtingen tot aanwending van strafrecht ter bescherming van fundamentele rechten* (oratie Nijmegen), Nijmegen: Wolf Legal Publishers, 2008, pp. 25–56 (i.e., *Repression because of human rights. About positive obligations for applying criminal law to protect fundamental rights* (lecture Nijmegen)); Feikje Vellinga-Schootstra & Wim H. Vellinga, 'Positive obligations en het Nederlandse straf(proces)recht' (Oratie Groningen), Deventer: Kluwer, 2008 (i.e., 'Positive obligations and Dutch criminal (procedural) law' (lecture Groningen)); David J. Harris, Michael O'Boyle, Ed P. Bates & Carla M. Buckley (eds.), *Harris, O'Boyle & Warbrick, Law of the European Convention on Human Rights*, Oxford: Oxford University Press, 2014, pp. 203–218.

395 ECtHR (Grand Chamber) 28 October 1998, *Osman/The UK*, no. 23452/94, para. 115. This concerns settled case law; see for an even earlier case ECtHR 9 June 1998, *L.C.B./The UK*, n. 23413/94, para. 36 and recently for example ECtHR 15 September 2015, *Lari/The Republic of Moldova*, no. 37847/13, para. 33–35.

The right to life from Article 2 ECHR also concerns itself with protection of life. The ECtHR emphasizes that states have the primary duty to provide that protection.[396] And even now states and government authorities are bound by both negative obligations (such as the obligations to abstain from arbitrary deprivation of liberty) and positive obligations (such as the obligation to protect life in legislation, by law enforcement and by using the criminal justice system). These positive obligations of protection also apply to threats to life presented by private actors such as other individuals.[397] These obligations can also be relevant in relation to both life-threatening violent crime by individuals and life-threatening health issues.

However, this does not mean that the above conclusions about Article 6 ICCPR regarding the cannabis issue also apply to Article 2 ECHR. The crucial question for that is whether the obligations ensuing from Article 2 ECHR to adopt positive measures to protect life already apply if there are general situations or developments that constitute a threat to life or life expectancy. Or do these obligations not arise until, and only if, there are concrete threats to the lives of concrete persons? This topic is explored below.

- *Protection against crime.* The above-mentioned consideration from the *Osman* judgment illustrates that the positive obligations pursuant to Article 2 ECHR can also apply if the life of an individual is in danger because of the criminal acts of another person.[398] It follows from this that if a life is taken or there is a death with an unnatural cause, the authorities are required to conduct a criminal inquiry, followed by prosecution, conviction, punishment and execution of punishment.[399] These obligations therefore also apply if cannabis cultivation and trade are dogged by for example (serious risks of) murder and manslaughter and life-threatening fires or seriously harmful infections as a result of unsafe installations in hemp nurseries.

  However, it is more important for the cannabis issue that the state also has obligations to ensure that the criminal taking of life is prevented. Two categories emerge from the Osman judgment in the above-mentioned consideration. Firstly, the obligation to take 'appropriate steps to safeguard' the lives of people, which we will dwell on presently. Secondly, 'in certain

---

396 See also, among other sources, ECtHR 3 November 2015, *Olszewscy/Poland*, no. 99/12, para. 58.

397 This is also covered by ECtHR (Grand Chamber) 28 October 1998, *Osman/The UK*, no. 23452/94.

398 ECtHR (Grand Chamber) 28 October 1998, *Osman/The UK*, no. 23452/94, para. 115.

399 In addition to the *Osman* judgment see also for example ECtHR 15 September 2015, *Lari/The Republic of Moldova*, no. 37847/13, para. 33–35; ECtHR 9 June 2009, *Opuz/Turkey*, no. 33401/02, para. 150; ECtHR (Grand Chamber) 30 November 2004, *Öneryildiz/Turkey*, no. 48939/99, para. 94; see also the literature mentioned in a footnote at the beginning of this subparagraph, which contains many references to case law.

well-defined circumstances' there can also be an obligation to take 'preventive operational measures'. A condition for the concrete applicability of this latter obligation is that the authorities (need to) know about 'a real and immediate risk' to the life of a certain individual posed by the criminal acts of another person.[400] This obligation does therefore not apply if there are general situations or developments that pose a threat to life or life expectancy. This operational obligation is not relevant in the case of preventing general risks such as murder and manslaughter or fires and seriously harmful infections involved with cannabis cultivation and trade.

On the contrary, the above-mentioned obligation to take appropriate steps to safeguard the lives of people is potentially relevant here. Firstly, this positive obligation is wide in its scope of application. The obligation does not only apply when there are fatalities, but also if there is a serious risk of this happening.[401] Moreover, the obligation to take measures according to the ECtHR applies in principle to the context of any activity, public or private, in which the right to life is at stake.[402] Thus, the obligation applies in any case to the special context of dangerous activities, where particular attention needs to be paid to regulation tailored to the special characteristics of such activities, especially regarding the level of risk for human lives.[403] There is more to this, though. The case law of the ECtHR shows that the obligation is important in connection with, among other areas: traffic safety;[404] safety on water;[405] natural disasters;[406] maritime safety,[407] safety on building sites[408] and dangerous environments such as landfill sites and other industries,[409] but also in the normal public space;[410] healthcare;[411] emergency services;[412] and the safety of dangerous (sports) activities the individual chooses to participate in.[413] This list is not exhaustive.[414] As we can see from the above-mentioned consideration in the *Osman* judgment, the obligation is certainly

---

400 See among other sources ECtHR 9 June 2009, *Opuz/Turkey*, no. 33401/02, para. 150; ECtHR 23 June 2015, *Selahattin Demirtaş/Turkey*, no. 15028/09, para. 27–31.

401 ECtHR 24 July 2014, *Brincat/Malta*, no. 60908/11, para. 103–117.

402 See also for example ECtHR 16 June 2011, *Ciechońska/Poland*, no. 19776/04, para. 63.

403 ECtHR 26 February 2015, *Prilutskiy/Ukraine*, no. 40429/08, para. 31.

404 ECtHR 27 November 2007, *Rajkowska/Poland*, no. 37393/02.

405 ECtHR 2 February 2016, *Cavit Tinarlioğlu/Turquie*, no. 3648/04, para. 60–78.

406 ECtHR 20 March 2008, *Budayeva/Russia*, no. 15339/02, para. 137.

407 ECtHR 16 January 2008, *Leray, Guilcher, Ameon, Margue et Mad/La France*, no. 44617/98.

408 ECtHR 26 August 2003, *Pereira Henrique/Luxembourg*, no. 60255/00, para. 54–63.

409 ECtHR (Grand Chamber) 30 November 2004, *Öneryildiz/Turkey*, no. 48939/99.

410 ECtHR 14 June 2011, *Ciechońska/Poland*, no. 19776/04, para. 67.

411 ECtHR 17 January 2008, *Dodov/Bulgaria*, no. 59548/00, para. 70, 79–83 and 87.

412 ECtHR 2 December 2008, *Furdik/Slovakia*, no. 42994/05, para. 1; see also ECtHR 16 January 2008, *Leray, Guilcher, Ameon, Margue et Mad/La France*, no. 44617/98.

413 About water sports see ECtHR 2 February2016, *Cavit Tinarlioğlu/Turquie*, no. 3648/04, and the references in it in para. 63 to judgments about all manner of other dangerous activities.

414 See also for example ECtHR 14 June 2011, *Ciechońska/Poland*, no. 19776/04, para. 63.

relevant for criminality that infringes the right to life. Also insofar as criminal activities in connection with cannabis cultivation and trade threaten the lives of persons (for example by murder and manslaughter or nursery fires and seriously harmful infections in residential areas), the positive obligations of Article 2 ECHR are therefore also important. However, the right to life does not give rise to positive obligations to protect against non-life threatening situations, such as organized crime as such, the fight against corruption in the upper world (undermining) and nuisance and damage.

That positive obligation to take measures is also broad in content. It concerns after all an obligation to take 'all' measures that are suitable for the required protection ('all appropriate steps').[415] Among other things, the obligation means that the authorities must provide a legislative and administrative framework capable of fending off threats to the right to life ('effective deterrence'). At any rate, states (as we have seen in the consideration from the *Osman* judgment presented above) must have 'effective criminal-law provisions [...] backed up by law-enforcement machinery for the prevention, suppression and sanctioning of breaches of such provisions.').[416] Depending on the situations involved, the authorities can also be required to provide licensing systems, supervision structures and practical measures that eliminate the threat to life to all intents and purposes.[417] Each time, the question is whether the measure is appropriate, that is to say: whether the measure can reasonably be regarded as a suitable (effective) means to deal with the risk.[418] In the light of this, we are of the view that there is no reason to suppose that policies and measures for drugs and/or cannabis could not qualify as an appropriate measure. This means that insofar as a certain drug and/or cannabis policy can prevent risks to the right of life, for example by actually reducing criminal activities connected with cannabis cultivation and trade such as murder and manslaughter or hemp nursery fires and seriously harmful infections, this policy in principle comes under the regime of positive obligations pursuant to Article 2 ECHR. However, this does not mean that Article 2 ECHR then inexorably necessitates implementation of that drug and/or cannabis policy.

It is also important that the authorities are not bound to eliminate every risk, not even if there are risks to life. The point here is that there is no obligation to achieve the 'full realization' of the right to life (in contrast

[415] See for example ECtHR (Grand Chamber) 30 November 2004, *Öneryildiz/Turkey*, no. 48939/99, para. 94; ECtHR 26 February 2015, *Prilutskiy/Ukraine*, no. 40429/08, para. 31.

[416] See also for example ECtHR 10 October 2000, *Akkoç/Turkey*, no. 22947/93, para. 87–94, in which the Court roundly criticizes the criminal law procedures in a certain region.

[417] See ECtHR (Grand Chamber) 30 November 2004, *Öneryildiz/Turkey*, no. 48939/99, para. 90.

[418] See ibid, para. 107.

to the obligation with respect to the right to health in the ICESCR and the ESC). First of all, the positive obligation to take measures is limited in the sense that states do not have to take unrealistic or disproportionately onerous measures. In particular, one must take into account the difficulties for authorities to keep an eye on modern society with the unpredictability of human behaviour and the operational choices that must be made, in terms of priorities and resources.[419] Secondly, individuals also bear responsibilities. If they neglect these, it may mean that the adverse consequences for the victim's life are not borne by the state.[420] That is certainly the case with drug use.[421] When we observe that authorities cannot be required to eliminate each and every risk to life, that is not to say that no measures need to be taken at all. Fundamentally, it is about states taking appropriate measures that can actually be implemented reasonably. To the extent that a certain policy on drugs and/or cannabis is an effective measure to protect life and the authorities are of the opinion that this policy is the appropriate solution, this policy falls within the regime of positive obligations to take preventive measures. However, if subsequently someone dies from overdosing on hard drugs in spite of that policy, this will not easily entail violation of Article 2 ECHR by the state. Thirdly, the ECtHR takes the view that the positive obligations pursuant to Article 2 ECHR must not be based on a paternalistic vision.[422] The Court points out that the notion of personal autonomy is an important part of the ECHR. Individuals have a choice to take up activities that are physically or morally harmful or risky. The Court points out that undue interference by the state in this freedom can be at odds with the convention. We will briefly return to this topic in section 2.4.11, when we look at the ECtHR's approach of alcohol, tobacco and drugs. What is important here is that if a state takes certain measures to protect life from a paternalistic point of view, these measures in principle will not qualify as measures that the state is required to take because of its positive obligations. Any regulated permission of cannabis cultivation and trade for the recreational user market, however, can hardly be seen as paternalistic. In that respect too, there is no reason to suppose that such a policy would not fall under the regime of positive obligations to take preventative measures. Worded in a positive way, it means that states could use such a policy to fulfil their positive obligations of protection.

---

419 See ECtHR 26 February 2015, *Prilutskiy/Ukraine*, no. 40429/08, para. 33; ECtHR (Grand Chamber) 30 November 2004, *Öneryildiz/Turkey*, no. 48939/99, para. 107; ECtHR 9 June 2009, *Opuz/Turkey*, no. 33401/02, para. 129.

420 ECtHR 2 February 2016, *Cavit Tinarlioğlu/Turquie*, no. 3648/04, para. 108.

421 ECtHR 4 January 2008, *Shelley/The UK*, no. 23800/06, para. 2 (sixth paragraph).

422 ECtHR 26 February 2015, *Prilutskiy/Ukraine*, no. 40429/08, para. 32.

We conclude that states can fulfil their positive obligations (derived from Article 2 ECHR by the ECtHR) to take all appropriate measures by adopting a policy on drugs and/or cannabis that protects life. This is the case, among other things, if there really is a slightly general serious risk in connection with cannabis cultivation and trade of concrete serious threats to the right of life because of, for example, murder and manslaughter and/or hemp nursery fires and seriously harmful infections, and that specific policy on drugs and/or cannabis is an effective measure to protect life from these risks, and the authorities are of the opinion that this policy is the most appropriate solution. This therefore also applies if that policy on drugs and/or cannabis entails that cannabis cultivation and trade for recreational users must be permitted under regulation.

- *Protection of life from health threats*. The ECtHR infers positive obligations to protect public health from Article 2 ECHR as well.[423] Protection against dangerous situations and activities in industry and nature also falls within the scope of these obligations.[424] The obligation to take '*all appropriate steps to safeguard*' the lives of people enters into this issue in the same way as detailed above, for which reason we will base our argument here on it. The question is whether the introduction of a policy on drugs and/or cannabis aimed at preventing soft drug users from sliding into a life-threatening habit of hard drug use can, under certain circumstances, qualify as fulfilling the positive obligation to protect life against health problems.

Firstly, it is important whether protection from life-threatening hard drug use in principle falls inside the scope of the positive obligations pursuant to Article 2 ECHR. As we have seen before, the positive obligation to take all appropriate steps has a wide range of application. We noted earlier that the healthcare sector also falls under it in some respects,[425] and the same goes for threats to life by dangerous substances such as asbestos,[426] toxic emissions,[427] exposure to radiation,[428] and insufficient protection against the transmission of contagious diseases such as hepatitis C.[429] Against this backdrop, it is implausible that the protection of citizens against life-threatening hard

423 Ingrid A.E.M. Leijten, *Core Rights and the Protection of Socio-Economic Interests by the European Court of Human Rights* (diss. Leiden), Leiden, 2015, pp. 351–359; David J. Harris, Michael O'Boyle, Ed P. Bates & Carla M. Buckley (eds.), *Harris, O'Boyle & Warbrick, Law of the European Convention on Human Rights*, Oxford: Oxford University Press, 2014, pp. 212–214.

424 See the elaborate overview of case law in ECtHR 2 February 2016, *Cavit Tinarlioğlu/Turquie*, no. 3648/04, para. 62–78.

425 ECtHR 17 January 2008, *Dodov/Bulgaria*, no. 59548/00, para. 70, 79–83 and 87.

426 ECtHR 24 July 2014, *Brincat/Malta*, no. 60908/11, para. 103–117.

427 ECtHR (Grand Chamber) 19 February 1998, *Guerra/Italy*, no. 14967/89, para. 60, 62.

428 ECtHR 9 June 1998, *L.C.B./The UK*, no. 23413/94, para. 36.

429 ECtHR 1 December 2009, *G.N./Italy*, no. 43134/05, para. 69; for references to cases about all sorts of other diseases, see ECtHR 24 July 2014, *Brincat/Malta*, no. 60908/11, para. 82.

drug use (or the seriously harmful infections discussed above) is irrelevant with regard to the positive obligation to take appropriate steps to safeguard the lives of people.

Secondly, we saw that this positive obligation is also broad in content: nearly all conceivable measures can be appropriate under this obligation. Thus, it is hard to see why a policy on drugs and/or cannabis to prevent deaths in society could not be valid method of fulfilling the positive obligation of protection. This will also have to apply if that policy aims to stop soft drug users from sliding into a life-threatening habit of hard drug use (or at preventing seriously harmful infections, as discussed before). In principle, this means that the separation of the soft drugs and hard drugs markets, insofar as this separation actually truly leads to fewer drug deaths, also falls within the regime of positive obligations to protect public health. However, this applies to a lesser extent, insofar as the drug user is partly responsible for the situation.

The obligation to protect life against serious health risks thereby supports the conclusion drawn before: states can fulfil their positive obligations (derived from Article 2 ECHR by the ECtHR) to take all appropriate measures by adopting a policy on drugs and/or cannabis that permits cannabis cultivation and trade under regulation. This is the case if there is a slightly general serious risk of death as a result of hard drug use, while the separation of the soft drugs and hard drugs markets is an effective measure to protect society against that risk and the authorities are of the opinion that this policy is the appropriate solution. The same conclusion applies, mutatis mutandis, as we have seen before, in the case of fighting seriously harmful infections caused by unsafe installations in hemp nurseries.

iv. Summary of Findings Regarding Article 6 ICCPR and Article 2 ECHR

From the obligation to protect life pursuant to Article 6 ICCPR and Article 2 ECHR, the Human Rights Committee and the ECtHR have concluded that states have the positive obligation to protect citizens from life-threatening crime and health risks. States must take (all) appropriate measures to prevent those dangers from presenting themselves. The introduction of a policy on drugs and/or cannabis that permits the cultivation and trade of cannabis for the recreational consumer market may under certain circumstances qualify as a fulfilment of the positive obligation of protection. This is also the case if the following conditions are met:

In the first place, there must really be a slightly general serious risk of and/or concrete serious threats to the lives of citizens. This condition is met if illegal cannabis cultivation and trade is accompanied by for example murder, manslaughter, hemp nursery fires and/or seriously harmful infections, such as Legionella or if a situation arises in which soft drug users slide into a life-threatening habit of hard drug use. However, the right to life does not give rise to positive obligations to protect against non-life threatening situations, such as organized crime as such, corruption in the upper world (undermining) and nuisance and damage.

Secondly, the above-mentioned policy on drugs and/or cannabis must be an effective measure to protect the lives of citizens against the aforementioned risks. That effectiveness need not be proved by data, but must be based on adequate research and an adequate evaluation by the authorities.

Finally, the authorities must be of the opinion that this policy, also taking into account the social peculiarities and the constellation of their state, is likely to be the most successful solution to reduce the risks. As we saw just now, they will also have to substantiate this view.

If all these conditions are met, a state can fulfil its positive obligation of protection pursuant to the right of life through a policy on drugs and/or cannabis that permits regulated cannabis cultivation and trade for the recreational consumer market. Whether this involves merely a possible solution or a mandatory solution, will be discussed in section 2.4.11.

2.4.9. SPECIFIC POSITIVE OBLIGATIONS FLOWING FROM THE RIGHT NOT TO BE SUBJECTED TO INHUMAN TREATMENT

The expositions in sections 2.4.1–2.4.7 about the general obligations that states have under the ICCPR and the ECHR also apply to the right not to be subjected to inhuman treatment.[430] So subsequently, we will now focus on the positive obligations connected with the right not to be subjected to inhuman treatment which bear on the cannabis issue.

i. The Protection Requirement in Article 7 ICCPR and Article 3 ECHR

Neither Article 7 ICCPR nor Article 3 ECHR explicitly states in any way that protection must be offered against inhuman treatment.[431] The provisions only say that 'No one shall be subjected' to it. Nevertheless, both the Human Rights Committee and the ECtHR require that the state offers protection against the acts prohibited by Article 7 ICCPR and Article 3 ECHR, whether committed by state authorities or by private persons.[432] The following discussion of jurisprudence

430 For a brief overview of the most relevant points, see the beginning of section 2.4.8.

431 For the text of the provisions see section 2.4.2.

432 See HRC, General Comment No. 20 (1992) 'Prohibition of torture and inhuman treatment', para. 2, and ECtHR 4 December 2003, *M.C./Bulgaria*, no. 39272/98, para. 149–166, and with further references David J. Harris, Michael O'Boyle, Ed P. Bates & Carla M. Buckley (eds.), *Harris, O'Boyle & Warbrick, Law of the European Convention on Human Rights*, Oxford: Oxford University Press, 2014, pp. 274–277.

and case law of these bodies about these provisions of the conventions seeks to answer the following question in particular:

> Does the positive obligation to protect citizens from crime that violates their physical integrity necessitate the prevention and fight against crime that goes hand in hand with cannabis cultivation and trade, such as assault and serious health risks incurred by citizens because of fire or seriously harmful infections caused by unsafe and illegal installations for illegal hemp nurseries?

Insofar as the answer turns out to be yes, a second question presents itself:

> Can the positive obligation for protection be fulfilled by a drug and/or cannabis policy that permits regulated cannabis cultivation and trade for recreational users?

These questions will now be dealt with in this order for the ICCPR and the ECHR. The regime of positive obligations in connection with the right not to be subjected to inhuman treatment is very similar to that of the right to life discussed above. To avoid repetition, the exposition below will be less elaborate than the previous one. To answer the above-mentioned questions, we will concentrate on the scope of the obligation of protection (protection must be offered against what exactly?) and what that protection must involve (which measures?). Because preventive measures are particularly relevant for the cannabis issue, we will primarily focus on these rather than repressive and redressive measures. Insofar as the second question above is answered in the affirmative, again the question rises whether it involves merely an acceptable method to meet the obligation or a mandatory one in principle. We will answer this question in section 2.4.12.

ii. Positive Obligations Pursuant to Article 7 ICCPR

As we explained in section 2.4.4.ii, Article 7 ICCPR covers acts that cause severe physical pain and/or mental suffering or have adverse physical or psychological effects, such as aggravated assault. That also applies if it is caused by private persons. In the above-mentioned section, we concluded that grievous bodily harm and causing severe burns and seriously harmful infections are covered in principle by the concept of 'inhuman treatment'. On the other hand, this is not the case for nuisance caused by cannabis cultivation and trade, unless this actually caused intense psychological suffering. Nor does the scope of the right not to be subjected to inhuman treatment in principle cover serious health problems caused by using hard drugs, unless these are directly caused by others, as would be the case with involuntary administration of hard drugs.

It now boils down to the question which measures states must take on account of the right not to be subjected to inhuman treatment in Article 7 ICCPR so as to prevent a situation where cannabis cultivation and trade lead to aggravated assault, dangerous fires and seriously harmful infections. In general, the same measures as discussed earlier in the context of the right to life are then required. The following applies to Article 7 ICCPR according to the Human Rights Committee:

> It is the duty of the State party to afford everyone protection through legislative and other measures as may be necessary against the acts prohibited by article 7, whether inflicted by people acting in their official capacity, outside their official capacity or in a private capacity.[433]

Measures are not restricted to specific measures: all sorts of useful measures ('other measures') can fall under the obligation to take measures, namely when these are relevant for preventing, punishing, investigating or redressing illegal serious violations of physical integrity.[434] Now too, the general obligation is important (discussed in section 2.4.7.v), namely that states are required to adopt legislative, judicial, administrative, educative and other appropriate measures to secure the human rights in the ICCPR. These obligations may relate to both slightly general (serious) risks for the physical and mental integrity of citizens and to concrete (serious) threats to that integrity. As far as the first category (of general (serious) risks) is concerned: according to the Human Rights Committee, states are required to take measures against for example domestic violence and female genital mutilation,[435] rape and indecent assault,[436] abduction of women[437] and the vulnerable position of elderly people in care homes.[438] In the light of this, it is hard to imagine that a policy on drugs and/or cannabis that offers protection against inhuman treatment would not qualify as a strategy to fulfil the obligation to take measures.

---

433 See HRC, General Comment No. 20 (1992) 'Prohibition of torture and inhuman treatment', para. 2.

434 See for example ibid, paras. 2, 8, 13, 14.

435 See for example HRC, Concluding Observations (Sweden), *UN Doc.* CCPR A/57/40 vol. I (2002), para. 79(7), 79(8); HRC, Concluding Observations (Yemen), *UN Doc.* CCPR A/60/40 vol. I (2005), para. 12 (obligation to address domestic violence through campaigns to raise awareness, criminal law and stiffer sentences).

436 See for example HRC, Concluding Observations (Hungary), *UN Doc.* CCPR A/57/40 vol. I (2002), para. 80(10); HRC, Concluding Observations (Peru), *UN Doc.* CCPR A/52/40 vol. I (1997), para. 160 and 167.

437 HRC, Concluding Observations (Venezuela), *UN Doc.* CCPR A/56/40 vol. I (2001), para. 77(17).

438 See for example HRC, Concluding Observations (Germany), *UN Doc.* CCPR A/59/40 vol. I (2004), para. 68(17).

However, the obligation to do so only arises if that policy can be deemed necessary ('as may be necessary'). As we have repeatedly seen before (in particular in sections 2.4.7.viii and ix), it is first and foremost up to the national authorities to decide what is necessary given the social peculiarities and the constellation of the state in question. If the state is of the opinion that a certain measure is necessary, it will have to be able to make a convincing case for this. The necessity and therefore also the effectiveness of the measure must be made plausible.

We therefore conclude that pursuant to Article 7 in conjunction with Article 2 ICCPR, states must take protective and/or preventative measures when the physical integrity of citizens is actually threatened by the consequences of illegal cannabis cultivation and trade. This is the case if there is (a substantial risk of) aggravated assault, dangerous fires and seriously harmful infections. If the state authorities after careful consideration and with cogent reasons are of the opinion that the best protection against it is offered by permitting cannabis cultivation and trade for the recreational user market through regulation, this policy of permission qualifies as a fulfilment of that state's positive obligation of protection.

iii. Positive Obligations Pursuant to Article 3 ECHR

As we explained in section 2.4.4.ii, Article 3 ECHR covers acts with 'a minimum level of severity', and this is usually the case if there is physical injury or intense physical or mental suffering, even if caused by private persons. So we concluded in section 2.4.4.ii that grievous bodily harm and causing severe burns and seriously harmful infections are in principle within the scope of the concept of 'inhuman treatment', but that this is not the case for nuisance caused by cannabis cultivation and trade or for serious health problems caused by using hard drugs.

Which measures must states take on account of the right not to be subjected to inhuman treatment in Article 3 ECHR so as to prevent cannabis cultivation and trade from leading to aggravated assault, dangerous fires and seriously harmful infections? Here too, in general states are required to take the same measures as those discussed with regard to the right to life, albeit that case law about positive obligations pursuant to Article 3 ECHR is more general in nature than that about Article 2 ECHR.[439] Settled case law of the ECtHR entails:

> Article 3, requires States to take measures designed to ensure that individuals within their jurisdiction are not subjected to ill-treatment, including ill-treatment administered by private individuals.[440]

---

[439] See the overviews in ECtHR 4 December 2003, *M.C./Bulgaria*, no. 39272/98, para. 149–166; ECtHR 3 March 2014, *Amadayev/Russia*, no. 18114/06, para. 68–72.

[440] ECtHR 4 December 2003, *M.C./Bulgaria*, no. 39272/98, para. 149; ECtHR 28 March 2000, *Mahmut Kaya/Turkey*, no. 22535/93, para. 115.

Among other things, it means that 'the framework of law' will have to provide adequate protection.[441] As we already saw in section 2.4.7.v, the state has a general obligation to take 'appropriate steps' and provide 'the implementation of a national system capable of securing compliance with the Convention'. At the same time, the principle is that acts that are contrary to Article 3 ECHR do not lead to liability on the part of the state party if they were not committed by state authorities.[442] Here, the ECtHR is referring to liability for the concrete act as such. This does not diminish the obligation of states to provide a general protective legal framework.

It goes without saying that the nature of 'the framework of law' does not have to be such that it guarantees there will never be any act any more that is contrary to Article 3 ECHR.[443] With regard to the positive obligation to prevent such acts in general, a state will only be liable to breaching that obligation if the national legal system failed to provide 'practical and effective protection'. Since a state is not required to prevent each and every eventuality, such a failure will only happen in reality for slightly general (serious) risks to the physical and mental integrity of citizens, for example when cannabis cultivation and trade actually lead to a (substantial risk of) aggravated assault, dangerous fires and seriously harmful infections. A drug and/or cannabis policy that addresses such consequences is to that extent a relevant measure from the regime of positive obligations of Article 3 ECHR. In this respect, it is also important, as we have already discussed in sections 2.4.7.viii and ix in particular, that it is first and foremost up to the national authorities to decide which measures are necessary, given the social peculiarities and the constellation of the state in question. It is also primarily for the national authorities to decide which situations in that state necessitate protection in the sense of Article 3 ECHR (the principle of primarity).

This leads us to the conclusion that the positive obligation of protection applies if a state makes a considered and substantiated decision that pursuant to Article 3 ECHR, protection is necessary against aggravated assault, dangerous fires and seriously harmful infections in connection with cannabis cultivation and trade. If the state authorities (again after careful consideration and with cogent reasons) are then of the opinion that the protection is best achieved by permitting cannabis cultivation and trade for the recreational user market through regulation, such a policy of permission must qualify as a fulfilment of the positive obligation of protection.

---

441 ECtHR 28 March 2000, *Mahmut Kaya/Turkey*, no. 22535/93, para. 115.

442 ECtHR 16 June 2015, *Vasil Hristov/Bulgaria*, no. 81260/12, para. 37.

443 ECtHR 3 March 2014, *Amadayev/Russia*, no. 18114/06, para. 72.

iv. Summary of Findings Regarding Article 7 ICCPR and Article 3 ECHR

Although Article 7 ICCPR and Article 3 ECHR do not explicitly establish an obligation of protection, the jurisprudence of the Human Rights Committee and that of the ECtHR means that states have a positive obligation to protect citizens against acts that run counter to these provisions. To prevent these acts or their consequences from manifesting themselves, states are required to take appropriate measures against them, partly by providing an adequate protective legal framework. The introduction of a policy on drugs and/or cannabis that permits the cultivation and trade of cannabis for the recreational consumer market may under certain circumstances qualify as a fulfilment of these positive obligation of protection. This is the case if – mutatis mutandis – the same conditions are met as those that we discussed earlier in relation to the right to life. Thus, first of all there must be a real slightly general (serious) risk for and/or concrete (serious threats) to the physical or mental integrity of citizens as a consequence of the acts by others. This involves acts causing serious physical pain and/or severe mental suffering and/or physical injury. The obligation of taking preventative measures is also applicable to acts by private persons, such As grievous bodily harm, causing severe burns and seriously harmful infections that occur in connection with or as a result of cannabis cultivation and trade. However, in principle the positive obligations to protect against inhuman treatment do not have any bearing on the nuisance caused by cannabis cultivation and trade nor on the serious health problems arising from the use of hard drugs. Secondly, the aforementioned policy on drugs and/or cannabis will have to be effective to protect the physical and mental integrity against the above-mentioned acts. The authorities will have to make that effectiveness plausible. Finally, here too the authorities must be of the opinion, after careful consideration and substantiation, that this policy, also taking into account the social peculiarities and the constellation of their state, is the best possible solution to reduce the risks. If all these conditions are met, a state can fulfil its positive obligation of protection (pursuant to their citizen's right not to be subjected to inhuman treatment) through a policy on drugs and/or cannabis that permits regulated cannabis cultivation and trade for the recreational consumer market. Whether this involves a possible solution or a mandatory solution, will be discussed in section 2.4.12.

2.4.10. SPECIFIC POSITIVE OBLIGATIONS FLOWING FROM THE RIGHT TO A PRIVATE LIFE

Finally, the discussions in sections 2.4.1–2.4.7 about the general obligations that states have under the ICCPR and the ECHR also apply to the right to a private life[444] Building on these expositions, we will now discuss the relevant positive obligations connected with the right to a private life which bear on the cannabis issue.

i. The Protection Requirement in Article 17 ICCPR and Article 8 ECHR

Whereas according to Article 17(2) ICCPR everyone has a right to protection by 'the law' against arbitrary or illegal interference in his or her private life, the text of Article 8 ECHR only requires 'respect' for privacy. Yet, not only the Human Rights Committee but also the ECtHR requires that the state offers protection against unlawful violations of privacy, also if these are committed by private persons.[445] In our discussion below of the jurisprudence of these bodies, the following questions take centre stage:

> Does the positive obligation to protect the citizen's right to privacy from unlawful violations of that right necessitate the prevention of and fight against serious nuisance and harm that go hand in hand with cannabis cultivation and trade, such as stench, noise, flooding, fire and seriously harmful infections and peripheral crime, such as assault and serious threats?
>
> Does the positive obligation to protect the physical and mental integrity of citizens on the grounds of the right to privacy necessitate the prevention of the use of hard drugs, and is the argument of the distinction between the soft drugs market and the hard drugs market relevant in this context?

Insofar as the answer to at least one of these questions is affirmative, a third question presents itself:

> Can the positive obligation for protection be fulfilled by a drug and/or cannabis policy that permits regulated cannabis cultivation and trade for recreational users?

In the discussion of these questions for the ICCPR and the ECHR respectively, it is important that the regime of positive obligations in connection with the right to a private life bears a great deal of similarity with the positive obligations that apply to the right to life and the right not to be subjected to inhuman treatment. To avoid repetition, the following will concentrate on the scope

---

444 For a brief overview of the most relevant points, see the beginning of section 2.4.8.

445 See HRC, General Comment No. 16 (1988) 'Right to privacy', para. 1, and ECtHR 4 December 2003, *M.C./Bulgaria*, no. 39272/98, para. 150–166 and 185–187, and with further references David J. Harris, Michael O'Boyle, Ed P. Bates & Carla M. Buckley (eds.), *Harris, O'Boyle & Warbrick, Law of the European Convention on Human Rights*, Oxford: Oxford University Press, 2014, pp. 523, 532–536.

of the protection obligation as much as possible (protection must be offered against what exactly?) and on the required nature of that protection (which measures?). Given the relevance for the cannabis issue, with these measures we will focus on preventative measures rather than repressive and redressive measures. Insofar as the third question above is answered in the affirmative, again the question rises whether it involves merely an acceptable method to meet the obligation or a mandatory one in principle. We will answer this question in section 2.4.11.

ii. Positive Obligations Pursuant to Article 17(2) ICCPR

As we saw above in section 2.4.4.iii, the scope of the protection of Article 17 ICCPR is unclear. However, we did establish that at any rate it is more limited than that of Article 8 ECHR which we will discuss later. It led us to the following conclusions: Insofar as nuisance and damage (such as considerable stench, noise, flooding, fire and seriously harmful infections) and peripheral criminality (such as assault and threats) lead to limitation of the enjoyment of a person's private life, this probably falls under the regime of positive obligations of Article 17 ICCPR. That is the case if that limitation of privacy is essential and fairly directly relates to the private life in the strict sense. In principle, that is the case with acts involving a person's home, but not necessarily with acts that are limited to an infringement of the physical and mental integrity of an individual. Thus, the relevance of Article 17 ICCPR for the cannabis issue is fairly limited. This is the more so because there is hardly any reason to suppose that according to the Committee Article 17 ICCPR also serves to protect citizens against the consequences of their uses of hard drugs. The argument of the distinction between the soft drugs and hard drugs markets is therefore probably not relevant here. This answers the second question in the previous subsection negatively.

Now the question is which measures states must take because of the right to a private life in Article 17 ICCPR so as to stop cannabis cultivation and trade from causing, among other things, considerable stench, noise, flooding, fire, seriously harmful infections, assault and/or threats in the private domain. This cannot be determined precisely. The positive obligation to protect citizens from acts of private persons who unlawfully interfere with the private lives of citizens has hardly been elaborated in the jurisprudence of the Committee. At any rate, the general obligation from Article 2 ICCPR as discussed in section 2.4.7.v is applicable. Therefore, the states parties are required to take all measures 'as may be necessary' to effectuate and/or guarantee the right. With regard to Article 17 ICCPR, the Committee basically only adds that states are required to take legislative and other measures to protect the right and to effectuate the prohibition on unlawful interference with a person's private life.[446] The parties responsible for that are the legislator, the administration, the judiciary and other relevant national organs. In itself, a policy on drugs and/or cannabis that offers protection against unlawful interference with someone's private life will therefore qualify as fulfilment of the obligation to take measures.

The question, though, is whether such a policy can be seen as necessary. After all, the Committee does not see the obligation of protection of Article 17 ICCPR as wide-ranging, but limits it to essential and fairly direct interference with privacy, for example in the case of direct disruption of the enjoyment of one's home. A policy on drugs and/or cannabis does not directly have anything to do with that as such. At the same time, it is first and foremost up to the national authorities to decide which measures will best prevent threats of infringements of this right. If a state makes a considered and substantiated decision that certain acts (such as considerable stench, noise, flooding, fire, seriously harmful infections, assault and/or threats touching upon the private domain) related to cannabis cultivation and trade can adequately be prevented by a certain drug policy, then the policy will have to qualify as fulfilment of the positive obligation of protection pursuant to Article 17 ICCPR. This also applies if that policy involves permitting the cultivation and trade of cannabis for the recreational user market. After all, it is the result that matters: achieving an effective general protection whereby unlawful interference with a person's private life is prevented.

iii. Positive Obligations Pursuant to Article 8(1) ECHR

As we explained in section 2.4.4.iii, Article 8(1) ECHR encompasses acts that impact on the physical or psychological integrity or identity of a person and have a 'minimum level of severity'. The positive obligation of protection mentioned in Article 8 ECHR overlaps with that of Article 3 ECHR.[447] We concluded in the above-mentioned section that considerable nuisance and damage caused by stench, noise, flooding, fire and seriously harmful infections well as peripheral crime such as assault and serious threats are relevant for this provision. In principle, the same applies to the risk posed to the physical and mental integrity of citizens caused by their use of hard drugs. The argument of the distinction between the soft drugs and hard drugs markets is therefore probably relevant for Article 8 ECHR. In view of the drug user's own responsibility, however, that applies to a lesser degree.

---

[446] HRC, General Comment No. 16 (1988) 'Right to privacy', para. 1.

[447] See among other sources ECtHR 4 December 2003, *M.C./Bulgaria*, no. 39272/98, para. 148–187.

Which preventative measures must be taken by states against these acts and consequences? Again, what matters most are the general obligations discussed in section 2.4.7.v that apply to all states parties pursuant to Article 1 ECHR. It concerns an obligation to achieve a result, so essentially states must take all appropriate steps to secure the convention rights. The case law of the ECtHR contains further requirements regarding the right to a private life, albeit that they are much less precise than those for the right to life in Article 2 ECHR discussed before. Settled case law of the ECtHR on Article 8 ECHR means that this provision can even require measures to protect privacy in situations that are restricted to interactions between private individuals to which the government as such is no party.[448] With respect to the time when such measures need to be taken, the following consideration of the Court provides some clarification:

> The Court has previously held, in various contexts, that the concept of private life includes a person's physical and psychological integrity and that the States have a *positive obligation to prevent breaches of the physical and moral integrity* of an individual by other persons when the *authorities knew or ought to have known* of those breaches [...]. The Court has also held that a positive obligation exists upon States to *ensure respect for human dignity and the quality of life* in certain respects (emphasis added).[449]

The ECtHR emphasizes in a general sense that states must prevent unlawful interference with privacy and that in certain ways they must ensure respect for human dignity and the quality of life. In other words, this concerns obligations to take measures before an actual instance of unlawful interference with privacy has taken place. The general obligation under Article 1 ECHR also means that in this sense general measures to protect privacy need to be taken, as we saw in the relevant discussion of that obligation. It also shows from the positive obligation imposed by the ECtHR to protect privacy with an 'effective judicial system'.[450] The Court also requires effective deterrents against grave acts such as rape for protection in the sense of Article 8 ECHR.[451] To that end, such acts must among other things be criminalized, and if such offences are committed, criminal enquiries, prosecution, conviction and sentencing must be possible.[452] All these requirements imply that the state must take all manner of measures to

448 For more references to case law see ECtHR 26 July 2011, *Georgel and Georgeta Stoicescu/Romania*, no. 9718/03, para. 48.

449 Ibid, para. 49.

450 See ibid, para. 52.

451 ECtHR 4 December 2003, *M.C./Bulgaria*, no. 39272/98, para. 150.

452 See among other sources ECtHR 4 December 2003, *M.C./Bulgaria*, no. 39272/98, para. 150–153; ECtHR 4 January 2007, *Szula/The UK*, no. 18727/06, para. 1.

prevent unlawful violations of the right under Article 8 ECHR and to be able to take action if such violations still happen despite these preventative measures. Does that also apply to non-acceptable consequences for someone's private life that are connected with cannabis cultivation and trade?

Considering the above-mentioned obligations to take general preventative measures, it is important what exactly is the meaning of the requirement that the authorities 'knew or ought to have known' about the violations. That meaning will have to depend on the type of measure the state is required to adopt. For example, the obligation to protect specific persons operationally from concrete interference with their private lives such as assault or serious threats may only arise if the authorities knew or should have known of the real and present danger for the individual involved.[453] However, in the case of the obligation to adopt general preventative measures, this requirement of course cannot be applied, since it would gravely undermine this obligation. After all, the state would otherwise only have to take measures against whatever threat to the right of privacy if the authorities were aware that this threat would specifically exist with regard to a specific person. The general preventative measures discussed above that states are compelled to adopt show that this is quite clearly not the Court's intention. It is also clear from the fact that the Court assumes violations of Article 8 ECHR because the government has not sufficiently prevented or checked situations that violate the right to a private life, when those authorities did not know which specific individuals were affected by these situations.[454] The crux of the matter is that the authorities know or ought to know that there are certain concrete risks for the right to a private life.[455] If that is the case, they will have to take general preventative measures against it. That means that when the authorities become aware of the fact that cannabis cultivation and trade involve serious levels of stench, noise, flooding, fire, seriously harmful infections, assault and/or threats, the state is compelled to adopt measures to address these problems. That also applies if the state knows or must know that the use of hard drugs has serious consequences for the physical and mental integrity of many people.

To decide which preventative measures must be adopted, the ECtHR offers some criteria.[456] Insofar as this is relevant here, the first thing that matters is the

453 ECtHR 16 July 2013, *Amadayev/Russia*, no. 61382/09, para. 71–75; ECtHR 24 July 2012, *Đorđević/Croatia*, no. 41526/10, para. 137–150; ECtHR 15 September 2009, *E.S./Slovakia*, no. 8227/04, para. 39–44; see also, albeit about Article 2 ECHR, ECtHR (Grand Chamber) 28 October 1998, *Osman/The UK*, no. 23452/94, para. 115–122.

454 See for example ECtHR 26 July 2011, *Georgel and Georgeta Stoicescu/Romania*, no. 9718/03, para. 53–63; ECtHR 16 November 2004, *Moreno Gomez/Spain*, no. 4143/02, para. 57–63.

455 See ECtHR 26 July 2011, *Georgel and Georgeta Stoicescu/Romania*, no. 9718/03, para. 56–57; ECtHR 16 November 2004, *Moreno Gomez/Spain*, no. 4143/02, para. 59.

456 The first four criteria mentioned below follow from, among other sources, ECtHR 26 July 2011, *Georgel and Georgeta Stoicescu/Romania*, no. 9718/03, para. 50–51, which refers to further case law.

importance of the interest at stake, as well as the question whether 'fundamental values' or 'essential aspects' of the private life are under threat. Secondly: with regard to the question whether adequate measures have been adopted, the Court also takes into account whether there is a discrepancy between the right and the administrative and legal practice and if the answer is yes, which consequences does this have for the individual? Thirdly, it is important to what extent a measure would encumber the authorities; measures that are impossible or disproportionately cumbersome for the authorities do not need to be taken in any case. Finally, states are not required to counteract each and every danger. That is already the case for risks to life and risks of inhuman treatment, and so this should be the case *a fortiori* when dealing with an unacceptable impact on privacy.[457]

What does this mean for the cannabis issue? We have explained above that if there are serious levels of stench, noise, flooding, fire, seriously harmful infections, assault, threats and/or serious health problems as a result of the use of hard drugs, this falls in the scope of Article 8 ECHR. As the consequences for the individual become more serious, the importance for the individual increases as well and stricter requirements for the measures that must be adopted will be imposed, in accordance with the first criterion. This applies in particular if for example the private domain of the individual's home is involved as well, since a 'fundamental value' and an 'essential aspect' of a private life is at stake even more clearly in that case. The second criterion is more cryptic. It seems to mean primarily that protection should not be arbitrary. It is unclear to what extent the discrepancies in the current cannabis policy are relevant here. We are referring to the circumstance that in the Netherlands the sale of cannabis is banned by law, whereas in practice it is tolerated under regulation, but this does not apply to the supply of cannabis to the seller. It may be of importance to the extent that this causes an imbalance in the protection of citizens. Thirdly, the taxation criterion: that does not play a role if the state itself chooses the measure. Apart from that, in principle neither a policy that prohibits cannabis cultivation and trade, nor a policy that permits it in a regulated form seems to be impossible or disproportionately cumbersome for the authorities. Yet, none of these approaches in itself or in combination with other measures can prevent all unlawful interference with privacy. However, that does not mean, according to the fourth criterion, that such a policy does not adequately fulfil the positive obligations. That policy, however, will then have to make a truly positive contribution to preventing the above-mentioned unlawful interference in order to qualify as an acceptable execution of the positive obligation.

457 See ECtHR (Grand Chamber) 28 October 1998, *Osman/The UK*, no. 23452/94, para. 115 (with regard to Article 2 ECHR); ECtHR 23 November 2010, *P.F. and E.F./The UK*, no. 28326/09, para. 40 (with regard to Article 3 ECHR); ECtHR 26 July 2011, *Georgel and Georgeta Stoicescu/Romania*, no. 9718/03, para. 51 (with regard to Article 8 ECHR).

The conclusion in the light of the foregoing is that the positive obligation of protection pursuant to Article 8 ECHR entails that states must provide preventative measures against serious levels of stench, noise, flooding, fire, seriously harmful infections, assault and threats involved with the cultivation of and trade in cannabis and/or against serious health problems caused by the use of hard drugs. If the state authorities (after careful consideration and with cogent reasons) are then of the opinion that the required effective protection is best achieved by permitting cannabis cultivation and trade for the recreational user market through regulation, such a policy must qualify as a fulfilment of the positive obligation of protection.

iv. *Summary of Findings Regarding Article 17(2) ICCPR and Article 8(1) ECHR*

Article 17(2) ICCPR, unlike Article 8(1) ECHR, explicitly requires protection by 'the law'. Yet, the positive protection required by the ECtHR on the basis of the latter provision requires a considerably wider scope than the obligation of protection that becomes manifest in the jurisprudence of the Human Rights Committee. Pursuant to Article 17 ICCPR, preventative protective measures probably only need to be provided for serious levels of stench, noise, flooding, fire, seriously harmful infections, assault and threats insofar as these limitations of privacy are genuinely essential and fairly directly impact on the private life in the strict sense of the word. This does not apply for the positive obligation of protection of Article 8 ECHR. It also applies if these consequences and acts primarily affect the physical or psychological integrity of a person, as long as they are of a serious nature. The applicability is reduced to some extent with regard to the risk for the physical and mental integrity of citizens caused by their use of hard drugs. The argument of the distinction between the soft drugs and hard drugs markets is therefore probably relevant for Article 8 ECHR. However, it is probably not relevant for Article 17 ICCPR.

Insofar as states must provide positive protection pursuant to the right to privacy, they are required to adopt effective general preventative measures as well. If implementation of a policy on drugs and/or cannabis that permits cultivation of and trade in cannabis for recreational use can genuinely prevent the above-mentioned unlawfully interference with the private lives of citizens, the state can thereby fulfil its positive obligation of protection. However, this is subject to meeting the conditions that already came to the fore in relation to the right to life and the right not to be subjected to inhuman treatment. Mutatis mutandis, that means in this case: 1. there must really be a slightly general serious risk and/or concrete serious threats to what a private life aims to protect; 2. the authorities will have to make plausible that the above-mentioned policy on drugs and/or cannabis is an effective measure to help stave off the above-mentioned threats; 3. the authorities must be of the opinion, after careful consideration and substantiation, that this policy, also taking into account the social peculiarities and the constellation of their state, is the most adequate solution to reduce the risks.

If all these conditions are met, a state can fulfil its positive obligation of protection pursuant to the right of privacy through a policy on drugs and/or cannabis that permits regulated cannabis cultivation and trade for the recreational consumer market. Whether this involves a possible solution or a mandatory solution, will be discussed in section 2.4.12.

2.4.11. DRUGS, ALCOHOL AND TOBACCO AND THE RIGHT TO HEALTH IN THE ICCPR AND THE ECHR

The ICCPR and the ECHR do not contain provisions that explicitly aim to protect against or combat alcohol, tobacco and drugs.[458] The protection or fight against these only plays a marginal part in the jurisprudence of the Human Rights Committee and the ECtHR. We have not been able to find clear positions of these organs on alcohol, tobacco and drugs, from which one can conclude that in their opinion cannabis use must be combated or conversely be permitted through legalization, decriminalization or a policy of tolerance.

In the case of *M.A.B., W.A.T. and J.-A.Y.T.*, the Human Rights Committee is of the opinion that the worship and distribution of a narcotic drug (in this case cannabis) does not fall within the scope of the right to religion in Article 18 ICCPR.[459] Neither does the right not to be subjected to arbitrary deprivation of liberty in Article 9 ICCPR preclude arrest on the grounds of possession or distribution of drugs. The committee does not state an opinion one way or another about the desirability of drug use or drug prohibitions.

The *Prince* case is also worth mentioning as it revolved around Rastafarians. The Committee makes it clear that if cannabis possession and use is part of a religion that is also recognized as such under Article 18 ICCPR, the state is entitled to prohibit such possession and use subject to the condition of the third paragraph of this provision.[460] In that case, prohibition is also allowed with respect to the equality principle and the non-discrimination principle in Article 26 ICCPR and the right to enjoy one's own culture and profess and practise one's religion in Article 27 ICCPR.[461] The Committee recognizes that a state has the right to prohibit cannabis if that state deems this to be necessary in order to protect public safety, public order, public health, public decency or the fundamental rights and freedoms of other people in the light of the harmful

458 However, Article 5(1)e ECHR recognizes the possibility of lawful detention of alcohol or drug addicts.
459 HRC 8 April 1994, *M.A.B., W.A.T. and J.-A.Y.T./Canada*, no. 570/93, para. 4.2.
460 HRC 31 October 2007, *Prince/South Africa*, no. 1474/06, para. 7.2–7.3.
461 Ibid, para. 7.5 and 7.4 respectively.

effects of cannabis. Here too, the Committee does not state an opinion one way or another about the desirability of drug use or drug prohibitions.

However, for the sake of its Concluding Observations in connection with the right to life, the Human Rights Committee has asked states whether they for example have legislation that prohibits the use of drugs for any reasons other than medical ones,[462] implement educational measures to prevent the use of narcotic drugs,[463] and take measures to discourage the trade in drugs.[464] However, this is hardly relevant for the cannabis issue, since in principle cannabis is not a life-threatening drug Furthermore, the Committee urges states to prevent and treat HIV/AIDS, also if it involves drug users.[465] This is relevant up to a point, in the sense that the argument of the division between the soft drugs market and the hard drugs market can be important with respect to preventing life-threatening diseases as a result of intravenous drug use.

Finally, we will mention that the Committee rejects a 'zero tolerance' drug policy. Instead, states should adopt an approach based on human rights in dealing with the problem of drug use. The emphasis should be on adequate healthcare, psychological support and rehabilitation drug users, including treatment of drug addiction, such as opioid substitution therapy and harm reduction programmes.[466] In doing so, the Committee chooses an approach based on individual and public health, instead of a prohibitive and repressive one.

In 2000, the ECtHR arrived at an interesting consideration in the *Marlow* case.[467] Marlow had published a book about the cultivation and production of cannabis. He was subsequently prosecuted and convicted for inciting cannabis cultivation. Marlow was of the opinion that among other things, his conviction breached his right to freedom of expression in Article 10 ECHR. The ECtHR ruled as follows:

> In making its assessment the Court cannot overlook the fact that there is an increased public acceptance of cannabis for medicinal and recreational purposes and a vociferous lobby in favour of decriminalizing certain types of use. A number of Contracting Parties have moved in this direction. However it is impossible to say that there is a European consensus on the desirability of decriminalization. In the respondent State, it still remains a criminal offence, *inter alia*, to possess, produce and, of relevance to the

462 HRC, Concluding Observations (Italy), *UN Doc.* CCPR A/36/40 (1981), para. 115.

463 HRC, Concluding Observations (Federal Republic of Germany), *UN Doc.* CCPR A/33/40 (1978), para. 341.

464 HRC, Concluding Observations (Panama), *UN Doc.* CCPR A/46/40 (1991), para. 431,433.

465 See the following, with references to considerations of the Human Rights Committee: Rick Lines, *International Human Rights Jurisprudence on Issues relating to Drug Use and Harm Reduction*, New York: Open Society Institute, 2007, pp. 3–4.

466 HRC, Concluding Observations (Georgia), *UN Doc.* CCPR C/GEO/CO/4 (2014), under C.

467 ECtHR 5 December 2000, *Marlow/The UK*, No. 42015/98, para. 1.

> instant case, to incite others to produce cannabis. In the Court's opinion, the decision to maintain on the statute book an offence of incitement to produce cannabis and to penalize authors of publications which serve this end must be considered to fall within the respondent State's margin of appreciation.

The Court concludes that there had been no violation of Article 10 ECHR in Marlow's case. The interesting thing about the consideration above is that the Court shows it is not blind to social developments in connection with cannabis, but that it still remains neutral with respect to the question whether these are desirable or not.[468] The fact that the Court has shifted its position in this respect, becomes clear when comparing its findings in this case with a case of four years earlier, from 1996. The *C./Belgium* case was about the extradition of plaintiff from Belgium because of his involvement with the sale of more than 17 kilograms of cannabis. The Court judged that the extradition was not in breach of Article 8 ECHR. The following was one of its considerations: 'The applicant had assisted in the sale of more than 17 kilograms of cannabis. In the light of the ravages of drugs among the population, and especially among young people, it is not surprising that the authorities show great firmness with regard to those who actively contribute to the spread of this scourge.'[469] According to the Court, it usually cannot reasonably be maintained that drug use and drug consumption constitute a serious threat to public order, not even if hard drugs are part of the equation.[470]

The current reserve displayed by the Court in a judgment about cannabis and the policies on it also shows in the fairly recent Dutch coffee shop case of *De Bruin*. The ECtHR considers the following in this:

> The Court takes note in the instant case of section 3 of the Opium Act, by virtue of which the retail of soft drugs is, per se, illegal [...]. This does not, in itself, raise any issue under the Convention: it should be recalled that the Convention leaves States free to designate as a criminal offence an act or omission not constituting the normal exercise of one of the rights that it protects [...]. It may well be that public authority tolerates transgressions of that prohibition to a certain extent, or subject to certain conditions.

468 Cf. European Commission of Human Rights 25 May 1997, *Larmela/Finland*, no. 26712/95.

469 ECtHR 7 August 1996, *C./Belgium*, no. 21794/93, para. 35. In the same sense, but then with regard to hard drugs (heroin) see ECtHR 12 January 2010, *Khan A.W./The UK*, no. 47486/06, para. 40; ECtHR 30 November 1999, *Baghli/France*, no. 34374/97, para. 48. Incidentally, in the case of hard drugs the Court is of the opinion: 'As it has pointed out on numerous occasions, in view of the ravages drugs cause it can see in particular why the authorities of the Contracting States are so firm towards those who contribute to the spread of this scourge, and it is fully aware of the need to combat drug trafficking and, accordingly, to secure fruitful cooperation between States in this area.'; see ECtHR (Grand Chamber) 29 March 2010, *Medvedyev/France*, no. 3394/03, para. 81.

470 ECtHR 26 June 2014, *Gablishvili/Russia*, no. 39428/12, para. 50 (heroin); ECtHR 13 February 2001, *Ezzouhdi/France*, no. 47160/99, para. 34 (heroin and cocaine).

> In this connection, it should be recalled that, save in so far as substantive provisions of the Convention may require the active prosecution of individuals reasonably suspected of being responsible for serious violations thereof [...], the decision whether or not to prosecute is not within the Court's remit. [...] It cannot follow, however, that a 'right' to commit acts prohibited by law can arise from the absence of sanctions, not even if public authority renounces the right to prosecute. Such renunciation, even if delivered in writing to a particular individual, is not to be equated with a licence granted in accordance with the law.[471]

So as far as the ECtHR is concerned, states are free to decide whether or not to criminalize the trade in drugs: they can do so, but they do not have to. The Court leaves the complex policy decisions on this issue to the national authorities.[472] The above consideration also illustrates that even if the national authorities have decided to criminalize acts involving soft drugs, there is no positive obligation to proceed with prosecution if the pertinent criminal offence has been committed. If there is a policy of tolerance in place, however, that does not mean either that states would not be allowed to prosecute those who committed the offence. With regard to prosecution for offences involving cannabis, states are also free to decide whether or not to do that. Not only are states at liberty to decide which policy they may adopt with regard to criminalization and prosecution regarding cannabis, but it may also deviate from the policy concerning alcohol, for example.[473]

A few cases relate to the question whether states are required to introduce bans on smoking, because of the positive obligation to protect the right to life in Article 2 ECHR and the right to a private life in Article 8 ECHR. In the *Botti* case, the Court points out that there are different ways to protect convention rights.[474] The choice of measures to ensure compliance of convention law in the relation between individuals in principle falls within the state's margin of appreciation. For that reason, the Court does not consider the absence of a general smoking ban to be incompatible with Article 2 ECHR and Article 8 ECHR. In the *Wöckel* case, the erstwhile European Commission of Human Rights on similar grounds arrived at the conclusion that the absence of a general ban on advertising for tobacco products and smoking does not constitute a shortcoming in the protection required by these provisions.[475]

---

471 ECtHR 19 September 2013, *De Bruin/The Netherlands*, no. 9765/09, para. 56–58.

472 See also Egbert Myjer & Peter Kempees, 'Thoughts on the Positive Impact of Negative Case-Law', in: Luis López Guerra, Carmen Morte Gómez, Anna Maria Mengual I Mallol & Guillem Cano Palomares (eds.), *El Tribunal Europeo de Derechos Humanos. Una visión desde dentro. En homenaje al Juez Josep Casadevall*, Valencia: Tirant lo Blanch, 2015, pp. 343–356 in para. 6.

473 ECtHR 19 September 2013, *De Bruin/The Netherlands*, no. 9765/09, para. 71.

474 ECtHR 2 December 2004, *Botti/Italy*, no. 77360/01, para. 1.

475 ECommHR 16 April 1998, *Wöckel/Germany*, no. 32165/96.

Finally, the *Barrett* case merits our attention.[476] It involved excessive alcohol consumption at a naval base. The Commission recognizes that if a state offers facilities for drinking alcohol in circumstances where there is an obvious and significant risk of excessive consumption, the absence of measures to discourage drinking is problematic in the light of Article 2 ECHR. However, in this case the checks and controls could not be faulted according to the Commission, and it also took into account the fact that states are best placed to decide which measures are necessary to protect life.

The ECtHR is far less pronounced about the desirability of 'harm reduction' measures than the Human Rights Committee. Nevertheless, it is clear that the Court also recognizes its importance and that it does not consider it incompatible with the ECHR.[477] The *Shelley* case concerns the complaint that the refusal of the authorities to introduce a needle exchange scheme in prisons runs counter to Articles 2, 3 and 8 ECHR.[478] In assessing the complaints, the Court positively takes into account that the authorities have taken a number of preventative measures (such as providing disinfection tablets) and that the authorities follow the developments about needle exchange schemes introduced elsewhere. In the final analysis, the Court ruled that the state's refusal to implement a similar programme falls within the 'margin of appreciation' in this case. So the ECtHR certainly does not object to introducing such 'harm reduction' measures. It even clearly intimates that it considers the needle exchange to be more effective than 'providing disinfectants'.[479]

The above illustrates once again that the ECtHR (and the erstwhile European Commission) do not easily force states to adopt a certain approach in the case of stimulants such as alcohol, tobacco and drugs. Incidentally, this is of a piece with the Court's position on Article 2 ECHR, namely that the positive obligations that apply there must not be informed by a paternalistic vision.[480] Ultimately, what matters is that risks connected with the above-mentioned stimulants must be controlled sufficiently In this respect, there is also room for policies that permit cannabis cultivation and trade under regulation and that achieves the separation of the soft drugs market from the hard drugs market, provided this actually offers protection for the right to life, the right not to be subjected to inhuman treatment and the right to a private life, among other things.

---

476 ECommHR 9 April 1997, *Barrett/The UK*, no. 30402/96, para. 1 and 2.

477 Cf. ECtHR 29 April 2003, *McGlinchey/The UK*, no 50390/99, para. 57 and 71 (prisoner dies as a result of, among other things, sudden withdrawal from heroin; violation because of insufficient medical care); ECtHR 27 May 2010, *Artyomov/Russia*, no. 14146/02, para. 190 (sufficient protection against the transmission of HIV, partly because the state 'employed a harm-reduction technique, namely condom distribution, together with universal precaution policies such as sterilising medical equipment for each patient').

478 ECtHR 4 January 2008, *Shelley/The UK*, no. 23800/06, para. 1.

479 Ibid, para. 2 (fifth paragraph).

480 ECtHR 26 February 2015, *Prilutskiy/Ukraine*, no. 40429/08, para. 32.

2.4.12. CONCLUSION REGARDING THE RIGHT TO LIFE, THE RIGHT NOT TO BE SUBJECTED TO INHUMAN TREATMENT AND THE RIGHT TO A PRIVATE LIFE

The rights secured by the ICCPR and the ECHR, namely the right to life (Article 6 ICCPR, Article 2 ECHR), the right not to be subjected to inhuman treatment (Article 7 ICCPR, Article 3 ECHR) and the right to privacy (Article 17 ICCPR, Article 8 ECHR) do not explicitly relate to drugs and/or cannabis. The Human Rights Committee and the ECtHR – unlike the ICESCR Committee and the European CSR – also hardly have any attention for the risks of these substances and the policies and measures about them. However, given the expositions above, that certainly does not mean that the provisions mentioned are irrelevant for the cannabis issue. We have now come to the point where we will answer the three key questions formulated in the introductory section of section 2.4.

i. First Question: Does the ICCPR or the ECHR Oppose Regulated Permission?

We have not found any indications that the ICCPR and/or the ECHR, or alternatively the jurisprudence about it from the Human Rights Committee and the ECtHR respectively oppose the introduction of a drug policy that permits the cultivation of and trade in cannabis for recreational use by adults, be it in the form of legalization, decriminalization or a policy of tolerance. The Human Rights Committee even shows itself to be an explicit advocate of a drug policy based on individual and public health and rejects a drug policy of 'zero tolerance'. At the same time, states are not allowed to remain passive if there are (likely to be) fatal casualties, for example as a direct consequence of the use of drugs available in society. If states therefore choose a policy of regulated permission, they must offer adequate general protection against unacceptable violations of the convention rights. The fact that the ICCPR and the ECHR do not have to be obstacles for a policy of regulated permission does not necessarily mean that such permission can qualify as a way to secure the right to life, the right not to be subjected to inhuman treatment and/or the right to a private life, or is even required by these rights. The following question relates to that.

ii. Second Question: Is Regulated Permission Required under the Right to Life, the Right not to be Subjected to Inhuman Treatment and the Right to Privacy?

Is a drug policy that permits the cultivation of and trade in cannabis for recreational use an acceptable and possibly even required vehicle for implementing the right to life, the right not to be subjected to inhuman treatment and the right to a private life, insofar as that drug policy would de facto protect the safety of citizens, prevent nuisance, and combat crime better than a more prohibitive drug policy? Given the answer to the previous question, roughly speaking there is again room for one of the following three alternative scenarios. And as before, the hypothesis is always that regulated permission results in a better protection of life, and privacy and protection against inhuman treatment. The first variant here is that the state may not only proceed with regulated permission, but effectively must do so, given the positive obligations of protection of the rights regarding life, inhuman treatment and privacy (may and must). The second variant is that the state then may and can fulfil the obligations to protect by permitting regulated cannabis cultivation and trade, but is not obliged to do so (may, can, not obliged). The third variant is that the rights referred to in the corresponding obligations of protection do not resist regulated permission, but that this cannot qualify as a fulfilment of these obligations (may, without relevance).

This latter variant (may, without relevance) does not apply at any rate. Admittedly, policies on drugs and/or cannabis only play a marginal part in the jurisprudence of the Human Rights Committee and the ECtHR, but such a policy can be of significant importance for the degree to which criminal acts and health-related consequences may occur involving drugs and/or cannabis. In this context, one can think of murder, manslaughter and causing death by negligence, overdose and contracting deadly diseases by intravenous drug use, grievous bodily harm, causing severe burns and seriously harmful infections, serious levels of stench, noise, flooding, fire, assault and threats, as well as serious health problems caused by the use of hard drugs. Under certain conditions, states have positive obligations to provide protection from such acts and consequences. Since a policy on drugs and/or cannabis may play a part in this, such a policy is consequently relevant from the point of view of positive obligations of protection.

At the same time, it is worth noting that there are no indications that the reduction of organized crime, reduction of cannabis exports and the fight against corruption in the upper world (undermining) are also relevant as such for the rights concerning life, inhuman treatment and privacy. The state may base its policy on drugs and cannabis on the importance of combating these phenomena, but the drive to prevent these in itself cannot qualify as a fulfilment of the positive obligations of protection. Only when these phenomena are accompanied by serious unsafety, nuisance and/or crime aimed at the physical or mental integrity of citizens can this be different, but then it is the fight against those consequences that is relevant from the point of view of these obligations of protection.

Ultimately, in our opinion the applicability of the first variant (may and must) is in principle the one that can be best defended in view of the foregoing. We came to the conclusion of that variant's applicability with regard to the right to health; see section 2.3.12. However, it is more obvious in that case than with the rights regarding life, inhuman treatment and privacy. After all, it is important that states do not have an obligation with these rights to achieve 'full realization', only an obligation to 'secure' these rights, to protect them effectively at the level and in the manner required by the Human Rights Committee and the ECtHR. To that end, the states parties are required to take (all) measures that are 'appropriate' to achieve the required level of protection. Seeing that in principle everything that is effective could function as an appropriate measure, the permission of cannabis cultivation and trade for the recreational user market will qualify as such, if such a policy best achieves the required protection. However, does the positive obligation of protection also imply that such a policy must be implemented? Basically, there are two ways to look at this. With the following exposition of the two points of view, the hypothesis is that the state, in accordance with its primary responsibility to decide which measures are most appropriate to fulfil the positive obligation of protection, taking into account the specific circumstances in the state (the principle of primarity) – draws the conclusion, in good faith ('pacta sunt servanda') and with sufficient substantiation, that regulated permission of the cultivation of and trade in cannabis for recreational use is the best way to fulfil the positive obligations of protection of the rights regarding life, inhuman treatment and privacy.

The first perspective. This is based on the assumption that the national authorities are only required to take appropriate measures within the 'margin of appreciation'. In this perspective, the margin functions as an instrument to determine content: from the very beginning, the margin is one factor that decides the scope of the human rights obligation imposed on states. The reasoning is that if subject to this margin, various approaches are possible, there is no obligation with respect to any of these approaches to implement them; the authorities are only required to choose one of them. Here is a theoretical example to illustrate this: Suppose that the margin leaves room for approach A (which prevents 100 unlawful breaches of the convention) and approach B (this one prevents 75) Approach A is therefore more effective than approach B. the authorities are not required to pick A nor are they required to pick B; they are only required to implement one or the other. With this perspective, each of these approaches fulfils the positive obligation of protection, but the authorities cannot claim with respect to either of them that they are compelled to adopt that particular approach, as there is always the absolutely permissible alternative of the other approach. With this perspective, one could argue that regulated permission of cannabis cultivation and trade cannot qualify as a positive obligation, even if this were the most effective way to fulfil the obligation of protection, since the authorities would still be allowed to opt for the prohibition and combating of cannabis and its consequences under criminal law.

The second perspective. This is based on the assumption that the authorities are required to take those appropriate measures that actually fulfils the positive obligation of protection most effectively. This means, building on the example of approaches A and B, that there is an obligation to implement approach A (which after all prevents 25 more unlawful breaches of the convention than approach B). The authorities cannot eliminate the obligation as such, but they can escape from it within the 'margin of appreciation'. For example, it is conceivable that the authorities are allowed to abstain from implementing approach A because of financial, political or moral considerations. With this perspective, the 'margin of appreciation' does not determine the scope of the obligations. On the contrary, the margin is an instrument that is primarily aimed at getting states to implement the measure that is the most effective, given the social peculiarities and the constellation of the state in question. The margin leaves states a certain freedom to refrain from measures that are experienced as unattractive or impossible given the nature of that society and its constellation; however, the state must then substantiate why this is the case. Therefore, the 'margin of appreciation' in this perspective does not detract in principle from the requirement to fulfil the positive obligation of protection in the most effective manner. With this perspective, the authorities can always take the position that they are required to adopt the most effective approach. It means that regulated permission of cannabis cultivation and trade can qualify as a positive obligation, if the rights regarding life, inhuman treatment and privacy were realized most effectively by this permission. That observation is in no way affected by the fact that states in appealing to the 'margin of appreciation' can nevertheless still opt to prohibit and combat cannabis and its consequences under criminal law, if this were less effective.

Although the first perspective approaches the functioning of positive obligations and of the 'margin of appreciation' in practice probably a little more than the second perspective, we believe that the second perspective can be defended best within the framework of the conventions. First of all because the 'object and purpose' of human rights conventions is to protect human rights effectively. The notion that states would be entirely free to choose an approach that is less effective than another available approach (compare the situation where approach B is twenty-five percent less effective than approach A) jars with this object and purpose. Secondly, the jurisprudence of both the Human Rights Committee and the ECtHR shows that states must take (sometimes: all) appropriate measures so as to secure and protect the convention rights. One may ask oneself whether measures that are less effective in preventing unlawful breaches of convention rights can still qualify as 'appropriate' on essentially the same basis as achievable and more effective measures. Thirdly, the first perspective ignores the rationale and purpose of the 'margin of appreciation'. With positive obligations, it is primarily aimed at being able to determine what – in the light of the social peculiarities and the constellation of the state – the 'appropriate steps' are to meet the obligation to secure convention rights.

Even if a state adopts less than optimal measures and in doing so remains within the margin, this is still only allowed to the extent that the state presents compelling reasons for doing so. Finally, in accordance with the principle of primarity it is first and foremost the state that decides what exactly protection must be offered against and how this should be done, so as to secure the convention rights. If a state in accordance with the principle of 'pacta sunt servanda' genuinely believes and convincingly argues that regulated permission of the cultivation of and trade in cannabis for recreational use is the best way to address serious nuisance, to fight crime and guarantee the safety and health of citizens, that state therefore in implementing that policy first and foremost meets the obligation to secure the convention rights. If such regulation has the support of a large part of society and comes about after democratic decision-making, it reinforces the assumption that this policy and those measures are indeed the appropriate steps that the authorities must take.

There is still another argument for the assertion that a policy on drugs and/or cannabis of regulated permission qualifies as a positive obligation if this fulfilled the obligation of protection most effectively. That is the argument that the government with such a policy breaches human rights much less than is the case with a prohibitive and repressive policy.[481] After all, the latter policy implies criminal prosecution of individuals as well. Among other things, this means the use of investigation methods that breach the right to a private life, and it is also likely to include arrest, provisional detention and prison sentences, which violate the right not to be deprived of liberty. The principle of subsidiarity (in the sense of necessity) requires that, as we observed in the discussion of the 'duty to respect', violations of human rights may only be permitted if there is not a less onerous means available with which the same goal can be reached. The fact that this must also apply in a general sense follows particularly from the 'object and purpose' of the ICCPR and the ECHR and the system of these conventions, while it finds further support in the fact that some provisions about human rights state this principle explicitly as well. This means that when a policy of regulated permission meets the

[481] For a general discussion about the way in which prohibitive and repressive drug policies are problematic from the point of view of human rights, see among other sources United Nations Development Programme, *Perspectives on the Development Dimensions of Drug Control Policy*, UNDP 2015; Steve Rolles et al., *The Alternative World Drug Report. Counting the Costs of the War on Drugs*, United Kingdom: Count the Costs, 2012, pp. 71–83; Damon Barrett & Manfred Nowak, 'The United Nations and Drug Policy: Towards a Human Rights-Based Approach', in: Aristotle Constantinides & Nikos Zaikos (eds.), *The Diversity of International Law: Essays in Honour of Professor Kalliopi K. Koufa*, Amsterdam: Brill & Martinus Nijhoff, 2009, pp. 449–477.

objective of countering cannabis use and hard drugs use at least as well as with a prohibitive and repressive policy, the former policy in principle is to be preferred from the point of view of human rights.

Furthermore, we take the view that there are no decisive arguments to assume that whereas states are allowed to proceed to the aforementioned regulation under the right to health, yet they cannot be required to do so (may, can, not obliged). The arguments presented for such a claim were already reviewed in section 2.3.12.ii in relation to the right to health. Mutatis mutandis, these arguments cannot be successful here either, for the same reasons. In addition to that, we will suffice with a few observations. With regard to the argument that regulated permission creates room for or facilitates cannabis use, it is important here that we already found that the ECtHR also does not in the least oppose 'harm reduction' measures that contribute to safer drug use. Then there is the argument that regulated permission of cannabis cultivation and trade is not mentioned as an obligation in the provisions of conventions and the jurisprudence about the rights regarding life, inhuman treatment and privacy. This argument cannot be successful, since this would undermine the responsibility to secure these rights positively to a considerable degree. Thirdly, the more politically tinged objection that if regulated permission of cannabis cultivation and trade for the Netherlands could qualify as an obligation, then subsequently all other States parties would also have to take such a step, does not hold water. Put succinctly, the primarity principle, the importance of democratic support and the 'margin of appreciation' ensure that states that are against regulated permission, will not have to go down that route.

Finally, we observe again that the three arguments reviewed just now (principle of primarity, democratic support, margin of appreciation) are also important for the question whether lower authorities in a state will be able to keep the national government and the national legislator beholden to implementing regulated permission under the law of the convention if the national government refuses to do that. We are of the opinion that the three arguments imply that this is not possible in principle. Incidentally, that is also impossible for individuals or private organizations.

iii. Third Question: Which Conditions do the Rights Regarding Life, Inhuman Treatment and Privacy Impose on Cannabis Policy?

Unlike the right to health in the ICESCR and the ESC, the rights in the ICCPR and the ECHR do not give rise to an obligation for states to provide an adequate health policy. These conventions and the specific human rights simply do not focus on that. To that extent, it is not surprising that policies which permit alcohol, tobacco and drugs or conversely combat these only play a marginal role in the jurisprudence of the Human Rights Committee and the ECtHR. It is evident from that jurisprudence that states at any rate do not have to choose for a prohibition of cannabis cultivation, trade and use. These bodies do not even require that states provide all manner of coherent measures so as to prevent such use. For the ECtHR, it also matters in this respect that states have their own responsibilities with regard to acts that pose risks to themselves. This certainly is the case with drug use.

This does not mean that states have no responsibility at all under the ICCPR and the ECHR to counteract the harmful effects of drugs, alcohol and tobacco – and therefore cannabis as well – for individual and public health. When these effects are in the domain of the rights regarding life and inhuman treatment in the ICCPR and the ECHR and the right to privacy in the sense of the physical and psychological integrity of the person in the ECHR (in principle this is not protected by the right to a private life in the ICCPR), then the concomitant positive obligations of protection may become relevant. Moreover, a drug policy conducted by a country will have to show respect for the human convention rights of persons in other countries. From that angle, there is a certain general urge within these conventions to discourage the use of substances such as cannabis. At the same time, the policy of discouragement must not be at odds with (the negative obligation to respect) the human rights in these conventions.

iv. Summary

The most defensible conclusion is that the state is required to implement – through legalization, decriminalization or a policy of tolerance – regulated permission of cannabis cultivation and trade, if this provides the most adequate protection for the rights regarding life, inhuman treatment and privacy in a state from the relevant forms of serious unsafety, nuisance, crime and health risks and if the conclusion that this is the case is supported by the state itself and by democratic decision-making. This follows from the positive obligation to secure the enjoyment of the above-mentioned rights at the required level of protection with (all) appropriate measures. The forms of serious unsafety, nuisance, crime and health risks to which the obligation of protection may apply under certain circumstances, comprise among other things cannabis cultivation and trade related murder, manslaughter and causing death by negligence, grievous bodily harm, causing severe burns and seriously harmful infections, serious levels of stench, noise, flooding, fire, assault and threats. Also overdose and contracting deadly diseases and serious health problems caused by the use of hard drugs may come under this. On the other hand, phenomena such as organized crime, cannabis export and the corruption of the upper world (undermining) cannot trigger the positive obligation of protection as such. Finally, it is worth noting that the rights mentioned do not impose special requirements on any policy of regulated permission.

2.5. CONCLUSION

Fundamentally, the cannabis issue is about the question whether regulation – through legalization, decriminalization or policy-based tolerance[482] – of cannabis cultivation and trade for recreational use can be advocated on the grounds of rights and obligations that ensue as positive law from international human rights treaties and conventions. The foregoing shows that this is possible. Moreover, it shows that a strong case, indeed the strongest case, can be made that such regulation under certain circumstances can even qualify as a positive obligation to protect human rights. Both the right to health in the ICESCR and the ESC and the rights regarding life, inhuman treatment and privacy in the ICCPR and the ECHR support this conclusion in different respects.

Roughly speaking, the most important conditions to accept such an obligation are as follows: 1. There must really be an interest that is relevant in the context of these human rights; 2. The state makes it plausible, in a genuine, convincing and substantiated manner that regulated permission offers the most adequate protection to that interest which has a relevance to human rights, also taking into account the social peculiarities and the constellation of the state involved; 3. The state's conclusion that this is the case is supported by democratic decision-making in the state.

For a discussion of the more specific meaning and practicalities of these conditions, we refer the reader to the conclusions in section 2.3.12.ii (in respect of the right to health) and section 2.4.12.ii (in respect of the rights regarding life, inhuman treatment and privacy), and those conclusions are based on the sections that precede them. We will now only highlight a few points from that discussion.

First, a short indication with regard to the arguments explained in sections 2.3.1 and 2.4.1 in favour of regulated permission that are relevant in the context of the rights discussed. For all these arguments, we work from the hypothesis that they are valid.

- For the right to health in Article 12 ICESCR and Article 11 ESC, the relevant arguments concern: safeguarding the quality of cannabis, monitoring the cannabis chain, protection of the health and lives of residents, protection of the health of juveniles, separating the soft drugs and hard drugs markets and more indirectly also cannabis as a less risky alternative stimulant.
- For the right to life in Article 6 ICCPR and Article 2 ECHR, the relevant arguments concern: reducing peripheral crime as well as the protection of health and life of residents (murder, manslaughter, causing death by negligence

[482] Which of these options best matches the obligations from the human rights conventions and the Drugs Conventions will be looked at in more detail in section 4.9.

such as hemp nursery fires and/or seriously harmful infections), and to a lesser degree the separation of the soft drugs market from the hard drugs market (to prevent overdoses or contracting fatal diseases as a result of using hard drugs).

- For the right not to be subjected to inhuman treatment in Article 7 ICCPR and Article 3 ECHR, the relevant arguments concern: reducing peripheral crime (such as grievous bodily harm and severe burns and seriously harmful infections). The arguments about nuisance and damage and the one about the separation between the soft drugs market and the hard drugs market are not relevant here in principle.
- For the right to privacy in Article 17 ICCPR, the relevant arguments concern: reduction of peripheral crime (assault and threats) and reduction of nuisance and damage (such as caused by serious levels of stench, noise, flooding, fire and seriously harmful infections), if there is a substantial and fairly direct limitation of the enjoyment of one's private life. The argument about the separation between the soft drugs market and the hard drugs market are not relevant here in principle.
- For the right to privacy in Article 8 ECHR, the relevant arguments concern: reduction of peripheral crime (aggravated assault and serious threats), reduction of nuisance and damage (such as caused by serious levels of stench, noise, flooding, fire and seriously harmful infections) and to a lesser degree the separation of the soft drugs market and the hard drugs market (the risk posed to the physical and mental integrity of citizens by their use of hard drugs).
- The arguments concerning the reduction of organized crime as such, reduction of cannabis export, combating the corruption of the upper world (undermining) were not found to have any relevance as such.

It is also important that the fact that a certain measure is not explicitly formulated in a provision of the convention or the international jurisprudence about it, does not mean that the state cannot be required to take that measure. This also applies if the measure takes the form of a drug and/or cannabis policy that permits regulated cannabis cultivation and trade for recreational users. In those cases where the obligation to implement this kind of policy may be assumed, this follows from the framework of general obligations and specific positive obligations arising from the convention rights that have been discussed.

The foregoing gives rise to an important condition if regulated permission of cannabis cultivation and trade is to be seen as a positive obligation. After all, this is only possible in principle if the state makes it plausible, in a genuine, convincing and substantiated manner, supported by democratic decision-making, that this approach secures the required protection of the convention rights in the most adequate way.

Moreover, that state will then have to provide adequate policies to discourage and limit recreational cannabis use and raise awareness of its risks. This is necessary not only to ensure that the policy on drugs and/or cannabis actually achieves the most adequate protection of human rights; the right to health itself creates an obligation to that end.

Finally, a few notes about the question whether low ranking authorities in a state – or individuals or private organizations – appealing to positive obligations relating to human rights could force the national authorities (the administration and legislator) to implement regulated permission of cannabis cultivation and trade if the national authorities refused to do that. Of course, this possibility cannot exist anyway if positive obligations relating to human rights could not be given priority over obligations under the UN narcotic drugs conventions. As we will look into this question of priority in Chapter 3, we will return to the possibilities for lower ranking authorities at the end of this book, in Chapter 4.[483]

Some findings from the foregoing will, however, be of crucial importance in that respect. This is particularly true for the conclusion that the national government itself in principle will need to be in favour of such permission for a positive obligation to come into being. To that extent, low ranking authorities and private parties will have no legal means at their disposal to force the national government to implement regulated permission of cannabis. More specifically, this is the case because first and foremost it is the state that has the responsibility to decide what requires protection and which measures are needed for that protection (principal of primarity), because it requires a more general democratic consensus and because the state has the option to escape that implementation within the 'margin of appreciation' if it does not see the implementation as desirable.

---

483 See section 4.5.

CHAPTER 3

INTERFERENCE BETWEEN HUMAN RIGHTS OBLIGATIONS AND OBLIGATIONS UNDER THE UN NARCOTIC DRUGS CONVENTIONS

3.1. INTRODUCTION

The central theme of the previous chapter was positive obligations pursuant to human rights conventions. We arrived at an affirmative answer to the key question whether regulation – through legalization, decriminalization or a policy of tolerance – of cannabis cultivation and trade for recreational use can be advocated on the grounds of rights and obligations that ensue as positive law from international human rights treaties and conventions. A strong case, and indeed the strongest case, can be made that such regulation under certain circumstances can even qualify as a positive obligation to protect human rights. This conclusion is supported by both the right to health in the ICESCR and the ESC and the rights regarding life, inhuman treatment and privacy in the ICCPR and the ECHR.

When we discussed and analysed the human rights conventions in the previous chapter, we did not take into account the obligations that states have under the UN narcotic drugs conventions. With regard to cannabis, the following conventions are particularly relevant: the Single Convention on Narcotic Drugs[1] as amended by the Protocol amending the Single Convention on Narcotic Drugs (Single Convention),[2] and the United Nations Convention Against Illicit Traffic in Narcotic Drugs and Psychotropic Substances (Illicit Traffic Convention).[3]

1 *Single Convention on Narcotic Drugs, 1961*, New York, 30 March 1961 (*Trb.* 1962/30, *Trb.* 1963/81).

2 *Protocol amending the Single Convention on Narcotic Drugs, 1961, 1972*, Geneva, 25 March 1972 (*Trb.* 1980/184, *Trb.* 1987/90).

3 *United Nations Convention Against Illicit Traffic in Narcotic Drugs and Psychotropic Substances, 1988*, Vienna, 20 December 1988 (*Trb.* 1989/97, *Trb.* 1990/94).

As we saw in our first book, *International Law and Cannabis I*, these drugs conventions undeniably aim to contribute to the interests of public health (object and purpose).[4] These conventions do so in three ways: 1. Availability of narcotic drugs as meaningful and/or effective medicine or research into this; 2. Treatment of and care for drug users so as to wean them off these narcotic drugs; 3. Protecting society against narcotic drugs by fighting and eliminating the production, trade, possession and use of these drugs for recreational purposes by means of criminal law and many other social prohibitions and measures. Therefore, the drugs conventions do not aim to guarantee public health in a general sense, they actually imply this guarantee must be achieved strictly by applying the three above-mentioned specific perspectives. As we concluded before: the UN narcotic drugs conventions actually reveal a limited, one-sided and rigid interpretation of public health interests.[5] With respect to drugs and/or cannabis for recreational use, the drugs conventions prescribe a prohibitive approach (if not one of zero tolerance) and they leave no room for a different view.[6]

Just as we did not pay any attention to the UN narcotic drugs conventions in the previous chapter, the discussion about these conventions in the aforementioned book on *International Law and Cannabis* was conducted exclusively from the internal perspective of those conventions, without involving human rights. Now is the right time to connect those regimes after all. By now, it has become clear that if examined separately, these two approaches lead to opposites outcomes with regard to the obligations that the state has vis-à-vis its policy on drugs and/or cannabis in the event that regulation of cannabis cultivation and trade for recreational use can achieve a higher level of protection of human rights than a prohibitive approach. In other words, there is interference between human rights conventions and drugs conventions within public international law (also: international law).[7] With this in mind, the following question takes pride of place in this chapter:

> To what extent can positive human rights obligations that justify or necessitate the regulated permission of cannabis cultivation and trade leave the national governments room under international law to interpret their obligations under the international drug control system differently or set these aside?

To answer this question, we will examine in this chapter which criteria and principles are offered by international law to arrive at a solution for the conflict between diametrically opposed obligations under conventions. We will apply those criteria and principles to the interference that appears to exist at first sight between the positive human rights obligations and the UN narcotic drugs conventions.

---

4 Piet Hein P.H.M.C. van Kempen & Masha I. Fedorova, *International Law and Cannabis I*, Cambridge: Intersentia 2019, Ch. 2.

5 Ibid, section 2.6.

6 Ibid, e.g. section 2.6; 5.2.1.

7 For a more elaborate interpretation of the concept of 'interference', see section 1.3.

Our analyses and reflections are again grounded in positive law. They are primarily based on the Vienna Convention on the Law of Treaties (VCLT),[8] the Charter of the United Nations (UN Charter),[9] the case law of the International Court of Justice (ICJ), the work of the International Law Commission (ILC) and the pertinent literature about this. In view of the character of international law, which is somewhat diffuse in many cases, the analyses, findings and conclusions in this chapter are supported with many references in footnotes, to provide a solid basis for the expositions.

Interference in public international law between sources (conventions, customary law, general principles of law) and between norms has been the subject of much debate.[10] This is beyond the scope of this book and so it is unnecessary to fully reproduce that discussion here. We will examine the discussion about the relationship between sources and in particular between norms of international law insofar as this is useful to arrive at an adequate answer to the question how the positive obligations arising from the human rights conventions discussed in Chapter 2 (the ICESCR, the ESC, the ICCPR and the ECHR) relate to the UN narcotic drugs conventions that are relevant here (the Single Convention and the Illicit Traffic Convention). Later, in section 3.3, we will briefly explain the structure which we will use to answer this question, because first the following is important for this.

3.2. APPROACHES TO INTERFERENCE BETWEEN INTERNATIONAL NORMS

When public international law norms interfere with each other, this may have various consequences. On one end of the spectrum of solutions is the possibility that one legal norm cancels the other because of a formal or substantive

8 *Vienna Convention of the law of treaties*, Vienna, 23 May 1969 (*Trb.* 1972/51).

9 *Charter of the United Nations*, San Francisco, 26 June 1945 (*Stb.* F 253 and *Stb.* F 321, and amended versions *Trb.* 1964/109, *Trb.* 1966/138 and *Trb.* 1972/96).

10 See International Law Commission, Report of the Study Group finalized by Martti Koskenniemi, 'Fragmentation of International Law: Difficulties arising from the Diversification and Expansion of International Law', *UN Doc.* A/CN.4/L/682, 13 April 2006 (also: ILC, 'Fragmentation of International Law', 2006). See also for example Charles Rousseau, 'De la Compatibilité des Norms Juridique Contradictoires dans l'Ordre International', *Revue générale de droit international public* 1932, vol. 39, pp. 133–192; W. Jenks, 'The Conflict of Law-Making Treaties', *British Yearbook of International Law* 1953, vol. 30, pp. 401–453; W. Czapliński & G. Danilenko, 'Conflict of Norms in International Law', *Netherlands Yearbook of International Law* 1990, vol. 21, pp. 3–42; Jan B. Mus, 'Conflicts between Treaties in International Law', *Netherlands International Law Review* 1998, vol. 45, pp. 208–232; Seyed-Ali Sadat-Akhavi, *Methods of Resolving Conflicts between Treaties*, Leiden/Boston: Martinus Nijhoff, 2003; Joost Pauwelyn, *Conflict of Norms in Public International Law: How WTO Law relates to Other Rules of International Law*, Cambridge: Cambridge University Press, 2003; Erich Vranes, 'The Definition of "Norm Conflict" in International Law and Legal Theory', *European Journal of International Law* 2006, vol. 17, pp. 395–418.

hierarchical relationship between both norms. In that case, the higher norm absolutely and categorically rules out the application of the hierarchically subordinate norm. In public international law, this may happen in the event of a clash between a *jus cogens* norm and an 'ordinary' norm. If no *jus cogens* norm is involved in the conflict between norms, the relationship between the two legal norms will be more relative in nature. In that case, there is a situation where one norm only temporarily overrides and suppresses the other norm rather than rendering it invalid as such. Nevertheless, the interference between norms is then resolved because one norm takes precedence over the other. At the other end of the spectrum, two interfering norms are equally applicable, while it is possible to interpret and apply the norms in such a way that they reinforce each other. In that case, the interference between norms can be resolved by harmonizing them.[11] In short: one end of the spectrum can be characterized as a strict *conflict approach*, whereas the other qualifies as an optimal *harmony approach*.

The question then is whether there can be moderate forms of suppression or harmonization between these two approaches. For example, can the interference be resolved because the weaker norm affects the interpretation and application of the prioritized norm, so that both norms apply to a certain extent, albeit that one is more powerful than the other? In general, it is difficult to determine under which circumstances it is impossible to 'reconcile' two interfering legal norms by a harmonizing interpretation and application, so that the interference will have to be resolved through a hierarchy or priority regime.

Some authors argue that interference of norms involves two mutually exclusive situations, in which the legal norms either accumulate or conflict: 'If two norms do not conflict, they necessarily accumulate (and vice versa).'[12] In this view, there is a clear limit on the possibility of harmonization between conflicting legal norms: 'interpretation of the terms in question may resolve apparent conflicts; it cannot resolve genuine conflicts'.[13]

The International Law Commission on the other hand takes the position that resolution of interference and interpretation are inseparable:[14]

> Whether there is a conflict and what can be done with prima facie conflicts depends on the way the relevant rules are interpreted. This cannot be stressed too much.

---

11 ILC, 'Fragmentation of International Law', 2006, para. 19.

12 Joost Pauwelyn, *Conflict of Norms in Public International Law: How WTO Law relates to Other Rules of International Law*, Cambridge: Cambridge University Press, 2003, p. 161. See also Ahmad Ali Ghouri, 'Determining Hierarchy Between Conflicting Treaties: Are There Vertical Rules in the Horizontal System?', *Asian Journal of International Law* 2012, vol. 2, no. 2, pp. 235–266 on p. 236.

13 Joost Pauwelyn, *Conflict of Norms in Public International Law: How WTO Law relates to Other Rules of International Law*, Cambridge: Cambridge University Press, 2003, p. 272.

14 ILC, 'Fragmentation of International Law', 2006, para. 412.

> Interpretation does not intervene only once it has already been ascertained that there is a conflict. Rules appear to be compatible or in conflict as a result of interpretation. Sometimes it may be useful to stress the conflicting nature of two rules or sets of rules so as to point to the need for legislative intervention. Often, however, it seems more appropriate to play down that sense of conflict and to read the relevant materials from the perspective of their contribution to some generally shared – 'systemic' – objective.[15]

Given the authority of the ILC and in particular its more realistic outlook on how law functions in reality, we assume that – with the exception of a case where the interference involves a *jus cogens* norm – there is to a greater or lesser extent nearly always room for harmonization in the event of interference between norms. Quite apart from that, interfering conventions can be easily harmonized if the will to do so exists among the states parties.[16] The approach of harmonization used here implies that there is a continuum between the strict conflict approach and the optimal harmony approach, which consists of less strict and optimal forms of these approaches. However, this does not say much about the possibilities and limitations that apply with the interference between human rights obligations and the UN narcotic drugs conventions.

With regard to the expositions about this matter in the following sections, it is useful to keep the following in mind. Every legal system at some time or other has had to deal with the question of the relationship between these norms. Still, the international legal order deviates significantly from national legal orders in many ways that are relevant for that question. This in particular complicates attempts to answer that question in the international context.[17] The structure of a national legal system in general is hierarchical like a pyramid; the relationship between two legal sources is clear or can be determined by the classical rules of precedence, such as the *lex specialis* rule (speciality), the *lex posterior* and *lex prior* rules (temporality) and the *lex superior* rule (the importance of the interest). The international legal order, on the other hand, is decentralized and fragmented: there is no real central or highest legislator, nor is there a traditional

15 Ibid.

16 Ibid, para. 42.

17 See among other sources Kerstin Odendahl, 'Application of successive treaties relating to the same subject matter', in: Oliver Dörr & Kirsten Schmalenbach (eds.), *Vienna Convention on the Law of Treaties, A Commentary*, Heidelberg/Dordrecht/London/New York: Springer, 2012, pp. 505–518 op 506; Dinah Shelton, 'Normative Hierarchy in International Law', *American Journal of International Law*, 2006, vol. 100, pp. 291–323 on p. 291; Theodor Meron, 'On a Hierarchy of International Human Rights', *American Journal of International Law* 1986, vol. 80, pp. 1–23 on p. 3; Anja Lindroos, 'Addressing Norm Conflicts in a Fragmented Legal System: The Doctrine of *Lex Specialis*', *Nordic Journal of International Law* 2005, vol. 74, pp. 27–66 on p. 27.

separation of powers, rather a multitude of equivalent legislators who create and apply norms in different, often independently operating forums.[18]

Because of the expansion of the corpus of norms in international law in all sorts of areas and the lack of a clear hierarchical superior legislative and/or judiciary power in an international context, there is a higher chance that the various legal norms are at odds with each other or even cause conflicts than in the national context. Moreover, the classical rules of precedence in international law do not function in the same way as they do in the national legal order that gave rise to these rules.[19] With this diversity in causes and forms of (potential) interference between legal norms in international law, various techniques to resolve conflicts can be applied to conflicts of legal norms with the intention to: 1. prevent them; 2. resolve them by using rules for conflict resolution; 3. harmonize them by using various interpretation methods.[20] In addition to this, the various techniques and/or rules of precedence can, by their very nature, be relevant in both the conflict resolution approach and the harmonization approach. For example, the *lex specialis* principle can play a role under circumstances in a harmonizing interpretation of the interfering norms, while the principle can serve as a rule for determining precedence in other cases.[21] All this entails that there is no neat and clear system for conflict resolution in international law.

3.3. ORDER OF TREATMENT

The foregoing also touches on the question of how interference between positive obligations for human rights and obligations under the drugs conventions need to be resolved. Before we address this question, we will expound a few topics around convention interference in a general sense. First of all, it must be determined when there is interference and/or a conflict of norms in a legal sense. This will be done in section 3.4. Subsequently, in section 3.5 we will turn our attention to the distinction between the hierarchy of sources and the

18 For an elaborate analysis, see among other sources Joost Pauwelyn, *Conflict of Norms in Public International Law: How WTO Law relates to Other Rules of International Law*, Cambridge: Cambridge University Press, 2003, pp. 13–24. See also the many references in ILC, 'Fragmentation of International Law', 2006, and also Andreas Fischer-Lescarno & Gunther Teubner, 'Regime-Collision: The Vain Search for Legal Unity in the Fragmentation of Global Law', *Michigan Journal of International Law*, 1999, vol. 25, pp. 999–1046 on pp. 1014–1017 (they talk about 'auto-constitutional regimes').

19 Michael Akehurst, 'The Hierarchy of the Sources of International Law', *British Yearbook of International Law*, vol. 47, 1974–1975, pp. 273–285; Ralf Michaels & Joost Pauwelyn, 'Conflict of Norms or Conflict of Laws?: Different Techniques in the Fragmentation of Public International Law', *Duke Journal of Comparative & International Law* 2012, vol. 22, pp. 349–376.

20 Cf. ILC, 'Fragmentation of International Law', 2006, para. 412.

21 Ibid, para. 56–58.

hierarchy of norms, as well as the absence of a formal hierarchy of sources in international law.

Building on this, we will then look specifically into the mechanisms for interference resolution in sections 3.6 and 3.7. At that stage, we will also include the interference between human rights conventions and drugs conventions in the context of the cannabis issue. First, the resolution of the so-called precedence clauses in the conventions will be dealt with (section 3.6). Secondly, the various rules regarding determining precedence will be the subject of discussion (section 3.7). Before we can discuss the *lex specialis*, *lex posterior* and *lex prior* and *lex superior* rules in the latter section and determine whether these can play a part within the cannabis issue, some general questions merit discussion. For example, a few crucial concepts, principles, criteria and restrictions related to the rules of precedence will be explained (sections 3.7.1–3.7.3). We will be able to go into even more detail regarding the interference between human rights conventions and drugs conventions aided by the results from sections 3.6 and 3.7.

The two approaches characterized before will be central to this. The short section 3.8 is about the first approach: the conflict approach. The focus will be on the functioning of the applicable priority and rules of precedence. The other approach, the harmony approach, is given extensive coverage in section 3.10. Building on the principles for systematic integration of interfering norms, we will be searching first for common ground between human rights obligations and the drugs conventions. Subsequently, we will assess to what extent the drugs conventions offer departure points for a harmonizing interpretation so as to achieve systematic integration of the interfering obligations. In the meantime, in section 3.9 we will discuss a few presumptions and principles from international law that call for the harmony approach.

Finally, in section 3.11 we will touch upon the question whether a state that permits regulated cultivation of and trade in cannabis so as to fulfil its positive human rights obligations generates liability for itself as a state in doing so. We will round off our analysis in section 3.12 with a conclusion of this chapter.

3.4. WHAT IS A 'CONFLICT' BETWEEN NORMS OF INTERNATIONAL LAW?

In this book, the term 'interference' simply stands for tension, friction, collision, conflict or something similar between conventions or norms of convention.[22] However, not every interference between conventions is relevant from an international law point of view. There has to be a 'conflict' between conventions or the norms of conventions. In the literature, a distinction is made between

22 See section 1.3.

a broad and narrow interpretation of the situation where there is a 'conflict' between international norms.[23] The way in which the phenomenon 'conflict' is defined affects the possibilities for applying the conflict approach and the harmony approach. Thus, the choice between the two definitions can also influence the manner in which the interference between positive human rights obligations and obligations under the drugs conventions can be resolved. That is why both definitions merit our attention here.

3.4.1. NARROW DEFINITION OF THE 'CONFLICT' OF NORMS

With the narrow definition of the phenomenon of a conflict of norms, the fundamental question traditionally is whether the state finds itself in a situation in which two obligations regarding the 'same subject matter' are applicable and it is impossible to fulfil both simultaneously.[24] Only if this is the case can we speak of a conflict of norms. Jenks introduced this restricted definition of conflict between international norms:

> A divergence between treaty provisions dealing with the same subject or related subjects does not in itself constitute a conflict. Two law-making treaties with a number of common parties may deal with the same subject with different points of view or be applicable in different circumstances or one of the treaties may embody obligations more far reaching than, but not inconsistent with, those of the other. A conflict in the strict sense of direct incompatibility arises only where a party to the two treaties cannot simultaneously comply with its obligations under both treaties.[25]

A conflict in the strict sense of the word therefore only arises with two mutually exclusive obligations.[26] That means that the conflict is only possible between

---

23 According to Marceau, the choice for a broad or narrow definition depends on 'one's conception of the international legal order'. Gabrielle Marceau, 'Conflict of Norms and Conflict of Jurisdictions: The Relationship between the WTO Agreement and MEAs and Other Treaties', *Journal of World Trade* 2001, vol. 35, pp. 1081–1131 on pp. 1082–1083.

24 Jasper Finke, 'Regime-collisions: Tensions between treaties (and how to solve them)', in: Christian J. Tams, Antonios Tzanakopoulos & Andreas Zimmermann (eds.), *Research Handbook on the Law of Treaties*, Cheltenham, UK/Northampton, USA: Edward Elgar, 2014, pp. 415–446 on p. 416; see also among other sources Gabrielle Marceau, 'Conflict of Norms and Conflict of Jurisdictions: The Relationship between the WTO Agreement and MEAs and Other Treaties', *Journal of World Trade* 2001, vol. 35, pp. 1081–1131 on p. 1084.

25 Clarence Wilfred Jenks, 'Conflict of Law-Making Treaties', *British Yearbook of International Law* 1953, vol. 30, pp. 401–453 on pp. 425–426.

26 See also Wolfram Karl, 'Conflicts between Treaties', in: R. Bernhardt (ed.), *Encyclopedia of Public International Law*, 1984, p. 468; Gabrielle Marceau, 'Conflict of Norms and Conflict of Jurisdictions: The Relationship between the WTO Agreement and MEAs and Other Treaties', *Journal of World Trade* 2001, vol. 35, pp. 1081–1131 on p. 1084.

norms that prescribe or prohibit a certain act ('obligation' or 'prohibition'), and not between, for example, norms that permit committing an act or omitting to do so ('permission' or 'exception').[27] After all, in the latter case a state can refrain from exercising the specific permission (or authority) and therefore there can be no conflict between two norms. That raises the question whether in the narrow definition there can be a conflict between positive human rights obligations and drugs conventions obligations, seeing that there is a 'margin of appreciation' in the former, whereas more constitutional clauses apply in the latter case, while those respective obligations at first sight relate to different topics at any rate. If the conclusion had to be that there is no conflict of norms sensu stricto, then there will be no room for the conflict approach with that narrow definition. We will briefly come back to this in section 3.8.

The underlying idea for maintaining the narrow definition is the 'presumption against conflict' and the necessity of promoting the coherence of the international legal order.[28] The reasoning behind this is that international legal norms are expressions of the sovereign will of states and this will cannot be deemed to be aimed at creating conflicts between norms.[29] However, as Jenks observes following the above-mentioned quote, that does not alter the fact that:

> A divergence which does not constitute a conflict may nevertheless defeat the object of one or both of the divergent instruments. [...] A divergence of this kind may in some cases, from a practical point of view, be as serious as a conflict; it may, for instance, render inapplicable provisions designed to give one of the divergent instruments a measure of flexibility of operation which was thought necessary to its practicability.[30]

Despite the interest behind the narrow interpretation of the phenomenon of conflict, it certainly is not experienced as non-problematic. That leads us to the following.

---

27 Joost Pauwelyn, *Conflict of Norms in Public International Law: How WTO Law relates to Other Rules of International Law*, Cambridge: Cambridge University Press, 2003, p. 159; Pauwelyn uses Kelsen's theory as a basis; for detailed information see Hans Kelsen, *General Theory of Norms*, Oxford: Oxford University Press, 1991 (translated from German by Michael Hartney, original edition *Allgemeine Theorie der Normen*, Wien: Manz-Verlag, 1979), pp. 96–101.

28 Clarence Wilfred Jenks, 'Conflict of Law-Making Treaties', *British Yearbook of International Law* 1953, vol. 30, pp. 401–453 on p. 428.

29 Joost Pauwelyn, *Conflict of Norms in Public International Law: How WTO Law relates to Other Rules of International Law*, Cambridge: Cambridge University Press, 2003, pp. 172–174.

30 Clarence Wilfred Jenks, 'Conflict of Law-Making Treaties', *British Yearbook of International Law* 1953, vol. 30, pp. 401–453 on pp. 426–427.

3.4.2. BROAD DEFINITION OF THE 'CONFLICT' OF NORMS

Advocates of a broader definition challenge the notion that there have to be two mutually exclusive obligations to warrant speaking of a conflict of norms.[31] For example, a conflict between an obligation and a right can also lead to a situation of conflict between these norms.[32] Pauwelyn for example defines the norm conflict as follows:

> Essentially, two norms are, therefore, in a relationship of conflict if one constitutes, has led to, or may lead to, a breach of the other.[33]

Pauwelyn also makes a distinction between: 1. inherent conflicts (in itself and by itself, a norm is not in conflict with another norm); and 2. conflicts that arise after the fulfilment of an obligation or the exercise of certain rights (inevitable conflicts if the fulfilment of an obligation leads to a failure to fulfil another obligation; and potential conflicts if the exercise of a certain right is at odds with another norm).[34]

In its report 'Fragmentation of International Law', the International Law Commission takes an even broader view:

> However, there are other, looser understandings of conflict as well. A treaty may sometimes frustrate the goals of another treaty without there being any strict incompatibility between their provisions. Two treaties or sets of rules may possess different background justifications or emerge from different legislative policies or aim at divergent ends.[35]

---

31 See among other sources Erich Vranes, 'The Definition of "Norm Conflict" in International Law and Legal Theory, *The European Journal of International Law* 2006, vol. 17, pp. 395–418; Christopher J. Borgen, 'Treaty Conflicts and Normative Fragmentation', in: Duncan B. Hollis (ed.), *The Oxford Guide to Treaties*, Oxford: Oxford University Press, 2012, pp. 448–471 on p. 455.

32 Hans Kelsen, 'Derogation', in: Ralph A. Newman (ed.), *Essays in Jurisprudence in honour of Roscoe Pound*, Indianapolis: Bobbs-Merrill Publication, 1962, pp. 339–355. See also Hans Kelsen, *General Theory of Norms*, Oxford: Oxford University Press, 1991 (translated from German by Michael Hartney, original edition *Allgemeine Theorie der Normen*, Wien: Manz-Verlag, 1979), pp. 100–101: 'It is true that the same norm which prohibits a certain behaviour cannot also command it, but it is perfectly possible for the same behaviour to be forbidden by a valid norm and commanded by another simultaneously valid norm. A conflict of norms will then exist, and the existence of conflicts of norm cannot be denied'.

33 Joost Pauwelyn, *Conflict of Norms in Public International Law: How WTO Law relates to Other Rules of International Law*, Cambridge: Cambridge University Press, 2003, pp. 175–176 (italicized in the original). See also Erich Vranes, 'The Definition of 'Norm Conflict' in International Law and Legal Theory, *The European Journal of International Law* 2006, vol. 17, pp. 395–418 on p. 415: 'There is a conflict between two norms, one of which may be permissive, if in obeying or applying one norm, the other is necessarily or possibly violated.'

34 Joost Pauwelyn, *Conflict of Norms in Public International Law: How WTO Law relates to Other Rules of International Law*, Cambridge: Cambridge University Press, 2003, p. 176.

35 ILC, 'Fragmentation of International Law', 2006, para. 24.

According to the ILC, a conflict manifests itself in the event of: 'a situation where two rules or principles suggest different ways of dealing with a problem.'[36] Both norms must be valid (in the sense of validity at the relevant moment) and applicable (in the sense of being binding in the concrete situation).[37] Applying such a wider, more encompassing definition has several advantages. For example, it covers a wider range of possible tensions, frictions and clashes – in short: forms of interference – between different substantive norms in international law which states may encounter. It also covers the institutional dimension of interference solution, such as the coordination between the various regimes in the implementation of the substantive norms.[38] The broad definition of the phenomenon of the norms conflict in international law thereby also provides a multi-dimensional perspective on the problem of interfering convention norms and creates room for all relevant factors to be included in the analysis. It also makes it possible to look for the most suitable solution in the concrete case on the sliding scale between absolute suppression of norms and perfect harmonization.

As we saw in the previous subsection, it is exactly because it is not clearly about a conflict in the narrow definition when dealing with interference between positive human rights obligations and obligations under the drugs conventions (at first sight anyway), that it is relevant for this book to proceed with the wider definition.

3.5. HIERARCHY OF SOURCES AND NORMS, AND THE LACK OF A FORMAL HIERARCHY

In principle, a distinction can be made between the hierarchy of sources and the hierarchy of norms of international law. The hierarchy of sources involves the order in which the various 'means of proof' of the existence of a legally binding norm must be consulted (such as conventions, customary law, general

36 Ibid, para. 25.

37 ILC, 'Report 58th Session. Chapter XII. Work of the Study Group on the Fragmentation of International Law: Difficulties arising from the Diversification and Expansion of International Law', 2006, *UN Doc.* A/61/10, (also: ILC, 'Report 58th Session: Chapter XII, Fragmentation of International Law', 2006), p. 407 (para. 251(2) (fn. 1012)): 'That two norms are valid in regard to a situation means that they each cover the facts of which the situation consists. That two norms are applicable in a situation means that they have binding force in respect to the legal subjects finding themselves in the relevant situation'.

38 Jasper Finke, 'Regime-collisions: Tensions between treaties (and how to solve them)', in: Christian J. Tams, Antonios Tzanakopoulos & Andreas Zimmermann (eds.), *Research Handbook on the Law of Treaties*, Cheltenham, UK/Northampton, USA: Edward Elgar, 2014, pp. 415–446 on p. 417.

principles of law).[39] The hierarchy of norms relates to the strength of the normative binding power of various (types of) norms in the structure of legal argumentation.[40]

In principle, there is no formal hierarchy in international law.[41] As a legal source, a convention is not *a priori* of a higher order than international customary law or a general principle of law. A hierarchical order between conventions, custom and general principles of law is not formulated in Article 38(1) ICJ Statute either.[42] The enumeration of sources in this provision rather reflects the order in which a judge would logically consult the sources: convention, international customary law and general principles of law.[43] This more 'logical' or 'natural' way of constructing a legal argument may imply the existence of an *informal* hierarchy of international sources.[44] After all, unlike customary law and principles of law, a convention contains an explicit expression of specific agreements reached by states, so that is easier in the case of a convention to determine what exactly the applicable norms are.

Although both the human rights obligations and the drugs conventions obligations that interfere with each other are derived from conventions, the observation that there is no formal hierarchy of sources in international law in principle is of some relevance here. The absence of that hierarchy entails that it is irrelevant whether a norm – such as the right to health or the obligation to

39 An authoritative recognition of sources of international laws is offered by Article 38 Statute of the International Court of Justice: international conventions, international custom, general principles of law and also judicial decisions and authoritative literature ('teachings of the most highly qualified publicists'). Schwarzenberger calls conventions, customary law and general principles of law the 'law-creating processes' and judicial decisions and literature the 'law-determining agencies'; see Georg Schwarzenberger, *International Law as Applied by International Courts and Tribunals*, 1957, vol. I, 3rd edition, London: Stevens & Sons Ltd., pp. 26–27; see also Vladimir Đuro Degan, *Sources of International Law*, The Hague/Boston/London: Martinus Nijhoff Publishers, 1997, p. 5.

40 For a more general discussion about the hierarchical relationships in legal argumentation in international law, see Martii Koskenniemi, 'Hierarchy in International Law: A Sketch', *European Journal of International Law* 1997, vol. 8, pp. 566–582 on p. 566: 'Legal reason is a hierarchical form of reason, establishing relationships of inferiority and superiority between units and levels of legal discourse'.

41 ILC, 'Fragmentation of International Law', 2006, para. 85, 488; see also with many further references to literature Joost Pauwelyn, *Conflict of Norms in Public International Law: How WTO Law relates to Other Rules of International Law*, Cambridge: Cambridge University Press, 2003, p. 94, and also, among other sources.: Prosper Weil, 'Towards Relative Normativity in International Law?', *The American Journal of International Law* 1983, vol. 77, pp. 413–442 on p 423; Juan Antonio Carrillo Salcedo, 'Reflections on the Existence of a Hierarchy of Norms in International Law', *European Journal of International Law* 1997, pp. 583–595 on p. 585.

42 James Crawford, *Brownlie's Principles of Public International Law*, Oxford: Oxford University Press, 2012, 22–23.

43 For the history of the creation of Article 38 ICJ Statute see Michael Akehurst, 'The Hierarchy of the Sources of International Law', *British Yearbook of International Law* 1974–1975, vol. 47, pp. 273–285.

44 For references see ILC, 'Fragmentation of International Law', 2006, para. 85, 86.

combat cannabis cultivation – has a foundation in an explicit convention norm as well as a basis in international customary law. Even if that is the case, this does not in itself afford that norm a formally higher hierarchical position, unless it involved a *jus cogens* norm.[45] However, this may be a somewhat different matter from a substantive point of view, as we will see in section 3.7.9.

3.6. EXPLICIT PRECEDENCE CLAUSES IN THE CONVENTIONS

As we observed, when trying to resolve interference between conventions and/or obligations from various conventions, one must first determine whether the conventions involved contain any rules to prevent or resolve the interference of norms. Many conventions actually contain provisions explicitly governing the relationships with other conventions.[46] Roughly speaking, this involves clauses giving priority to the convention itself and clauses establishing priority for certain other conventions. There are various subcategories within each of these categories, but these are not important for the following.

The question now is whether the human rights conventions discussed in Chapter 2 and the relevant UN narcotic drugs conventions contain such clauses, and if yes, whether they are sufficiently clear to resolve the interference between human rights obligations and obligations arising from drugs conventions for the cannabis issue. That is not the case.

The relevant UN narcotic drugs conventions, namely the Single Convention and the Illicit Traffic Convention, do not contain any explicit precedence clauses that are relevant when the norms from the drugs conventions interfere with norms from other conventions (external effect).[47]

This is slightly different for the UN human rights conventions. Article 24 ICESCR and the identical Article 46 ICCPR contain precedence clauses that do relate to external instruments. However, the provision only decrees that none of the provisions in these conventions may be interpreted as impairing the provisions of the UN Charter[48] and of the constitutions of the specialized

45 With regard to *jus cogens*, see section 3.2.

46 For a more elaborate discussion of possible explicit clauses to prevent and resolve conflicts between various convention norms, see among other sources Christopher J. Borgen, 'Resolving Treaty Conflicts', *The George Washington International Law Review* 2005, vol. 37, pp. 573–648 on pp. 584–587; Duncan B. Hollis, 'Treaty clauses', in: Duncan B. Hollis (ed.), *The Oxford Guide to Treaties*, Oxford: Oxford University Press, 2012, pp. 655–770 on pp. 723–730.

47 Admittedly, the Illicit Traffic Convention does contain an internal precedence clause: Article 25 states that the provisions in the Illicit Traffic Convention do not derogate from the rights and obligations of states parties under the Single Convention.

48 See for information on that section 3.7.8.

agencies of the United Nations. This also applies then insofar as these provisions describe the responsibilities of those bodies with regard to the matters covered in the ICESCR and the ICCPR. For example, other human rights conventions or regional human rights bodies – such as the European CSR and the ECtHR – are not protected by this clause.[49] This also holds true for other bodies – within or outside the United Nations – insofar as their duties do not relate to the matters covered in the ICESCR and the ICCPR. Seeing that the UN narcotic drugs conventions do not contain provisions about human rights, the clause does not apply to the INCB and the CND for example either. Even if that were the case, this would only mean that the ICESCR and the ICCPR are not allowed to impair the responsibilities and powers given to these bodies.[50]

However, there is more to it than that. It is worth knowing that during the creation of the ICESCR and the ICCPR, a proposal was tabled to include in the precedence clause a reference to the Convention on the Prevention and Punishment of the Crime of Genocide[51] (the Genocide Convention).[52] This is interesting, because this convention to some extent is comparable with the UN narcotic drugs conventions. While it is true that the seriousness of the acts it aims to stop (genocide) are of a different magnitude than the acts on which the UN narcotic drugs conventions focus (production of and trade in drugs), the Genocide Convention is a criminal law based convention and that is partly true for the UN narcotic drugs conventions as well. Both belong to the 'branch'[53] of international (including transnational[54]) criminal law.[55] For that reason it is useful to discuss them here.

The proponents of including the Genocide Convention in the precedence clause pointed at the importance of this convention and to the fact that this convention does not contain a provision similar to Article 103 of the UN Charter.[56] The opponents of the amendment asserted that 'the primary purpose

49 See Ben Saul, David Kinley & Jacqueline Mowbray, *The International Covenant on Economic, Social and Cultural Rights*, Oxford: Oxford University Press, 2014, p. 269.

50 Cf. Ibid.

51 *Convention on the Prevention and Punishment of the Crime of Genocide*, Paris, 9 December 1948 (*Trb.* 1960/32, *Trb.* 1966/179).

52 The amendment read as follows: 'Similarly, it shall not be interpreted in such a way as to impair the provisions of the Convention on the Prevention and Punishment of the Crime of Genocide.'; see Annotations on the Text of the Draft International Covenants on Human Rights, *UN Doc.* A/2929, 1 July 1955, p. 102 (para. 180).

53 See section 3.7.1 below.

54 Neil Boister, '"Transnational Criminal Law"?', *European Journal of International Law* 2003, vol. 14, 953–976.

55 See ILC, *Yearbook of the International Law Commission, 1971*, vol. II, part two (1973), *UN Doc.* A/CN.4/SERJV/1971/Add.l (Part 2), in particular para. 442–446; see also Alexander Orakhelashvili, *Peremptory Norms in International Law*, Oxford: Oxford University Press, 2008, p. 101.

56 See Annotations on the Text of the Draft International Covenants on Human Rights, *UN Doc.* A/2929, 1 July 1955, p. 102 (para. 181). More information on Article 103 Charter of the United Nations; see section 3.7.8.

of the article was to safeguard not the Charter or the constitutions of the specialized agencies, but the distribution of responsibilities between the United Nations and the specialized agencies', which would render a reference to the Genocide Convention irrelevant.[57] Moreover, it would not be appropriate to refrain from referring to other relevant international conventions as well then. That would mean that 'considerable research would be needed to ensure a full listing of all the existing conventions which had a direct bearing on the rights enunciated in the covenant', which list could not possibly be complete and definitive.[58] The proposal to amend the provision in Article 24 ICESCR and Article 46 ICCPR was withdrawn because of the potentially unfavourable political consequences of the proposal being rejected or accepted by a narrow majority only.[59]

It is clear from this summary explanation from the history of the convention that first, when the ICESCR and the ICCPR were created, no 'definite possibility of a discrepancy' between the human rights conventions and the drugs conventions of that time was foreseen.[60] Secondly, apart from that, it would appear that no one saw a clear *specialis/generalis* relationship (or the other way around) between, on the one hand, the ICESCR and the ICCPR and, on the other hand, the Genocide Convention and other conventions that might be relevant for the rights in the human rights conventions (as may be the case for drugs conventions).[61] It is also worth noting that one did not even protect or did not want to protect the Genocide Convention from the situation in which states could shirk their obligations under this convention by appealing to provisions in the ICESCR and the ICCPR. Taking into account the different order of the drugs conventions, there are even fewer reasons to assume that this would have been the intention for those conventions in one way or another. It was therefore left to the rules of precedence of international law, which we will discuss presently.

Finally, the two European human rights conventions. The ESC does not contain any provisions to arrange the relationship to other international

---

57 Ibid, p. 102 (para. 182).

58 Ibid.

59 Ibid, p. 102 (para. 183).

60 For information about the drugs conventions at the time – including the *International Opium Convention* of 1925, which ceased to be valid with the entry into force of the Single Convention on 13 December 1964, see the latter's Article 44(1)(c) – e.g. Tom Blom, *Opiumwetgeving en drugsbeleid*, Deventer: Kluwer, 2015, pp. 1–40 (i.e., Tom Blom, 'Opium laws and drug policy', Deventer: Kluwer, 2015, pp. 1–40).

61 This is not because no one took account of such relationships; after all, that relationship was recognized in the case of the International Labour Organisation's Convention No 87 concerning Freedom of Association and Protection of the Right to Organize (ILO, 1948), which is referred to in Article 8(3) ICESCR and Article 22(3) ICCPR; see Annotations on the Text of the Draft International Covenants on Human Rights, *UN Doc.* A/2929, 1 July 1955, p. 56 (para. 152) and 102 (para. 182).

instruments or norms. The same goes for the ECHR. It is true that the preamble of this convention refers to the Universal Declaration of Human Rights (UDHR), but it does not contain a precedence clause with respect to other conventions. Insofar as the relationship to other human rights conventions is concerned, this is hardly surprising, since the ECHR is the first binding human rights instrument to be created, on 4 November 1950. The UN narcotic drugs conventions did not exist at the time either, although as we observed before, there were other drugs covenants and treaties in force at the time.

The conclusion is that the relevant human rights conventions and drugs conventions do not contain precedence clauses that are relevant for the interference between these conventions.

3.7. CLASSIC RULES ABOUT DETERMINING PRIORITY AND PRECEDENCE

If the interference between conventions and/or obligations from different conventions cannot be resolved through convention precedence clauses as a result of the absence, lack of clarity or the non-applicability of those clauses, one can resort to the classic rules about determining precedence. This concerns rules regarding:

- specificity (*lex specialis* versus *lex generalis*);
- temporality (*lex posterior* and *lex prior*); and
- status (*lex superior*, for which *jus cogens*, *erga omnes* obligations and Article 103 UN Charter are relevant, among other things).

Other principles and the Vienna Convention on the Law of Treaties play a part in the meaning of these rules as well. Before we discuss the various rules in order below, there are a few general background concepts and limitations about these rules that deserve our attention.

3.7.1. 'SYSTEMS', 'SUBSYSTEMS', 'BRANCHES', 'SUBSETS' AND INSTITUTIONAL UNITS

Certain concepts such as 'system', 'subsystem' and 'branches' and sometimes also 'subsets' are bandied about in the international literature about rules of precedence. These concepts have no legal meaning in themselves and they do not have their origin in conventions for example either. In addition to this, these concepts are in many cases not defined by the authors who use them. Partly because of that, it is not always clear in which sense these concepts are used and whether the concepts actually refer to the same thing in different texts. Against the backdrop of the literature used in this book and in which these concepts are found, we assume that the concepts usually have the meanings described below. At any rate, these are the meanings used for this book. In addition to the four concepts mentioned, we will also define the concept of 'institutional units', as this is relevant later in this chapter, for example in relation to the four other concepts. Incidentally, we also point out that the purpose of this discussion is not to establish exactly and in detail what the concepts cover, nor is this necessary for the cannabis issue. Incidentally, as far as we know, no one has established this in the literature on international law to date.

- *System*. This concept usually refers to a complete legal system. International law constitutes such a system.[62] This also holds for the national legal system of an individual country.
- *Subsystems*. This entails specialized systems that are part of a larger system. This concerns systems that belong to the general system of international law, but that does not mean that they are always perfectly in line with it.[63] With a subsystem, as the term implies, there is a certain system and consistent configuration, with a relatively autonomous complex of rules and principles, institutes and legal practice.[64]

  The first type of subsystem is to do with functionally defined theme areas – also called regimes'[65] – such as international human rights law, trade law, environmental law, criminal law, diplomacy law and maritime law.[66] Perhaps the UN drug control system (with its own monitoring mechanisms and dispute settlement, which in international literature is discussed as a

62 ILC, 'Report 58th Session: Chapter XII, Fragmentation of International Law', 2006, p. 407 (para. 251(1) (fn. 1012)). See also Joost Pauwelyn, 'Fragmentation of International Law', in: *Max Planck Encyclopedia of Public International Law*, Oxford: Oxford University Press (online; last updated: September 2006, para. 27).

63 For information on the derogation of the 'branch' of international human rights law with regard to general international law and the institutional ambitions of that 'branch', see for example Martti Koskenniemi & Päivi Leino, 'Fragmentation of International Law? Postmodern Anxieties', *Leiden Journal of International Law* 2002, vol. 15, no. 3, pp. 553–579 on pp. 567–570.

64 ILC, 'Report 58th Session: Chapter XII, Fragmentation of International Law', 2006, p. 404 (para. 243); see also ILC, 'Fragmentation of International Law', 2006, para. 152. See also Axel Marschik, 'Too Much Order? The Impact of Special Secondary Norms on the Unity and Efficacy of the International Legal System', *European Journal of International law* 1998, vol. 9, pp. 212–239 on p. 212: 'Regimes of international law which combine certain primary norms with a distinct set of secondary norms designed to ensure the operation of those primary norms have since been termed 'subsystems' of international law'.

65 For more information about this, see Stephen D. Krasner, 'Structural Causes and Regime Consequences: Regimes as Intervening Variables', in: Stephen D. Krasner (ed.), *International Regimes*, Ithaca/London: Cornell University Press, 1983, pp. 1–21 on pp. 1–5.

66 See Joost Pauwelyn, 'Fragmentation of International Law', in: *Max Planck Encyclopedia of Public International Law*, Oxford: Oxford University Press (online; last updated: September 2006, para. 2).

separate subject) can also be considered a subsystem;[67] otherwise one could qualify it as a 'subset' of the 'branch' that is constituted by international law regarding fighting (international or transnational) crime (for more information about this, see below). Incidentally, this concerns a subsystem which – just like the ICESCR and the ICCPR, but unlike the law of the World Trade Organization (WTO)[68] – is an integral part of the system of the United Nations. Subsystems in a functional theme area may overlap with functionally specialized organizations, such as the WTO and the International Labour Organization (ILO).

The second type of subsystem relates to geographical areas, for example the human rights system of the United Nations (global) and the human rights system of the Council of Europe (regional) or even the ECHR system as such[69] (regional).[70] This second type of subsystem can result in a divergence between functionally defined theme areas and/or branches. This is usually referred to as fragmentation.[71]

- *Branches.* These are branches of international law. There are those who appear to treat 'branches' and 'subsystems' as synonyms.[72] Others use the term in a broader sense: a branch by and large covers all international law in a certain theme area. The following are examples of branches: international law relating to human rights law, trade law, environmental law, diplomacy law, maritime law, space law and the law of treaties.[73] For example, the

67 Literature in which this point of view is asserted explicitly has so far eluded us in our search, but it is interesting that for example international terrorism law – which has clear similarities with international law on drugs – is regarded as a separate 'branch' (for an explanation of this concept see below); also in this respect, see Daniel Moeckli, 'The Emergence of Terrorism as a Distinct Category of International Law', *Texas International Law Journal* 2008, vol. 44, pp. 157–183.

68 This is important because many of the problems described in the literature about the application of human rights in the system of the WTO do not present themselves for the drug control system or not in the same way, so that the discussion about this can be disregarded in this book; with respect to the WTO, see for example Joost Pauwelyn, *Conflict of Norms in Public International Law: How WTO Law relates to Other Rules of International Law*, Cambridge: Cambridge University Press, 2003; Sarah Joseph, *Blame it on the WTO?: A Human Rights Critique*, Oxford: Oxford University Press, 2011.

69 The situation that the ECHR itself comprises a subsystem is a conclusion drawn by Magdalena Forowicz, *The Reception of International Law in the European Court of Human Rights*, Oxford: Oxford University Press, 2010, pp. 16–18.

70 Cf. Bruno Simma & Dirk Pulkowski, 'Of Planets and the Universe: Self-contained Regimes in International Law', *Europeans Journal of International Law* 2006, vol. 17, no. 3, pp. 483–529 on pp. 483, 516.

71 This is the subject of ILC, 'Fragmentation of International Law', 2006.

72 For example, see Manuel Rama-Montaldo, 'Universalism and Particularisms in the Creation Process of International Law', in: Sienho Yee & Jacques-Yvan Morin, *Multiculturalism and International Law. Essays in Honour of Edward McWhinney*, Leiden/Boston: Martinus Nijhoff Publishers, 2009, pp. 129–167 on p. 144.

73 Compare for example the enumerations in Davorin Lapas, 'Some remarks on fragmentation of international law: disintegration or transformation?', *Comparative and International Law*

ICESCR, the ICCPR, the ESC, the ECHR and the corresponding monitoring mechanisms all fall in the branch of human rights law. Within this branch, the Council of Europe or even the ECHR system as such are subsystems.[74] International law to fight (international or transnational) crime is also recognized as a branch.[75] The UN drug control system can then also be seen as a part of that branch,[76] possibly as a 'subsystem' (see above) or otherwise as a 'subset' (see below). In this book, we will also use the terms 'subsystem' and 'branch' as distinct concepts.[77] This does not alter the fact that they may completely overlap in concrete cases: international law within a branch can be so systematic and coherent that the entire branch also constitutes a subsystem. With respect to the branch of human rights, this is not the case in our opinion, in view of the systematic, procedural and substantive differences between the legal regimes of for example the ICCPR, the ECHR and the Inter-American and African human rights treaties.

- *Subsets.* Sometimes the concept of 'branches' is used in a stricter sense than in this book, for example by designating international refugee law and international humanitarian law as branches of international human rights

Journal of Southern Africa (Comp. & Int'l L.J. S. Afr.) 2007, vol. 40, pp. 1–29 on 21 and 23; Daniel Moeckli, 'The Emergence of Terrorism as a Distinct Category of International Law', Texas International Law Journal 2008, vol. 44, pp. 157–183 on p. 158. In 1971, the ILC identified seventeen 'topics' or 'branches' in which international law could be divided at the time; see ILC, *Yearbook of the International Law Commission, 1971*, vol. II, part two (1973), *UN Doc.* A/CN.4/SERJV/1971/Add.l (Part 2), in particular para. 13, 16.

74 See in that sense Magdalena Forowicz, *The Reception of International Law in the European Court of Human Rights*, Oxford: Oxford University Press, 2010, p. 17; Axel Marschik, 'Too Much Order? The Impact of Special Secondary Norms on the Unity and Efficacy of the International Legal System', European Journal of International law 1998, vol. 9, pp. 212–239 on p. 224 ('human rights regimes present interesting examples of subsystems') and 235 ('subsystems such as human rights treaties'); Joost Pauwelyn, 'Fragmentation of International Law', in: *Max Planck Encyclopedia of Public International Law*, Oxford: Oxford University Press (online; last updated: September 2006, para. 3 and 4; and apparently also Jana Ondrovičová, 'Book review of: 'P. Šturma, S. Hýbnerová, J. Ondřej, V. Balaš, V. Bílková & V. Honusková: Competing Jurisdiction of International Judicial Bodies (Prague: Charles University in Prague, Faculty of Law, 2009, 117 pp.), *Czech Yearbook of International Law* 2010, pp. 255–258 on p. 255.

75 See, among other sources, Davorin Lapas, 'Some remarks on fragmentation of international law: disintegration or transformation?', *Comparative and International Law Journal of Southern Africa (Comp. & Int'l L.J. S. Afr.)* 2007, vol. 40, pp. 1–29 on p. 13; Eduardo Vetere, 'Opening statement', in: *The Application of the United Nations Standards and Norms in Crime Prevention and Criminal Justice*, Papers of Expert Group Meeting, Vienna: UNODC, 2003, pp. 7–9 on p. 8, in which the 'whole spectrum of crime prevention and criminal justice aspects' is presented as an entire unit and under which 'criminal justice subsystems' are recognized.

76 Cf. ILC, *Yearbook of the International Law Commission, 1971*, vol. II, part two (1973), *UN Doc.* A/CN.4/SERJV/1971/Add.l (Part 2), in particular para. 446.

77 Incidentally, the ILC also distinguishes subsystems from branches; see ILC, 'Fragmentation of International Law', 2006, para. 152.

law.[78] However, in this context the term 'subsets' is also used[79] and that is the term we will use. A 'subset' is then a smaller coherent unit which is part of a larger theme area or a branch. Insofar as the UN drug control system lacks independence and uniqueness for it to be deemed a 'subsystem', as a 'subset' it does at any rate fall within the branch of international and transnational criminal law, with respect to the point where this system interferes with human rights conventions, namely: the fight against drugs for recreational use.[80]

- *Institutional units.* This concept is important because international law is created through a large number of regulatory forums. For example, the United Nations and the Council of Europe. These – and many other – international organizations derive their regulatory powers from an institutional basis document (for the UN and the CoE that is the Charter/Statute) and that makes them institutional units. Various different organs may function within an institutional unit, including organs that monitor compliance with conventions. This is the case in both the United Nations (for example the human rights committees, the INCB and the CND) and the Council of Europe (for example, the European CSR and the ECtHR). A subsystem may completely overlap an institutional unit, but it does not have to be that way. After all, a subsystem may be part of an institutional unit (if one sees the ECHR system as a subsystem, it is still a part of the Council of Europe), whereas it is also possible that a subsystem is carried by various institutional units (this would be the case if the entire branch of human rights law were qualified as a subsystem).

In the light of the foregoing, in principle we will discuss the human rights system of the United Nations and that of the Council of Europe as two different subsystems that both fall within the branch of human rights law. Moreover, we will also designate the UN drug control system as a subsystem in principle. Furthermore, we regard the United Nations and the Council of Europe as institutional units, which comprise the ICESCR, the ICCPR and the UN narcotic drugs conventions, and the ESC and the ECtHR, respectively.

3.7.2. RULES OF PRECEDENCE IN GENERAL

Of the classical rules about determining precedence in international law, *lex specialis*, *lex posterior/prior* and to a certain degree *lex superior* are based on

[78] Seira Yun, 'Breaking Imaginary Barriers. Obligations of Armed Non-State Actors Under General Human Rights Law – the Case of the Optional Protocol to the Convention on the Rights of the Child', *Journal of International Humanitarian Legal Studies* 2014, vol. 5, pp. 213–257 on 218 and 220 (fn. 29).

[79] Ibid, pp. 213, 215, 220, 256.

[80] Cf. ILC, *Yearbook of the International Law Commission, 1971*, vol. II, part two (1973), *UN Doc.* A/CN.4/SERJV/1971/Add.l (Part 2), in particular para. 446.

a trio of general principles: 1. the contractual freedom of states; 2. the principle of *pacta sunt servanda*;[81] and 3. the principle of *pacta tertiis nec nocent nec prosunt*.[82,83]

According to Pauwelyn, the principle of contractual freedom of states plays a decisive part in most cases and the most recent expression of the will of the states usually takes precedence.[84] For example, that will can be expressed in the so-called precedence clauses discussed above in section 3.6. Particularly when that is not the case, or not clearly the case, or when the clause does not apply because the state is not a party to either convention to which the clause relates (*pacta tertiis nec nocent nec prosunt*), the applicability of the aforementioned three basic principles and the way in which they work will depend to a large extent on the circumstances of the specific case. Merely because of that, the applicability of the rules of precedence and the way in which they work will depend on the particulars of the case. Additionally, these rules of precedence may apply simultaneously. Consequently, the application of the rules of precedence may vary from case to case, since the way in which the rules work is influenced by the above-mentioned basic principles.[85] Eventually, taking into account the concrete circumstances of interference, one must determine which rules of precedence are applicable, to what extent and in which respect. Two important restrictions apply that must always be borne in mind.

First, it is important that there is no hierarchical relationship between or for the application of these classic rules of precedence themselves. There is no higher norm of international law that states that a more specific rule always takes precedence over or must give precedence to a later rule.[86] The functioning

81 See this principle in relation to the obligation to comply with conventions in Article 26 of the Vienna Convention on the Law of Treaties: 'Every treaty in force is binding upon the parties to it and must be performed by them in good faith'.

82 In connection with conventions, see Article 34 of the Vienna Convention on the Law of Treaties: 'A treaty does not create either obligations or rights for a third State without its consent'.

83 Joost Pauwelyn, *Conflict of Norms in Public International Law: How WTO Law relates to Other Rules of International Law*, Cambridge: Cambridge University Press, 2003, p. 328.

84 Ibid.

85 See among other sources ILC, 'Fragmentation of International Law', 2006, para. 250, 325, 410.

86 See among other sources Ralf Michaels & Joost Pauwelyn, 'Conflict of Norms or Conflict of Laws?: Different Techniques in the Fragmentation of Public International Law', *Duke Journal of Comparative & International Law* 2012, vol. 22, pp. 349–376; Dinah Shelton, 'Normative Hierarchy in International Law', *The American Journal of International Law* 2006, vol. 100, pp. 291–323 on p. 294: 'Conceptual problems abound because almost every purported principle of precedence (e.g. *lex specialis derogat lex generali*) has exceptions and no rule establishes when to apply the principle and when to apply the exception.'; Martii Koskenniemi, 'Hierarchy in International Law: A Sketch', *European Journal of International Law* 1997, vol. 8, pp. 566–582; Clarence Wilfred Jenks, 'Conflict of Law-Making Treaties', British Yearbook of International Law 1953, vol. 30, pp. 401– 453 on p. 407: 'no particular principle or rule can be regarded as of absolute validity'.

of these rules is not mechanical[87] but relative and determined by context.[88] Decisive factors are:[89]

- the wills of the parties;
- the nature of the instrument and its object and purpose; and
- reasonable application with minimal disruption for the workings of the legal system.[90]

Secondly, it is relevant whether the interference between conventions is about the situation where the conventions were neither created within the same institutional unit nor from within the same subsystem. If that is the case (and this involves a so-called 'inter-system' conflict), this will often hamper the application of the rules of precedence significantly; a better situation for the functioning of the rules of precedence occurs in an 'intra-system' relationship.[91] The multitude of equivalent international regulators that create and apply norms in different, often independently operating organizations, and also the absence of a clear hierarchy of legal sources and a hierarchical institutional structure in public international law entails that the classical rules of precedence must be applied differently in the case of interference between conventions and/or norms than they would in national systems or even within the specialized, more or less independently operating 'subsystems' of public international law.[92] Within such subsystems, it will be easier to interpret the subject of the conventions or the will of the states parties than between these various 'subsystems'. That applies in particular in situations where the states signing the convention have not paid attention to potential inter-systemic conflicts between norms.

Finally, the following needs to be pointed out. In certain cases, it may be important who the parties to the conventions are that are involved

87 ILC, 'Fragmentation of International Law', 2006, para. 36, 250, 488.

88 Ibid, para. 62 and also 410: 'The way the relevant techniques *(lex specialis; lex posterior, lex superior)* operated was dependent on what should be considered as the relevant aspects of each case'.

89 Ibid, para. 410.

90 For more information on this, see sections 3.9 and 3.10.1.iii.

91 Ralf Michaels & Joost Pauwelyn, 'Conflict of Norms or Conflict of Laws?: Different Techniques in the Fragmentation of Public International Law', *Duke Journal of Comparative & International Law* 2012, vol. 22, pp. 349–376 on 357, 363, 366–367; see also for example Ahmad Ali Ghouri, 'Determining Hierarchy Between Conflicting Treaties: Are There Vertical Rules in the Horizontal System?', *Asian Journal of International Law* 2012, vol. 2, no. 2, pp. 235–266 on p. 254.

92 For an explanation of the concept of 'self-contained regimes' (systems, subsystems and branches), see for example ILC, 'Fragmentation of International Law', 2006, para. 152 (see also 118, 132, 489); moreover, see Bruno Simma & Dirk Pulkowski, 'Of Planets and the Universe: Self-contained Regimes in International Law', *Europeans Journal of International Law* 2006, vol. 17, no. 3, pp. 483–529.

in interference.[93] In principle, it is not relevant for the analysis of this book to establish precisely which states are party to the two conventions the norms of which clash. First of all, this book is about analysis and assessment of positive human rights obligations and drugs conventions obligations as such. The book does not aim to clarify a specific concrete conflict between two or more states with regard to the interference between these obligations. However, even if this were different, in most cases that would not lead to different results, and that brings us to a second point: both the Single Convention and the Illicit Traffic Convention on the one hand and the ICESCR and the ICCPR on the other hand can be characterized by practically universal participation. This obviously is not the case for the European human rights conventions (the ESC and the ECHR), but there is an almost unanimous acceptance at a European level. In addition to this, the ICESCR and the ICCPR on the one hand and the ESC and the ECHR on the other hand are mostly similar with respect to the obligations relevant for the cannabis issue. However, they are not identical, as we saw in Chapter 2.

3.7.3. THE CRITERION OF THE 'SAME SUBJECT MATTER' TEST

Previously, we briefly discussed the question whether the interfering conventions and/or convention norms cover the same subject matter in relation to the definition of conflict. That question may also be relevant when deciding whether the rules of precedence discussed later may apply. For that reason, we will already dwell in general on this criterion or the so-called 'same subject matter' test here.

Finding out whether the subject is the same can be approached in different ways. For example, one can give prominence to the theme of interfering conventions and/or convention norms.[94] In this strict approach of the criterion, human rights conventions and drugs conventions do not have the 'same subject matter', since the themes are human rights and drugs, respectively. This strict interpretation entails that the most problematic interferences, such as conflicts between human rights conventions and humanitarian law or between environmental agreements and trade agreements, fall outside the scope of this provision.[95] So the question is whether a wider approach is possible and indeed, called for. Most international conventions can always be qualified in different

93 See Article 30(4) of the Vienna Convention on the Law of Treaties, which deals with successive treaties that relate to the same subject matter; see also Ahmad Ali Ghouri, 'Determining Hierarchy Between Conflicting Treaties: Are There Vertical Rules in the Horizontal System?', *Asian Journal of International Law* 2012, vol. 2, no. 2, pp. 235–266 on p. 249.

94 ILC, 'Fragmentation of International Law', 2006, para. 22.

95 See among other sources Christopher J. Borgen, 'Resolving Treaty Conflicts', *The George Washington International Law Review* 2005, vol. 37, pp. 573–648 on p. 614.

ways from various perspectives. Instead of establishing a link to the 'nature of the instrument', it is also possible to qualify an instrument in terms of 'the *interest* from the perspective of which the instrument is assessed by the observer.'[96]

A wider approach is therefore possible by making the objective of the convention the decisive factor, instead of its subject matter.[97] Depending on how generally the object and purpose of human rights conventions and drugs conventions for example are formulated, it may be possible to conclude that they cover the same subject matter. Should the objective of drugs conventions for example be designated as guaranteeing public health by combating drugs and securing the availability of medicines? In that case, the subject matter is perhaps different from that of the human rights conventions. This could be different if its purpose were more generally seen as guaranteeing public health or even the well-being of people.[98] In that case, its objective strongly resembles that of the human rights conventions and then it would be the same subject matter. In sections 3.10.1.ii and 3.10.2.ii, we will return to the object and purpose of the conventions in question.

An even broader approach is used by the International Law Commission, among others, which follows the example of Vierdag and assumes that the subject matter is the same if an attempt to apply two rules of the same complex of facts or acts simultaneously leads to incompatible results.[99] This may be the case if two conventions and/or norms of conventions touch upon the same question, albeit from various objectives and angles. Even with a strict interpretation of the theme and the objective of human rights conventions and drugs conventions, these instruments do after all relate to the same subject matter if they are normatively relevant for a drugs and/or cannabis policy. Because it is often assumed in the literature that this approach of the ILC is the applicable approach, we will make this our starting point. Nevertheless, we point out that the criterion of the 'same

---

96 See among other sources ILC, 'Fragmentation of International Law', 2006, para. 254.

97 Cf. ILC, 'Fragmentation of International Law', 2006, para. 256: 'The distinction between treaties dealing with the "same subject-matter" and treaties within the same "regime" may appear slight, but it constitutes an important practical shift of perspective. In the former case, focus is on the object that is being regulated while in the latter case, focus is on the intent of the States parties and the institutions they have established'.

98 Cf. INCB, *Report of the International Narcotics Control Board for 2015*, New York: United Nations, 2016, p. 1 (no. 1). 'The ultimate goal of the three international drug control conventions is to protect public and individual health and welfare'.

99 ILC, 'Fragmentation of International Law', 2006, para. 22–23 (see also 116–118 and 253–254), with reference to E.W. Vierdag, 'The Time of the "Conclusion" of a Multilateral Treaty: Article 30 of the Vienna Convention on the Law of Treaties and Related Provisions', *British Yearbook of International Law* 1988, vol. 59, pp. 75–111 on p. 100. See also, among other sources, Anja Lindroos, 'Addressing Norm Conflicts in a Fragmented Legal System: The Doctrine of *Lex Specialis*', *Nordic Journal of International Law* 2005, vol. 74, pp. 27–66 on pp. 44–48; Jan Klabbers, 'Beyond the Vienna Convention: Conflicting Treaty Provisions', in: Enzo Cannizzaro (ed.), *The Law of Treaties Beyond the Vienna Convention*, Oxford: Oxford University Press, 2011, pp. 192–205 on pp. 193–194.

subject matter' in this approach has little capacity for making distinctions. For a convincing application of rules of precedence, it may then be useful or necessary to make further assessments as to whether there is indeed a strong link between the conventions subject wise.

3.7.4. SPECIAL VERSUS GENERAL: SUBJECT OF THE CONVENTIONS (*LEX SPECIALIS*)

The principle of *lex specialis derogat lex generali* can be relevant when differentiating between content and for prioritization in the case of interference of conventions or their norms.[100] Although this principle has no basis in the Vienna Convention on the Law of Treaties, it is a 'standard technique of legal reasoning' and a 'widely accepted maxim of legal interpretation and technique for the resolution of normative conflicts.'[101] The principle also means that if a legal subject is regulated by both a general norm and a more specific rule, the latter rule takes precedence. Incidentally, this does not imply that the *specialis* is superior to the general rule in terms of content.[102]

i. Rationale for the Lex Specialis *Rule*

The premise of this precedence clause is that if a situation is covered by a specific rule, there is little point in resorting to the general rule. In this respect, it is also important that the special norms usually are more relevant and more effective than general ones.[103] The power of the *lex specialis* rule can be found in its capacity to resolve interference concretely, clearly and definitively, to take into account the specific circumstances of the case and to express the intention of the parties.[104] In particular, the emphasis on 'consent' and the intention of the parties make the *lex specialis* a suitable instrument for resolving normative conflicts in

---

100 ILC, 'Fragmentation of International Law', 2006, para. 61. Although this research is merely about the *lex specialis* rule in the case of interference between conventions, it may also play a role in other relationships; see para. 68: 'The maxim may operate (a) within a single instrument; (b) between two different instruments; (c) between a treaty and a non-treaty standard and (d) between two non-treaty standards.'; see also para. 66.

101 Ibid, para. 119 and 56.

102 Likewise, Antonios Tzanakopoulos, 'Collective Security and Human Rights', in: Erika De Wet & Jure Vidmar (eds.), *Hierarchy in International Law: The Place of Human Rights*, Oxford: Oxford University Press, 2012, pp. 42–70 on pp. 45–46.

103 ILC, 'Fragmentation of International Law', 2006, para. 59–60. See also Joost Pauwelyn, *Conflict of Norms in Public International Law: How WTO Law relates to Other Rules of International Law*, Cambridge: Cambridge University Press, 2003, p. 387.

104 ILC, 'Fragmentation of International Law', 2006, para. 119.

international law.[105] After all, the contractual freedom of states entails that states can invoke specific rules in derogation of general international law.[106]

ii. Two Variants of the General/Specific Relationship

A specific norm can relate to a general norm in two ways: as an application of it or an exception to it. 'A particular rule may be considered an *application* of a general standard in a given circumstance. The special relates to the general as does administrative regulation to law in domestic legal order. Or it may be considered as a *modification, overruling* or a *setting aside* of the latter.'[107]

The first possibility therefore is that the *specialis* must be read as an extension, update or a technical specification of the more general norm.[108] In that case, the general and specific norms point in the same direction[109] and the specific norm falls within the scope of the general norm.[110] The application of the *specialis* then takes place through interpretation in agreement with the (object and purpose of the) generalis. In that case, there is no interference and the *lex specialis* rule cannot be used as a rule of precedence.[111] With regard to the relationship between human rights obligations and drugs conventions obligations, it is hard to defend that one norm serves to specify the more general other norm. After all, neither of the obligations has been established explicitly as further specification of the obligations in the other, while in principle they actually point in opposite directions as far as the cannabis issue is concerned.

The other possibility means that the rule regarding *lex specialis* is interpreted more rigorously: 'to cover the case where two legal provisions that are both valid and applicable, are in no express hierarchical relationship, and provide incompatible direction on how to deal with the same set of facts.'[112] In contrast to the first possibility, this is exactly where the *lex specialis* rule works as a technique to solve norm interference. The solution comes down to applying the

---

105 Anja Lindroos, 'Addressing Norm Conflicts in a Fragmented Legal System: The Doctrine of *Lex Specialis*', *Nordic Journal of International Law* 2005, vol. 74, pp. 27–66 on pp. 36–37.

106 ICJ, Judgment of 20 February 1969, *I.C.J. Reports* 1969, para. 472 (*North Sea Continental Shelf cases – Federal Republic of Germany v. Denmark & Federal Republic of Germany v. The Netherlands*); ICJ, Judgment of 24 February 1982, *I.C.J. Reports* 1982, para. 24 (*Case concerning the Continental Shelf – Tunisia v. Libyan Arab Jamahiriya*).

107 ILC, 'Fragmentation of International Law', 2006, para. 88 (footnotes omitted).

108 Jan B. Mus, 'Conflicts between Treaties in International Law', *Netherlands International Law Review* 1998, vol. 45, pp. 208–232 on p. 218.

109 ILC, 'Fragmentation of International Law', 2006, para. 56.

110 Gerald Fitzmaurice, 'The Law and Procedure of the International Court of Justice 1951–1954: Treaty Interpretation and other Treaty Points', *British Yearbook of International Law* 1957, vol. 33, pp. 203–293 on p. 236.

111 See also, with further references, Anja Lindroos, 'Addressing Norm Conflicts in a Fragmented Legal System: The Doctrine of *Lex Specialis*', *Nordic Journal of International Law* 2005, vol. 74, pp. 27–66 on pp. 44–45.

112 ILC, 'Fragmentation of International Law', 2006, para. 57.

specific exception rather than the general rule. In subsection iv below, we are looking at the question whether and if yes, in which respect, the relationship between human rights conventions and the drugs conventions is of the general/specific kind or vice versa.

iii. Limitations to the Applicability of the Lex Specialis *Rule*

The potential applicability of the rule in international law is at any rate subject to the following, partly interconnected limitations.[113]

First of all, the functioning of the *lex specialis* is seen as problematic[114] and is even excluded by some[115] in cases where the norms are not based on a 'common system'. The *lex specialis* rule may play a role in interference between general international law and one of its subsystems.[116] However, this will be difficult if not impossible in case the interference relates to conventions and/or norms of conventions that belong to different subsystems.[117] It is important that this

---

113 See also Anja Lindroos, 'Addressing Norm Conflicts in a Fragmented Legal System: The Doctrine of *Lex Specialis*', *Nordic Journal of International Law* 2005, vol. 74, pp. 27–66 on pp. 42–44.

114 Anja Lindroos, 'Addressing Norm Conflicts in a Fragmented Legal System: The Doctrine of *Lex Specialis*', *Nordic Journal of International Law* 2005, vol. 74, pp. 27–66 on pp. 41–42; Jan Klabbers, 'Beyond the Vienna Convention: Conflicting Treaty Provisions', in: Enzo Cannizzaro (ed.), *The Law of Treaties Beyond the Vienna Convention*, Oxford: Oxford University Press, 2011, pp. 192–205 on p. 201; Jasper Finke, 'Regime-collisions: Tensions between treaties (and how to solve them)', in: Christian J. Tams, Antonios Tzanakopoulos & Andreas Zimmermann (eds.), *Research Handbook on the Law of Treaties*, Cheltenham, UK/Northampton, USA: Edward Elgar, 2014, pp. 415–446 on p. 423. In the same sense, but then in relation to the *lex posterior* rule: ILC, 'Fragmentation of International Law', 2006, para. 256.

115 Ralf Michaels & Joost Pauwelyn, 'Conflict of Norms or Conflict of Laws?: Different Techniques in the Fragmentation of Public International Law', *Duke Journal of Comparative & International Law* 2012, vol. 22, pp. 349–376 on p. 355: 'the lex superior principle requires a common system within which a hierarchy of norms can be established; it does not function between systems.'; Ahmad Ali Ghouri, 'Determining Hierarchy Between Conflicting Treaties: Are There Vertical Rules in the Horizontal System?', *Asian Journal of International Law* 2012, vol. 2, no. 2, pp. 235–266 on p. 254; Silvia Zorzetto, 'The Lex Specialis Principle and its Uses in Legal Argumentation. An Analytical Inquire', *Eunomía. Revista en Cultura de la Legalidad*, September 2012–February 2013, no. 3, pp. 61–87 on p. 64.

116 According to Davorin Lapas, 'Some remarks on fragmentation of international law: disintegration or transformation?', *Comparative and International Law Journal of Southern Africa (Comp. & Int'l L.J. S. Afr.)* 2007, vol. 40, pp. 1–29 on p. 25.

117 See Erika de Wet & Jure Vidmar, 'Conclusions', in: Erika De Wet & Jure Vidmar (eds.), *Hierarchy in International Law: The Place of Human Rights*, Oxford: Oxford University Press, 2012, pp. 300–310 on p. 305; Andreas R. Ziegler & Bertram Boie, 'The Relationship between International Trade Law and International Human Rights Law', in: Erika De Wet & Jure Vidmar (eds.), *Hierarchy in International Law: The Place of Human Rights*, Oxford: Oxford University Press, 2012, pp. 272–299 on p. 290; Anja Lindroos, 'Addressing Norm Conflicts in a Fragmented Legal System: The Doctrine of *Lex Specialis*', *Nordic Journal of International Law* 2005, vol. 74, pp. 27–66 on p. 44.

is the case with interference between human rights conventions and drugs conventions. After all, they belong to different subsystems. Even if one held the view that the UN narcotic drugs conventions do not constitute a subsystem, they still do not belong to a human rights subsystem and not even the branch of human rights law. That means that we are looking at an 'inter-system' conflict, and that we should therefore not expect an easy application of the *lex specialis* rule. However, the interference takes place within an institutional unit: both the UN narcotic drugs conventions and the ICESCR and ICCPR have their foundations within the United Nations. Insofar as we are dealing with interference with regard to the ESC and the ECHR, this is not an intra-conflict but an 'inter-system' conflict, where the application of the *lex specialis* rule is also problematic, to say the least.

Secondly, the *lex specialis* rule proves particularly useful if there is a clear link between the interfering conventions and/or norms in terms of content or substance. There is formally a substantive link if the conventions relate to the same subject matter or at any rate to the same functionally defined theme area.[118] It is usually assumed, by the ILC as well, that the *lex specialis* rule can only apply if the two norms involve the same subject matter.[119] Therefore, it is important that the respective subjects of the conventions or norms are very similar if not identical. Earlier on we saw that most of the authors assume, as does the ILC, that the subject matter is the same if an attempt to apply two rules of the same complex of facts or acts simultaneously leads to incompatible results. To that extent, the *lex specialis* rule, as we have observed before, has the potential to play a part in situations where human rights conventions and drugs conventions are normatively relevant for a drug and/or cannabis policy. However, as the 'same subject matter' test has a rather limited capacity for making distinctions with the above-mentioned interpretation of the criterion, its usefulness has by no means been ascertained. In other words, the fact that the subject matter is the

118 Anja Lindroos, Addressing Norm Conflicts in a Fragmented Legal System: The Doctrine of *Lex Specialis*, *Nordic Journal of International Law* 2005, vol. 74, pp. 27–66 on pp. 44–46. If the subject matter is the same, there can also be speciality with regard to the number of subjects whose behaviours are regulated by the convention; the convention that applies to fewer subjects, may then under conditions qualify as *specialis* for the convention that covers more subjects, incidentally particularly if they fall within the same subsystem; see with further references ILC, 'Fragmentation of International Law', 2006, para. 112; and also, although slightly differently, Joost Pauwelyn, *Conflict of Norms in Public International Law: How WTO Law relates to Other Rules of International Law*, Cambridge: Cambridge University Press, 2003, pp. 390–391.

119 ILC, 'Fragmentation of International Law', 2006, para. 116 (see also pp. 46, 75, 89), with reference to Gerald Fitzmaurice, 'The Law and Procedure of the International Court of Justice 1951–1954: Treaty Interpretation and other Treaty Points', *British Yearbook of International Law* 1957, vol. 33, pp. 203–293 on p. 237; International Law Commission, 'Draft articles on Responsibility of States for Internationally Wrongful Acts, with commentaries', *UN Doc.* A/56/10, 2001 (additionally: ILC, 'Articles on Responsibility of States for Internationally Wrongful Acts, with commentaries', 2001), comm. Article 55 (para. 4–5).

same from a formal point of view does not mean that there is also a strong link in terms of content. We will return to this in subsection iv.

Thirdly, the *lex specialis* rule can at best only play a part if it can be established that one of the interfering rules is of a more general nature, whereas the other one's character is specific. This need not always be the case. For certain subjects, states will establish all sorts of specific rights and obligations without there being general norms for the subject. In that case, there will be no *specialis*, so the rule is unusable.[120] The question therefore is whether one can identify a relationship of a general nature – special in the interference between human rights obligations and obligations arising from drugs conventions.

As far as the latter is concerned (and this leads us to a fourth limitation), the *lex specialis* rule is of little use. After all, it provides no criteria for the assessment which norms qualify as *generalis* and which ones as *specialis*.

iv. Does the Lex Specialis *Rule Apply to the Cannabis Issue?*

In the foregoing, a number of questions about the *lex specialis* rule already came to the fore in connection with the interference between human rights obligations and the obligations arising from drugs conventions. Nevertheless, several questions remain unanswered, including the most important one: can the (obligations from the) human rights conventions and the (obligations from the) drugs conventions be considered to be in a relationship of a general/specific nature, and if yes, in which respect? After all, if such a relationship does not exist either formally or substantively, the *lex specialis* rule is not usable as we have observed. This question must be answered in the negative, for the following reasons.

- *Formal approach*. First of all, from a formal point of view, there is no *specialis/generalis* relationship between the interfering conventions. The four human rights conventions (ICESCR, ICCPR, ESC and ECHR) do not contain any information explicitly or implicitly that they must be interpreted as further specification of the obligations that states have with regard to drugs or other conventions that also pertain to criminal law. Apart from that, the text and the preambles of these conventions do not contain – with the exception of a detail that is not relevant here[121] – any mention or reference to drugs.[122] As we saw in section 3.6 above, during the creation of the ICESCR and the ICCPR no *specialis/generalis* relationship (or the other way around) was used as a starting point between on the one hand the human rights conventions and on the other

---

120 See ILC, 'Fragmentation of International Law', 2006, para. 121. See also Anja Lindroos, 'Addressing Norm Conflicts in a Fragmented Legal System: The Doctrine of *Lex Specialis*', *Nordic Journal of International Law* 2005, vol. 74, pp. 27–66 on p. 42.

121 See Article 5(1)e ECHR, which recognizes the possibility of lawful detention of alcohol or drug addicts.

122 See sections 2.3.10 and 2.4.11.

hand conventions that might be relevant for the rights in the human rights conventions (for example the drugs conventions).

It is a slightly different situation for the recognition from within the drugs conventions that human rights can be relevant. This does not involve the Single Convention so much: its text and preamble do not explicitly refer to international human rights, human rights conventions or a specific human right. However, in the preparatory work on this convention, there are occasional references to human rights. The gist of these is usually that the obligations from the drugs conventions are not in conflict with or are not allowed to cause a conflict with human rights.[123] We have seen no evidence for any opinion about a possible *specialis/generalis* relationship between these conventions. The Illicit Traffic Convention, however, does contain an explicit reference to human rights. According to Article 14(2) of the Illicit Traffic Convention, the states parties in taking measures to prevent and eradicate illicit cannabis cultivation must 'respect fundamental human rights and shall take due account of traditional licit uses, where there is historic evidence of such use, as well as the protection of the environment.' This provision confirms the obligation to honour human rights, but it does not establish a *specialis/generalis* relationship between human rights and the Illicit Traffic Convention. As far as we have been able to ascertain, no attention was paid to any such relationship during the creation of the convention. However, the preparatory work on this convention contains a few references to specific individual rights in relation to specific subjects.[124] Almost invariably, the point made is that the obligations from the drugs conventions are not in conflict with or are not allowed to cause a conflict with human rights.

---

123 See United Nations, 'Conference for the adoption of a Single Convention on Narcotic Drugs. New York – 24 January–25 March 1961, Official Records, Volume I', *UN Doc.* E/CONF. 34/24, p. 14 and 196–197 (among other things 'to ensure the protection of human rights'); see also United Nations, 'United Nations Conference to consider amendments to the Single Convention on Narcotic Drugs, 1961. Geneva – 6–24 March 1972, Official Records, Volume I', New York, 1974, *UN Doc.* E/CONF. 63/10, p. 69 (para. 626) ('individual rights', 'right to personal freedom'), pp. 34, 47 ('freedom of the individual') and p. 70 (para. 630) ('the proposal in no way constituted a threat to personal freedoms'); United Nations, 'United Nations Conference to consider amendments to the Single Convention on Narcotic Drugs, 1961. Geneva – 6–24 March 1972, Official Records, Volume II', New York, 1973, *UN Doc.* E/CONF. 63/10/Add.1, pp. 157–161 (para. 12, 14, 20, 22, 48, 50, 57) ('freedom of expression', 'freedom of the press', 'freedom of thought'), p. 163 (para. 14) ('freedom of the press') and p. 198 (para. 8) ('respect for personal freedom').

124 See United Nations, 'Conference for the Adoption of a Convention against Illicit Traffic in Narcotic Drugs and Psychotropic Substances. Vienna, 25 November–20 December 1988, Official Records, Volume I', *UN Doc.* E/CONF. 82/16, p. 18 (para. 101) ('right to property' and 'presumption of innocence'), p. 25 (para. 200) ('measures adopted must be compatible with fundamental human rights')', p. 26 (para. 201) ('respect for human rights was an unquestionable requirement'), p. 34 (para. 45) ('human rights'), p. 65 (para. 93) ('the right of asylum or a violation of individual human rights') and p. 65 (para. 95) (The 'Review Group' about the draft convention 'agreed that the Convention was not intended to prejudice the right to asylum in conformity with international law'.)

Incidentally, this was recently confirmed for the UN drug control system by the INCB: 'Drug control action must be consistent with international human rights standards'.[125] Here too, a *specialis/generalis* relationship was neither confirmed nor implied.

- *Substantive approach.* From a substantive point of view, there is no *specialis/ generalis* relationship (or vice versa) either between the human rights and drugs conventions interfering in the cannabis issue. Admittedly, the foregoing implies that the drugs conventions must be applied with due regard for human rights, but that does not mean that the one is de facto a *specialis* of the other.

As became clear earlier, this poses a problem for applying the *lex specialis* rule, in that there is no 'common system' that lies at the heart of the human rights conventions and the drugs conventions. In any event, the conventions do not belong to the same 'branches': the first fall under international human rights law, whereas the drugs conventions – at the point where they interfere with human rights conventions – tie in most closely with international law on fighting crime. It is only with regard to the interference between the drugs conventions and the ICESCR and the ICCPR (and therefore not the ESC and the ECHR) that this problem may be less complicated, since they all fall within an institutional unit: the United Nations. However, that is not really the case, since in practice there is no harmonization between these convention regimes in terms of subject matter, nor has it taken place during their creation. That is also relevant in relation to the following.

The fact that under the current wide interpretation of the criterion of the 'same subject matter', human rights conventions and the drugs conventions cover the same topic where they interfere with each other with respect to a drug and/or cannabis policy, does not mean that there is a strong link between the conventions with respect to subject matter. Such a strong relationship is not easy to construe either. Again, such efforts would be thwarted by the fact that the conventions belong to different 'branches'. Even if one sees through that and presents a more general argument based on the object and purpose of the interfering conventions, this does not lead to a strong general link. It is true that in a general sense both convention regimes aim to protect the well-being of people, but that is true, directly or indirectly, for nearly all conventions. That is why this characterization is found wanting in its capacity to make distinctions in relation to the *lex specialis* rule.[126] The question then is whether, to be more precise, the common denominator lies in the protection of individual and public health. At any rate, that appears

---

125 INCB, *Report of the International Narcotics Control Board for 2015*, New York: United Nations, 2016, p. 6 (no. 36). For more information on this, see section 3.7.9.i.

126 In relation to harmonizing interpretation in order to arrive at the systematic integration of the systems, this common goal may be important, though; see section 3.10.

to be the objective of the drugs conventions in general.[127] However, this characterization is not adequate for the human rights conventions. The reason is that it only touches the core of the right to health. Health is not without meaning for the right to life, the right not to be subjected to inhuman treatment and the right to privacy, but this is far too narrow a description of its objective. Individual or public health has no bearing whatsoever on most other rights, so the rule of *lex specialis* cannot be used for that reason either. As regards the interference in the cannabis issue, the only somewhat pertinent substantive connection that can be construed is the one between the drugs conventions and the right to health. However, this does not detract from the other obstacles to the application of the *lex specialis* rule.

Finally, it is not easy to detect a *specialis/generalis* relationship, even if one restricts oneself to the interference between the drugs conventions and the right to health and negotiates the above-mentioned obstacles. After all, the question is which of the convention regimes would be deemed the general one. The two regimes are not related systematically, rather they are two different subsystems of different branches. If one in spite of this still wants to shoehorn the conventions involved – or more narrowly: the right to health and the UN drug control system – into a speciality relationship, this does not lead to unambiguous points of view. After all, it is possible to argue in two different directions, and in both cases the results are far from convincing. In the first scenario, the right to health is taken to be the general provision and the UN drug control system is treated as its specific implementation. Insofar as that system is all about fighting drugs production and trade for recreational use, this would be seen as a special implementation of the obligation to secure for everyone physical and mental health of 'the highest attainable standard' (Article 12(1) ICESCR) and 'to remove as far as possible the causes of ill-health' (Article 11(1) ESC. The problem with this approach is that the obligations arising from the drugs conventions only tenuously tie in with the tenor of the right to health and the way in which it is implemented more concretely in international law.[128] An important difference for example is that whereas the drugs conventions force states parties to prohibit and repress the production of and trade in drugs for recreational use, the right to health allows states discretion in principle, so that no obstacles arise for the state in its obligation to realize the highest attainable standard of health. In addition to this, we take the view that it is rather far-fetched to see the extensive UN drug control system as a *specialis* of one single individual right, the more so because no such connection is made in the system or in that right. Furthermore, at the time that the Single Convention was created in 1961, the right to health only had a codified basis at UN level in the non-legally binding Universal Declaration of

127 For more information on this, see section 3.10.1.ii.
128 See section 2.3.

Human Rights (UDHR) (see Article 25 UDHR[129]). After all, the ICESCR did not come into effect until 1966.[130] Taking this into account, one could then see the right to health as the *specialis* to the UN drugs conventions, which means we find ourselves arguing from the opposite direction. The biggest objection to that line of reasoning is that the right to health happens to be related to individual and public health in a much wider way than the UN drug control system.

Taking the foregoing into account, we conclude that the interference between the human rights conventions and the drugs conventions does not meet the requirements for the application of the *lex specialis* rule, while from a substantive point of view as well, that rule cannot be used to resolve the interference.

3.7.5. NEW VERSUS OLD: CHRONOLOGY OF THE CREATION OF CONVENTIONS (*LEX POSTERIOR*)

The adage *lex posterior derogat legi priori* translates as: the later law overrides the earlier one. In principle, it means that a rule of law created after another rule that conflicts with that more recent rule, the latter will prevail with regard to the scope of the conflict.[131] In contrast to the *lex specialis* rule, the *lex posterior* rule has an explicit basis[132] in – one of the most discussed[133] provisions from – the Vienna Convention on the Law of Treaties; Article 30, which will be discussed later.

i. *Rationale for the* Lex Posterior *Rule*

The rationale of the rule, as far as international law is concerned, lies in the idea that international rules are an expression of the will of states, which in

129 See section 2.3.2.

130 Incidentally, the ESC came into force only a little more than half a year later than the Single Convention, but apart from that, it really does not make sense that the UN drug control system is intended as a *specialis* for a right under the regional ESC.

131 Aaron X. Fellmeth & Maurice Horwitz, *Guide to Latin in International Law*, Oxford: Oxford University Press, 2009, at: 'Lex posterior derogat (legi) priori': 'A maxim meaning that a legal rule arising after a conflicting legal rule prevails over the earlier rule to the extent of the conflict'.

132 Christopher J. Borgen, 'Resolving Treaty Conflicts', *The George Washington International Law Review* 2005, vol. 37, pp. 573–648, on p. 603: 'thus, Article 30 (3) effectively codifies the lex posterior rule'.

133 Kerstin Odendahl, 'Application of successive treaties relating to the same subject matter', in: Oliver Dörr & Kirsten Schmalenbach (eds.), *Vienna Convention on the Law of Treaties, A Commentary*, Heidelberg/Dordrecht/London/New York: Springer, 2012, pp. 505–518 on pp. 507–508; Alexander Orakhelashvili, 'Article 30', in: Olivier Corten & Pierre Klein, *The Vienna Convention on the Law of Treaties, A Commentary*, Oxford: Oxford University Press, 2011, vol. I, pp. 764–800; ILC, 'Fragmentation of International Law', 2006, para. 257–264.

their sovereign equality enjoy contractual freedom: later agreements therefore take precedence over earlier ones,[134] unless the will of states demonstrates a preference for another outcome.[135] The rule does not imply that the later convention is superior to the earlier one for substantive reasons.[136]

ii. Dating of the Interfering Conventions

In order to determine the temporal order of successive conventions, one must establish the moment when a convention actually comes into being. The question is which moment is used as the decisive criterion: is it the moment the convention is adopted, the opening for signature, entry into force, signature and/or ratification by the required number of states parties? In general, the moment of adoption of the convention is seen as decisive.[137] More concretely, the effect of the application of Article 30 of the Vienna Convention on the Law of Treaties, which we will discuss now, for each individual state party will depend on the moment that the convention enters into force for that state.[138]

iii. Limitations to the Applicability of the Lex Posterior *Rule*

In essence, Article 30 of the Vienna Convention on the Law of Treaties states – subject to Article 103 Charter of the United Nations,[139] and insofar as this is relevant here – for 'successive treaties relating to the same subject-matter' that:[140]

---

134 See International Law Commission, 'Draft Articles on the Law of Treaties, with commentaries', *Yearbook of the International Law Commission* 1966, vol. II (also: ILC, 'Draft Articles on the Law of Treaties, with commentaries', 1966), comm. Article 26, p. 216 (para. 9); Joost Pauwelyn, *Conflict of Norms in Public International Law: How WTO Law relates to Other Rules of International Law*, Cambridge: Cambridge University Press, 2003, p. 96.

135 ILC, 'Fragmentation of International Law', 2006, para. 252.

136 Likewise, Antonios Tzanakopoulos, 'Collective Security and Human Rights', in: Erika De Wet & Jure Vidmar (eds.), *Hierarchy in International Law: The Place of Human Rights*, Oxford: Oxford University Press 2012, pp. 42–70 on pp. 45–46. However, for another opinion see Alexander Orakhelashvili, 'Article 30', in: Olivier Corten & Pierre Klein, *The Vienna Convention on the Law of Treaties, A Commentary*, Oxford: Oxford University Press, 2011, vol. I, pp. 764–800 on p. 786, who considers the moment of entry into force as decisive.

137 Kerstin Odendahl, 'Application of successive treaties relating to the same subject matter', in: Oliver Dörr & Kirsten Schmalenbach (eds.), *Vienna Convention on the Law of Treaties, A Commentary*, Heidelberg/Dordrecht/London/New York: Springer, 2012, pp. 505–518 on 509–510; ILC, 'Fragmentation of International Law', 2006, para. 232.

138 E.W. Vierdag, 'The Time of the "Conclusion" of a Multilateral Treaty: Article 30 of the Vienna Convention on the Law of Treaties and Related Provisions', *British Yearbook of International Law* 1988, vol. 20, pp. 74–111 on p. 95, with a reference to I. Sinclair, *The Vienna Convention on the Law of Treaties*, Manchester: Manchester University Press, 1984, p. 98.

139 See for information on that section 3.7.8.

140 See also Richard D. Kearney & Robert E. Dalton, 'The Treaty on Treaties', *American Journal of International Law* 1970, vol. 64, pp. 495–561 on p. 517.

1. 'when a treaty specifies that it is subject to, or that it is not to be considered as incompatible with, an earlier or later treaty, the provisions of that other treaty prevail' (second paragraph);
2. 'When all the parties to the earlier treaty are parties also to the later treaty but the earlier treaty is not terminated or suspended in operation [...], the earlier treaty applies only to the extent that its provisions are compatible with those of the later treaty' (third paragraph);
3. When the parties to the earlier treaty do not include all the parties to the later one, the rule under (b) also applies between states that are parties to both treaties, whereas states that are not party to both treaties are governed by the treaty to which all these states are parties (fourth paragraph).

The framework of Article 30 of the Vienna Convention on the Law of Treaties is therefore limited to 1. conventions,[141] which 2. are successive and 3. relate to the same subject matter (the 'same subject matter' test), where another factor may be 4. what the conventions themselves say about the relationship between each other and 5. whether the parties to the interfering conventions are the same ('contracting parties' test).[142] With this restricted applicability, Article 30 of the Vienna Convention on the Law of Treaties therefore offers a limited solution for interference between conventions.[143] This also has a bearing on the interference between conventions with regards to the cannabis issue, as we will see later.

That is the case even more so because it is dubious – as the International Law Commission concludes in spite of the rule under c. – that the *lex posterior* rule has any meaningful part to play if parties to two successive conventions differ from each other.[144] In this respect, it is relevant in our opinion that in that case the idea that the will of parties is the foundation for the rule becomes untenable. After all, it is hard to maintain that the creation of the latter convention implies

---

141 As such, the *lex posterior* rule may also apply between other legal sources than merely conventions, but as the cannabis issue is in principle a case of interference between conventions, we can leave that safely out of the equation; for more information on this, see for example Jan Wouters, 'Bronnen van het internationaal recht', in: Nathalie Horbach, Rene Lefeber & Olivier Ribbelink (eds.), *Handboek Internationaal Recht*, Den Haag: T.M.C. Asser Press, 2007, pp. 119–122 (i.e., Jan Wouters, 'Sources of International Law' in: Nathalie Horbach, Rene Lefeber & Olivier Ribbelink (eds.), *Handbook for International Law*, Den Haag: T.M.C. Asser Press, 2007, pp. 119–122).

142 Cf. Ahmad Ali Ghouri, 'Determining Hierarchy Between Conflicting Treaties: Are There Vertical Rules in the Horizontal System?', *Asian Journal of International Law* 2012, vol. 2, no. 2, pp. 235–266 on p. 249, who identifies three tests: 'the subject matter test', the 'chronology test' and 'the contracting parties test'.

143 Christopher J. Borgen, Treaty Conflicts and Normative Fragmentation, in: Duncan B. Hollis (ed.), *The Oxford Guide to Treaties*, Oxford: Oxford University Press, 2012, pp. 448–471 on p. 450.

144 ILC, 'Fragmentation of International Law', 2006, para. 243.

that the will of the parties to the previous convention has changed, if not at least all those states that were party to the earlier convention are also party to the later convention.[145] In principle, the same will apply if the conventions came into being within different institutional units.[146] After all, the application of the *lex posterior* rule would in that case mean that the activity of one international 'regulator' (for example the United Nations) could change the will of the other international 'regulator' (for example the Council of Europe or the European Union) or at least could determine that it has changed.

In addition to this, the *lex prior* rule, which prescribes the priority of a norm established earlier, has not been codified as such in Article 30 or any other provision in the Vienna Convention on the Law of Treaties.[147,148] However, the second paragraph of this provision states, among other things, that the earlier convention prevails if the later convention states explicitly that it is subject to the earlier convention or at least cannot be considered to be incompatible with it. That is the case in Article 25 of the Illicit Traffic Convention, which says that the provisions from this convention 'shall not derogate from any rights enjoyed or obligations undertaken by Parties to this Convention' under the Single Convention. The *lex prior* rule flows from the principle of *pacta sunt servanda*, which requires states, among other things, to honour their commitments in good faith (Article 26 of the Vienna Convention on the Law of Treaties). Although the principle of *pacta sunt servanda* is not the basis of the *lex posterior* rule – that, after all, is the will of the parties – and is even at odds with that principle,[149] it

145 Cf. Joost Pauwelyn, *Conflict of Norms in Public International Law: How WTO Law relates to Other Rules of International Law*, Cambridge: Cambridge University Press, 2003, pp. 368–370, who uses the phrase of '*fiction of 'legislative intent*''; see also pp. 377–378, 380.

146 See also Ralf Michaels & Joost Pauwelyn, 'Conflict of Norms or Conflict of Laws?: Different Techniques in the Fragmentation of Public International Law', *Duke Journal of Comparative & International Law* 2012, vol. 22, pp. 349–376 on p. 353, p. 356, pp. 365–369.

147 The draft of the Harvard Draft on Law of Treaties, the precursor to the Vienna Convention on the Law of Treaties, did mention the principle of *lex prior*. See Alexander Orakhelashvili, 'Article 30', in: Olivier Corten & Pierre Klein, *The Vienna Convention on the Law of Treaties, A Commentary*, Oxford: Oxford University Press, 2011, vol. I, pp. 764–800.

148 And the adage '*lex posterior generalis non derogat priori specialis*' that is not relevant here (because of the non-applicability of the *lex specialis* rule for the cannabis issue) has not been included in (Article 30) of the Vienna Convention on the Law of Treaties either. See for its meaning Aaron X. Fellmeth & Maurice Horwitz, *Guide to Latin in International Law*, Oxford: Oxford University Press, 2009: 'A principle according to which a rule of *lex specialis* that conflicts with a later general treaty provision or rule of customary law is not usually considered to be repealed or amended. The rationale for this rule is that, in adopting general rules, the international community should not be assumed to intend to expunge preexisting nuances of the law'.

149 Cf. Christopher J. Borgen, 'Resolving Treaty Conflicts', *The George Washington International Law Review* 2005, vol. 37, pp. 573–648 on p. 590: 'there is at the very least a tension between the notions of *lex posterior* (favoring the later treaty) and *pacta sunt servanda* (favoring the earlier treaty), if not an outright clash of norms'.

must be assumed, however, that states are not allowed to invoke the *lex posterior* rule in bad faith at any rate.[150]

iv. Does the Lex Posterior *Rule Apply to the Cannabis Issue?*

In view of the above-mentioned requirements for applicability of the *lex posterior* rule in Article 30 of the Vienna Convention on the Law of Treaties, we conclude that this provision is not applicable to the interference between human rights conventions and drugs conventions. The most important obstacles for this are – as will become clear presently – the 'same subject matter' test, the absence of any provision in the conventions about how they relate to each other and in the variety of states parties to the Single Convention, the Illicit Traffic Convention, the ICESCR, the ICCPR, the ESC and the ECHR. None of this takes away the fact – as will become clear below – that Article 30 does have meaning for the cannabis issue from an analogical point of view.

First, the 'same subject matter' requirement. In principle, with regard to the interference between the human rights conventions and the drugs conventions, the same comments as those made before in subsection 3.7.4.iv in relation to the *lex specialis* rule apply. Thus, it is not easy to construe a strong substantive link in terms of subject matter between these conventions. Only with regard to the relationship between the drugs conventions and the right to health is this possible in a somewhat convincing way. We therefore draw the conclusion that because of the huge difference in subject matter of the conventions alone (apart from the relationship to the right of health), it is difficult for the *lex posterior* rule[151] if not de facto impossible[152] to play a role in the cannabis issue.

Secondly, it is important that none of the human rights conventions explicitly state that it is subject to the UN narcotic drugs conventions or the other way round. Also, none of the conventions state that it is 'not to be considered as incompatible' with the other earlier or later conventions (see section 3.6 above). That means that Article 30(2) of the Vienna Convention on the Law of Treaties does not apply formally. Nevertheless, it is interesting that (as we discussed in section 3.7.4.iv above) Article 14(2) of the Illicit Traffic Convention specifies that states parties in adopting measures against illicit cannabis cultivation

---

150 Ibid, p. 642.

151 Cf. ILC, 'Fragmentation of International Law', 2006, para. 255–256; ILC, 'Report 58th Session: Chapter XII, Fragmentation of International Law', 2006, p. 417 (para. 251 (26)).

152 Cf. for example Andreas R. Ziegler & Bertram Boie, 'The Relationship between International Trade Law and International Human Rights Law', in: Erika De Wet & Jure Vidmar (eds.), *Hierarchy in International Law: The Place of Human Rights*, Oxford: Oxford University Press, 2012, pp. 272–299 on p. 290, p. 296; Erika De Wet & Jure Vidmar, 'Conclusions, in: Erika De Wet & Jure Vidmar (eds.), *Hierarchy in International Law: The Place of Human Rights*, Oxford: Oxford University Press 2012, pp. 300–310 on p. 306.

'shall respect fundamental human rights', that the preparatory work for both the Single Convention and the Illicit Traffic Convention contains several references to human rights that implicitly or explicitly suggest states' awareness of the importance that the obligations under the drugs conventions should not violate human rights, and that implementation and execution of the drug control system according to the INCB must be carried out in accordance with human rights norms and must promote such norms. Analogical application of Article 30(2) of the Vienna Convention on the Law of Treaties means that the human rights conventions then have priority over the UN narcotic drugs conventions.

Finally, the states parties to, on the one hand, the ICESCR, the ICCPR, the ESC and/or the ECHR and, on the other hand, the Single Convention and/or the Illicit Traffic Convention do not match. This means that the *lex posterior* rule from Article 30 of the Vienna Convention on the Law of Treaties is not generally applicable to the interference between the conventions,[153] in this case the interference in respect of the cannabis issue for a policy on drugs and/or cannabis. Insofar as the interference between the conventions takes centre stage in a conflict between specific states, this may yet be different because of the fourth paragraph of the provision, as it contains rules for the situation in which not all the parties to the earlier convention are also parties to the later one. But even then, the problem remains that in any case the drugs conventions (UN) and the ESC and the ECHR (CoE) did not originate within the same institutional unit, and the drugs conventions and all four human rights conventions belong to different branches and even to different subsystems. It is also because of that reason (as became clear in subsection iii) that it is difficult[154] or de facto even impossible[155] for the *lex posterior* rule to play a role in the cannabis issue. Consequently, there is no point in examining what the various temporality relationships look like between, on the one hand, the ICESCR (1966), the ICCPR (1966), the ESC (18 October 1961, 1996) and/or the ECHR (1950) and, on the other hand, the Single Convention (30 March 1961, 1971) and/or the Illicit Traffic Convention (1988).

---

153 Jan Klabbers, 'Beyond the Vienna Convention: Conflicting Treaty Provisions', in: Enzo Cannizzaro (ed.), *The Law of Treaties Beyond the Vienna Convention*, Oxford: Oxford University Press, 2011, pp. 192–205 on p. 198.

154 See for example ILC, 'Fragmentation of International Law', 2006, para. 255–256; ILC, 'Report 58th Session: Chapter XII, Fragmentation of International Law', 2006, p. 417 (para. 251(26)).

155 See for example Andreas R. Ziegler & Bertram Boie, 'The Relationship between International Trade Law and International Human Rights Law', in: Erika De Wet & Jure Vidmar (eds.), *Hierarchy in International Law: The Place of Human Rights*, Oxford: Oxford University Press, 2012, pp. 272–299 on p. 290, p. 296; Erika De Wet & Jure Vidmar, 'Conclusions, in: Erika De Wet & Jure Vidmar (eds.), *Hierarchy in International Law: The Place of Human Rights*, Oxford: Oxford University Press, 2012, pp. 300–310 on p. 306.

3.7.6. HIGHER VERSUS LOWER (*LEX SUPERIOR*): GENERAL

Where there is no formal hierarchy in international law (with the exception of *jus cogens*),[156] it does to some degree have a substantive hierarchy. It follows from and is connected with the – not entirely uncontroversial – notion of an international legal order.[157] Important starting points for such an *ordre public* are found in principle in the concepts of '*jus cogens*' rules (mandatory, non-derogable rules) and '*erga omnes*' obligations (obligations that each state has towards all other states and the fulfilment of which is in the interests of all states[158]).[159] The superior status of the *jus cogens* norms in international law assumes the existence of an international order, based on shared values, of the 'community of states as a whole'.[160] This assumption is not entirely unproblematic. Still, this does not alter the fact – as the International Law Commission finds – that:

> Irrespective of the difficulty of finding a general vocabulary that would express the role of the sense of importance of particular norms, the practice of international law has always recognized the presence of some norms that are superior to other norms and must therefore be given effect.[161]

The existence and validity of the *jus cogens* norms – and consequently of a formal hierarchy in international law – is also a given to the extent that it is also

---

156 See section 3.5.

157 There is a good deal of literature on the idea that international law is going through a process of 'constitutionalization'; see among other sources Erika De Wet & J. Vidmar (eds.), *Hierarchy in International Law: The Place of Human Rights*, Oxford: Oxford University Press, 2012; Jan Klabbers, Anne Peters & Geir Ulfstein (eds.), *The Constitutionalisation of International Law*, Oxford: Oxford University Press, 2010; Dinah Shelton, 'Normative Hierarchy in International Law', *The American Journal of International Law*, 2006, vol. 100, pp. 291–323. For an exposition on the constitutional character of the UN Charter, see among other sources Bardo Fassbender, *The United Nations Charter as the Constitution of the International Community*, Leiden/Boston: Martinus Nijhoff Publishers, 2009.

158 See section 3.7.9.vi.

159 Prosper Weil, 'Towards Relative Normativity in International Law?', *The American Journal of International Law*, 1983, vol. 77, pp. 413–442 on 421 (where he establishes the development) and 425 (where he is critical about it).

160 See among other sources Jure Vidmar, 'Norm Conflicts and Hierarchy in International Law: Towards a Vertical International Legal System?', in: Erika de Wet & Jure Vidmar (eds.), *Hierarchy in International Law: The Place of Human Rights*, Oxford: Oxford University Press, 2012, pp. 13–41 on p. 14; Juan Antonio Carillo Salcedo, 'Reflections on the Hierarchy of Norms in International Law', *European Journal of International Law* 1997, vol. 8, pp. 583–595 on p. 588; Bruno Simma & Andreas L. Paulus, 'The 'International Community': Facing the Challenge of Globalization', *European Journal of International Law* 1998, vol. 9, pp. 266–277; Jonathan I. Charney, 'Universal International Law', *The American Journal of International Law* 1993, vol. 87, pp. 529–551 on p. 543.

161 ILC, 'Fragmentation of International Law', 2006, para. 326.

recognized as a 'peremptory norm of general international law' in Article 53 and Article 64 of the Vienna Convention on the Law of Treaties.[162]

The *lex superior* rule is not only expressed through the *jus cogens* norms, but also in the precedence clause of Article 103 of the UN Charter.[163] This provision in essence confers a higher status to the obligations specified in the charter.

Human rights norms are also an important part of the discussion about the hierarchical positioning of norms of public international law.[164] Many opinions can be found in the legal practice and literature in particular about the superior position of (some) human rights norms. Especially because of the interference in the 'cannabis issue' between human rights conventions and drugs conventions, it is relevant to what extent human rights norms occupy a higher position with regard to other norms of international law, if they do so at all.

The three most important points of departure for the existence of a normative hierarchy in international law will be elaborated below. They concern: 1. the *jus cogens* obligations; 2. the precedence of obligations from the UN Charter; and 3. the special status of certain norms of international law outside the first two concepts mentioned before. In all three cases, it boils down to establishing whether positive human rights obligations trump obligations under the drugs conventions or rather the other way round.

3.7.7. *LEX SUPERIOR I*: ABSOLUTE PRECEDENCE OF '*JUS COGENS*' NORMS

A norm with *jus cogens* status is a general international law norm which enjoys absolute validity and may therefore not be derogated from. It is therefore 'non-derogable' nor can there be valid 'reservations' about it.[165] Such a norm prevails over all other norms, including norms under conventions and customary law. That is why it is important here to see if the positive human rights obligations that are relevant for the cannabis issue or the drugs conventions obligations are *jus cogens*. After all, if that is the case for either of them, it would categorically displace and suppress the other opposing obligations.

---

162 Ibid, para. 362.

163 Dinah Shelton, 'Normative Hierarchy in International Law', *American Journal of International Law* 2006, vol. 100, pp. 291–323 on 293–294 (also pay attention there to fn. 11).

164 See among other sources Dinah Shelton, 'Hierarchy of Norms and Human Rights: Of Trumps and Winners', *Saskatchewan Law Review* 2002, vol. 65, pp. 301–331; Theodor Meron, 'On a Hierarchy of International Human Rights', *American Journal of International Law* 1986, vol. 80, pp. 1–23.

165 For more information see Ineke Boerefijn, 'Impact on the Law on Treaty Reservations', in: Menno T. Kamminga & Martin Scheinin, *The Impact of Human Rights Law on General International Law*, Oxford: Oxford University Press, 2009, pp. 63–98 on pp. 78–79.

i. *A Closer Look at* Jus Cogens *in General*

A *jus cogens* norm belongs to customary law (or it is the result of international consensus),[166] but it can at the same time be embedded in a convention. The concept of *jus cogens* is akin to the concept of *erga omnes*, which means: obligations that every state has with respect to all other states.[167] This is because *jus cogens* norms have an *erga omnes* effect; however, conversely this is not necessarily the case.[168] The absolute precedence of *jus cogens* rules does not rely on a formal hierarchy of sources; after all, there is no such hierarchy in international law, that is to say: sources in the sense of conventions, customary law, and general principles of law.[169] Moreover, *jus cogens* is not a norm: it is a status qualification of a norm. The absolute precedence of *jus cogens* rules therefore relies on the recognition of the material superiority of the norm: *lex superior derogat legi inferiori*.[170] This principle is expressed through the *jus cogens* rule, which is recognized in the Vienna Convention on the Law of Treaties with regard to its relationship to conventions. According to Article 53 of the VCLT, a peremptory norm of general international law is:

> a norm accepted and recognized by the international community of States as a whole as a norm from which no derogation is permitted and which can be modified only by a subsequent norm of general international law having the same character.

Also according to Article 53 of the Vienna Convention on the Law of Treaties, conventions that conflict with a peremptory norm of general international law at the time of their conclusion are void. Furthermore, Article 64 of the Vienna Convention on the Law of Treaties states: 'If a new peremptory norm of general international law emerges, any existing treaty which is in conflict with

---

166 Malcolm Evans (ed.), *International Law*, Oxford: Oxford University Press, 2014, p. 59.

167 See section 3.7.9.vi below.

168 According to, among other people, Michael Byers, 'Conceptualising the Relationship between Jus Cogens and Erga Omnes Rules', *Nordic Journal of International Law* 1997, vol. 66, pp. 211–239 on p. 211, pp. 236–237; Jure Vidmar, 'Norm Conflicts and Hierarchy in International Law: Towards a Vertical International Legal System?, in: Erika de Wet & Jure Vidmar (eds.), *'Hierarchy in International Law: The Place of Human Rights'*, Oxford: Oxford University Press, 2012, pp. 13–41 on pp. 23–24; Alexander Orakhelashvili, *Peremptory Norms in International Law*, Oxford: Oxford University Press, 2008, p. 245. However, for another view, apparently with a rather specific interpretation of what constitutes obligations, see Paolo Picone, 'The Distinction between Jus Cogens and Obligations Erga Omnes', in: Enzo Cannizzaro (ed.), *The Law of Treaties Beyond the Vienna Convention*, Oxford: Oxford University Press, 2011, pp. 411–424 on p. 417, 421.

169 See section 3.5.

170 Aaron X. Fellmeth & Maurice Horwitz, *Guide to Latin in International Law*, Oxford: Oxford University Press, 2009: '"Higher law."(1) A body of law of greater legitimacy than another body of law. (2) A body of law that supersedes another, conflicting body of law.'

that norm becomes void and terminates.' It illustrates that *jus cogens* norms by their very nature take absolute, normative precedence over all other norms. It applies here in the sense that agreements reached between states that conflict with a *jus cogens* norm must be deemed void.

Apart from the Vienna Convention on the Law of Treaties, the International Court of Justice (among other organizations)[171] also recognizes the existence of *jus cogens* law, sometimes referring to this term. For example, it is used explicitly in the *Questions relating to the Obligation to Prosecute or Extradite* case.[172] According to the Court, the *Diallo* case is about 'rules of general international law which are binding on States in all circumstances, even apart from any treaty commitments'.[173] More substantial qualifications can also be found in the Court's jurisprudence. In the *Corfu Channel* case,[174] the Court restricts the sovereignty of states with a reference to 'elementary considerations of humanity'. And in the *Legality of the Threat or Use of Nuclear Weapons* case,[175] the Court considers that many rules of humanitarian law are 'so fundamental to the respect of the human person and "elementary considerations of humanity"' that these 'fundamental rules are to be observed by all States whether or not they have ratified the conventions that contain them, because they constitute *intransgressible principles* of international customary law' (emphasis added). Finally, the *Case concerning the Military and Paramilitary Activities in and against Nicaragua* is also relevant. In this case, the Court finds that the international prohibition of aggression has the validity of customary law, for which ruling the Court also finds further confirmation in the fact that this prohibition has been qualified as *jus cogens* by the International Law Commission, among other institutions.[176] The fact that the Court presents

---

171 Cf. International Law Commission, 'Draft Articles on the Law of Treaties, with commentaries', *Yearbook of the International Law Commission* 2001, vol. II (also: ILC, 'Draft Articles on the Law of Treaties, with commentaries', 2001), comm. Article 40, p. 112 (para. 2): 'The concept of peremptory norms of general international law is recognized in international practice, in the jurisprudence of international and national courts and tribunals and in legal doctrine.' See also Francisco Forrest Martin, 'Delineating a Hierarchical Outline of International Law Sources and Norms', *Saskatchewan Law Review* 2002, vol. 65, pp. 333–368 on pp 342–343, with references to jurisprudence of the ECtHR, I-ACionHR, I-ACtHR and ICTY.

172 ICJ, Judgment of 20 July 2012, *I.C.J. Reports* 2012, p. 422 on 457 (para. 99) (*Questions relating to the Obligation to Prosecute or Extradite – Belgium v. Senegal*).

173 ICJ, Judgment of 30 November 2010, *I.C.J. Reports* 2010, p. 639 on 671 (para. 87) (*Ahmadou Sadio Diallo – Republic of Guinea v. Democratic Republic of the Congo*).

174 ICJ, Judgment of 9 April 1949, *I.C.J. Reports* 1949, p. 22 (*Corfu Channel Case – The United Kingdom v. Albania*).

175 ICJ, Advisory Opinion 8 July 1996, *I.C.J. Reports* 1996, p. 257 (para. 79) (*Legality of the Threat or Use of Nuclear Weapons*). Repeated in ICJ, Advisory Opinion 9 July 2004, *I.C.J. Reports* 2004, p. 136 on 199 (para. 157) (*Legal Consequences of the Construction of a Wall in the Occupied Palestinian Territory*).

176 See also ICJ, Judgment 27 June 1986, *I.C.J. Reports* 1986, p. 14 on 100–101 (para. 190) (*Case concerning the Military and Paramilitary Activities in and against Nicaragua – Nicaragua v. United States*).

this fact to support its own conclusion indicates that it does not disagree with that qualification.

The question which international law is to be accorded *jus cogens* status is difficult to answer in a general sense.[177] Martin lists the following rights and obligations that must be deemed *jus cogens* under international law: the international prohibition of aggression, the right to life, the right to be treated with dignity, the prohibition of ex post facto laws ('*nulla poena sine lege praevia*'), the prohibition of genocide, the prohibition of war crimes, the prohibition of slavery, the prohibition of discrimination based on race, colour, sex, language, religion, or social origin, the prohibition of deprivation of liberty on the grounds of contractual debts, the prohibition of crimes against humanity, the right to be recognized as a person, the freedom of conscience and the right to self-determination.[178] Although therefore not all rights and obligations from human rights conventions have *jus cogens* status, it is obvious that most of the norms that do have this status are human rights or are related to them.[179]

ii. Jus Cogens *Status for Positive Human Rights Obligations?*

Out of the four human rights which were in the limelight in Chapter 2, the right to health and the right to a private life are not included in the enumeration above (see below about the right to life and the prohibition of inhuman treatment). As we are not dealing-with non-derogable rights here, these cannot qualify as *jus cogens* norms.[180] As there is otherwise no obvious reason to suppose that these have *jus cogens* status, they can be eliminated from the present analysis.

On the other hand, the other human rights discussed in Chapter 2 do feature in the above-mentioned list: it is fairly generally assumed that the right to life[181]

---

177 Cf. Prosper Weil, 'Towards Relative Normativity in International Law?', *The American Journal of International Law* 1983, vol. 77, pp. 413–442 on pp. 428–426.

178 Francisco Forrest Martin, 'Delineating a Hierarchical Outline of International Law Sources and Norms', *Saskatchewan Law Review* 2002, vol. 65, pp. 333–368 on pp. 346–347; incidentally, he also lists so-called regional *jus cogens* norms: freedom from arbitrary detention, the rights of the family, the right to a name, the rights of the child, the right to a nationality and the right to participate in governance. See also, with further references to international case law and literature, the overviews in ILC, 'Fragmentation of International Law', 2006, para. 374–376; Annika Tahvanainen, 'Hierarchy of Norms in International and Human Rights Law', *Nordisk Tidsskrift For Menneskerettigheter* 2006, vol. 24, no 3, pp. 191–205 on p. 195.

179 In that sense see also Francisco Forrest Martin, 'Delineating a Hierarchical Outline of International Law Sources and Norms', *Saskatchewan Law Review* 2002, vol. 65, pp. 333–368 on p. 347.

180 It is remarkable, though, that sometimes it is assumed that all human rights have *jus cogens* status; cf. among other sources Maurizio Ragazzi, *The Concept of International Obligations Erga Omnes*, Oxford: Oxford University Press, 2000, p. 70.

181 For recognition of the *jus cogens* status of the right to life, see also, among other sources, the Inter-American Commission on Human Rights: I-ACionHR 16 October 1996, *Victims of the Tugboat '13 de Marzo'/Cuba*, case 11.436, report 47/96, para. 79.

and the prohibition of inhuman treatment[182] have *jus cogens* status.[183] Does this mean that the positive obligations ensuing from these rights that can be used to argue for regulated permission of cannabis cultivation and trade have the status of *jus cogens* and that therefore the obligations from the drugs conventions that conflict with them are null and void?

To draw such a conclusion would be indicative of too simple an approach. Quite apart from the fact that international case law is very reluctant to declare provisions void merely because they are at odds with *jus cogens* law,[184] there is an important question whether the status of *jus cogens* applies to the full scope of the norm, therefore including all applicable negative and positive obligations that result from it. In our view, it is essential that positive obligations necessitate activity, an assessment of the situation and even to the application of means and/or resources.[185] Martin remarks that the fact that a right covers positive obligations to act does not necessarily mean that this right cannot have *jus cogens* status. We think that conclusion is correct. The right to life, the prohibition of inhuman treatment and the prohibition of genocide, among other things, all entail positive obligations, when it is obvious that they are seen as *jus cogens*. Martin draws the following conclusion from this:

> It simply means that such *jus cogens* norms require implementing international instruments and domestic legislation or action, which may in some cases be subject to a certain margin of appreciation or degree of deference. It does not mean that such norms

182 For recognition of the *jus cogens* status of the prohibition of inhuman treatment and/or torture see also among other sources: ILC, 'Fragmentation of International Law', 2006, para. 374; Jure Vidmar, 'Norm Conflicts and Hierarchy in International Law: Towards a Vertical International Legal System?, in: Erika de Wet & Jure Vidmar (eds.), *'Hierarchy in International Law: The Place of Human Rights'*, Oxford: Oxford University Press, 2012, pp. 13–41 on p. 26; ICJ, Judgment of 20 July 2012, *I.C.J. Reports* 2012, p. 422 on 457 (para. 99) (*Questions relating to the Obligation to Prosecute or Extradite – Belgium v. Senegal*); ICTY, Judgment of 10 December 1998, *Prosecutor v. Anto Furundžija*, Case No. IT-95-17/1, Trial Chamber II, para. 153–157; ECtHR (Grand Chamber) 21 November 2001, *Al-Adsani/The UK*, no. 35763/97, para. 61.

183 For recognition of the *jus cogens* status for both, see among other sources the references in: Annika Tahvanainen, 'Hierarchy of Norms in International and Human Rights Law', *Nordisk Tidsskrift For Menneskerettigheter* 2006, vol. 24, no 3, pp. 191–205 on p. 195; Teraya Koji, 'Emerging Hierarchy in International Human Rights and Beyond: From the Perspective of Non-derogable Rights', *European Journal of International Law* 2001, vol. 12, no. 5, pp. 917–941 on p. 927.

184 See for example Moshe Hirsch, 'Interactions between Investment and Non-investment Obligations', in: Peter Muchlinski, Federico Ortino & Christoph Schreuer (eds.), *The Oxford Handbook of International Investment Law*, Oxford: Oxford University Press, 2008, pp. 154–181 on p. 179.

185 This problem is also pointed out by Francisco Forrest Martin, 'Delineating a Hierarchical Outline of International Law Sources and Norms', *Saskatchewan Law Review* 2002, vol. 65, pp. 333–368 on p. 348; Theodor Meron, 'On a Hierarchy of International Human Rights', *American Journal of International Law* 1986, vol. 80, pp. 1–23 on p. 11.

> do not have *jus cogens* status. […] The state must provide some form of remedy, and failure to do so means that the state has violated its *jus cogens* obligation.[186]

This conclusion is essentially open to challenge and must be rejected in our opinion. First, it is questionable whether the negative obligation and the positive obligation always relate to the same norm. For example, what about the norm that the state must refrain from torture and the norm that the state must protect individuals from torture by third parties? Does this involve one and the same norm, or are there actually two norms at play? If the latter is the case, and that seems the position that is most easily defended, in the light of the following,[187] then it must be decided whether the cases in which the prohibition of inhuman treatment was assigned *jus cogens* status, applied to the first, the second or both norms. The fact that treating what is essentially one set of norms as if it was one norm leads to incorrect conclusions also manifests itself with Shelton, who argues against the concept of *jus cogens* on the basis of incorrect reasoning.[188] She points out that it is assumed in international case law that the prohibition of crimes against humanity including the prohibition of torture – which qualify as *jus cogens* – do not lead to nullity of state and diplomatic immunity. That is correct. Still, that does not mean that the prohibitions mentioned do not constitute *jus cogens*. It only means that the state and diplomats cannot be prosecuted for crimes against humanity and torture. It does not mean at all that the entities to which immunity is due are allowed to commit the prohibited acts. The prohibition as such, that is to say the negative obligation of not committing crimes against humanity and not engaging in torture, of course also applies without any qualification for entities with immunity. The positive obligation connected to these prohibitions – the obligation to prosecute and punish the perpetrators of these acts – does not have absolute force, as the uninterrupted effect of immunities shows. In our view, Shelton has therefore not presented a particularly strong case against the concept of *jus cogens*. On the other hand, her argument, indirectly, demonstrates convincingly that a prohibition with *jus cogens* status (that is to say a negative obligation), does not automatically mean that any positive obligations attached to it also have *jus cogens* status.[189]

Secondly, it seems important to us that a norm can only qualify as *jus cogens* if it involves a norm that is accepted and recognized by the international

---

186 Francisco Forrest Martin, 'Delineating a Hierarchical Outline of International Law Sources and Norms', *Saskatchewan Law Review* 2002, vol. 65, pp. 333–368 on p. 349.

187 See also Jure Vidmar, 'Norm Conflicts and Hierarchy in International Law: Towards a Vertical International Legal System?, in: Erika de Wet & Jure Vidmar (eds.), *'Hierarchy in International Law: The Place of Human Rights'*, Oxford: Oxford University Press, 2012, pp. 13–41 on pp. 35–36.

188 Dinah Shelton, 'Hierarchy of Norms and Human Rights: Of Trumps and Winners', *Saskatchewan Law Review* 2002, vol. 65, pp. 301–331 on pp. 323–326.

189 Cf. ECtHR (Grand Chamber) 21 November 2001, *Al-Adsani/The UK*, no. 35763/97, para. 61–66.

community of states as a norm that does not allow derogation.[190] With regard to the negative obligations with the right to life (the state is prohibited from taking the life of an individual without justification) and the prohibition of inhuman treatment (the state is prohibited from torturing individuals or treating them inhumanly), that general acceptance may be assumed, also in view of the wording of these rights in the conventions. Does that also apply to the positive obligations, though? These have not been elaborated on and usually are not even mentioned in the provisions of human rights conventions regarding civil rights, such as the right to life, prohibition of inhuman treatment and the prohibition of slavery.[191] There is no full consensus about their scope and content in the international human rights jurisprudence either. Or is it sufficient that the international community of states accepts *in abstracto* that for example the right to life and the prohibition of inhuman treatment also presuppose positive obligations? In other words, without it being clear what exactly these positive obligations are about? We take the view that this approach does not sit well with the unique status of *jus cogens* (absolutely mandatory) and its effect (nullity of provisions conflicting with it).

There is a third point that has some bearing on this. It is exactly with positive obligations that states nearly always have the so-called 'margin of appreciation', even if they do not have that for the negative obligation attached to the same right.[192] Although this does not affect the existence of the positive obligation as such, it does imply that it is hard to qualify it as applicable in absolute terms. Moreover, even with positive obligations regarding rights that should be upheld even in an emergency (therefore non-derogable rights), it very much remains to be seen if that prohibition of derogation also covers the positive obligations that go hand-in-hand with that right. While it is still possible during an emergency for the authorities to refrain from violations of 'non-derogable rights', it will be very difficult under those circumstances to protect the rights effectively against threats from third parties. Even if the positive obligation should still remain in force formally (as they would also be deemed 'non-derogable'), they can actually become nothing more than an empty shell. That too, does not square with the idea of an absolute norm.

In the light of the foregoing we conclude that positive human rights obligations do not automatically acquire *jus cogens* status merely because the law from which these obligations arise has that status. To put it differently: positive human rights obligations, in our opinion, must be seen as norms that are to be identified independently in principle and which can only be assumed

190 See Article 53 Vienna Convention on the Law of Treaties; see also ILC, 'Draft Articles on the Law of Treaties, with commentaries', 2001), comm. Article 26, p. 85 (para. 5).

191 See Article 6 ICCPR and Article 2 ECHR (right to life), Article 7 ICCPR and Article 3 ECHR (prohibition of inhuman treatment) and Article 8 ICCPR and Article 4 ECHR (prohibition of slavery).

192 See section 2.4.7.ix.

to have *jus cogens* status if there is explicit proof for that or is accepted as such in, for example, international case law. We have not been able to find any solid substantiation for the assertion that the positive obligations ensuing from the rights to life and the right not to be subjected to inhuman treatment, which are relevant for the cannabis issue, have the status of *jus cogens*. At the same time, this does not mean that it is entirely without importance for the cannabis issue that at any rate the negative rights regarding life and inhuman treatment have *jus cogens* status. As we have seen before, most norms that have this status involve human rights or are related to them. To that extent, the *jus cogens* doctrine creates the impression that human rights are a category within international law that carries extra weight.

iii. Jus Cogens *Status for Obligations under Drugs Conventions?*

The list at the beginning of this subsection does not contain any obligations that explicitly or directly relate to drugs and/or cannabis. We have not found any other source either that grants *jus cogens* status to obligations under the UN narcotic drugs conventions. According to Boister, the assumption that drug-related offences must qualify as crimes pursuant to international customary law is not supported by state practice or *opinio juris*. He even considers it absurd to argue that the offences defined in the drugs conventions entail *erga omnes* obligations or constitute *jus cogens* norms.[193] We do not see any grounds for that either. At the time when the drugs conventions were established, the purpose was not codification of customary law.[194] Just as it is untenable to claim that the drugs conventions have by now been rendered obsolete or irrelevant by state practice,[195] there is no room either for the position that the content of the conventions has by now become customary law.[196] This is also gainsaid by the fact that a number of states parties have proceeded to legalization, decriminalization or policy-based tolerance of production, trade and/or possession of drugs and/or cannabis

---

193 Neil Boister, *The Suppression of Illicit Drugs Through International Law*, Nottingham: University of Nottingham, 1998, pp. 250–251. See also the criteria presented by him, which drug crimes do not satisfy, in Neil Boister, '"Transnational Criminal Law"?', *European Journal of International Law* 2003, vol. 14, pp. 953–976 on pp. 965–966.

194 Mark A. Leinwand, 'The International Law of Treaties and United States Legalization of Marijuana', *Columbia Journal of Transnational Law* 1971, vol. 10, no. 2, pp. 413–441 on p. 414: 'There are no traditional or customary norms in international law regarding drugs. The international legal norms that do exist are embodied in international agreements and treaties.' See also S.K. Chatterjee, *Legal Aspects of International Drug Control*, The Hague/Boston/London: Martinus Nijhoff Publishers, 1981, pp. 204–207, 530–531.

195 See Piet Hein P.H.M.C. van Kempen & Masha I. Fedorova, *International Law and Cannabis I*, Cambridge: Intersentia, 2019, section 2.5.

196 See also Juan Carlos Sainz-Borgo, 'The International Criminal Court, Drug Trafficking and Crimes against Humanity: A local Interpretation of the Rome Statute', *The Journal Jurisprudence* 2012, pp. 373–388 on p. 386.

on the assumption that they have a right to do so under international law.[197] Furthermore, another obstacle to assuming the status of *jus cogens* is the fact that the drugs conventions themselves show that the obligations they contain are not absolute. For example, various obligations are subject to the constitutional principles of the member states. This is the case for the Single Convention with regard to the obligations of criminalization in Article 36 and the Illicit Traffic Convention with respect to the obligations of criminalization in Articles 3(1)(c) and 3(2). Furthermore, Article 14(2) of the Illicit Traffic Convention states that fighting cannabis cultivation must take place with due regard for fundamental human rights. In addition to this, in view of Article 53 of the Vienna Convention on the Law of Treaties it is important that both the Single Convention (Article 47) and the Illicit Traffic Convention (Article 31) recognize that each party to the convention can table a proposal for modification of the convention. No provision in the convention is excluded from the possibility. To sum up: drugs conventions and the norms they contain do not belong to *jus cogens* law.

iv. Conclusion

There is insufficient solid substantiation for the assertion that the positive obligations ensuing from the rights to life and the right not to be subjected to inhuman treatment, which are relevant for the cannabis issue, have the status of *jus cogens*. That status certainly does not pertain to the right to health and the right to a private life, nor to the positive obligations attached to them. The obligations in drugs conventions do not belong to *jus cogens* law either.

3.7.8. *LEX SUPERIOR II*: PRECEDENCE PURSUANT TO ARTICLE 103 UN CHARTER

Whereas a *jus cogens* norm leads to nullity of provisions conflicting with the norm, the applicability of the absolute prevalence rule of Article 103 UN Charter has a more relative effect. Agreements between states that conflict with the obligations under the Charter will in principle not become invalid by applying Article 103, but will have to cede priority to those obligations from the Charter.[198] Article 103 UN Charter states:

---

197 For example, see the recent overview in Niamh Eastwood, Edward Fox & Ari Rosmarin, *A Quiet Revolution: drug decriminalization across the globe*, Release Publication, 2016.

198 See ILC, 'Fragmentation of International Law', 2006, para. 333–335. See also Andreas Paulus & Johann R. Leiß, 'Article 103', in: Bruno Simma, Daniel-Erasmu Khan, Georg Nolte & Andreas Paulus (eds.), *The Charter of the United Nations*, Oxford: Oxford University Press, 2012, pp. 2110–2137 on p. 2116; Jure Vidmar, 'Norm Conflicts and Hierarchy in International Law: Towards a Vertical International Legal System?', in: Erika de Wet & Jure Vidmar (eds.), *Hierarchy in International Law: The Place of Human Rights*, Oxford: Oxford University Press, 2012, pp. 13–41 on p. 19.

> In the event of a conflict between the obligations of the Members of the United Nations under the present Charter and their obligations under any other international agreement, their obligations under the present Charter shall prevail.[199]

Thus, the question is whether the positive human rights obligations that are relevant for the cannabis issue or rather the obligations arising from the drugs conventions qualify as obligations pursuant to the UN Charter. To the extent that this were the case, it means that those obligations pursuant to Article 103 UN Charter prevail over opposing obligations that are not covered by the Charter.

i. More on Article 103 UN Charter in General

This provision aims to ensure the effectiveness of the 'Charter system' and to eradicate obstacles to the implementation of charter obligations insofar as those obstacles arise from 'ordinary' convention norms.[200] To this end, in the event of a conflict between norms[201] (which cannot be resolved by interpretation[202]), Article 103 gives absolute precedence to the obligations of the states parties under the Charter in relation to any other obligations (unless these are *jus cogens* obligations[203]). This precedence provision therefore overrides the effect of the other classical rules of precedence, including the *lex specialis* rule and the *lex posterior* rule.[204] Article 103 therefore creates a hierarchical relationship between the sources of international law, although this is limited to one specific source: the UN Charter.[205] As became clear earlier, application of Article 103 UN Charter does not lead to nullity of the other conflicting norms, but will merely give priority to the obligations pursuant to the Charter. It is usually assumed in the literature that there is no violation of the 'lower-ranking' obligation, if a state cannot fulfil it since Article 103 must be applied because of another 'charter-based' obligation.[206]

---

199 Emphasis added.

200 Andreas Paulus & Johann R. Leiß, 'Article 103', in: Bruno Simma, Daniel-Erasmus Khan, Georg Nolte & Andreas Paulus (eds.), *The Charter of the United Nations*, Oxford: Oxford University Press, 2012, pp. 2110–2137 on p. 2123.

201 For the meaning of 'conflict', see section 3.4.

202 Andreas Paulus & Johann R. Leiß, 'Article 103', in: Bruno Simma, Daniel-Erasmus Khan, Georg Nolte & Andreas. Paulus (eds.), *The Charter of the United Nations*, Oxford: Oxford University Press, 2012, pp. 2110–2137 on pp. 2120, 2123.

203 See Ibid, on pp. 2119–2120, 2121, 2129.

204 Ibid, on p. 2116.

205 Jure Vidmar, 'Norm Conflicts and Hierarchy in International Law: Towards a Vertical International Legal System?', in: Erika de Wet & Jure Vidmar (eds.), *Hierarchy in International Law: The Place of Human Rights*, Oxford: Oxford University Press, 2012, pp. 13–41 on p. 19.

206 Hans Van Houtte, 'Treaty Protection against Economic Sanctions', *Revue belge de droit international* 1984–1985, vol. 18, pp. 34–56 on p. 51; Marko Milanović, 'Norm Conflict in International Law: Whither Human Rights?', *Duke Journal of Comparative and International Law* 2009, vol. 20, no. 1, pp. 69–131 on p. 77; Terry D. Gill, 'Legal Aspects of the Transfer of

ii. *Obligations in the Sense of Article 103 UN Charter*

The exact scope of Article 103 is not absolutely clear or without controversy.[207] Particularly since the *Lockerbie* cases before the International Court of Justice and later in the context of measures to fight terrorism, there has been a good deal of debate about the scope of the decisions taken by the Security Council and therefore – at least indirectly – the scope of Article 103.[208] Nonetheless, we can assume the following.

Article 103 UN Charter refers to two categories of obligations: those under the Charter itself and those under other international agreements. With regard to the latter: the element of 'obligations under *any other international agreement*' is interpreted broadly. Most of the time, it is assumed that it also covers customary law,[209] and that applies at any rate to conventions and all sorts of other agreements that are binding for states.[210] To that extent, both the human

---

Authority in UN Peace Operations', *Netherlands Yearbook of International Law* 2011, vol. 42, pp. 37–70 on p. 60. Otherwise, see Kristen E. Boon, Aziz Huq & Douglas C. Lovelace (eds.), *Terrorism. Commentary on Security Documents vol. 107, U.N. Response to Al-Qaeda*, Oxford: Oxford University Press, 2010, p. 432. See also section 3.11.

207 See among other sources Robert Kolb, 'Does Article 103 of the Charter of the United Nations Apply Only to Decisions or Also to Authorizations Adopted by the Security Council?', Zeitschrift für ausländisches öffentliches Recht und Völkerrecht 2004, vol. 64, no. 1, pp. 21–35 on p 21; including an overview of opinions Rain Liivoja, 'The Scope of the Supremacy Clause of The United Nations Charter', *International and Comparative Law Quarterly* 2008, vol. 57, pp. 583–612 on pp. 584–585.

208 Andreas Paulus & Johann R. Leiß, 'Article 103', in: Bruno Simma, Daniel-Erasmus Khan, Georg Nolte & Andreas Paulus (eds.), *The Charter of the United Nations*, Oxford: Oxford University Press, 2012, pp. 2110–2137 on p. 2113. In *Lockerbie*, the ICJ had to address the question whether a resolution of the Security Council forcing the extradition of suspected terrorists should prevail over the provisions of the Convention for the Suppression of Unlawful Acts against the Safety of Civil Aviation, Montreal 1971; see ICJ, Provisional Measures, Order of 14 April 1991, *I.C.J. Reports* 1992, p. 114 on 126 (para. 42) (*Questions of Interpretation and Application of the 1971 Montreal Convention arising from the Aerial Incident at Lockerbie – Libyan Arab Jamahiriya v. United States of America*).

209 See ILC, 'Fragmentation of International Law', 2006, para. 344–345 (and the references in footnotes 475–477): 'the prevailing opinion [is] that Article 103 should be read extensively – so as to affirm that charter obligations prevail also over United Nations Member States' customary law obligations.' See in a similar sense Jure Vidmar, 'Norm Conflicts and Hierarchy in International Law: Towards a Vertical International Legal System?', in: Erika de Wet & Jure Vidmar (eds.), *Hierarchy in International Law: The Place of Human Rights*, Oxford: Oxford University Press, 2012, pp. 13–41 on pp. 18–19.

210 Separate Opinion of Judge Jessup, in: ICJ, Preliminary Objections, Judgment of 21 December 1962, *I.C.J. Reports* 1962, p. 319 (*South West Africa Cases – Ethiopia v. South Africa*), p. 407: 'there appears to be no reason to interpret this Article as excluding any treaty, convention, accord, or other type of international engagement or undertaking.'; Rain Liivoja, 'The Scope of the Supremacy Clause of The United Nations Charter', *International and Comparative Law Quarterly* 2008, vol. 57, pp. 583–612 on 601, see also on pp. 602–612; Jure Vidmar, 'Norm Conflicts and Hierarchy in International Law: Towards a Vertical International Legal System?', in: Erika de Wet & Jure Vidmar (eds.), *Hierarchy in International Law: The Place of Human Rights*, Oxford: Oxford University Press, 2012, pp. 13–41 on pp. 18–19.

rights conventions that are relevant here and the drugs conventions can qualify as 'other international agreement'.

The other category concerns 'the obligations under the Charter'. These obligations are given precedence by Article 103, and not to the UN Charter as such. The question then is what must be understood by Charter obligations. First of all, this may comprise both the primary obligations from the Charter and the secondary obligations that arise from the primary ones. The primary obligations cover all obligations that manifest themselves explicitly in the Charter, such as the general obligations in Article 2 and the obligation to comply with the decisions of the Security Council and the International Court of Justice (Article 25 and Article 94 respectively).[211] The obligations incorporated in those decisions do not qualify as primary obligations but as secondary obligations and fall as such within the scope of Article 103.[212] It is interesting that there is consensus that this may now also apply to decisions of the Security Council, among other bodies, which do not cover obligations but for example merely authorizations.[213] In other words, the concept of 'obligations' must be interpreted rather broadly.[214] To that extent, there is no reason to suppose that the obligations pursuant to human rights obligations and drugs conventions could not come under the umbrella of this concept.

At the same time, Article 103 may also apply to other secondary obligations. According to ICJ Judge Ammoun, this is the case for example for 'obligations resulting from the provisions of the Charter and from its purposes'.[215] In particular when one also deduces obligations from the Charter's objectives, the scope of Article 103 may become so vast that eventually all law established

---

211 See among other sources Joost Pauwelyn, *Conflict of Norms in Public International Law: How WTO Law relates to Other Rules of International Law*, Cambridge: Cambridge University Press, 2003, p. 339.

212 See for example Andreas Paulus & Johann R. Leiß, 'Article 103', in: Bruno Simma Daniel-Erasmus Khan, Georg Nolte & Andreas Paulus (eds.), *The Charter of the United Nations*, Oxford: Oxford University Press, 2012, pp. 2110–2137 on p. 2116 and pp. 2124–2125 with a reference to case law of the ICJ.

213 Ibid, on p. 2125.

214 For more information see Rain Liivoja, 'The Scope of the Supremacy Clause of The United Nations Charter', *International and Comparative Law Quarterly* 2008, vol. 57, pp. 583–612 on pp. 588–589; Robert Kolb, 'Does Article 103 of the Charter of the United Nations Apply Only to Decisions or Also to Authorizations Adopted by the Security Council?', *Zeitschrift für ausländisches öffentliches recht und Völkerrecht* 2004, vol. 64, no. 1, pp. 21–35.

215 Separate Opinion of Vice-President Ammoun, in: ICJ, Advisory Opinion of 21 June 1971, *I.C.J. Reports* 1971, p. 16 (*Legal Consequences for States of the Continued Presence of South Africa in Namibia (South West Africa) Notwithstanding Security Council Resolution 276 (1970)*), para. 18. See also, among other sources, A Andreas Paulus & Johann R. Leiß, 'Article 103', in: Bruno Simma Daniel-Erasmus Khan, Georg Nolte & Andreas Paulus (eds.), *The Charter of the United Nations*, Oxford: Oxford University Press, 2012, pp. 2110–2137 on p. 2124; Kjetil Mujezinovic Larsen, *The Human Rights Treaty Obligations of Peacekeepers*, Cambridge: Cambridge University Press, 2012, pp. 314–315; Gabriel Orellana Zabalza, *The Principle of Systemic Integration*, Wien: Lit Verlag GmbH & Co, 2012, p. 85.

within the United Nations would be covered by this provision. That would not be in agreement with the text of Article 103. Moreover, it would deprive the rule of precedence in this provision of its value or meaning, as in that case nearly everything would take precedence and thereby de facto nothing.

Therefore, we agree with Pauwelyn that obligations 'under any agreement or act concluded *in the context of a UN body*' do not qualify as obligations pursuant to the Charter.[216] The mere fact that the ICESCR, the ICCPR and UN narcotic drugs conventions came about under the auspices of the United Nations does not in itself make those obligations 'obligations under the Charter'. The question is whether they actually are, albeit for other reasons. In the final analysis, that is indeed the case, even if it concerns the positive obligations based on these conventions. First of all, the following is important in this respect.

iii. Recognition of the 'Human Rights' in the UN Charter

It is incontrovertibly true that the UN Charter lays the foundation for modern international law regarding human rights.[217] The Charter refers explicitly to human rights in a number of provisions:

1. Preamble: it confirms the '*faith*' of the peoples of the United Nations in '*the fundamental human rights*, and '*the dignity and worth of the human person*'. (emphasis added)
2. Objectives of the United Nations: Article 1(3) stipulates that one of the objectives of the United Nations is: 'To achieve international co-operation in solving international problems of an economic, social, cultural, or humanitarian character, and in *promoting and encouraging respect for human rights and for fundamental freedoms* for all without distinction as to race, sex, language, or religion'. (emphasis added)
3. Duties of the General Assembly: Article 13(1)(b) UN Charter gives the General Assembly the authority to order studies and to make suggestions aimed at *promoting* the objective mentioned in the previous subsection, including 'assisting in the *realization of human rights and the fundamental freedoms* for all.' (emphasis added)
4. Duties of the United Nations: pursuant to Article 55(c) UN Charter, 'the United Nations shall *promote*', among other things ('with a view to the creation of conditions of stability and well-being') 'universal *respect for, and observance of, human rights and fundamental freedoms* for all'. (emphasis added)

---

216 Joost Pauwelyn, *Conflict of Norms in Public International Law: How WTO Law relates to Other Rules of International Law*, Cambridge: Cambridge University Press, 2003, p. 338.

217 See for example Thomas Buergenthal, 'The Normative and Institutional Evolution of International Human Rights', *Human Rights Quarterly* 1997, vol. 19, no. 4, pp. 703–723 on p. 703.

5. Duties of the UN member states: Article 56 reads: 'All Members *pledge themselves* to take joint and separate action in co-operation with the Organization for the achievement of the purposes set forth in Article 55.' (emphasis added)
6. Duties of the ECOSOC: pursuant to Article 62(2), the Economic and Social Council may '*make recommendations* for the purpose of *promoting respect for, and observance of, human rights and fundamental freedoms* for all.' And pursuant to Article 68, ECOSOC shall set up commissions '*for the promotion of human rights*'. (emphasis added)
7. Duties of the trusteeship system: Article 76(c) shows that it is the objective of this body too, 'to *encourage* respect for human rights and for fundamental freedoms for all'. (emphasis added)

iv. The Obligation to Respect Human Rights in the UN Charter

None of the provisions mentioned above contain an unequivocal obligation for states to protect human rights or take measures to that effect. It appears from the preparatory work of the UN Charter that the cautious approach in the text of the Charter provisions is the result of reluctance among member states to include hard requirements to protect human rights.[218] This reluctance also shows in the choice of bodies which have explicitly been given a mandate in the area of human rights, namely: the General Assembly and the Economic and Social Council. The point is that neither of these have the authority to take binding decisions.[219]

The one body which has the authority to take binding decisions is the Security Council. In the framework of Chapter VII of the UN Charter, it can also take binding decisions to realize human rights but only 'when the degree and scope of their violation are such as to constitute a threat to international peace and security', so in principle, this option is irrelevant for the cannabis issue.[220]

---

218 For an elaborate discussion of all the proposals for embedding human rights in the UN Charter more deeply, see Katarina Månsson, 'Reviving the "Spirit of San Francisco": The Lost Proposals on Human Rights, Justice and International Law to the UN Charter', *Nordic Journal of International Law* 2007, vol. 76, pp. 217–239; see also Herrch Lauterpacht, *International Law and Human Rights*, Archon Books, 1968 (1950), p. 146, who refers to some proposals from states and also to literature, including Charles K. Webster, 'The Making of the Charter of the United Nations', *History* 1947, vol. 32, no. 115, pp. 16–38 on p. 35.

219 HerschLauterpacht, *International Law and Human Rights*, Archon Books, 1968 (1950), p. 147. See also Catherine Brölmann, 'Law-Making Treaties: Form and Function in International Law', *Nordic Journal of International Law* 2005, vol. 74, pp. 383–404 on pp. 386–387: 'States drafting the UN Charter had strongly opposed conferring on the Organization the power to enact binding international rules. Likewise, proposals to give the General Assembly powers to impose certain general conventions on States by some form of majority vote had been rejected'.

220 Hersch Lauterpacht, *International Law and Human Rights*, Archon Books, 1968 (1950), p. 147.

- *Human rights: obligations, not just assumptions.* The foregoing illustrates that the position of human rights could have been given more weight in the wording of the Charter than is actually the case. Does that mean that their position can be said to be 'weak'?[221] That seems to be an untenable claim to us. Throughout the Charter, there are as many as seven explicit references to 'human rights' and there are several indirect ones.[222] The member states do not merely confirm their faith in them; according to the provisions of the Charter, promoting and stimulating respect for human rights is one of the main objectives of the United Nations, while promoting the achievement of human rights and the fundamental freedoms are explicitly mentioned as a duty of the United Nations, the General Assembly and ECOSOC. In addition to this, all UN member states 'pledge themselves' both jointly and separately, 'to take action' together with the United Nations 'for the achievement' of the objective of 'universal respect for, and observance of, human rights and fundamental freedoms for all' (see Article 56 in conjunction with Article 55).

  Does this then mean that the reference to human rights in the UN Charter should be seen as nothing more than an expression of relevant principles, as some kind of 'programme of action' for the organization, without those principles having to be treated as legally binding?[223] In our opinion, this view is hard to defend, in the light of the text of the provisions and of the object and purpose of the Charter. After all, one of the explicit objectives is 'promoting and encouraging respect for human rights and for fundamental freedoms'. Lauterpacht therefore observes that the assumption that there is no legal obligation for states to honour human rights is not only 'destructive of both the legal and the moral authority of the Charter as a whole' and its 'spirit', but also 'runs counter to a cardinal principle of construction according to which treaties must be interpreted in good faith.'[224]

  This is even clearer with respect to the issues the UN member states have committed themselves to. After all, in Article 56 in conjunction with

221 See in that sense Thomas Buergenthal, 'The Normative and Institutional Evolution of International Human Rights', *Human Rights Quarterly* 1997, vol. 19, no. 4, pp. 703–723 on pp. 705–706: 'the human rights provisions of the Charter [...] were purposefully drafted to be weak and vague'.

222 See for example the Articles 23, 24, 52 and 56 UN Charter.

223 See Olivier De Schutter, *International Human Rights Law: Cases, Materials, Commentary*, Cambridge: Cambridge University Press, 2010, p. 49, who refers to both advocates and opponents of this approach, the former of which includes: Manley O. Hudson, 'Integrity of International Instruments', *American Journal of International Law* 1948, vol. 42, no. 1, pp. 105–108; Hans Kelsen, *The Law of the United Nations*, London: The London Institute of World Affairs, 1950. See also Egon Schwelb, 'The International Court of Justice and the Human Rights Clauses of the Charter', *American Journal of International Law* 1972, vol. 66, pp. 337–351.

224 Hersch Lauterpacht, *International Law and Human Rights*, Archon Books, 1968 (1950), pp. 149, 151.

Article 55, they pledge themselves to take action so as to promote universal respect and observance of human rights. The authentic French and Spanish versions refer to 's'engagent' and 'comprometen'. Where the English text in this respect is slightly ambiguous, the French and Spanish version point towards an agreement or undertaking that has been entered into. The obligation refers to 'the achievement of the purposes' in Article 56. The purposes are listed in paragraphs a, b and c in Article 55. In our opinion, the wording of Articles 55 and 56 reveals an important substantive difference between them. Where the purposes in the first provision are connected to the single duty for the United Nations to promote them, the states committed themselves in Article 56 to achieve those objectives ('achievement'). It is important that the text in Article 56 refers to the (multiple) purposes mentioned in Article 55 and not to the (single) task in it. Thus, pursuant to Article 56 in conjunction with Article 55, the member states have committed to the single obligation to achieve the purposes – including universal respect for and observance of human rights – and therefore not just to promote them.

The texts of the provisions thereby indicate that there is an obligation of achievement for member states in the sense of Article 103 UN Charter. But even if one used the less easily defensible interpretation that states are only required to promote the rights rather than achieve these purposes, it is still only reasonable to assume that there is an obligation to respect and observe human rights. After all, it is hard to argue that a state which acts contrary to its human rights obligations could still claim in good faith that it fulfils its obligation to promote these rights.

- *Recognition by UN institutions and in the literature.* For other reasons, it is assumed by many others as well that the Charter provisions referring to human rights – such as Article 56 in conjunction with Article 55 – entail a legal obligation for member states regarding human rights in the sense of Article 103 UN Charter.[225] For example, the Special Rapporteurs on globalization and its impact on the full enjoyment of all human rights state:

> States – beginning with the Charter of the United Nations and the International Bill of Human Rights – are subjected to a primary obligation to promote and protect

[225] Apart from the literature to be mentioned below, see among other sources Jordan J. Paust, 'Human Rights on the Battlefield', *The George Washington International Law Review* 2015, vol. 47, pp. 509–561 on pp. 519–520, 530–531; Seung Hwan Choi, '"Human Dignity" as an Indispensable Requirement for Sustainable Regional Economic Integration', *Journal of East Asia and International Law* (*J. E. Asia & Int'l L*) 2013, vol. 6, pp. 81–105 on p. 87, pp. 90–91; Destaw A. Yigzaw, 'Hierarchy of Norms: The Case for the Primacy of Human Rights over WTO Law', *Suffolk Transnational Law Review* 2015, vol. 38, pp. 33–68 on pp. 62–64; Eibe H. Riedel & Jan-Michael Arend, 'Article 55 (c)', in: Bruno Simma, Daniel-Erasmus Khan, Georg Nolte & Andreas Paulus (eds.), *The Charter of the United Nations*, Oxford: Oxford University Press, 2012, pp. 1565–1602 on p. 1573. See also the reference to the positions of countries in that sense in Georg Nolte, 'Article 2 (7)', in: Bruno Simma,

> human rights and that those obligations cannot be negotiated away when States function in another forum. […] We may add that where States Member of the United Nations are concerned, if any other obligations conflict with international agreements to which they are party, their obligations under the Charter shall prevail. [source text is followed by a footnote (no. 141) to Article 103 of the Charter of the United Nations.] Their obligations under the Charter supersede other international legal obligations. In sum, they have no choice but to give primacy, *inter alia*, to human rights obligations.[226]

With regard to the Charter provisions referring to human rights, De Schutter comes to the conclusion that the case law of the International Court of Justice makes it clear that these provisions constitute legal obligations.[227] Among other things, he points out a consideration by the Court in the *Legal Consequences for States of the Continued Presence of South Africa in Namibia (South West Africa)* case.[228] In this case, the Court found that South Africa (a member state of the UN), under the UN Charter:

> had pledged itself to observe and respect […] human rights and fundamental freedoms for all without distinction as to race. To establish instead, and to enforce, distinctions, exclusions, restrictions and limitations exclusively based on grounds of race, colour, descent or national or ethnic origin which constitute a denial of fundamental human rights is a flagrant violation of the purposes and principles of the Charter.[229]

Additionally, it is worth pointing out a consideration by the Court in the *United States Diplomatic and Consular Staff in Tehran* case.

> Wrongfully to deprive human beings of their freedom and to subject them to physical constraint in conditions of hardship is in itself manifestly incompatible

Daniel-Erasmus Khan, Georg Nolte & Andreas Paulus (eds.), *The Charter of the United Nations*, Oxford: Oxford University Press, 2012, pp. 280–311 on p. 296.

226 Progress report of the Special Rapporteurs on globalization and its impact on the full enjoyment of all human rights, J. Oloka-Onyango and Deepika Udagama, *UN Doc.* E/CN.4/Sub.2/2001/10, 2 August 2001, para. 58.

227 Olivier De Schutter, *International Human Rights Law: Cases, Materials, Commentary*, Cambridge: Cambridge University Press, 2010, pp. 49–50; see also Schwelb, 'The International Court of Justice and the Human Rights Clauses of the Charter', *The American Journal of International Law* 1972, vol. 66, pp. 337–351 on p. 348. By the way, De Schutter (on p. 49) also points out that those who are sceptical about assuming legal obligations 'were often confusing the question whether the Charter's provisions were self-executing, with the question whether they were legally binding; and they were premised on the indeterminate character of the content of the "human rights and fundamental freedoms" referred to in the Charter, which the Universal Declaration of Human Rights precisely sought to make explicit'.

228 ICJ, Advisory Opinion of 21 June 1971, *I.C.J. Reports* 1971 (*Legal Consequences for States of the Continued Presence of South Africa in Namibia (South West Africa) Notwithstanding Security Council Resolution 276 (1970)*).

229 Ibid, p. 16 on 57 (para. 131); see also p. 46 (para. 92), in which the ICJ points out that the UN in General Assembly in General Assembly resolution 2145 (XXI) asserts that 'the Mandated Territory by South Africa has been conducted in a manner contrary' to, among others things, the UN Charter and the Universal Declaration of Human Rights.

> with the principles of the Charter of the United Nations, as well as with the fundamental principles enunciated in the Universal Declaration of Human Rights.[230]

The Court finds in the above-mentioned cases that violating human rights means acting contrary to the Charter among other things, and that finding is only possible if there is an obligation to act differently. Fairly soon after the creation of the Charter, Lauterpacht too concludes that UN member states are under a legal obligation to act in accordance with the 'purposes' of the Charter. 'It is their legal duty to respect and observe fundamental human rights and freedoms.'[231] A resolution from the UN General Assembly from as early as 1958 confirms this.[232]

- *Lack of further specification of human rights does not preclude accepting obligations.* Sometimes, the idea that the United Nations Charter establishes legally binding obligations to honour and observe human rights is opposed with the argument that the relevant catalogue of human rights are not specified in the Charter.[233] If this argument were to hold water, one must also wonder whether the Charter contains any obligations that are aimed at 'international peace and security', as this notion is even vaguer than the reference to 'human rights and fundamental freedoms'. As it is beyond doubt that the Charter does contain obligations about this, the vagueness about human rights cannot mean that there are no legal obligations in that respect. Apart from this, as Lauterpacht correctly observes, the question whether a provision comprises a legal obligation is an inherently different question from the one how effective a provision is if it does not clearly define what exactly the obligation entails.[234] Here we are looking at the latter question.
- *UN Security Council resolution 1267 (1999) does not constitute a counter argument.* Finally, a few comments about this resolution, that led to many discussions in the literature and resulted in both national and international

230 ICJ, Judgment of 24 May 1980, *I.C.J. Reports* 1980, p. 3, para. 91 (*United States Diplomatic and Consular Staff in Tehran – United States of America v. Iran*).

231 Hersch Lauterpacht, *International Law and Human Rights*, Archon Books, 1968 (1950), p. 147; see also p. 148.

232 UN General Assembly Resolution 1248 (XIII), 'Question of race conflict in South Africa resulting from the policies of apartheid in the Government of the Union of South Africa', adopted 13th plenary meeting on 30 October 1958, *UN Doc.* A/3962.

233 For example, cf. Hans Van Houtte, 'Treaty Protection against Economic Sanctions', *Revue belge de droit international* 1984–1985, vol. 18, pp. 34–56 on p. 54. See also the reference to the positions of countries in Georg Nolte, 'Article 2 (7)', in: Bruno Simma, Daniel-Erasmus Khan, Georg Nolte & Andreas Paulus (eds.), *The Charter of the United Nations*, Oxford: Oxford University Press, 2012, pp. 280–311 on p. 296.

234 Hersch Lauterpacht, *International Law and Human Rights*, Archon Books, 1968 (1950), pp. 148–149. See also Daniel Heilmann, 'The International Control of Illegal Drugs and the U.N. Treaty Regime: Preventing or Causing Human Rights Violations?', *Cardozo Journal of International and Comparative Law* 2011, vol. 19, pp. 237–290 on p. 276.

case law.[235] Because of the situation in Afghanistan at the time, this resolution is an exception in that it contains very strict obligations for states.[236] Consequently, states had to freeze assets of persons and entities that had links with the Taliban and/or Al-Qaida and had been placed on the UN terrorist list for that reason. The text of the resolution and the underlying system left no room to wriggle out of the obligation, not even if its implementation would lead to violation of human rights.[237] Persons and entities that had been placed on that list within the UN system had no access to an independent and impartial judicial authority in the sense of the right to a fair trial.

The crux is that the obligations in Resolution 1267 pursuant to Article 103 prevailed over conflicting obligations. Our assumption here is that within the system of the UN Charter, this also applied if the conflict involved a UN human rights norm.[238] Does that assumption imply that those human rights norms do not fall within the scope of Article 103 after all? We do not think that this is the case. First, it is important to realize that from a legal point of view, it cannot be ruled out at all that there is also a conflict of norms within the framework of Article 103. Under normal circumstances, it must then be determined which of those obligations eventually merits priority, on the basis of the rules of precedence discussed in this chapter. Resolution 1267, however, concerned very specifically formulated obligations with a view to protecting international peace and security, versus human rights norms. With the very strictly worded obligations, the resolution not only caused the conflict, it thereby also implicitly made clear that the obligations in it would prevail. In fact, the Security Council absolutely gave more weight to international peace and security than to the protection of human rights in this case.

Be that as it may, it is hard to see that this entails that Article 103 UN Charter does not apply to human rights as well. Moreover, the Security Council, in particular with respect to fighting terrorism, confirms that 'Member States must ensure that any measures taken [...] comply with all their obligations

---

235 For more information about this see for example Marko Milanović, 'Norm Conflict in International Law: Whither Human Rights?', *Duke Journal of Comparative and International Law* 2009, vol. 20, no. 1, pp. 69–131 on 79–92; Erika De Wet, 'From Kadi to Nada: Judicial Techniques Favouring Human Rights over United Nations Security Council Sanctions', *Chinese Journal of International Law* 2013, vol. 12, pp. 787–807.

236 Resolution 1267 with its very strict obligation is fairly unusual, because resolutions nearly always leave states at least some discretion in fulfilling the obligations, so that they can also meet requirements under human rights obligations.

237 See among other sources Antonios Tzanakopoulos, 'Collective Security and Human Rights', in: Erika De Wet & Jure Vidmar (eds.), *Hierarchy in International Law: The Place of Human Rights*, Oxford: Oxford University Press, 2012, pp. 42–70 on 43, 56, 57, 61. In that sense, see also ECtHR (Grand Chamber) 12 September 2012, *Nada/Switzerland*, no. 10593/08, para. 172.

238 Therefore, it is not relevant here to what extent and why an appeal to the ECHR or European Union law could be an obstacle to applying the resolution; for more information on this, see the literature mentioned in the footnotes above.

under international law, in particular international human rights, refugee and international humanitarian law'.[239] To that extent, the effect of human rights via Article 103 is also bolstered by such binding resolutions.

- *Conclusion.* In the light of the text of the Charter provisions referring to human rights, the object and purpose of the UN Charter and the case law of the International Court of Justice about it, we conclude that those provisions create obligations for the member states, among other parties, to respect and observe human rights. That means that pursuant to Article 103 UN Charter, those human rights obligations prevail over other obligations from other international agreements that conflict with them. However, that does not yet establish for which specific human rights obligations this applies and to what extent the ICESCR, the ICCPR, the ECHR and the ESC are relevant in that respect.

v. *Precedence of Positive Human Rights Obligations Pursuant to Article 103 UN Charter?*

The question is whether positive obligations pursuant to the rights with respect to health, life, inhuman treatment and privacy take precedence in the sense of Article 103 UN Charter. This question can only be answered in the affirmative if these positive obligations qualify under 'human rights and fundamental freedoms' in the sense of the Charter.

All told, an enormous number of human rights can be found in, among other things, conventions, non-binding instruments such as recommendations and documents with Rules, Principles and Guidelines as well as in case law. Partly because of the exceptional priority that obligations have in the sense of Article 103 UN Charter, it is implausible that thanks to this provision all those human rights prevail over all sorts of international obligations that are not related to human rights. Article 103 does not imply that anything that could be seen as a human rights obligation falls within the scope of this provision, regardless of when, in which format, how or by whom they were created.[240]

What is certain is that at any rate, certain human rights obligations must fall under the Charter, because otherwise it is difficult to understand why the references to 'human rights' have been included in the Charter. In view of the following, it is perfectly possible to argue (and we believe it is the most convincing argument) that the four human rights discussed in Chapter 2 regarding health, life, inhuman treatment and privacy qualify as human rights in the sense of the Charter and therefore fall within the scope of Article 103 UN Charter. It is also possible to argue convincingly that this also applies to the

---

239 Security Council Resolution 2170 (2014), *UN Doc.* S/RES/2170, 15 August 2014. Earlier for example Security Council Resolution 1456 (2003), *UN Doc.* S/RES/1456, 20 January 2003.

240 Jose E. Alvarez, 'How Not to Link: Institutional Conundrums of an Expanded Trade Regime', *Widener Law Symposium Journal* 2001, vol. 7, no. 1, pp. 1–19 on pp. 5–6.

positive obligations arising from these rights that may be relevant for regulated permission of cannabis cultivation and trade.

- *Are the rights from the ESC and the ECHR covered by Article 103 UN Charter?* First of all, we note that this is not directly the case where the recognition of these rights in the ESC and the ECHR is concerned and their clarification in the case law of the European CSR and the ECtHR. After all, these Conventions are not part of United Nations law, and given their regional nature, non-European UN member states can neither accept nor reject them. That does not alter the fact that recognition of the relevant human rights and positive obligations in the ESC and the ECHR that are relevant for the cannabis issue can support the universal application of those rights and obligations. To that extent, these Conventions too can be relevant to and give further effect to the UDHR.

  Additionally, the ECtHR points out that it follows from the UN Charter that the UN Security Council has an obligation to act in accordance with 'human rights and fundamental freedoms'. According to the ECtHR, this entails that it must be assumed that the Security Council 'does not intend to impose any obligation on member States to breach fundamental principles of human rights' and that therefore its resolutions must be interpreted in a way 'which is most in harmony' with the ECHR. In other words: the ECtHR apparently considers the ECHR as a relevant factor for the obligation on the UN Security Council to respect human rights.[241]
- *Are the rights from the UDHR, the ICESCR and the ICCPR covered by Article 103?* The recognition of the four rights within the framework of the United Nations is a different matter from that of the recognition of these rights within the ESC and the ECHR.

  In the first place, the text of the Charter refers in fairly general terms to 'human rights' and does not specify their relevance to for example human rights belonging to the 'general principles'[242] or the 'peremptory norms' (*jus cogens*) of general international law. From a textual point of view, there are good reasons to bring a fairly wide cluster of human rights under the Charter rather than a small set. Moreover, Articles 1, 13, 55, 56 (indirectly), 62 and 76 also refer to 'fundamental freedoms'. Human rights designated as freedoms in the UDHR, the ICCPR and the ECHR are the rights regarding expression, religion and association, for example. Several of these were already identified as freedoms in the French *Déclaration des Droits de l'Homme et du Citoyen*

241 ECtHR (Grand Chamber) 7 July 2011, *Al Jedda/The UK*, no. 27021/08, para. 102, confirmed in ECtHR (Grand Chamber) 12 September 2012, Nada/Switzerland, no. 10593/08, para. 171–172.

242 Usually, it is the other way round: 'human rights' in the Charter are an expression of 'general international law'; see Andreas Paulus & Johann R. Leiß, 'Article 103', in: Bruno Simma, Daniel-Erasmus Khan, Georg Nolte & Andreas (eds.), *The Charter of the United Nations*, Oxford: Oxford University Press, 2012, pp. 2110–2137 on p. 2131.

of 1789 and the Bill of Rights of 1789 in the United States. The fact that the Charter also explicitly relates to freedoms, implies that it covers at least a slightly wider collection of human rights.

Secondly, we note that the International Court of Justice admittedly recognizes 'the primary necessity of interpreting an instrument in accordance with the intentions of the parties at the time of its conclusion', but also takes the view that an international instrument is 'not static, but [...] by definition evolutionary'.[243] This would then also have to apply to the Charter.[244] Because of that, but also quite apart from that, it is relevant that the UN General Assembly has the task of *promoting* 'assisting in *the realization of human rights and fundamental freedoms* for all.' The Universal Declaration of Human Rights (UDHR) (as early as 1948) and also the ICESCR and the ICCPR (of 1966) are some of the results of that.[245] The ICESCR and the ICCPR in their preambles also point to the human rights obligations under the UN Charter. Another consideration is that while not all UN member states are party to the ICESCR and the ICCPR, the majority of them are.[246] The position which can be best defended in our view is that the catalogue of human rights that find recognition in the UDHR, ICESCR and the ICCPR in principle give effect to the reference in the Charter to 'human rights and fundamental freedoms'.

Some are more reluctant. It is often assumed in the literature that the UDHR at any rate gives effect to the Charter or is seen as an authoritative interpretation thereof.[247] All four human rights discussed in Chapter 2 are included in the Declaration. Article 25 UDHR states, among other things, that everyone has the right 'to a standard of living adequate for the health and well-being of himself

243 ICJ, Advisory Opinion of 21 June 1971, *I.C.J. Reports* 1971, p. 16 on 31 (para. 53) (*Legal Consequences for States of the Continued Presence of South Africa in Namibia (South West Africa) Notwithstanding Security Council Resolution 276 (1970)*). See also ICJ, Judgment of 25 September 1997, *I.C.J. Reports* 1997, p. 7 on pp. 67–68 (para. 112) (*Case Concerning the Gabcikovo-Nagymaros Project – Hungary v. Slovakia*).

244 According to A. Peters, 'Article 25', in: Bruno Simma, Daniel-Erasmus Khan, Georg Nolte & Andreas Paulus (eds.), *The Charter of the United Nations*, Oxford: Oxford University Press, 2012, pp. 787–854 on p. 824.

245 See C.-A. Fleischhauer & B. Simma, 'Article 13', in: Bruno Simma, Daniel-Erasmus Khan, Georg Nolte & Andreas Paulus (eds.), *The Charter of the United Nations*, Oxford: Oxford University Press, 2012, pp. 525–551 on p. 551.

246 The ICESCR counts 164 states as signatories and the ICCPR 168; see: https://treaties.un.org/ (visited on: 17 April 2016).

247 See also, with further references, Noëlle Quénivet, 'Binding the United Nations to Human Rights Norms by Way of the Laws of Treaties', *The George Washington International Law Review* 2010, vol. 42, pp. 587–621 on p. 599; and also, among other sources, A. Peters, 'Article 25', in: Bruno Simma, Daniel-Erasmus Khan, Georg Nolte & Andreas Paulus (eds.), *The Charter of the United Nations*, Oxford: Oxford University Press, 2012, pp. 787–854 on p. 824; Olivier De Schutter, *International Human Rights Law: Cases, Materials, Commentary*, Cambridge: Cambridge University Press, 2010, p. 49; Michael Singer, 'Jurisdictional Immunity of International Organizations: Human Rights and Functional Necessity Concerns', *Virginia Journal of International Law* 1953, vol. 36, pp. 53–165 on p. 97.

and of his family, including [...] medical care'. Pursuant to Article 3 UDHR, everyone has the 'right to life, liberty and security of person'. Article 5 UDHR stipulates that no one shall be subjected 'to torture or to cruel, inhuman or degrading treatment or punishment'. And Article 12 UDHR states among other things that no one shall be subjected to 'arbitrary interference with his privacy, family, home or correspondence' and that 'everyone has the right to the protection of the law' against such interference. Another factor that is relevant for the importance of the UDHR as implementation of the Charter is that the International Court of Justice in the *United States Diplomatic and Consular Staff in Tehran* case (quoted in the previous subsection) judged that certain actions of a member state are 'manifestly incompatible' with the Charter and the UDHR. Such a consideration can only have meaning, relevance and legitimacy if there is apparently an obligation (for states) not to act contrary to the Declaration.

Others take an even stricter position that – at any rate, or only – human rights that belong to customary law fall within the scope of the human rights references in the Charter and therefore within the scope of Article 103.[248,249] Apart from the fact that this condition – as we noted before – does not match the text of the Charter provisions referring to human rights very well, it is dubious whether imposing such a condition leads to essentially different conclusions with regard to the four human rights that are relevant here. In section 3.7.7.ii we saw that the negative obligations ensuing from the right to life and the prohibition of inhuman treatment have *jus cogens* status. That means that at any rate they belong to customary law as well in that respect. While it is not very easy to establish whether law is also customary law, it is usually (but not always[250]) assumed in the literature (partly because of considerations

248 Mary Ellen O'Connell, Jordan Paust & Rosa Pauks (panel), in: 'The Second Major General John L. Fugh Symposium', *Military Law Review* 2015, vol. 223, p. 440 on pp. 486–487; Jordan J. Paust, 'The Bush-Cheney Legacy: Serial Torture and Forced Disappearance in Manifest Violation of Global Human Rights Law', *Barry Law Review* 2012, vol. 18, no. 1, pp. 61–85 on pp. 69–70.

249 See – somewhat of an exception – for an even more restrictive view Jose E. Alvarez, 'How Not to Link: Institutional Conundrums of an Expanded Trade Regime', *Widener Law Symposium Journal* 2001, vol. 7, no. 1, pp. 1–19 on pp. 5–11. Alvarez does not indicate which rights still remain within the scope of the Charter. His argument seems to imply eventually that this cannot be assumed for any single right (with the exception perhaps of *jus cogens* rights), so that his conclusion is not tenable in view of the fact that the Charter repeatedly and unconditionally refers to 'human rights and fundamental freedoms'.

250 The notion that all universal human rights are customary law is rejected by Bruno Simma & Philip Alston, 'The Sources of Human Rights Law: Custom, Jus Cogens, and General Principles', *Australian Year Book of International Law* 1988–1989, vol. 12, pp. 82–108, but they do eventually qualify universal human rights as 'general principles' of international law, which are also valid legal sources according to Article 38(1) ICJ Statute. For another negative conclusion, see Alain Pellet, '"Human Rightism" and International Law' (Lecture delivered on 18 July 2000 at Geneva), in: *Gilberto Amado: Memorial Lectures*, Brasília, FUNAG, 2012, pp. 267–284 on p. 276.

of UN bodies and positions taken by states) that human rights in the UDHR also count as customary law.[251] Thus, in addition to the right to life and the right not to be subjected to inhuman treatment, the right to health and the right to a private life would, in principle, have the status of customary law as well.[252] If the ICESCR and the ICCPR do not already qualify directly as customary law themselves,[253] they can be seen as a further elaboration of the rights in the UDHR.[254]

- *Are the positive obligations within the scope of Article 103 UN Charter?* In view of the foregoing, it is difficult to defend the position that the four human rights that are relevant here (regarding health, life, inhuman treatment and privacy) do not fall under the 'human rights and fundamental freedoms' in the sense of the UN Charter. On the other hand, also on the basis of the foregoing, there are powerful arguments why this is the case. This means that we assume that these four rights can prevail in the sense of Article 103 UN Charter. However, this does not yet mean that this automatically applies to the positive obligations arising from these rights that may be relevant for regulated permission of cannabis cultivation and trade. It would appear that there are at least two positions that can be defended.

  On the one hand, it can be argued that positive obligations do not fall within the scope of the Charter. The provisions in the Charter refer to 'human rights and fundamental freedoms,' not explicitly to positive obligations concerning them. The Charter also emphasizes respect for and observance of

---

251 See Louis B. Sohn, 'The Human Rights Law of the Charter', *Texas International Law Journal* 1992, vol. 12, pp. 129–140 on 131–134, and also with further references Eibe H. Riedel & Jan-Michael Arend, 'Article 55 (c)', in: Bruno Simma, Daniel-Erasmus Khan, Georg Nolte & Andreas Paulus (eds.), *The Charter of the United Nations*, Oxford: Oxford University Press, 2012, pp. 1565–1602 on pp. 1578–1579; Richard B. Lillich, 'The Growing Importance of Customary International Human Rights Law, *Georgia Journal of International and Comparative Law* 1995–1996, vol. 25, pp. 1–30.

252 See in that sense specifically with respect to the right to health: Eleanor D. Kinney, 'The International Human Right to Health: What Does this Mean for Our Nation and World?', *Indiana Law Review* 2001, vol. 34, pp. 1457–1475 on pp. 1464–1467, 1475; and for the right to a private life: Alexandra Rengel, 'Privacy as an International Human Right and the Right to Obscurity in Cyberspace', *Groningen Journal of International Law* 2014, vol. 2, no. 2, pp. 33–54 on pp. 37–42 (particularly p. 42).

253 Thus, for example, Kinney on p. 1464; Thomas Buergenthal, 'The Normative and Institutional Evolution of International Human Rights', *Human Rights Quarterly* 1997, vol. 19, no. 4, pp. 703–723 on pp. 704–705; Louis B. Sohn, 'The Human Rights Law of the Charter', *Texas International Law Journal*, 1977, vol. 12, pp. 129–140 on p. 135; Jordan J. Paust, 'Human Rights on the Battlefield', *The George Washington International Law Review* 2015, vol. 47, pp. 509–561 on p. 520.

254 For an elaborate analysis see Eibe H. Riedel & Jan-Michael Arend, 'Article 55 (c)', in: Bruno Simma, Daniel-Erasmus Khan, Georg Nolte & Andreas Paulus (eds.), *The Charter of the United Nations*, Oxford: Oxford University Press, 2012, pp. 1565–1602 on pp. 1576–1585; Louis B. Sohn, 'The Human Rights Law of the Charter', *Texas International Law Journal* 1992, vol. 12, pp. 129–140 on pp. 134–136.

human rights. One must also bear in mind that at the time, the rights regarding life, inhuman treatment and private life were approached and understood predominantly from the perspective of the negative obligations for the state, while the positive obligations about the right to health were even more limited.

On the other hand, one must realize that the UN Charter, as we noted, is also 'not static, but [...] by definition evolutionary', so that the meaning of formulations it contains also depends on legal and social developments. By now, positive obligations are undeniably part and parcel of positive international human rights law, including the ICCPR, whether one agrees with it or not.[255] In this light, the general references in the Charter to 'human rights and fundamental freedoms' by now comprise positive obligations as well. Here too, the same proviso applies that this cannot cover each and every positive obligation, irrespective of when, in which form and how and by which organization they were established. In our opinion, the minimum requirement would be that the obligation may be assumed to qualify by now as a solid obligation under the convention, such as the ICESCR or the ICCPR. The positive obligations identified in Chapter 2 have been embedded so firmly in the international jurisprudence about those rights and thereby in the human rights system, that this is indeed the case in our view. Meanwhile, there is also the fact that states have a 'margin of appreciation' especially with regard to the positive obligations or otherwise have some freedom to decide how they fulfil these obligations.[256] Partly because of that, it is possible for states to escape a positive obligation to permit regulated cannabis cultivation. As we already saw before, however, in subsection *ii* – the notion of 'obligations' in Article 103 UN Charter must be interpreted fairly broadly these days, so that it may also include authorizations. In that respect, a positive human rights obligation is more powerful: whilst states have a 'margin of appreciation' in fulfilling their obligations, this does not in principle detract from the obligation to give maximum effect to the implementation of the positive obligation of protection.[257]

We conclude that one can argue convincingly that the positive obligations arising from the four rights that may be relevant for regulated permission of cannabis cultivation and trade, qualify as obligations in the sense of Article 103 UN Charter.

---

255 For a critical stance on this, see Piet Hein P.H.M.C. van Kempen, 'Four Concepts of Security – A Human Rights Perspective', *Human Rights Law Review* 2013, vol. 13, no. 1, pp. 1–23; Piet Hein P.H.M.C. van Kempen, *Repressie door mensenrechten. Over positieve verplichtingen tot aanwending van strafrecht ter bescherming van fundamentele rechten*, Nijmegen: Wolf Legal Publishers, 2008 (i.e., *Repression because of human rights. About positive obligations to apply criminal law to protect fundamental rights*, Nijmegen: Wolf Legal Publishers, 2008).

256 See sections 2.3.7.x, 2.4.7.ix and 2.4.12.ii.

257 For more information. see section 2.4.12.ii (from: The second perspective).

vi. Do Obligations under Drugs Conventions Take Precedence Pursuant to Article 103 UN Charter?

Where the UN Charter refers on many occasions to 'human rights and fundamental freedoms', its text does not contain any specific reference to drugs. The possibility that this is a conscious choice is already plausible for the very reason that the earlier Covenant of the League of Nations of 1919 explicitly mentions the general supervision of the implementation of instruments with respect to 'the traffic in opium and other dangerous drugs' as a responsibility of the League of Nations.[258] Also the fight against crime or international cooperation in criminal law are not mentioned explicitly in the UN Charter. However, there is a number of more general objectives in the framework of which one can place the drugs conventions.

Article 1 of the UN Charter states the objectives of the United Nations, such as bringing about international cooperation 'in solving international problems of an economic, social, cultural, or humanitarian character', and according to the Articles 13, 55, 56 and 62 responsibilities in this area have been assigned to the General Assembly, the United Nations, the UN member states and ECOSOC respectively. However, the purpose and the related responsibilities are not primarily (not implicitly either) aimed at solving drugs problems or the creation of drugs conventions.[259]

It is perhaps more relevant that the Charter with the Articles 13, 55, 56 (indirectly), 57 and 62 also has obligations with respect to health ('health fields', 'health problems', 'health matters'. It would appear that the creation of the UN narcotic drugs conventions needs to be seen first and foremost in that context.[260] We believe that the obligations from the drugs conventions have such a tenuous and indirect link with the Charter that they can hardly be considered obligations in the sense of Article 103 UN Charter.

Moreover, the opposite conclusion would deprive Article 103 of its meaning. After all, that would mean that everything that is happening within the United Nations on the basis of the general purposes and descriptions of responsibilities

---

258 See Article 23(c) of the Covenant of the League of Nations of 28 April 1919.

259 Compare the extensive commentaries on these provisions in Bruno Simma, Daniel-Erasmus Khan, Georg Nolte & Andreas Paulus (eds.), *The Charter of the United Nations*, Oxford: Oxford University Press, 2012, none of which feature the drugs problems, drugs or the fight against them with respect to this objective, with one exception: the INCB is designated as a functional commission created by ECOSOC in order to coordinate and promote the cooperation on social issues; see the article in that book by Volker Röben, 'Article 62', pp. 1678–1696 on p. 1693.

260 See Tobias Stoll, 'Article 55 (a) and (b)', in: Bruno Simma, Daniel-Erasmus Khan, Georg Nolte & Andreas Paulus (eds.), *The Charter of the United Nations*, Oxford: Oxford University Press, 2012, pp. 1535–1564 on p. 1561; Daniel Heilmann, 'The International Control of Illegal Drugs and the U.N. Treaty Regime: Preventing or Causing Human Rights Violations?', *Cardozo Journal of International and Comparative Law* 2011, vol. 19, pp. 237–290 on p. 274.

could be seen as a priority obligation according to this provision.[261] That is the case even more so here in particular, because the status of 'health' in the Charter is lower than that of 'human rights and fundamental freedoms'; after all, 'health' is not an explicit part of the main purposes from Article 1 of the Charter. Consequently, it is problematic to try and place the obligations under the drugs conventions in the scope of the Charter by relying on an 'object and purpose' argument.

Finally, we point out that it is not only the drugs conventions that can be seen as a way to carry out the duties regarding 'health', but that is also true for the human right to health.[262] If in spite of the foregoing one still wanted to construe an obligation under the Charter via 'health', the question presents itself whether its implementation must take place on the basis of the right to health or the drugs conventions. And that again brings one back to the question which of these takes precedence.

vii. Conclusion

It must be assumed that the rights regarding health, life, inhuman treatment and a private life are all human rights in the sense of the UN Charter and therefore fall within the scope of its Article 103. At any rate, this applies to the rights in the sense of the UDHR, the ICESCR and the ICCPR (the ESC and the ECHR do not play a direct part here, although recognition of the rights in these charters/ conventions supports their universality). It can be argued convincingly that Article 103 also applies to the positive obligations arising from these rights that may be relevant for regulated permission of cannabis cultivation and trade. Conversely, it cannot be argued reasonably that the obligations pursuant to the drugs conventions are also obligations in the sense of the Charter.

All this does not mean, however, that obligations from the drugs conventions that conflict with positive human rights obligations can simply be brushed aside on the grounds of Article 103. After all, it is important (as we shall see in section 3.9) that a 'presumption of compatibility' applies, among other things.[263] Basically, this presumption implies that obligations must be interpreted in such a way that a conflict between them is prevented and thereby a violation of at least one of them.

---

261 See for information on this subsection 3.7.8.ii. above.

262 Consequently, this right also features in Eibe H. Riedel & Jan-Michael Arend, 'Article 55 (c)', in: Bruno Simma, Daniel-Erasmus Khan, Georg Nolte & Andreas Paulus (eds.), *The Charter of the United Nations*, Oxford: Oxford University Press, 2012, pp. 1565–1602 on p. 1560.

263 See the following in relation to Article 103 UN Charter Andreas Paulus & Johann R. Leiß, 'Article 103', in: Bruno Simma, Daniel-Erasmus Khan, Georg Nolte & Andreas Paulus (eds.), *The Charter of the United Nations*, Oxford: Oxford University Press, 2012, pp. 2110–2137 on pp. 2118–2119.

3.7.9. *LEX SUPERIOR III*: SPECIAL SUBSTANTIVE STATUS FOR HUMAN RIGHTS OR OBLIGATIONS FROM DRUGS CONVENTIONS?

There is a great deal of discussion in the literature about the question whether certain categories of international law norms that are not *jus cogens* – and are not related to Article 103 UN Charter – carry more weight in a substantive sense than other norms of that kind. Below, we will assess both the obligations arising from human rights and the obligations under drugs conventions to see if they have such a special substantive status. In this respect, the concept of *erga omnes* obligations comes into play. What is also important is the distinction between 'ordinary' multilateral treaties, which essentially only comprise bilateral obligations, and 'special' multilateral treaties, which are considered to be normative or 'law-creating' or creating 'objective regimes' and which contain so-called 'integral obligations'.

i. Special Substantive Status for Human Rights According to UN Institutions

When reading documents of important UN bodies and entities, the jurisprudence and the literature, one often comes across the assertion that human rights have a special substantive status and/or they must be given precedence over any other international law that is not *jus cogens*. In this respect, the following point of view of the UN Special Rapporteur on the right to health is very interesting for the cannabis issue:

> A number of United Nations bodies enforce the three drug control treaties and are required to promote and protect human rights, as identified in Articles 1 and 55 of the Charter of the United Nations. When the goals and approaches of the international drug control regime and international human rights regime conflict, it is clear that human rights obligations should prevail. The General Assembly has consistently adopted resolutions declaring that international drug control must be carried out in conformity with the Charter, and 'with full respect for human rights' (see resolutions 62/176 and 63/197).[264]

The Special Rapporteur speaks in broad terms about the international human rights regime and the ensuing obligations, so that the prevalence of human rights that is recognized by him apparently also applies to positive human rights obligations. Furthermore, the conclusion of the Special Rapporteur that the implementation of the obligations under the drugs conventions can only take place with due regard to

264 Report of the Special Rapporteur on the right of everyone to the enjoyment of the highest attainable standard of physical and mental health, Anand Grover, *UN Doc.* A/65/255, 6 August 2010, para. 10.

human rights is indeed supported by this Resolution and many other Resolutions of the UN General Assembly. For example, Resolutions 66/183 and 67/193 confirm:

> that countering the world drug problem is a common and shared responsibility that must be addressed in a multilateral setting, that it requires an integrated and balanced approach and that it must be carried out in full conformity with the purposes and principles of the Charter of the United Nations and other provisions of international law, the Universal Declaration of Human Rights and the Vienna Declaration and Programme of Action on human rights, and, in particular, with full respect for [...] all human rights and fundamental freedoms.[265]

The first interesting aspect of this consideration is that respect for *all* human rights and fundamental freedoms is required. This suggests an even broader set of human rights to be respected than those that are part of the UDHR, since otherwise a reference to that Declaration would have sufficed. The mere mention of the Declaration means that the four human rights discussed in Chapter 2 (regarding health, life, inhuman treatment and privacy) are indisputably among the rights that are to be respected.[266] Nevertheless, in view of the general and broad reference to all human rights, it must be assumed that 'countering the world drug problem' can also only take place within human rights law pursuant to the ICESCR and ICCPR.

Secondly, the reference to the Vienna Declaration and Programme of Action deserves our attention. Item 1 of that declaration lends special weight to human rights and the obligations that states have in that respect:

> Human rights and fundamental freedoms are the birthright of all human beings; their protection and promotion is the first responsibility of Governments.[267]

Earlier, in section 3.7.8.iv, we quoted the Special Rapporteurs on globalization and its impact on the full enjoyment of all human rights. In essence, according to them, if there is a conflict between human rights obligations and other international obligations, states 'have no choice but to give primacy, *inter alia*, to human rights obligations'.[268] This also applies if there is a conflict with

---

265 UN General Assembly Resolution 66/183, 'International cooperation against the world drug problem', adopted 66nd plenary meeting on 19 December 2011, *UN Doc.* A/RES/66/183, 3 April 2012, para. 2 and 14(a); UN General Assembly Resolution 67/193, 'International cooperation against the world drug problem', adopted 67th plenary meeting on 20 December 2012, *UN Doc.* A/RES/67/193, 23 April 2013, para. 2 and 17(a).

266 See section 3.7.8.v.

267 U.N. World Conference on Human Rights, Vienna, 14–25 June 1993, 'Vienna Declaration and Programme of Action', *UN Doc.* A/CONF.157/24, 12 July 1993.

268 Progress report of the Special Rapporteurs on globalization and its impact on the full enjoyment of all human rights, J. Oloka-Onyango and Deepika Udagama, *UN Doc.* E/CN.4/Sub.2/2001/10, 2 August 2001, para. 58.

obligations from another branch of subsystem such as international trade law.[269] This would then also have to apply with regard to the drug control system.

The UN bodies that monitor the UN narcotic drugs conventions recognize that implementation of the obligations under the drugs conventions must take place within the framework of human rights.

In the first place, that applies to the International Narcotics Control Board. The INCB emphasizes the following:

> Drug control action *must be consistent with international human rights* standards.'[270] 'The drug control system is a balanced system, driving towards improving public health and welfare, based on the underlying principles of proportionality, collective responsibility and compliance with international human rights standards. Implementing this system means putting the health and welfare of mankind at the core of drug policies, applying comprehensive, integrated and balanced approaches to elaborating drug control policy, *promoting human rights standards*, giving higher priority to prevention, treatment, rehabilitation and the reduction of the negative consequences of drug abuse, and strengthening international cooperation based on shared responsibility.[271] (emphasis added).

The INCB apparently sees human rights as an integral part of the drug control system, which can and must be applied in accordance with international human rights standards. In this respect, it is also important (as we discussed in section 3.7.4.iv) that Article 14(2) of the Illicit Traffic Convention specifies that states parties in adopting measures against illicit cannabis cultivation 'shall respect fundamental human rights', and that the preparatory work for both the

---

269 Final report of the Special Rapporteurs on globalization and its impact on the full enjoyment of all human rights, J. Oloka-Onyango and Deepika Udagama, *UN Doc.* E/CN.4/Sub.2/2003/14, 25 June 2003, Annex, para. 6. See also for example UN Sub-Commission for the Prevention of Discrimination and the Protection of Minorities, Resolution 1998/12 on 'Human rights as the primary objective of trade, investment, and financial policy', UN Doc. E/CN.4/Sub.2/RES/1998/12, 20 August 1998, para. 1, in which 'the realization of the human rights and fundamental freedoms' from the UDHR, the ICESCR, ICCPR and other international and regional human rights instruments is qualified as 'the first and most fundamental responsibility and objective of States in all areas of governance and development'.

270 INCB, *Report of the International Narcotics Control Board for 2015*, New York: United Nations, 2016, p. 6 (no. 36). See also *Report for 2017*, p. 44 (no. 251) and 45 (no. 258); *Report for 2014*, p. iii, 1 (nos. 1–2) and 8–9 (para. 35–38), which annual report is the first with a specific paragraph on 'Respect for human rights'; *Report for 2013*, p. iv; *Report for 2012*, p. 3 (no. 17); *Report for 2010*, p. vii; *Report for 2008*, p. 7 (no. 31). The importance of respecting human rights was given more prominence for the first time in the *Report for 2007*, p. 2 (no. 7), p. 5 (nos. 20–21) and in particular p. 9 (nos. 37–38); compare this to the *Report for 1996*, p. 9 (no. 31), which only casually referred to the protection of human rights as something to be taken into account.

271 INCB, *Report of the International Narcotics Control Board for 2015*, New York: United Nations, 2016, p. iv (Foreword).

Single Convention and the Illicit Traffic Convention contains several references to human rights that implicitly or explicitly suggest state's awareness of the importance that the obligations under the drugs conventions should not violate human rights.

There is no reason to assume that this does not also apply to the positive human rights obligations (as is the case for the positive obligations discussed in Chapter 2) that have found permanent recognition under human rights conventions and consequently belong to these convention systems. After all, these positive obligations also qualify as 'international human rights standards'. In addition to this, the INCB to this end refers explicitly to human rights conventions and notes that the parties to the drugs conventions if necessary 'should [...] seek out the advice of human rights treaty bodies for the implementation of such [human rights] norms.'[272] This recognition of the relevance of the judgments and opinions of the human rights monitoring bodies is important, because it is exactly also in the jurisprudence of those bodies that positive human rights obligations have been developed.

Finally, the Commission on Narcotic Drugs matters here. The CND has also confirmed repeatedly 'that the world drug problem has to be addressed in full conformity with' among other things, the UN Charter, the UDHR and in particular all human rights and fundamental freedoms.[273]

The considerations quoted above do not mean that the UN General Assembly, the INCB and the CND are saying that as far as they are concerned, obligations under the drugs conventions such as those for criminalization, prosecution for and fighting cannabis cultivation and trade can be ignored. Every time when human rights are discussed in connection with the drugs conventions, they do make it clear that those human rights need to be prioritized. Unlike the Special Rapporteur on the right to health, these bodies apparently hardly see a possibility for a conflict between the two, if at all. Their assumption after all is not only that the drugs conventions must be implemented in accordance with human rights standards (to which the positive human rights obligations belong as well), but that this is also possible. Since there is at any rate in first instance genuine interference between human rights obligations and obligations under

272 INCB, *Report of the International Narcotics Control Board for 2014*, New York: United Nations, 2015, p. 9 (no. 38).

273 CND Resolution 56/16, 'Enhancing international cooperation to strengthen efforts in West Africa to counter illicit drug trafficking', *UN Doc.* E/CN.7/2013/14, preamble. See also for example CND Resolution 58/4, 'Promoting the implementation of the United Nations Guiding Principles on Alternative Development', *UN Doc.* E/CN.7/2015/15, preamble; CND, 'Joint Ministerial Statement of the 2014 High-Level Review by the Commission on Narcotic Drugs of the Implementation by Member States of the Political Declaration and Plan of Action on International Cooperation towards an Integrated and Balanced Strategy to Counter the World Drug Problem, CND 57th session, Vienna, 13 and 14 March 2014', para. 1 and 23.

the drugs conventions within the cannabis issue, it is important to have a closer look at the question whether a special substantive status is due to one of them.

ii. Basis of the Special Substantive Status of Human Rights: General

It does not follow unambiguously and explicitly from international law that 'human rights and fundamental freedoms' as a category of norms deserve special importance. However, in addition to what follows from the previous subsection, there are various grounds to be found in international law to assume that this is the case. These are not only important for the ICESCR and the ICCPR, but they do have at any rate indirect and sometimes also direct relevance for the ESC and ECHR. As we will see below in subsection xi, a few qualifying comments are called for with regard to that special status.

iii. Basis: Recognition in UN Charter and Council of Europe Statute

There is explicit recognition for 'human rights and fundamental freedoms' in the UN Charter, and promoting and stimulating respect for these rights and freedoms is even recognized in it as one of the main purposes of the United Nations.[274] The same goes for the Council of Europe, which mentions 'the maintenance and further realization of human rights and fundamental freedoms' as one of its aims in Article 1 of the Statute of the Council of Europe. This also points out the special importance of human rights, but it does not – unlike Article 103 UN Charter – grant a hierarchical position of superiority to human rights.[275] All this also applies to the four human rights discussed in Chapter 2 (regarding health, life, inhuman treatment and privacy). That will include (which can be argued convincingly[276]) the concomitant positive obligations that are relevant for the cannabis issue.

iv. Basis: Recognition as 'Jus Cogens'

As we saw earlier, while not all rights and obligations from human rights conventions have *jus cogens* status, it is obvious that most of the norms that do have this status are human rights or are related to them.[277] One might say that more generally, this illustrates that human rights are something special, particularly because the difference in importance between *jus cogens* human rights and many other human rights is rather gradual than essential.

274 See sections 3.7.8.iii, iv and v.
275 Cf. Dinah Shelton, 'Hierarchy of Norms and Human Rights: Of Trumps and Winners', *Saskatchewan Law Review* 2002, vol. 65, pp. 301–331 on p. 307.
276 See section 3.7.8.v.
277 See section 3.7.7.i.

v. *Basis: Recognition as Customary Law*

It became clear earlier that human rights mentioned in the UDHR also belong to customary law.[278] This concerns the law that has binding force for all states, regardless of the question whether it has actually been codified in a treaty or not. Customary law is therefore universally applicable. Consequently, that is also the case for the four human rights discussed in Chapter 2. Although customary law does not occupy a higher place in the hierarchy than treaty law, the fact that this law applies universally illustrates again that it is something extraordinary, as this is not the case for most international treaty law.

vi. *Basis: Recognition as* 'Erga Omnes'

Most *erga omnes* obligations relate to the area of human rights and humanitarian law,[279] although not all human rights norms constitute *erga omnes* obligations, that is to say: obligations each state has with respect to other states and the compliance with which is in the interest of all states.[280,281] The tight connection between the concept of *erga omnes* and human rights is not surprising. It is exactly the violation of human rights by a country that can easily cause unrest in other countries and even pose a risk to international peace and security, and this is reflected in the preambles to the ICESCR, the ICCPR, the ESC and the ECHR.[282] *Erga omnes* norms can belong to customary law or treaty law.[283] Furthermore, *jus cogens* norms have an *erga omnes* effect; conversely, this is not necessarily the case.

Referring to the UN Charter and the UDHR, some authors argue that human rights in general have by now acquired *erga omnes* effect or that at any rate the general obligation to respect human rights has that effect.[284] One of the reasons

---

278 See section 3.7.8.v.

279 ILC, 'Fragmentation of International Law', 2006, para. 391; Maurizio Ragazzi, *The Concept of International Obligations Erga Omnes*, Oxford: Oxford University Press, 2000, p. 135.

280 Aaron X. Fellmeth & Maurice Horwitz, *Guide to Latin in International Law*, Oxford: Oxford University Press, 2009: '"Toward all" [...] obligations owed by a state to all other states or the international community at large [...]. All states are considered to have a legal interest in deterring violations of erga omnes obligations'.

281 Incidentally, this paragraph is not about the more limited *erga omnes inter partes* or *erga omnes contractantes*, where the *erga omnes* effect only applies between parties to the convention. Cf. Ulf Linderfalk, 'International Legal Hierarchy Revisited – The Status of Obligations *Erga Omnes*', *Nordic Journal of International Law*, 2011, vol. 80, pp. 1–23 on p. 11.

282 See the preambles to the ECHR for example.

283 Michael Byers, 'Conceptualising the Relationship between Jus Cogens and Erga Omnes Rules', *Nordic Journal of International Law* 1997, vol. 66, pp. 211–239.

284 See the discussion and references in Maurizio Ragazzi, *The Concept of International Obligations Erga Omnes*, Oxford: Oxford University Press, 2000, pp. 141–145, who arrives at a less far-reaching conclusion himself: 'each obligation should be assessed on its own merits, with a view to ascertaining whether or not it is an obligation *erga omnes*'.

provided is that the rationale for respecting human rights does not lie in the subjective interests of states, but rather in those of individuals who together form 'the international community'.[285] If one wanted to go this far (and there certainly is something to be said for it), then it is also possible to assume that this applies in principle to the positive obligations that go hand-in-hand with those rights and which have been fully recognized in international and regional human rights conventions systems. That would also apply then to the positive obligations discussed in Chapter 2. In the absence of support for this general acceptance in jurisprudence and legal practice for the entire branch of human rights law, we will however – as yet – not assume such a general applicability of the *erga omnes* concept (however, see the next subsection).

According to the International Court of Justice in the *Barcelona Traction* case, *erga omnes* obligations arise from 'the basic rights of the human person' among other things.[286] After an analysis of this ruling and of the terms basic rights with respect to the terms 'human rights' and 'fundamental human rights', Ragazzi comes to the conclusion that the category of 'basic rights' is narrower and that 'the character *erga omnes* does not apply indiscriminately to all principles and rules protecting human rights.'[287] In addition to the prohibitions of genocide, slavery and racial discrimination, it could possibly cover the prohibitions of murder, enforced disappearance, torture and inhuman treatment, prolonged arbitrary deprivation of liberty and 'a consistent pattern of gross violations of internationally recognized human rights'.[288] Breaching these prohibitions imply very serious violations of human rights and the emphasis is on the negative obligation for the state to refrain from such acts.

Can it be assumed on the basis of the (perhaps by now[289] too) restrictive approach of the International Court of Justice that the positive obligations

---

285 Ian D. Seiderman, *Hierarchy in International Law*, Antwerpen/Groningen/Oxford: Intersentia/Hart, 2001, p. 129, 145, pp. 276–277.

286 ICJ, Judgment of 5 February 1970, *I.C.J. Reports* 1970, p. 3 on 32 (para. 33–34) (*Case Concerning the Barcelona Traction, Light and Power Company, Limited – Belgium v. Spain, Second Phase*).

287 Maurizio Ragazzi, *The Concept of International Obligations Erga Omnes*, Oxford: Oxford University Press, 2000, pp. 139–140. Otherwise, see Theodor Meron, *Human Rights and Humanitarian Norms as Customary Law*, Oxford: Oxford University Press, 1991, pp. 188–201; Ian D. Seiderman, *Hierarchy in International Law*, Antwerpen/Oxford: Intersentia/Hart, 2001, p. 124 (see also pp. 131–135), who contests that legal importance should be attached to the qualification of 'basic rights'.

288 Cf. Maurizio Ragazzi, *The Concept of International Obligations Erga Omnes*, Oxford: Oxford University Press, 2000, pp. 140–141, with a reference to Restatement 702 of *Restatement of the Law Third: The Foreign Relations Law of the United States*, American Law Institute, 1987.

289 Already some 25 years ago, the following conclusion was drawn by Theodor Meron, *Human Rights and Humanitarian Norms as Customary Law*, Oxford: Oxford University Press, 1991, p. 199: 'In sum, both international practice and scholarly opinion seem to have moved well beyond the *erga omnes* dictum of *Barcelona Traction*'.

discussed in Chapter 2 and which are relevant for the cannabis issue also constitute *erga omnes* obligations? It seems to us that this position is defensible up to a point, as far as this concerns persons who perish because of violence or fires or who suffer injuries through inhuman treatment when the state is in a position to prevent this. After all, these events could easily be considered serious breaches of human rights.

Although the *erga omnes* status too does not imply that a norm is superior, they are norms of extraordinary importance and of a special nature, according to the International Court of Justice.[290] One ground for assuming such a status is also the fact that the norm 'is one of the essential principles of contemporary international law'.[291] In respect of the special nature, Byers concludes:

> *Jus cogens* rules and *erga omnes* rules seek to protect and promote the common interests of States to a much more obvious degree than most rules of international law. They are constitutional rules which help define the fundamental characteristics of the international legal system: they play an important role in determining how rules of international law are developed, maintained and changed, and in protecting those human rights or civil liberties which are considered essential to the self-identity of the international legal system, and the international society it serves.[292]

The fact that a norm is part of customary law and has *erga omnes* status, does not grant this norm precedence over other norms, but it does indicate its special importance.

vii. Basis: Recognition as 'Integral Obligations'

Most conventions comprise obligations that parties to the convention have towards each other in a network of mutual relationships. In addition to this, there are conventions containing more absolute obligations that are therefore not merely reciprocal between parties.[293] A distinction can be made here between integral obligations (actions of each party to the convention are

[290] ICJ, Judgment of 5 February 1970, *I.C.J. Reports* 1970, p. 3 on 32 (para. 33) (*Case Concerning the Barcelona Traction, Light and Power Company, Limited – Belgium v. Spain, Second Phase*): 'In view of the importance of the rights involved, all States can be held to have a legal interest in their protection; they are obligations *erga omnes*.' See also Jure Vidmar, 'Norm Conflicts and Hierarchy in International Law: Towards a Vertical International Legal System?, in: Erika de Wet & Jure Vidmar (eds.), '*Hierarchy in International Law: The Place of Human Rights*', Oxford: Oxford University Press, 2012, pp. 13–41 on p. 14, pp. 23–25.

[291] ICJ, Judgment of 30 June 1995, *I.C.J. Reports* 1995, p. 90 on 102 (para. 29) (*Case concerning East Timor – Portugal v. Australia*).

[292] Michael Byers, 'Conceptualising the Relationship between Jus Cogens and Erga Omnes Rules', *Nordic Journal of International Law* 1997, vol. 66, pp. 211–239 on p. 239.

[293] ILC, 'Fragmentation of International Law', 2006, para. 385.

independent of those of all other parties, as is the case for human rights conventions; see below) and interdependent obligations: actions of each party to the convention depend on actions of all other parties, which applies to disarmament conventions for example).[294] Integral conventions are 'normative', law-creating conventions – or as Brölmann calls them: 'the true 'law-making' instruments' – and they create 'objective' obligations.[295] The concept of integral obligations is strongly related to that of *erga omnes* obligations, but they are not identical. Unlike *erga omnes* obligations, integral obligations are always based on a multilateral convention and they only apply between the parties to the convention.[296]

The existence of such 'integral' conventions and treaties and/or treaty obligations is not reflected in the Vienna Convention on the Law of Treaties, but is recognized by the International Law Commission.[297] Moreover, such recognition is also substantiated by the case law of the International Court of Justice. In the *Reservations to the Convention on Genocide* case, the Court confirms that the object and purpose of conventions must be taken into consideration and that there are conventions that undeniably have been adopted for 'a purely humanitarian and civilizing purpose':

> In such a convention the contracting States do not have any interests of their own; they merely have, one and all, a common interest, namely, the accomplishment of those high purposes which are the raison d'être of the convention. Consequently, in a convention of this type one cannot speak of individual advantages or disadvantages to States, or of the maintenance of a perfect contractual balance between rights and duties. The high ideals which inspired the Convention provide, by virtue of the common will of the parties, the foundation and measure of all its provisions.[298]

Such conventions work independently and therefore regardless of the actions by the parties to the conventions or their invocations of these conventions. With such conventions, states undertake to behave in a certain 'parallel' way, not

---

294 Catherine Brölmann, 'Law-Making Treaties: Form and Function in International Law', *Nordic Journal of International Law* 2005, vol. 74, p. 388, 395.

295 Ibid, pp. 383–404 on p. 388, pp. 401–402.

296 See also K. Sachariew, 'State Responsibility for Multilateral Treaty Violations: Identifying the "Injured State" and its Legal Status', *Netherlands International Law Review* 1988, vol. 35, no. 3, pp. 273–289 on p. 276 (fn 13).

297 ILC, 'Fragmentation of International Law', 2006, para. 248, 269, 311–313; ILC, 'Articles on Responsibility of States for Internationally Wrongful Acts, with commentaries', 2001, comm. Article 33 (para. 2), comm. Article 42 (para. 5).

298 ICJ, Advisory Opinion of 28 May 1951, *I.C.J. Reports* 1951, p. 15 on 23 (*Reservations to the Convention on the Prevention and Punishment of the Crime of Genocide*); see also ICJ, Judgment of 26 February 2007, *I.C.J. Reports* 2007, p. 43 on 110 (para. 161) (*Application of the Convention on the Prevention and Punishment of the Crime of Genocide – Bosnia and Herzegovina v. Serbia and Montenegro*).

towards or in relation to each other, but within their own legal order.[299] Human rights conventions are important examples of conventions establishing integral obligations.[300] Such obligations then include positive obligations that have been fully recognized under human rights conventions, because these have come to be part of the convention system. This means that the positive obligations (discussed in Chapter 2 and which are relevant to the cannabis issue) from the ICESCR, the ICCPR, the ESC and the ECHR, are 'integral obligations'.

With such 'integral' human rights conventions, the parties to the convention subject themselves in the general interest to obligations, not in relation to other states, but to all individuals within their jurisdiction[301] and the international community as a whole. This is one of the areas where the concept of integral obligations shows a strong connection with the concept of *erga omnes*. Indeed, international courts in the field of human rights (such as the ECtHR and the Inter-American Court for Human Rights) are also of the opinion that human rights conventions are of a special nature.[302] The foregoing squares with the fact that the Human Rights Committee and the ECtHR for example take the view that the general rules for reservations are not automatically applicable to human rights conventions.[303]

---

299 Bruno Simma, 'International Crimes: Injury and Countermeasures. Comments on Part 2 of the ILC Work on State Responsibility', in: Joseph H.H. Weiler, Antonio Cassese & Marina Spinedi (eds.), International Crimes of State, Berlin/New York: Walter de Gruyter, 1989, pp. 283–318 on p. 286.

300 ILC, 'Fragmentation of International Law', 2006, para. 248, 262, 312, 493(1); ILC, 'Articles on Responsibility of States for Internationally Wrongful Acts, with commentaries', 2001, comm. Article 48 (para. 7). See also Catherine Brölmann, 'Law-Making Treaties: Form and Function in International Law', *Nordic Journal of International Law* 2005, vol. 74, pp. 383–404 on p. 383, 388, 397, 402; Bruno Simma, 'International Crimes: Injury and Countermeasures. Comments on Part 2 of the ILC Work on State Responsibility', in: Joseph H.H. Weiler, Antonio Cassese & Marina Spinedi (eds.), International Crimes of State, Berlin/New York: Walter de Gruyter, 1989, pp. 283–318 on p. 286; Joost Pauwelyn, 'A Typology of Multilateral Treaty Obligations: Are WTO Obligations Bilateral or Collective in Nature?', *European Journal of International Law* 2003, vol. 14, no. 5, pp. 907–951 on pp. 933–934 for example. See also Ahmad Ali Ghouri, 'Is Characterization of Treaties a Solution to Treaty Conflicts?', *Chinese Journal of International Law* 2012, vol. 11, pp. 247–280 on p. 263 (para. 26–27) and pp. 279–280 (para. 62); M. Craven, 'Legal differentiation and the concept of the human rights treaty in international law', *European Journal of International Law* 2000, vol. 11, pp. 489–519.

301 Catherine Brölmann, 'Law-Making Treaties: Form and Function in International Law', *Nordic Journal of International Law* 2005, vol. 74, pp. 383–404 on pp. 401–402.

302 See the previously mentioned article by Brölmann, with further references, and also ILC, 'Fragmentation of International Law', 2006, para. 163, 428, 437.

303 See for example HRC, General Comment No. 24, 'Issues relating to reservations made upon ratification or accession to the Covenant or the Optional Protocols thereto, or in relation to declarations under article 41 of the Covenant', 4 November 1994, *UN Doc.* CCPR C/21/ Rev.1/Add.6 (1994), para. 17; ECtHR 23 March 1985, *Loizidou/Turkey*, no. 15318/89, para. 70, 89.

viii. Basis: Several Other Special International Recognitions

In international law, there are all sorts of provisions of the treaties that grant a special status to human rights. Our first example is Article 60 of the Vienna Convention on the Law of Treaties, which excludes human rights provisions from the possibilities to terminate a treaty or to suspend its operation as a consequence of the treaty having been breached.[304] Furthermore, Article 21(3) of the Statute of the International Criminal Court (ICC) states that the interpretation of the law by the Court must be compatible with internationally recognized human rights. Our last example is Article 50 of the Articles on State Responsibility.[305] According to this provision, a state which has suffered because of an act deemed wrongful under international law is not allowed to take countermeasures that fly in the face of the obligations to protect fundamental human rights.

ix. Basis: European Human Rights Prevail Over Global International Law

The special substantive status of human rights norms is in principle based on the special values these norms represent. In that respect, it does not matter what the formal basis of the norms is, in which instrument they have been integrated, whether it concerns international, regional or national law and whether the instrument is binding or not. However, indirectly and de facto the formal basis is important, at any rate with regard to the question whether a norm truly deserves that status from a substantive point of view. Whether one can establish that the special substantive status of the norm is generally recognized, will in many cases also depend on the instrument, that is to say its authority, its binding force and the number of states that are party to it. It would be beyond the scope of this book to explain here what exactly the value of the ESC and the ECHR is. Nevertheless, we note that particularly the ECHR system is one of the most influential human rights systems in the world and is therefore probably the most authoritative. In addition to this, the rights and obligations established through the ECHR are supported in other regional human rights systems as well as the human rights system of the United Nations. This absolutely applies to the core of the positive obligations that we dealt with in Chapter 2, as became clear there with regard to the relationship

304 The fact that the provision also bears on human rights treaties is discussed in Thomas Giegerich, 'Article 60', in: Oliver Dörr & Kirsten Schmalenbach (eds.), *Vienna Convention on the Law of Treaties*, Berlin/Heidelberg: Springer-Verlag, 2012, pp. 1021–1049 on p. 1047 (no. 85).

305 ILC, 'Articles on Responsibility of States for Internationally Wrongful Acts, with commentaries', 2001.

between the ICESCR and the ICCPR.[306] As important regional human rights conventions, the ESC and in particular the ECHR can be considered relevant implementations of the UDHR.

The ECtHR goes much further in this respect. For example, in the *Al-Saadoon and Mufdhi* case, the United Kingdom justified its actions (this concerned an extradition to Iraq) by relying on its obligations under international law. The ECtHR rejected the defence on the grounds of the following considerations:

> The Court must [...] have regard to the special character of the Convention as a treaty for the collective enforcement of human rights and fundamental freedoms. [...] It has been accepted that a Contracting Party is responsible under Article 1 of the Convention for all acts and omissions of its organs regardless of whether the act or omission in question was a consequence of domestic law or of the necessity to comply with international legal obligations. [...] The State is considered to retain Convention liability in respect of treaty commitments subsequent to the entry into force of the Convention.[307]

It is interesting that the UN Charter pre-dates the ECHR. Yet, the ECtHR does not consider obligations under the UN Charter to be superior to obligations under the European Convention.[308] As the drugs conventions are of an even later date than the ECHR, and they are also more extended implementations of the UN Charter,[309] there is even less reason to assume that the ECtHR would rank the obligations under the drugs conventions more highly than the European Convention.

Meanwhile, the Grand Chamber of the ECtHR in the *Nada* case implies that states may perhaps not be bound to their obligations under the ECHR if they act on the basis of an absolute obligation in the sense of the UN Charter and insofar as that obligation leaves them no flexibility at all to act in a way other than in

306 For more information, also about the American Convention on Human Rights and the African Charter on Human and Peoples' Rights, see among other sources Piet Hein P.H.M.C. van Kempen, 'The Recognition of Legal Persons in International Human Rights Instruments: Protection Against and Through Criminal Justice?', in: Mark Pieth & Radha Ivory (eds.), *Corporate Criminal Liability. Emergence, Convergence, and Risk*, New York/Dordrecht/Heidelberg/London: Springer 2011, pp. 355–389 on pp. 379–386; Fernando Felipe Basch, 'The Doctrine of the Inter-American Court of Human Rights Regarding States' Duty to Punish Human Rights Violations and Its Dangers', *American University International Law Review* 2007, vol. 23, pp. 195–229.

307 ECtHR (Grand Chamber) 2 March 2010, *Al-Saadoon and Mufdhi/The UK*, no. 61498/08, para. 127–128.

308 The Court deliberately steers clear of the question 'of the hierarchy between the obligations of the States Parties to the Convention under that instrument, on the one hand, and those arising from the United Nations Charter, on the other'; see ECtHR (Grand Chamber) 12 September 2012, *Nada/Switzerland*, no. 10593/08, para. 196, 197.

309 See section 3.7.8.vi.

breach of the ECHR.[310] Even that, however, is far from certain. The ECtHR did not cede priority to the Charter in the *Al-Dulimi and Montana Management Inc/Switzerland* case either and ruled there was a violation of the right to access to a court in the sense of Article 6 ECHR.[311] Switzerland acted on the basis of an obligation in the sense of Article 103 UN Charter, which is included in Resolution 1483 of the UN Security Council.[312] This resolution concerned the freezing of assets of Saddam Hussein and other senior officials of Iraq's former regime in the interest of 'international peace and security'. One interesting aspect of this case is that the ECtHR ruled that this is about a non-flexible absolute obligation where the resolution left no room to allow an appeal to the courts.[313] Even more remarkable is that four out of the seven judges in their (Partly) Dissenting Opinions judged that in the conflict between the obligation stemming from Resolution 1483 and the obligations flowing from the ECHR, the obligation under the Resolution takes precedence in this case anyway.[314] Nevertheless, the violation of Article 6(1) ECHR was confirmed with a majority of four votes to three.[315]

For the time being, the ECtHR lets the human rights obligations from the ECHR prevail over even absolute obligations in the sense of the UN Charter. In doing so, the Court assigns an effect to the human rights obligations of the ECHR similar to that established by Article 103 UN Charter for charter obligations. But even if a non-flexible absolute obligation under the UN Charter could relieve a state from the obligations under the ECHR, this exception does not apply to obligations under the drugs conventions. After all, those obligations do not count as obligations in the sense of the UN Charter.[316] Additionally, they cannot be considered to be absolute in the sense that they could force states to violate human rights.[317]

---

310 ECtHR (Grand Chamber) 12 September 2012, *Nada/Switzerland*, no. 10593/08, para. 196–197; see also ECtHR (Grand Chamber) 7 July 2011, *Al Jedda/The UK*, no. 27021/08, para. 101–110; and only about the second requirement ECtHR (Grand Chamber) 15 October 2015, *Perinçek/Switzerland*, no. 27510/08, para. 258–268.

311 ECtHR 26 November 2013, *Al-Dulimi and Montana Management Inc./Switzerland*, no 5809/08, para. 123–135. Incidentally, the case was referred to the Grand Chamber.

312 Security Council Resolution 1483 (2003), *UN Doc.* S/RES/1483, 22 May 2003.

313 ECtHR 26 November 2013, *Al-Dulimi and Montana Management Inc./Switzerland*, no 5809/08, para. 117.

314 See the Partly Dissenting Opinion of Judge Sajó (eventually supported the confirmation of the violation) and the Dissenting Opinion of Judge Lorenzen joined by Judges Raimondi and Jočienė (according to whom there was no violation).

315 This extraordinary situation has arisen because Judge Sajó in his Partly Dissenting Opinion takes the view that the primacy of the resolution obligation should have led to inadmissibility of the complaint but subsequently (when the majority of the Chamber declared the complaint admissible) believed that there was a violation in spite of the fact that the resolution obligation prevails over the ECHR.

316 See section 3.7.8.vi.

317 For more information on this see section 3.7.9.i above and section 3.10.2 below.

The foregoing implies that the applicable human rights and positive obligation ensuing from the ECHR have a special status, also in respect of global international law. At any rate, the member states are bound to the ECHR in that sense. In view of the fact that the formal status of the ESC is equivalent to that of the ECHR, we are of the opinion that the above must be assumed to apply to the ESC as well.

x. Basis of the Special Substantive Status of Human Rights: Conclusion

Human rights enjoy a special status. That is the conclusion one must draw, given the rationale and purposes of the major public international law organizations such as the United Nations and the Council of Europe, the system of international law with its concepts of, among other things, *jus cogens*, *erga omnes*, customary law and integral obligations, specific provisions in general agreements such as the Vienna Convention on the Law of Treaties, the ICC Statute and Articles on State Responsibility, as well as international case law. This special status does not bestow human rights primacy – unless they involve a *jus cogens* norm or if Article 103 UN Charter applies – but it does imply that special importance is attached to human rights. In principle, this applies to human rights in the ICESCR and the ICCPR as well as those in the ESC and the ECHR. If human rights are involved in interference between norms or when an attempt is made to achieve 'systematic integration' through interpretation, this can be a factor to be taken into account.

xi. Qualifying the Special Substantive Status of Human Rights

Human rights are not an end in themselves, merely a means to an end. Even though human rights belong to the most important instruments to protect human dignity, the well-being, freedom, position, equality and fair treatment of people, this does not render other instruments for that purpose irrelevant. They often seek to achieve similar goals, be it directly or indirectly. Under certain circumstances, these other instruments can even produce better results with respect to realizing those interests, and at any rate simply disabling or suppressing these instruments in favour of human rights could make it more difficult to protect and serve those interests. For example, international law in the area of international peace and security, economy and trade, transnational criminal law and diplomatic relationships, are also important for the interests of individuals and the communities that they form together. Incidentally, the same goes for national law. It is therefore risky and it reveals an over-simplistic approach to bestow absolute validity *in abstracto* on certain instruments such as human rights conventions.

Human rights conventions, just like other conventions come about as an agreement between states. They belong to international law and in that respect they do not form an autonomous system that is superior to everything else, even though they can be considered subsystems.[318] Human rights instruments, just like the drugs conventions, are not suitable as guidelines for all the issues and problems that society and politics have to address. There are simply too narrow and specific for that.[319] To that extent, positive obligations stemming from human rights instruments merely constitute – coercive – means that the state has at its disposal in addition to other possibilities in dealing with societal issues such as the effects of drugs production, trade and use. The primarity principle can also be seen against this background.[320]

With the above observations we are not saying that human rights are currently endowed with too special a status in international law. The point is that these observations must be borne in mind when analysing and applying the international law system in the event of interference between norms. Neither the human rights subsystem itself nor international law – with the exception of *jus cogens* – presupposes the absolute validity of human rights, in particular where positive obligations of human rights are concerned. Arguments based on that presumption are therefore at odds with international law. This also means that the interference between norms within the cannabis issue cannot simply be resolved by assuming absolute validity or absolute priority of human rights obligations.

xii. Special Substantive Status for the Obligations under the Drugs Conventions?

As we saw previously, the UN Charter does not refer directly or indirectly to drugs or drugs conventions and that drug control is not one of the explicit objectives of this organization.[321] That, by the way, also applies to the Charter of the Council of Europe. Furthermore, there appeared to be no reason to assume that the obligations under the drugs conventions have *jus cogens* status or belong to customary law.[322]

Things are considerably less clear with regard to the question whether the obligations under the drugs conventions enjoy *erga omnes* status or qualify as 'integral obligations'. To answer that question, two main approaches can be followed: a narrow substantive one, and a wider formal one.

- *Narrow substantive approach.* This approach is based on case law by the International Court of Justice and therefore has the stronger legal foundation;

318 James Crawford, *Brownlie's Principles of Public International Law*, Oxford: Oxford University Press, 2012, 634–635.

319 Alain Pellet, '"Human Rightism" and International Law' (Lecture delivered on 18 July 2000 at Geneva), in: *Gilberto Amado: Memorial Lectures*, Brasília, FUNAG, 2012, pp. 267–284 on p. 272.

320 Cf. Ibid, p. 281. For the primarity principle see sections 2.3.7.ix and 2.4.7.viii.

321 See section 3.7.8.vi.

322 See section 3.7.7.iii.

this is also the approach that we use for human rights in subsection ii. According to the Court, these norms can only be accorded *erga omnes* status if they are of great substantive importance. After all, they have to be so important that all states benefit from their protection, which is the case for the prohibitions of international aggression and genocide and for 'the principles and rules concerning the basic rights of the human person, including protection from slavery and racial discrimination'[323] and 'the right of peoples to self-determination'.[324,325] We believe it takes considerable effort to argue that obligations stemming from the UN narcotic drugs conventions – or other obligations to fight (transnational) offences that do not qualify as international crimes[326] – can be put on a level footing with *erga omnes* norms, in particular insofar as they relate to cannabis. Finally, an important point here is that with all the norms mentioned by the Court (and that applies to human rights as well), individuals are the bearers of the rights from which the obligations stem, whereas that is not the case with the obligations stemming from the drugs conventions or at any rate not directly.

As we saw before, Boister also firmly believes that the punishable offences mentioned in drugs conventions do not constitute obligations of an *erga omnes* nature.[327] He asserts that in view of the wording of the drugs conventions they do not constitute international crimes and that it was not the intention of the parties to the convention to do this either.[328] This position is supported by the Human Rights Committee for example, which holds the view that drug offences do not qualify as 'the most serious crimes'.[329] According to Dominice, it is not true either that the obligations in multilateral conventions are also *erga omnes* obligations, and they are not 'multilateral obligations' and/or 'integral

---

323 ICJ, Judgment of 5 February 1970, *I.C.J. Reports* 1970, p. 3 on 32 (para. 33–34) (*Case Concerning the Barcelona Traction, Light and Power Company, Limited – Belgium v. Spain, Second Phase*); see also section 3.7.9.vi above.

324 ICJ, Advisory Opinion of 9 July 2004, *I.C.J. Reports* 2004, p. 136 on 172 (para. 88) and 199 (para. 155–157) (*Legal Consequences of the Construction of a Wall in the Occupied Palestinian Territory*).

325 Cf. Jure Vidmar, 'Norm Conflicts and Hierarchy in International Law: Towards a Vertical International Legal System?, in: Erika de Wet & Jure Vidmar (eds.), *'Hierarchy in International Law: The Place of Human Rights'* 2012, Oxford: Oxford University Press, pp. 13–41 on p. 23.

326 International offences include war crimes, genocide, crimes against humanity and torture.

327 Neil Boister, *The Suppression of Illicit Drugs Through International Law*, Nottingham: University of Nottingham, 1998, pp. 250–251.

328 See also Neil Boister, '"Transnational Criminal Law"?', *European Journal of International Law* 2003, vol. 14, pp. 953–976 on pp. 965–966. See also Neil Boister, *An Introduction to Transnational Criminal Law*, Oxford: Oxford University Press, 2018, Chapter 6.

329 HRC, Concluding Observations (Thailand), *UN Doc.* CCPR/CO/84/THA (2005), para. 14; see also UNODC, 'Drug control, crime prevention and criminal justice: A Human Rights perspective', Note by the Executive Director, *UN Doc.* E/CN.7/2010/CRP.6, E/CN.15/2010/CRP.1 3 March 2010, para. 25, in which it is asserted that the 'weight of opinion indicates that drug offences (such as possession and trafficking) and those of a purely economic nature' do not qualify as 'most serious crimes'.

obligations' either, which is to say: obligations of which the consequences when unfulfilled do not only concern the party to the convention that is affected by it, but also the entire international community.[330] That status, for example, does not belong to the obligations in reciprocal (legal) assistance treaties, which is what the Illicit Traffic Convention is to a large extent, for example. Also, when other parties to the convention have a certain interest in compliance with the convention by one party towards another party, this does not imply that one is dealing with *erga omnes* obligations or 'multilateral obligations' and/or 'integral obligations'.[331]

The International Law Commission does not assume such a broad applicability of the *erga omnes* concept to multilateral conventions either. Article 48 of the Articles on State Responsibility recognizes that every state other than the state affected by a violation of the convention can invoke the liability of the violating state, if the obligation in question 'is owed to the international community as a whole' ('collective obligations'). However, the ILC interprets this in a restrictive way by basing itself on what the International Court of Justice qualifies as *erga omnes* obligations, although the ILC also recognizes that the 'scope of the concept will necessarily evolve over time'.[332] Because this is not yet clearly the case in legal practice (contrary to the literature; see below), the approach taken by the ILC also leads to the conclusion that the drugs conventions do not contain *erga omnes* obligations.[333]

- *Wider, formal approach.* This approach is based on the interest pursued by multilateral conventions. This 'object and purpose' approach is not so much about the weight of that interest but about the question whether that interest is always a collective interest of all the parties to the convention. For example, Advocate General Lenz at the European Court of Justice takes the view that the

330 See Christian Dominice, 'The international responsibility of states for breach of multilateral obligations', *European Journal of International Law* 1999, pp. 353-363 on pp. 354, 363. Dominice talks about 'multilateral obligations', which he defines as obligations the non-fulfilment of which not only concerns the party to the convention that is affected by it, but also the entire international community (see also p. 358). Therefore, this concerns what was called 'integral obligations' above. The two terms can also be found in Joost Pauwelyn, 'A Typology of Multilateral Treaty Obligations: Are WTO Obligations Bilateral or Collective in Nature?', *European Journal of International Law* 2003, vol. 14, no. 5, pp. 907–951 on p. 911.

331 Kamen Sachariew, 'State Responsibility for Multilateral Treaty Violations: Identifying the "Injured State" and its Legal Status', *Netherlands International Law Review* 1988, vol. 35, no. 3, pp. 273–289 on pp. 278–279.

332 ILC, 'Articles on Responsibility of States for Internationally Wrongful Acts, with commentaries', 2001, comm. Article 1 (para. 4), comm. Chapter III (para. 3), comm. Article 48 (para. 6 and 9).

333 The situation is different for example for the prohibition of terrorism, partly in view of the fact that this is a 'threat to international peace and security' according to the UN Security Council; for more information on this, with references, see Thomas Weatherall, 'The Status of the Prohibition of Terrorism in International Law: Recent Developments', *Georgetown Journal of International Law* 2015, vol. 46, pp. 589–627 on pp. 619–620.

Single Convention creates 'multilateral obligations'. The first of the two most important arguments presented by him is that this drugs convention requires a coordinated global effort against narcotic drugs, witness its preamble. The second reason is that a failure to take the required measures may have consequences for all the parties to the convention.[334]

With regard to the second point, this is indeed possible, but it will often not be the case. Thus, one can argue equally well that with a concrete breach of the convention by one state, one will have to see which other states are affected by it. Moreover, breaches of obligations under drugs conventions – unlike breaches of human rights obligations – do not automatically create a disadvantage for specific states or specific individuals. However, Bothe arrives at the conclusion that the obligation in the drugs conventions have an *erga omnes* effect because a breach of these obligations usually does not affect a concrete state or a concrete individual, but the public health interest of all states. For that reason, Bothe called the international drug control system an 'objective' system; or therefore an 'integral system'.[335]

There is actually nothing that can be presented to counter the first argument of advocate general Lenz (conventions require coordinated and global effort). The question, though, is whether this is sufficient ground to justify the term 'multilateral obligations'. After all, the consequence of this could be that in principle all transnational criminal law treaties containing obligations of criminalization would have to be qualified as conventions containing 'multilateral' and/or 'integral obligations'. In this perspective, conventions that force parties to standardization of law have an integral effect,[336] even if the objective of standardization does not cover particularly serious interests in a substantive sense.

---

334 Conclusion of A-G Lenz of 4 October 1994, Case C-324/93, *European Court Reports* 1995 I-00563, ECLI:EU:C:1994:357, para. 33.

335 Michael Bothe, 'Conflict Settlement in the Field of International Drug Control', in: Daniel Bardonnet (ed.), *Le Règlement Pacifique des Différends Internationaux en Europe: Perspectives D'avenir*, Dordrecht/Boston/London: Martinus Nijhoff Publishers, 1991, pp. 145–158 on pp. 146, 150. For a similar line of reasoning to substantiate the assertion that conventions to protect the environment contain obligations with *erga omnes* effect, see Karl Zemanek, 'New Trends in the Enforcement of Erga Omnes Obligations', *Max Planck Yearbook of United Nations Law* 2000, 1–52 op 6. Cf. also S.K. Verma, *An Introduction to Public International Law*, Delhi: Prentice-Hall, 1998, p. 276, who believes that the Single Convention has 'universal application' or a 'public law character'. Verma bases this assertion exclusively on the obligation of parties to the convention to prohibit the export of (legal) narcotic drugs to a non-state party if the estimates of that country are exceeded as a result (see Article 21 of the Single Convention and also Article 14 of the Single Convention). Although the convention thereby exerts pressure on non-state parties, this really concerns a legal obligation for states parties only, not for non-states parties.

336 See Bruno Simma, 'International Crimes: Injury and Countermeasures. Comments on Part 2 of the ILC Work on State Responsibility', in: Joseph H.H. Weiler, Antonio Cassese & Marina Spinedi (eds.), *International Crimes of State*, Berlin/New York: Walter de Gruyter, 1989, pp. 283–318 on p. 286.

- *Evaluation and conclusion.* In the latter, wider and formal approach, the crux is whether the object and purpose of a multilateral convention is aimed at a shared interest and whether that interest has particular substantive weight. With this approach, unlike the narrow, substantive approach, one cannot deduce from the qualification 'erga omnes' or 'multilateral obligation' that the norm is accorded a particular status, and has more weight than other norms. More than that, this approach implies a considerable extension of the criterion of the International Court of Justice.

  Should one apply this wide approach to the drugs conventions, there is no reason any more either to base oneself on a narrow interpretation of 'basic rights' in the Court's case law. Thus, it must be assumed that all generally accepted human rights and the corresponding positive obligations have an *erga omnes* effect. That also applies then to the positive human rights obligations that are relevant from the perspective of interference with drugs conventions' obligations. In that case, these positive obligations and the obligations under the drugs conventions obtain the same qualification, but that does not imply any substantive value judgment about those obligations, as we observed before. We reject that approach for the following reasons.

  The narrow, substantive approach of the *erga omnes* concept has its origins in case law of the International Court of Justice and the work of the International Law Commission. On the other hand, the wider approach appears to be presented in the literature exclusively and only by a few people. With this state of affairs, we assume in this book that the first approach is the legally valid one. Another argument for this assumption is that the provisions in the UN narcotic drugs conventions themselves do not give a definitive answer to the question whether the convention has *erga omnes* status. It is interesting that the drugs conventions, unlike the ICCPR and the ECHR,[337] do not have a specific complaints procedure which will enable parties to the convention to refer any alleged breach of the provisions of the convention to the INCB, not even if they are affected by that breach.[338] On the other hand, arrangements have been made to settle disputes in case a concrete dispute arises between two or more parties to the convention about the interpretation or implementation of the convention (Article 48 of the Single Convention and Article 32 of the Illicit Traffic Convention). The procedure for settling disputes therefore centres on the bilateral relationships between parties to the convention and does not imply that it also concerns *erga omnes* obligations or 'multilateral obligations' and/or 'integral obligations'. Furthermore, we have not found any clear indications in

---

[337] See Article 41 ICCPR (optional recognition of right of complaint) and art. 33 ECHR (compulsory recognition of right of complaint).

[338] However, pursuant to Article 14 of the Single Convention, the INCB may receive data from governments, but it is not clear whether those data may relate to other states; even if that were the case, this is not a procedure aimed at dealing with complaints by states about other states.

the preparatory work either that (some of) the parties to the convention regard the obligations in the Single Convention and/or the Illicit Traffic Convention as *erga omnes* norms. Finally, it must be noted that whereas human rights conventions are aimed directly at the protection of each individual in each contracting state (which calls for integral obligations), the practical foundation of creating the drugs conventions primarily appears to be the will to counteract the transnational effects of illicit drugs trafficking (which goal can be achieved by means of bilateral obligations).[339] Also in view of this, it is less obvious to see the obligations in drugs conventions as having *erga omnes* and 'integral' effect. This means that we assume that the obligations from the drugs conventions do not contain norms that have such status.

xiii. Conclusion

In different ways, human rights are shown to have special substantive status and/or a special substantive weight under international law. Conversely, there are very few indications – if any – that this is the case for the obligations under the drugs conventions.

First of all, authorities such as the UN General Assembly, the INCB, the CND and the Special Rapporteur on the right to health make it clear that the drugs conventions may only be implemented with due regard for human rights. This assessment is borne out by the findings of the Special Rapporteurs on globalization and its impact on the full enjoyment of all human rights. To that extent, all these institutions clearly give priority and/or precedence to human rights obligations in relation to obligations under drugs conventions. This includes both the negative human rights obligations and the positive obligations discussed in Chapter 2, those flowing from the rights related to health, life, inhuman treatment and privacy. Where the Special Rapporteur on the right to life takes the view that human rights norms and obligations under the drugs conventions may conflict with each other, the UN General Assembly, the INCB and the CND assume that the drugs conventions must, and can be, applied in accordance with human rights standards.

The special status of human rights is also reflected in the rationale and main purposes of the major public international law organizations, in the system of international law, in specific provisions from general agreements, as well as international case law. That special status extends indirectly to positive human rights obligations and partly even directly, to the extent it concerns an *erga omnes* effect, the concept of 'integral obligations' and the status that human rights have by virtue of their position in the UN Charter and according to the case law of the ECtHR.

339 For more information, see section 3.10.2.iii.

At the same time, the special substantive status of human rights needs to be qualified. This is not about a position that formally grants priority to human rights – with the exception of *jus cogens*. This means that the *lex superior* rule does not function here as a rule of precedence but as a principle of interpretation and consideration. One must bear in mind that the interference between norms within the cannabis issue cannot simply be resolved by assuming absolute validity or absolute precedence of human rights obligations.

3.7.10. CONCLUSION: HUMAN RIGHTS OBLIGATIONS HAVE PRIORITY OR EVEN TAKE PRECEDENCE

There is no *specialis/generalis* relationship (or vice versa) between the human rights and drugs conventions interfering in the cannabis issue, neither in a formal sense nor in a substantive one. The interference can therefore not be resolved by means of the *lex specialis* rule.

The same is true for the *lex posteriori* and *prior* rules as they are expressed in Article 30 of the Vienna Convention on the Law of Treaties. Their applicability is thwarted among other things by the 'same subject matter' test, the absence of any provision in the conventions about how they relate to each other and in the variety of states parties to the Single Convention, the Illicit Traffic Convention, the ICESCR, the ICCPR, the ESC and the ECHR. Nevertheless, it follows from Article 14(2) of the Illicit Traffic Convention, the preparatory work of both the Single Convention and the Illicit Traffic Convention and the judgments of the INCB and the CND, that implementation of the drugs conventions must take place in accordance with human rights standards. This can be interpreted as an indication how the relationship between earlier and later conventions must be seen. If Article 30 of the Vienna Convention on the Law of Treaties is applied to the cannabis issue analogically, then this means that the human rights conventions have priority over the UN drugs conventions.

The *jus cogens* concept (norms which have absolute validity and which are non-derogable) does not provide a clear solution either for the interference between human rights obligations and obligations under the drugs conventions. While it is true that the right to life and the prohibition of inhuman treatment have *jus cogens* status, there is insufficient ground to claim that this also applies for the positive obligations arising from those rights. Such a status certainly does not pertain to the right to health and the right to a private life, nor to the obligations under the drugs conventions.

However, Article 103 UN Charter is relevant here. Obligations in the sense of that provision have precedence over obligations conflicting with them. Obligations from the drugs conventions do not fall within the scope of Article 103 UN Charter, but the situation is different for human rights obligations. As far as the rights regarding health, life, inhuman treatment and privacy from the ICESCR and the ICCPR are concerned, these are all human rights in the sense of the UN Charter. This means that at any rate, the negative obligations to respect these rights fall within the scope of the rule of precedence of Article 103. In addition, it is possible to argue convincingly that this also applies to the positive obligations arising from these rights that may be relevant for regulated permission of cannabis cultivation and trade. Those obligations then prevail over obligations from drugs conventions pursuant to Article 103. This concerns a specific arrangement of the *lex superior* rule as a rule of precedence.

The priority position of human rights also comes to the fore in various UN institutions. For example, authorities such as the UN General Assembly, the INCB, the CND and the Special Rapporteur on the right to health as well as the Special Rapporteurs on globalization and its impact on the full enjoyment of all human rights are of the opinion that the drugs conventions may only be implemented with due regard for human rights. The Special Rapporteur on the right to life makes it clear that human rights obligation really have precedence over – and not merely carry more weight than – obligations under the drugs conventions.

Finally, it is apparent in various other respects that human rights have a special substantive status, unlike the drugs conventions. To be sure, this is not about human rights having absolute priority in the sense that they are automatically to be given hierarchical precedence beyond the Article 103 UN Charter priority rule or when they have *jus cogens* status. Rather, human rights have a special weight on the basis of substantive criteria in relation to other international norms, which has to be taken into account when interpreting these norms or resolving conflicts between them. The *lex superior* rule works here primarily as a principle of interpretation and consideration. That special status is reflected in the rationale and the main purposes of the great public international law organizations (such as the UN and the CoE), the system of international law (among other things *jus cogens*, *erga omnes*, customary law and 'integral obligations'), in specific provisions in general agreements as well as European and other international case law. At any rate, that special status extends indirectly to positive human rights obligations as well. To some extent, it is also the case directly, namely where it concerns an *erga omnes* effect, the concept of 'integral obligations' and the position of human rights in the UN Charter and according to the ECtHR.

In short: while there are hardly any indications to assign special priority or weight to the obligations under the drugs conventions, there is ample justification for that in international law with regard to human rights obligations. That applies in principle to both negative and positive obligations and in relation to the ICESCR and the ICCPR as well as the ESC and the ECHR. It is undeniable that the drugs conventions can only be implemented within the frameworks that result from human rights and fundamental freedoms.

3.8. THE CANNABIS ISSUE: SOLUTION VIA THE CONFLICT APPROACH

The discourses in Chapter 2 are based on the hypothesis that regulated permission of cannabis cultivation and trade meets the positive obligations stemming from the rights regarding health, life, inhuman treatment and privacy better than an approach in which that cultivation and trade is prohibited and combated. That hypothesis is also the basis of this chapter. Within the cannabis issue, there is an interference and/or conflict between positive human rights obligations and obligations under the international drug control system. In section 3.2, we showed that this interference can be resolved from two different perspectives, namely: the so-called conflict approach and the so-called harmony approach. The question is which result is produced with the conflict approach and whether that approach is supported by international law. We will see below that the latter is not the case.

The fact that human rights obligations have priority over obligations under the drugs conventions has been firmly embedded in international law in various ways. In certain respects, the positive human rights obligations even have absolute priority in relation to the drugs conventions.[340] In any case, the drugs conventions can only be implemented within the margins prescribed by the human rights conventions, including the ICESCR, the ICCPR, the ESC and the ECHR. In the literature too, it is assumed that human rights obligations have priority or even prevail over obligations under drugs conventions.[341]

Application of the conflict approach results in one legal norm cancelling the other because of a formal or substantive hierarchical relationship between both norms. The conclusions from the foregoing make it clear that the application of the conflict approach to the cannabis issue means that the drugs conventions must give way to the positive human rights obligations that are relevant here. That would mean that states could proceed to permit regulation of cannabis cultivation trade if this achieves a better realization of the right to health, the right to life, the right not to be subjected to inhuman treatment and the right to a private life. Conversely, insofar as regulated permission of cannabis cultivation and trade can be based on positive human rights obligations, obligations under drugs conventions that are barriers to this cannot be fulfilled.

---

340 See section 3.7 and see section 3.7.10 for the conclusion.

341 See among other sources Rick Lines & Richard Elliott, 'Injecting drugs into human rights advocacy', International Journal of Drug Policy 2007, vol. 18, pp. 453–457 on p. 455; Daniel Heilmann, 'The International Control of Illegal Drugs and the U.N. Treaty Regime: Preventing or Causing Human Rights Violations?', *Cardozo Journal of International and Comparative Law* 2011, vol. 19, pp. 237–290 also on p. 275. Cf. John Walsh & Geoff Ramsey, *Uruguay's Drug Policy: Major Innovations, Major Challenges*, Washington: Brookings, 2015, p. 11.

The discussion whether this even leads to nullity of the provisions in the drugs conventions or indeed the very drugs conventions as a whole remains outside the scope of this book. Because of the primacy of the principle of systemic integration, which is discussed below, the conflict approach will have to be rejected. Apart from that, it is worth noting that if one starts from a narrow definition of norms conflict, there is no such conflict with regard to the interference between human rights obligations and the drugs conventions. There is no room for the conflict approach in that case.[342]

3.9. SYSTEMIC INTEGRATION: PRESUMPTION OF COMPATIBILITY AND PRESUMPTION AGAINST CONFLICT: AXIOMS FOR HARMONIZATION

In international law, the primacy of the principle of systemic integration, the presumption of compatibility and the presumption against conflict applies. Actually, these are techniques to prevent rather than solve conflicts.[343] The presumption against conflict ties in with the idea that states normally do not intend to enter into agreements that conflict with other obligations.[344] At the heart of the presumption against conflict lies the notion of a coherent and consistent legal system. The assumption is that the norms, conventions and subsystems within international law are compatible, in other words in harmony with each other. That compatibility is not always evident and will need to be achieved through interpretation in cases that do not immediately conform to this idea. The principle of systemic integration comes into play with that interpretation. That applies even if one of the interfering obligations has *jus cogens* status or falls within the scope of Article 103 UN Charter. Even then it remains to be seen whether it is possible to interpret the norms in such a way that the other norm can remain functional as much as possible, without derogation from a *jus cogens* norm in the process.[345]

The primacy of the principle of systemic integration stems from the system of international law, has a strong foundation in legal practice and international

---

342 See section 3.4.1.

343 Andreas Paulus & Johann R. Leiß, 'Article 103', in: Bruno Simma, Daniel-Erasmus Khan, Georg Nolte & Andreas Paulus (eds.), *The Charter of the United Nations*, Oxford: Oxford University Press, 2012, pp. 2110–2137 on p. 2118.

344 ILC, 'Report 58th Session: Chapter XII, Fragmentation of International Law', 2006, p. 414 (para. 19); Sarah Joseph, *Blame it on the WTO?: A Human Rights Critique*, Oxford: Oxford University Press, 2011, p. 47; Joost Pauwelyn, *Conflict of Norms in Public International Law: How WTO Law relates to Other Rules of International Law*, Cambridge: Cambridge University Press, 2003, pp. 240–241.

345 See Andreas Paulus & Johann R. Leiß, 'Article 103', in: Bruno Simma, Daniel-Erasmus Khan, Georg Nolte & Andreas Paulus (eds.), *The Charter of the United Nations*, Oxford: Oxford University Press, 2012, pp. 2110–2137 on pp. 2118–2121.

case law and is expressed in Article 31(1) and 31(3)(c) of the Vienna Convention on the Law of Treaties.[346] Pursuant to this provision, in interpreting terms in conventions one must take into account 'any relevant rules of international law applicable in the relations between the parties'. Those rules of international law may be found in other conventions, customary law and/or the general principles.[347]

In the ECHR, the principle of systemic integration is shown as follows, with a reference to the above-mentioned provision:

> The Convention [...] cannot be interpreted in a vacuum. The Court must be mindful of *the Convention's special character as a human rights treaty*, and it must also take the relevant rules of international law into account [...]. The Convention should *so far as possible* be interpreted *in harmony with other rules of international law* of which it forms part (emphasis added).[348]

The following axioms stem from the primacy of the principle of systemic integration, the presumption of compatibility and the presumption against conflict:

1. *Interpretation from current international law.* Although it is necessary to interpret international instruments such as conventions in accordance with the will of the parties at the time the instrument was created, these instruments must be interpreted and applied in the framework of the entire legal system that is in force at the time of interpretation.[349] That is the more so if concepts used in the convention are open or evolutionary in character[350] or if they concern the previously mentioned 'integral' or 'normative' conventions.[351]

---

346 ILC, 'Fragmentation of International Law', 2006, para. 410–480.

347 Ibid, see the references in it.

348 ECtHR (Grand Chamber) 21 November 2001, *Al-Adsani/The UK*, no. 35763/97, para. 55. Confirmed in, among other sources, ECtHR (Grand Chamber) 16 September 2014, *Hassan/The UK*, no. 29750/09, para. 77; ECtHR (Grand Chamber) 12 September 2012, *Nada/Switzerland*, no. 10593/08, para. 170.

349 ICJ, Advisory Opinion of 21 June 1971, *I.C.J. Reports* 1971, p. 16 on 31 (para. 53) (*Legal Consequences for States of the Continued Presence of South Africa in Namibia (South West Africa) Notwithstanding Security Council Resolution 276 (1970)*). See also ICJ, Judgment of 25 September 1997, *I.C.J. Reports* 1997, p. 7 on pp. 67–68 (para. 112) (*Case Concerning the Gabcikovo-Nagymaros Project – Hungary v. Slovakia*); The Arbitral Tribunal, Decision of 24 May 2005, Reports of International Arbitral Awards, vol. XXVII, pp. 35–125 on 66–67 (para. 57–60) (*Award in the Arbitration regarding the Iron Rhine ('IJzeren Rijn') Railway between the Kingdom of Belgium and the Kingdom of the Netherlands*). See also Campbell McLachlan, 'The Principle of Systemic Integration and Article 31 (3) (c) of the Vienna Convention', *International and Comparative Law Quarterly* 2005, vol. 54, pp. 279–320 on pp. 282–284, 316–319.

350 ILC, 'Report 58th Session: Chapter XII, Fragmentation of International Law', 2006, pp. 415–416 (para. 22–23).

351 Catherine Brölmann, 'Law-Making Treaties: Form and Function in International Law', *Nordic Journal of International Law* 2005, vol. 74, pp. 383–404 on pp. 393–394.

Furthermore, the interpretation of law can be partly dependent on for example social, economic and technical developments.[352]

2. *Looking for shared objectives and values.* A useful ground rule is that if different subsystems and/or convention regimes apply to a certain issue, what is important is not so much the question to which of these the subject most belongs, but rather which of these is the most suitable for application to the issue at hand.[353] To this end, one may consider whether the conventions involved have a shared object and purpose[354] or – on an even more abstract level – whether they seek to protect shared values,[355] and which one of the conventions best realizes the shared objectives and values.[356]
3. *Striving towards maximum retention of norms and other legal sources.* An interpretation of conflicting norms that enables both norms to have maximum effect is to be preferred.[357] It is also important that questions for which the convention or the conventions do not provide a definitive answer must be resolved on the basis of customary law and the general principles of law (cf. Article 38 ICJ).[358]

---

352 See ICJ, Judgment of 13 July 2009, *I.C.J. Reports* 2009, p. 213 on 244 (para. 70–71) (*Dispute regarding Navigational and Related Rights – Costa Rica v. Nicaragua*); ILC, 'Report 58th Session: Chapter XII, Fragmentation of International Law', 2006, pp. 415–416 (para. 23).

353 See Andreas Fischer-Lescano & Gunther Teubner, 'Regime-Collisions: the Vain Search for Legal Unity in the Fragmentation of Global Law', *Michigan Journal of International Law* vol. 25, pp. 999–1046 on pp. 1021–1023; Ralf Michaels & Joost Pauwelyn, 'Conflict of Norms or Conflict of Laws?: Different Techniques in the Fragmentation of Public International Law', *Duke Journal of Comparative & International Law* 2012, vol. 22, pp. 349–376 on p. 369.

354 After all, Article 31(1) of the Vienna Convention on the Law of Treaties states that a convention must be interpreted in its 'context and in the light of its object and purpose'. See also ILC, 'Fragmentation of International Law', 2006, para. 95: '*Both rules are now rationalized under the same purpose*'; and also para. 97.

355 See Ahmad Ali Ghouri, 'Determining Hierarchy Between Conflicting Treaties: Are There Vertical Rules in the Horizontal System?', *Asian Journal of International Law* 2012, vol. 2, no. 2, pp. 235–266.

356 See also the way in which the ECtHR in the event of applicability of another regime (in this case that of the European Union) in addition to the ECHR, contemplates to which extent the other regime 'is considered to protect fundamental rights, as regards both the substantive guarantees offered and the mechanisms controlling their observance, in a manner which can be considered at least equivalent to that for which the Convention provides [...]. By "equivalent" the Court means "comparable"; any requirement that the organisation's protection be 'identical' could run counter to the interest of international cooperation pursued [...]. However, any such finding of equivalence could not be final and would be susceptible to review in the light of any relevant change in fundamental rights protection.', according to ECtHR (Grand Chamber) 30 June 2005, *Bosphorus Hava Yollari Turizm ve Ticaret Anonim Sirketi/Ireland*, no. 45036/98, para. 155.

357 See also, with further references, Andreas Paulus & Johann R. Leiß, 'Article 103', in: Bruno Simma, Daniel-Erasmus Khan, Georg Nolte & Andreas Paulus (eds.), *The Charter of the United Nations*, Oxford: Oxford University Press, 2012, pp. 2110–2137 on p. 2118.

358 ILC, 'Report 58th Session: Chapter XII, Fragmentation of International Law', 2006, p. 414 (para. 19–20).

These ground rules help implement the harmony approach if there is interference between conventions and/or norms, like the one that can be seen in the cannabis issue between positive human rights obligations and the UN narcotic drugs conventions. We will therefore take heed of these axioms below.

3.10. THE CANNABIS ISSUE: SOLUTION VIA THE HARMONY APPROACH

Positive human rights obligations are given special weight, and they have priority and sometimes even absolute precedence over the obligations under the drugs conventions, and this is firmly and widely embedded in international law, as we have demonstrated above. Within the strict framework of the drugs conventions (which is to say, within the strictly internal legal perspective as taken in the first book on *International Law and Cannabis I*[359]), there is no room for regulated permission of cannabis cultivation and trade. Because of the positive human rights that are relevant here, that room will have to be forcibly created in the drugs conventions after all.

Because of the inequality between the obligations interfering in the cannabis issue, it will not be possible to achieve perfect harmony between the human rights obligations and the obligations under the drugs conventions. However, that certainly does not mean that a certain degree of harmony and harmonization is impossible. We will therefore now first look at what the axioms discussed in the previous section mean for the interference in the cannabis issue in a more general way. We will then look at the obligations from the drugs conventions in more detail in a concrete way. The focus of our attention will be on how these obligations can be left intact as much as possible, while at the same time states have the possibility to fulfil their positive human rights obligations with regulated permission of cannabis cultivation and trade.[360] The interference is therefore solved through harmonizing interpretation.[361]

---

359 See Piet Hein P.H.M.C. van Kempen & Masha I. Fedorova, *International Law and Cannabis I*, Cambridge: Intersentia, 2019.

360 Elsewhere we argue that *inter se* modification of treaties can function as an international framework within which states can effectuate their positive human rights obligations that are relevant for the international drug control system, see Piet Hein P.H.M.C. van Kempen & Masha Fedorova, 'Regulated Legalization of Cannabis through Positive Human Rights Obligations and *Inter se* Treaty Modification', *International Community Law Review*, vol. 20, 2018, pp. 493–526.

361 Cf. Nele Matz-Lück, 'Harmonization, Systemic Integration, and "Mutual Supportiveness" as Conflict-Solution Techniques: Different Modes of Interpretation as a Challenge to Negative Effects of Fragmentation?', *Finnish Yearbook of International Law* 2006, vol. 17, pp. 39–53 on pp. 42–45.

3.10.1. THE AXIOMS OF SYSTEMIC INTEGRATION AND THE CANNABIS ISSUE

We will now discuss the meaning of the four axioms of systemic integration that were established in section 3.9 for the interference between positive human rights obligations and the obligations under the drugs conventions.

i. Interpretation from Current International Law

With regard to human rights conventions and drugs conventions, there are at least two developments that are important for the relationship between them.

- *Development in knowledge about effectiveness of a drug policy.* The underlying assumption in the drugs conventions that health risks around recreational drug use are best combated by a strictly prohibitive approach has by now been called into question. In the academic literature, the legal practice and also within governments, a huge variety of facts and arguments are presented that seek to qualify or discredit this assumption. The Special Rapporteur on the right to health also arrives at such a conclusion:

  > The current international system of drug control has focused on creating a drugfree world, almost exclusively through use of law enforcement policies and criminal sanctions. Mounting evidence, however, suggests this approach has failed, primarily because it does not acknowledge the realities of drug use and dependence. While drugs may have a pernicious effect on individual lives and society, this excessively punitive regime has not achieved its stated public health goals, and has resulted in countless human rights violations.[362]

  The question is whether that is directly relevant for the interpretation – and therefore the actual meaning – of the drugs conventions. It is not possible to answer that question decisively. There are arguments to presume that data about the (in)effectiveness of the fight against drugs can be or even must be taken into account in the interpretation and application of the drugs conventions.

  As we saw before, according to the International Court of Justice, among other sources, the meaning of international law can also depend on social, economic and technical developments for example. This appears to leave room to also take into account the (in)effectiveness of certain obligations under conventions in the interpretation of the norms that they are based on. It cannot be said with certainty that the Court also intends that room to be there.

[362] Special Rapporteur Health, A/65/255, 2010, p. 2 (Summary) and in more detail para. 14–16. See also Report of the Special Rapporteur on the right of everyone to the enjoyment of the highest attainable standard of physical and mental health, Dainius Pūras, UN Doc. A/HRC/29/33, 2 April 2015, para. 27. See also section 2.3.11.

The same is true in relation to, for example, the test of proportionality which is recognized in international law.[363] Admittedly, there will have to be some clarity for the application of the test as to the extent to which a measure can actually achieve the intended objective, but it is not entirely certain whether that test also applies to the implementation of obligations from instruments such as the drugs conventions.

The notion that the (in)effectiveness of certain obligations under conventions need to be taken into account in the interpretation of convention norms is at any rate borne out in the rule that conventions must be interpreted in such a way that they are effective instead of ineffective.[364] Since that effectiveness also depends on the reality in society, this rule presupposes that this reality may and must influence the interpretation of convention norms.

Article 15(1)(b) of the ICESCR also deserves attention here. Pursuant to this provision, states that are party to this convention recognize the right of everyone to 'enjoy the benefits of scientific progress and its applications'. In this respect, states must ensure that the results of scientific and technological progress are used in the interests of reinforcing, among other things, the economic and social development of peoples and the realization of human rights and fundamental freedoms.[365] In this light as well, pursuant to international law it is necessary to take into account scientific knowledge about the actual effects of implementation of the obligations under the drugs conventions when interpreting these conventions, for example the effects on public health as well as the actual nature and seriousness of the risks of cannabis.

Finally, we point out that the effectiveness of measures is also relevant for the question whether positive human rights obligations can necessitate the application of the measure. Indeed, all of Chapter 2 is based on the hypothesis that regulated permission of cannabis cultivation and trade leads

---

363 See for example ICJ, Judgment of 19 November 2012, *I.C.J. Reports* 2012, p. 624 on 715–717 (para. 239–247) (*Territorial and Maritime Dispute – Nicaragua v. Colombia*); ICJ, Advisory Opinion of 9 July 2004, *I.C.J. Reports* 2004, p. 136 on 193 (para. 136) (*Legal Consequences of the Construction of a Wall in the Occupied Palestinian Territory*). See also the references regarding the EU, the ECHR and the WTO in Alec Stone Sweet & Jud Mathews, 'Proportionality Balancing and Global Constitutionalism', *Columbia Journal of Transnational Law* 2008, vol. 47, pp. 72–164 on pp. 138–159.

364 See Hersch Lauterpacht, 'Restrictive Interpretation and the Principle of Effectiveness in the Interpretation of Treaties', *British Yearbook of International Law* 1949, vol. 26, pp. 48–85 on p., 52; Ulf Linderfalk, *On the Interpretation of Treaties*, Dordrecht: Springer, 2007, pp. 217–221, 290–291.

365 See point 1 of the Declaration on the Use of Scientific and Technological Progress in the Interests of Peace and for the Benefit of Mankind, *UN Doc.* A/RES/3384(XXX), 10 November 1975); see also the Report of the Special Rapporteur in the field of cultural rights, Farida Shaheed, The right to enjoy the benefits of scientific progress and its applications, *UN Doc.* A/HRC/20/26, 14 May 2012, para. 50; Audrey R. Chapman, 'Towards an Understanding of the Right to Enjoy the Benefits of Scientific Progress and Its Applications, *Journal of Human Rights* 2009, vol. 8, pp. 1–36 on pp. 9–10.

to more effective results with regard to individual health and public health, safety and fighting crime. Only if that hypothesis it is proven to work, can the corresponding positive human rights obligations apply. In that respect too, it would be curious if in that case effectiveness could be ignored in the interpretation of obligations under the drugs conventions that necessitate positive measures to fight drugs and/or cannabis for reasons of public health and the well-being of people.

We therefore consider it defensible that if there are clear data that obligations under the drugs conventions are less effective than is assumed, this must play a part in the interpretation of the drugs conventions, pursuant to international law. We will briefly come back to this in section 3.10.2.ii.

- *Development of positive human rights obligations*. As far as the right to health is concerned, this development is hardly spectacular. The very wording of this right in Article 12 in conjunction with Article 2 ICESCR and in Article 11 ESC makes it clear that states have positive obligations to take measures so as to realize this right.[366] Moreover, that wording is fairly open and general in nature. Therefore, it is understandable that the ICESCR Committee and the European CSR have from the very beginning fleshed out these positive obligations. However, in respect of the primarily or even entirely negatively worded rights regarding life, inhuman treatment and privacy in the ICCPR and the ECHR, it was significantly less obvious that these rights would also lead to extensive development of positive obligations. That development primarily only began at the end of the 1990s, in other words after the creation of the drugs conventions.

  However, none of this is an argument for ignoring the positive obligations that have been derived from the right to life, the right not to be subjected to inhuman treatment and the right to a private life. After all, the first axiom – which is partly based on Article 31 of the Vienna Convention on the Law of Treaties, the case law of the International Court of Justice and the literature – means that conventions must be interpreted and applied in the framework of the entire legal system that is in force at the time of interpretation. The positive obligations identified in Chapter 2 have been embedded so firmly in the international case law about those rights that they are undeniably part of applicable positive international human rights law. These obligations will therefore have to be included in the interpretation of the drugs conventions. In the light of the foregoing, this consequently applies *a fortiori* to the positive obligations stemming from the right to health. For the sake of completeness, we observe that the INCB also recognizes the relevance of the judgments of monitoring bodies with human rights conventions.[367]

366 See sections 2.3.7 and 2.3.8.

367 INCB, *Report of the International Narcotics Control Board for 2014*, New York: United Nations, 2015, p. 9 (no. 38): 'Member States should give due consideration to the human rights norms relevant in the context of each element of a comprehensive, integrated and balanced

ii. Shared Objectives and Values

The importance of the object and purpose of a convention is founded, among other things, on case law of the International Court of Justice and on the Vienna Convention on the Law of Treaties.[368] Neither of these, however, defines what exactly these concepts should be taken to mean. It roughly concerns the objectives of the convention and the nature of the instruments to realize these.[369]

- *Object and purpose of the drugs conventions.* With regard to the object and purpose of the Single Convention and the Illicit Traffic Convention, three main levels of abstraction can be identified.

  First level. The most abstract purpose that is still expressed explicitly in the drugs conventions is 'health and welfare of mankind' or 'of human beings'.[370] This recognizes at any rate public health and the social well-being, and perhaps also individual health as the primary basic values of the conventions. In the most abstract sense, the object of the conventions is narcotic drugs.

  Second level. On a more concrete level, the purpose, as we explained in our first book, *International Law and Cannabis I*, comes down to the following:[371] 1. Availability of narcotic drugs as meaningful and/or effective medicine or research into this; 2. Treatment of and care for drug users so as to wean them off these narcotic drugs; 3. Protecting society against narcotic drugs by fighting and eliminating the production, trade, possession and use of these drugs for recreational purposes by means of criminal law and many other social prohibitions and measures. The more concrete object of the conventions consists of cannabis products, coca products and poppy products, since these are also explicitly mentioned in the conventions themselves.

  Third level. For each of the three purposes mentioned above, the conventions show even more concrete purposes. For this research, the third purpose is of course important. In view of the preambles, the text, the system and the preparatory work of the Single Convention and the Illicit Traffic Convention, the eradication of cannabis for recreational use is also part of the object and

---

approach, according to their legal obligations. They should also, if necessary, seek out the advice of human rights treaty bodies for the implementation of such norms'.

368 See among other sources ICJ, Advisory Opinion of 28 May 1951, *I.C.J. Reports* 1951, p. 15 on p. 21, pp. 23–24 (*Reservations to the Convention on the Prevention and Punishment of the Crime of Genocide*); and for example Article 31 of the Vienna Convention on the Law of Treaties. See also, with further references to the way in which the object and purpose is established Piet Hein P.H.M.C. van Kempen & Masha I. Fedorova, *International Law and Cannabis I*, Cambridge: Intersentia, 2019, section 2.3.4.iv.

369 Cf. for example David S. Jonas & Thomas N. Saunders, 'The Object and Purpose of a Treaty: Three Interpretive Methods', *Vanderbilt Journal of Transnational Law* 2010, vol. 43, no. 3, pp. 565–609 on pp. 579–580.

370 See the preambles to the Single Convention and the Illicit Traffic Convention.

371 Piet Hein P.H.M.C. van Kempen & Masha I. Fedorova, *International Law and Cannabis I*, Cambridge: Intersentia, 2019, section 2.6.

purpose of these conventions. At the heart of this aim of eradication lies the assumption that the interests of public health and crime control in particular are most adequately served by achieving this aim.[372] In order to achieve this aim of eradication, the conventions provide a prohibitive, repressive and multi-layered enforcement system, which, among other things, imposes a wide range of diverse obligations related to criminal law, and administrative and other obligations on the parties to the convention.[373] In short: the convention focuses on eliminating the circulation of narcotic drugs for other purposes than medical or scientific ones.[374] So that applies to cannabis for recreational use as well.

- *Commonality between human rights conventions and drugs conventions.* On the first level of the purpose of the drugs conventions, there is a clear commonality with the purpose of the human rights conventions.[375] Although the latter do not always state it literally and explicitly in the preambles, these are also directly aimed at the well-being of mankind.[376] That is also true for all fundamental rights and freedoms in them and for all the corresponding positive obligations. With regard to the right to health, there is also a clear similarity with the primary purpose of the drugs conventions with respect to the health of mankind or human beings. This is partly applicable to the rights regarding life, inhuman treatment and privacy, namely to the extent that they forbid the state to affect health adversely and force the state to take positive measures to benefit health. Otherwise, these human rights tie in with the purpose of well-being. The human rights conventions and the drugs conventions absolutely seek to protect shared values.

  The commonality is more limited on the second level. The first sub-purpose (among other things the availability of narcotic drugs as medicine) and the second sub-purpose (treatment and care of drug users) match a 'human rights-based approach' rather well. However, it is more important that this is only partly the case for the third sub-purpose (to protect society against recreational narcotic drugs by fighting and eliminating them). So there is a partial connection. The fact that a drugs and/or cannabis policy where cannabis cultivation and trade are permitted under regulation may be called for by virtue of positive obligations does not mean that there is no longer any room to combat recreational drugs and/or cannabis. On the contrary. The fact that permission is regulated, actually implies that cultivation and trade that do not take place within the regulatory frameworks, must be considered illegal

372 Ibid.
373 Ibid.
374 Ibid.
375 See in that sense INCB, *Report of the International Narcotics Control Board for 2014*, New York: United Nations, 2015, p. 8 (no. 37): 'the human rights treaties employ the same language and rationale as used in the preambles to the drug control treaties'.
376 In a literal sense, see the preamble of the ESC; then for the sake of comparison also see, among other items, Article 4 ICESCR.

and must therefore be fought. After all, that regulation does not only seek to create room for cultivation and trade, but also to ensure that this does not exist outside the regulatory frameworks. Both the drugs conventions and the positive human rights obligations oppose serious drug and/or cannabis related criminality. In addition to this, when the right to health can be realized most effectively by permitting cannabis cultivation and trade under regulation, this right simultaneously still requires the state to discourage recreational drug use.[377] On the second purpose level of the drugs conventions, there certainly is not a perfect similarity with the human rights purposes, but there is a reasonable degree of commonality.

For the third level of purposes of the drugs conventions, this is an entirely different situation. Both a fundamental assumption of this purpose level (the risks of recreational drugs for public health are best combated by a prohibitive and repressive approach) and the core of this purpose level (complete eradication of recreational drugs), is completely at odds with regulated permission of cannabis cultivation and trade because of positive human rights obligations. Moreover, the drugs conventions are not directly aimed at protecting citizens against the consequences of drugs crime, for example.

In section 3.10.2.ii we will come back to the object and purpose as a starting point for harmonization.

iii. Striving Towards Maximum Retention of Norms

The interpretation of the interfering norms should preferably take place in such a manner that they are retained as much as possible. In view of the both abstract and concrete priority of the positive human rights obligations, this cannot involve a compromise where concessions are made with respect to the required protection of human rights. However, the prioritization of human rights does not force states to disable the drug system with regard to cannabis completely. As we saw before, an illegal circuit around cannabis may still remain operational even if cannabis cultivation and trade were permitted under regulation. That illegal circuit could in principle be subject to all the norms of the drugs conventions that contain obligations to combat and eradicate cannabis and to co-operate internationally in that area. The legal circuit would be the cannabis cultivation and trade taking place within the regulatory framework. The drugs conventions also contain various rules and regulations for legal drugs (under the drugs conventions these are currently the narcotic drugs with exclusively 'medical and scientific purposes'). We will have to see to what extent these are reasonably applicable to cannabis which falls within the regulatory framework.

---

[377] See section 2.3.10.

3.10.2. STARTING POINTS FOR HARMONIZATION IN THE UN DRUG CONTROL SYSTEM

In the introduction to this chapter, while referring to our first book on *International Law and Cannabis I*, we noted that the UN narcotic drugs conventions reveal a limited, one-sided and rigid view of public health interests and impose a strictly prohibitive approach. From the internal perspective of these conventions, this was inevitable, as we demonstrated in the aforementioned book. However, that will have to change by virtue of the external perspective of positive human rights obligations that are relevant here. The question is to what extent the drugs conventions offer departure points for harmonization, so that the situation where obligations under conventions simply need to be rendered inoperative can be avoided as much as possible. There appear to be several of such departure points.

i. INCB Approach

It is interesting that the UN General Assembly, and of late, also the INCB, has formulated a more nuanced approach than that manifested in the drugs conventions themselves. In the quotations included above (in section 3.7.9.i), they opine that the drug issue calls for a 'multilateral setting' and 'comprehensive, integrated and balanced approaches' and that 'the health and welfare of mankind [need to be] at the core of drug policies'.[378] Thus, a certain foundation for harmonization has been established within the drug control system too.

ii. Object and Purpose of the Drugs Conventions

As we have already noted, one of the key questions in the harmony approach is whether the interfering conventions have a common object and purpose and whether they set out to protect shared values. In the previous section (3.10.1.ii), it transpired that there is a clear case of common attempts to protect health and the well-being of people, and this can also be seen in policies to combat illegal cannabis cultivation and trade as well as the discouragement of recreational cannabis use. However, there is a stark contrast with respect to the third sub-purpose of the drugs conventions: prohibition and repression of all recreational cannabis (the drugs conventions) versus regulated permission of cannabis cultivation and trade (positive human rights obligations).

---

[378] See also INCB, *Report of the International Narcotics Control Board for 2014*, New York: United Nations, 2015, p. 9 (no. 38): 'Member States should give due consideration to the human rights norms relevant in the context of each element of a comprehensive, integrated and balanced approach, according to their legal obligations'.

A ground rule in the harmony approach is that the approach of conventions that best realize shared objectives and values decide the direction in the application of the principle of systemic integration. This brings us to an empirical question: which approach actually offers the best protection? This is in part the same question as the one covered by the hypothesis in this book: does a system of regulated permission of cannabis cultivation and trade for the recreational user market lead to better and/or more effective positive protection of individual and public health, life, people's physical and psychological integrity and privacy?

As we have repeatedly stated, this book's hypothesis is that the answer to this question is affirmative.[379] This hypothesis has three consequences here.

The first consequence is that the positive obligations discussed in Chapter 2 regarding the rights related to health, life, inhuman treatment and privacy are applicable. Given their special weight and to some extent their priority position, these positive obligations have priority over the obligations under the drugs conventions that interfere with them.

Secondly, the hypothesis entails that as far as protection of individual and public health as well as the well-being of people are concerned, the human rights approach works better than a strictly prohibitive and repressive approach imposed by the drugs conventions. That is also the case insofar as discouragement of recreational drug use is the common goal. The right to health forces states to develop a detailed policy of discouragement that is based on actual reality and the social constellation, more so than the drugs conventions do. To couch it in different terms: the drugs conventions require a total prohibition of recreational drugs on the basis of the assumption that this works best, whereas the right to health requires that measures be taken that actually discourage drug use most effectively. That policy of discouragement would therefore have to be shaped and informed by the right to health, although measures from the drugs conventions could conceivably play a part in that. Furthermore, it is important that regulation of cannabis cultivation and trade for the recreational user market implies that there may still be illegal cultivation and trade. To combat these, the drugs conventions provide a considerably more robust framework than the human rights obligations. In this respect, the principle of systemic integration supposes that the obligations under the drugs conventions must underpin actions and policies.

Thirdly, the hypothesis implies that drugs conventions are not as effective as they supposedly are. In subsection 3.10.1.i above, we saw that is there is a case for taking this into account in the interpretation of the drugs conventions. That would mean that even from within the drugs conventions themselves – so without having to rely on positive human rights obligations – there is cause

379 See section 4.3 on the substantiation a state must provide regarding effectiveness if it were to implement such regulated permission.

to interpret and apply these drugs conventions in such a way that the primary purposes (public health and well-being) can be achieved better. There are concrete departure points for this in the drugs conventions as well. According to the preamble to the Single Convention, the convention is aimed at 'effective measures against abuse of narcotic drugs', while the Illicit Traffic Convention is guided by the desire 'to conclude a comprehensive, effective and operative international convention'. Particularly in the latter convention, effectiveness of measures and cooperation are key to various provisions.

iii. Focus on Transnational Problems and Approach

The aims of the obligations under the drugs conventions undeniably include prohibiting and fighting narcotic drugs also if the production, trade and the use of such substances only affects the internal legal order of a state.[380] Nonetheless, there are various departure points to interpret the conventions primarily from the angle of transnational interests and objectives. The following is important in this respect.

First, the acts that the drugs conventions require to be criminalized do not constitute international crimes, which are so fundamentally serious that fighting them is necessary, regardless of where and by whom they are committed.[381] The rationale of the drugs conventions actually lies in a practical assumption, namely that effective national control of drug abuse is not possible if other states do not monitor the production and trade of narcotic drugs within their own territory and if there is no international coordination about this.[382] This requires 'a coordinated global effort' and therefore 'international cooperation'.[383] Where the drugs conventions categorically reject drugs for recreational use, the practical foundation for the creation of these conventions appears to be primarily the will to counter the transnational effects of illegal drugs trade.

This is also evident from Article 14 of the Single Convention. This provision gives the INCB powers to ensure the implementation of the obligations under the conventions if the Board 'has objective reasons to believe that the aims of this Convention are being *seriously endangered* by reason of the failure of any Party [...] to carry out the provisions of this Convention' (emphasis added).

---

380 See for example Article 4 of the Single Convention: 'The parties shall take such legislative and administrative measures as may be necessary: (a) To give effect to and carry out the provisions of this Convention within their own territories'; but also, among other things,: '(b) To co-operate with other States in the execution of the provisions of this Convention; and (c) [...]'.

381 See sections 3.7.7.iii and 3.7.9.xii.

382 Neil Boister, *An Introduction to Transnational Criminal Law*, Oxford: Oxford University Press, 2018, par. 6.1.

383 See Preamble of the Single Convention.

According to the official UN Commentaries to the conventions, those aims are 'seriously endangered' if 'lack of control or defective control in one country or territory appears to endanger the effectiveness of control in another country or territory'. The commentary goes on to state that the INCB will not be able to apply the procedure of Article 14 of the Single Convention in principle if 'failure to comply with the treaty provisions has only a domestic impact'.[384] Also relevant here is for example the preamble to the Illicit Traffic Convention. This underlines that organized criminal activities in illicit traffic 'undermine the legitimate economies and threaten the stability, security and sovereignty of States,' and that 'illicit traffic is an international criminal activity'. The preamble hereby focuses on both a national and international interest. The preamble also brings to the fore the problem that illicit traffic in narcotic drugs increasingly makes 'inroads into various social groups'.

The foregoing illustrates in our view that the primary concern is that each state party must prevent the production, distribution and trade in drugs within their own territory from affecting other states adversely. Should a state party manage to prevent these negative effects, then it has already achieved the practical purpose of the drugs conventions to a considerable extent. Furthermore, that state will need to ensure that its own stability, safety and sovereignty are not endangered, which of course goes hand-in-hand with an international interest. In itself, this does not provide any clues as to which measures need to be taken. This is very much a result-oriented objective. The question then is whether a state that achieves this objective without fulfilling its obligations under the convention actually meets the requirements of the convention better than a state that does fulfil its obligations under the convention but cannot achieve the result as a consequence. We take the view that an affirmative answer to this question is defensible. What is also important is that the hypothesis of this book is that regulated permission of cannabis cultivation and trade would actually lead to better protection of public health, better results in the fight against crime and preventing the consequences of crime than a prohibitive and repressive policy.[385] That hypothesis also entails that regulation can be more effective in countering the corruption of the upper world by illegal cannabis cultivation and trade. That too, fits in with the objective to avoid 'the steadily increasing inroads into various social groups' made by illicit traffic.

---

384 United Nations, *Commentary on the Single Convention on Narcotic Drugs*, 1961, New York: 1973, p. 178 (no. 2). To read about the status of the commentaries, see Piet Hein.P.H.M.C. van Kempen & Masha I. Fedorova, *International Law and Cannabis I*, Cambridge: Intersentia, 2019, section 2.1.ii.

385 See section 1.5.5 for information on the hypothesis and sections 2.3.1 and 2.4.1 for the arguments.

With the foregoing, the drugs conventions offer departure points to interpret the obligations they contain much more from the point of view of transnational and international interests and cooperation. In our thinking, however, given the contents of the drugs conventions and that of the positive human rights obligations that are relevant here, there is only room for such an interpretation if the following two conditions are met. First of all, regulated permission of cannabis cultivation and trade by one state within its own territory must not lead to a decrease in protection for other states. Secondly, that regulation must lead to better results in the state's own territory than a prohibitive approach, with regard to public health and the well-being of people.

iv. Human Rights and Constitutional Clauses

On the more concrete level of provisions in conventions, a departure point may be created under pressure of the positive human rights obligations, to be precise: the legal obligations to protect public health, life, the physical and psychological integrity of people and their private lives. The more general starting points are the following.

- *Human rights clause Article 14(2) Illicit Traffic Convention.* According to this provision that we have already mentioned several times, each party 'shall take appropriate measures' to prevent on its own territory 'illicit cultivation' of cannabis plants among other things 'and to eradicate [such] plants [...]' if they are 'cultivated illicitly' in the territory. And also: 'The measures adopted shall respect fundamental human rights [...].' In short, this stipulation requires that the fight against illicit cultivation must take place with due consideration for human rights. The text of this provision does not say that human rights must be taken into account in deciding what is 'illicit cultivation' and what is not. Strictly speaking, this clause cannot cover a drug and/or cannabis policy that permits a regulated cannabis cultivation and trade in order to give effect to positive human rights obligations.

  To allow harmonization, one could also interpret the provision in a wider sense. The reasoning is that fighting cannabis cultivation does not take place with due regard for human rights if the state pursuant to positive human rights obligations is actually bound to permit cultivation under regulation. The implication of this reading is that Article 14(2) of the Illicit Traffic Convention consequently requires that states provide a policy of regulation in order to prevent the situation in which the fight against cultivation as a whole must be declared contrary to human rights. Any cultivation outside the regulatory framework – which is the 'illicit cultivation' that Article 14(2) of the Illicit Traffic Convention refers to – can then be taken on as per usual and with due regard for human rights.

This approach has far-reaching consequences. First and foremost, it leads to an essentially different interpretation of what must be considered 'illegal' under the conventions. In principle, that is no longer all cannabis that does not serve 'medical or scientific purposes'.[386] From now on, 'illegal' cannabis would be cannabis that is not covered by the regulatory framework. The most important provisions that relate explicitly to 'illegal' narcotic drugs or acts related to them can be found in Article 3 of the Illicit Traffic Convention (obligation of criminalization), Article 12 (measures against substances used for the manufacture of narcotic drugs), Article 13 (measures against materials and equipment) and Article 14 (measures against cultivation).

A second far-reaching consequence is that if Article 14(2) of the Illicit Traffic Convention ceases to permit the fight against regulated cannabis cultivation, a systematic reading of the drugs conventions must entail that the fight against among other things, the production, distribution, trade and possession of cannabis is no longer permitted insofar as this falls within the regulatory framework. The assumption is of course that the convention must be interpreted in such a way that it cannot be applied if positive obligations dictate that the state has to permit regulated cannabis cultivation. With that state of affairs, it is hard to argue that the convention still requires the fight against regulated permitted distribution, trade and possession of cannabis if that regulation also finds its origin in positive human rights obligations. In this perspective, Article 14(2) of the Illicit Traffic Convention would do away with the obligations to fight cannabis cultivation and trade, provided these take place within the regulatory framework.

- *Constitutional clauses.* Various provisions in the Single Convention and the Illicit Traffic Convention are so-called constitutional clauses. They mean that each state party is exonerated from fulfilling obligations that such clauses apply to if they run counter to the constitutional system, constitutional limitations or constitutional principles. The Single Convention has six of such clauses and there are three of them in the Illicit Traffic Convention.[387]

  The most important consequences of these clauses are the following. Only subject to the Constitution:
  - does international legal assistance need to be provided in the fight against illicit traffic (Article 35 of the Single Convention);
  - does criminalization need to be provided for intentional cultivation, distribution, trade and possession of cannabis (Article 36(1) and (2) of the Single Convention);

---

386 Piet Hein P.H.M.C. van Kempen & Masha I. Fedorova, *International Law and Cannabis I*, Cambridge: Intersentia, 2019, sections 2.2.3 and 2.3.3.

387 Incidentally, see Ibid, para. 2.3.2.vi, which shows that Article 2(1) of the Illicit Traffic Convention is a clause that is irrelevant here after all, in spite of its words 'in conformity with the fundamental provisions of their respective domestic legislative systems'.

- does criminalization need to be provided to combat property acquired through offences as well as materials and equipment and substances used for cannabis cultivation among other things (Article 3(1)(c) of the Illicit Traffic Convention);
- does criminalization need to be provided for incitement, participation in and attempts to commit offences related to cannabis among other things (Article 3(1)(c) of the Illicit Traffic Convention);
- does criminalization need to be provided for, among other offences, the intentional cultivation, possession and purchase of cannabis for personal use (Article 3(2) of the Illicit Traffic Convention; for information about Article 3(1) of the Illicit Traffic Convention see below in this subsection);
- do the obligations need to be met that arise from obligations to which the constitutional clause applies.

In the first book on *International Law and Cannabis I* we established in relation to the constitutional clause that it would appear that a state may only refrain from criminalizing acts if such criminalization would cause a genuine breach of fundamental principles. In this interpretation (from the internal perspective of the drugs conventions), there is absolutely no room for most states to decriminalize cannabis cultivation, possession and trade, let alone to legalize it.[388] However, again the external perspective of positive human rights obligations, as well as the interests of the drugs conventions served by harmonization, necessitates systemic integration by innovative interpretation.

For that reason and in the light of the following, we believe there is a lot to be said for interpreting the terms 'constitution' and 'constitutional' no longer in a strictly national sense, but to include European and international constitutional law as well. The consequence of that would be that from now on the internationally recognized human rights and the ensuing positive obligations would impact on the drugs conventions via the constitutional clauses. This is in line with the development in which international human rights have acquired an increasing constitutional relevance in national legal orders. Moreover, it is consistent with the constitutional character of human rights in the development of international legal orders.[389] Furthermore, there is no reason from a substantive point of view why fundamental rights from national constitutions may detract from obligations on the drugs conventions, but this is not possible for international – even universally recognized – catalogues of fundamental rights.

---

388 Ibid, pp. 57, 58, 177–178.

389 See for example ECtHR (Grand Chamber) 30 June 2005, *Bosphorus Hava Yollari Turizm ve Ticaret Anonim Sirketi/Ireland*, no. 45036/98, para. 156, in which the Court mentions 'the Convention's role as a "constitutional instrument of European public order" in the field of human rights'. See also Erika de Wet, 'The International Constitutional Order', International and Comparative Law Quarterly 2006, vol. 55, pp. 51–76.

By recognizing international human rights and fundamental freedoms under the constitutional clause, it is also easier to give effect to the views of bodies such as the UN General Assembly, the INCB and the CND that the drugs conventions must be implemented in full accordance with human rights and that the promotion of human rights is an intrinsic part of the implementation of the conventions.[390]

Finally, a few comments about Article 3(1)(a) and (b) of the Illicit Traffic Convention. There is no evidence in the Illicit Traffic Convention that the constitutional clause also applies to this particular provision. In essence, this Article concerns the obligation to criminalize the intentional 1. commission of offences such as cultivation, production, distribution and trade with regard to cannabis or possession 'contrary to the provisions of 'the Single Convention, 2. the manufacture, transport or distribution of equipment, materials or of substances [...], knowing that they are to be used in or for the 'illicit cultivation, production or manufacture of narcotic drugs', 3. organizing, managing or financing of any of the offences enumerated, and 4. conversion of property derived from offences listed above.

The obligations under 3. and 4. are only relevant to the extent that they apply under 1. or 2. The obligation under 2. only relates to 'illegal' acts, as the text indicates. If one interprets the drugs conventions in such a way that cannabis cultivation and other offences within the regulatory framework no longer qualify as 'illegal', the obligations under 2 no longer apply then.

It is not as straightforward for the obligations under 1. After all, according to the UN Commentary, the states parties deliberately decided not to include a constitutional clause in Article 3(1) of the Illicit Traffic Convention because they 'were anxious to make the present text fully mandatory, allowing parties no loopholes'.[391] Another consideration was that the clause was deemed to be 'almost certainly unnecessary' as there was no evidence of constitutional obstacles with regard to this. That assessment turns out to be incorrect in hindsight, at least when one also adopts an international point of view when reading the constitutional clause, which a harmonizing interpretation gives rise to as explained above. Admittedly, there is no reason to refrain from criminalizing the actions mentioned; the problem though is that Article 3(1) of the Illicit Traffic Convention has been worded in such a way that it does not allow a legal circuit of actions relating to recreational drugs and/or cannabis within a regulatory framework as well. Since such a circuit may be called for on account of positive human rights obligations, there is a reason to interpret the provision differently. It also offers a starting point for that.

---

390 See section 3.9.1.i.

391 United Nations, Commentary on the United Nations Convention Against Illicit Traffic in Narcotic Drugs and Psychotropic Substances, Vienna: 1988, p. 50 (no. 3.5).

Article 3(1) of the Illicit Traffic Convention contains an obligation to criminalize all sorts of acts 'contrary to the provisions' of the Single Convention. However, the obligations for criminalization in the Single Convention are always subject to the constitutional clause; see Article 36 of the Single Convention. Thus, acts which may be permitted on account of the clause in this provision could be qualified as not at odds with the Single Convention. That would then apply for the acts taking place subject to a regulatory framework for cannabis that is supported by positive human rights obligations. According to Article 3(1) of the Illicit Traffic Convention, the obligations for criminalization it contains will no longer apply, as these acts will no longer be contrary to the Single Convention.

v. *Legal versus Illegal Cultivation and Trade*

If regulated permission of cannabis cultivation and trade is not based on a policy of tolerance but is embedded in legalizing legislation, cultivation and trade within the regulatory framework will be legal and cultivation and trade outside that framework will be illegal. It will be possible to marry up the interpretations of provisions of conventions. Wherever the conventions contain obligations with regard to 'illegal' or 'illicit' acts or of 'illicit traffic', these obligations only apply to acts that are not legalized and therefore take place outside the regulatory framework. The opposite applies where the convention talks about 'legal', such as legal authority for possession of drugs in Article 33 of the Single Convention. Indeed, this is not about creating so-called 'claw-back' clauses, on the basis of which neighbouring states can simply wriggle out of obligations under the drugs conventions by legalizing acts in the national legal order. After all, this interpretation of the convention can only be applied to the extent that the regulatory framework can be assumed to be supported by human rights obligations.

3.10.3. STARTING POINTS FOR REGULATION GIVEN SPECIFIC OBLIGATIONS UNDER THE DRUGS CONVENTIONS

In addition to the necessary interpretation and implementation of the obligations under the drugs conventions in the light of positive human rights obligations, there is actually also room to use certain obligations under the drugs conventions as a basis or even a requirement. There are not only substantive reasons to do this, the principle to strive towards maximum retention of norms also calls for it. We will briefly discuss the most important ones of these obligations. Some of them are a natural consequence of the foregoing.

i. No Negative Consequences for Other Countries

An important requirement is that regulated permission of cannabis cultivation and trade for the recreational user market must at any rate not lead to negative consequences for other countries. This means that the protection of other countries with such regulation should be no less – indeed, preferably even more effective – than that offered under a prohibitive approach that fully accords with the drugs conventions. Therefore, a closed system and/or chain for cultivation, trade and possibly also use of cannabis will have to be provided, i.e. closed in the sense that cannabis cannot leak away to illegal markets, so this does not have to exclude the possibility of legal export to and import from other jurisdictions that do allow so.[392] As it is inconceivable that the positive human rights obligations would oppose this, while preventing transnational effects is the practical cornerstone of the drugs conventions, full implementation of these conventions must be achieved in this respect. It also means that illegal cannabis cultivation and trade (that is outside the regulatory framework) must continue to be combated in accordance with the conventions and that to this end, cooperation with other states will have to be continued.

ii. Combating Illegal Cannabis Cultivation and Trade

Cannabis cultivation and trade that do not take place within the regulatory framework must be qualified as illegal. All obligations in the drugs conventions regarding criminalization, prosecution, administrative prohibition, confiscation and other ways of combating such cultivation and trade will need to be fulfilled with regard to these illegal activities.[393]

iii. Measures to Discourage Cannabis Use

Pursuant to Article 38 of the Single Convention, states parties are required to take measures against the use of narcotic drugs. Among other things, these measures need to be aimed at the 'early identification, treatment, education, after-care, rehabilitation and social reintegration' of problem drug users, on the training of personnel working in these areas, and to promote an understanding among the relevant professions and the public of the problems

---

392 Cf. Martin Jelsma, Neil Boister, David Bewley-Taylor, Malgosia Fitzmaurice & John Walsh, *Balancing Treaty Stability and Change: Inter se modification of the UN drug control conventions to facilitate cannabis regulation* (GDPO Policy Report 7, March 2018) p. 1–43 at 34.

393 For more information and more detail on that, see Piet Hein P.H.M.C. van Kempen & Masha I. Fedorova, *International Law and Cannabis I*, Cambridge: Intersentia, 2019, Chapter 2 and the overview in section 2.6.

of drugs with a view to preventing these problems. These measures fit in well with the positive obligation arising from the right to health to discourage drug use.[394] Therefore, the obligations under Article 38 of the Single Convention must be carried out in full.

iv. System of Estimates, Licensing System and Supervision

The so-called 'system of estimates' provided by Articles 12–21bis of the Single Convention seeks to make strict supervision of all phases of the legal drugs economy possible. Article 19 of the Single Convention requires states to furnish the INCB each year with estimates on the quantities of drugs to be consumed for medical and scientific purposes; and on the stocks of drugs held as at 31 December of the year to which the estimates relate. This system aims to ensure that narcotic drugs for medical and scientific purposes are available in sufficient measure and not in excessive quantities. Particularly in the light of the latter intention, to monitor the closed character of the system and/or the chain and because of the principle of maximum retention of norms, it seems only logical to apply this system to cannabis cultivation, trade and stocks as well within the regulatory framework.

Additionally, at any rate a licensing system will have to be established for the cultivation and production as well as the trade and distribution of cannabis (Articles 29 and 30 of the Single Convention). Incidentally, Article 30 of the Single Convention also imposes requirements about packaging and labelling of narcotic drugs. In addition to this, one would have to pay attention to the question how the obligation to create a national cannabis agency (which would be responsible for issuing licences, among other things) could be carried out most effectively within the regulatory framework (Article 28 in conjunction with Article 23 of the Single Convention). That also applies for the measures of supervision and inspection regarding persons and institutions involved with the cultivation, distribution and trade (Article 34 of the Single Convention) and for the measures regarding international trade (Article 31 of the Single Convention). Export to other countries will only be possible insofar as the laws and regulations of the other country allow this.

Finally, it is worth noting that pursuant to Article 28(1) in conjunction with Article 23(2) of the Single Convention, cannabis cultivation may be left to private cultivators. Under a strict application of the system of these provisions, however, there is no room to place the cannabis chain entirely in the hands of private entities. In section 4.10 we will look in more detail at the question whether these provisions require a full implementation once the state decides to permit regulated cannabis cultivation and trade. At this point, we will merely point out

[394] See section 2.3.10.

that also in view of Article 34(a) of the Single Convention, persons who are issued with a licence for cannabis cultivation and persons who are employed by such cultivators, cannot have criminal records in respect of drugs regulation, according to the official UN Commentary on the Single Convention.[395]

3.10.4. CONFLICT WITH OBLIGATION TO LIMIT TO 'MEDICAL AND SCIENTIFIC PURPOSES'

So far, we have not dealt with another – crucial – part of the drugs conventions. Various provisions in the conventions constitute obligations to limit the circulation of narcotic drugs 'exclusively' to those narcotic drugs that serve 'medical or scientific purposes'. Because cannabis for recreational use does not meet these criteria, the convention effectively stands in the way of permitting this use (legalization) or tolerating it (decriminalization and/or policy-based tolerance) in whichever form or shape.[396]

The most important provision here is Article 4 of the Single Convention (general obligations), pursuant to which the states parties are required to take 'such legislative and administrative measures as may be necessary' and subject to the provisions of the Convention, 'to limit exclusively to medical and scientific purposes the production, manufacture, export, import, distribution of, trade in, use and possession of drugs.' The obligation to limit narcotic drugs to medical or scientific purposes also follows from the system of estimates (see the Articles 12(5), 19 and 21 of the Single Convention), the exception where the obligation to combat cannabis cultivation is concerned (Article 22(2) of the Single Convention) and the powers of the INCB (see Article 9 of the Single Convention). The question is whether it is possible to eliminate this obstacle as well via a harmonizing interpretation, so that regulation of cannabis cultivation and trade for the recreational user market becomes possible.

i. Solution via Article 9 of the Single Convention?

A first angle of approach would be to seek alignment with the aforementioned Article 9 of the Single Convention, which concerns the powers of the INCB. Pursuant to this provision, the INCB endeavours 'to limit the cultivation, production, manufacture and use of drugs to an adequate amount required for medical and scientific purposes, to ensure their availability for such purposes

395 United Nations, *Commentary on the Single Convention on Narcotic Drugs*, 1961, New York: 1973, p. 281 (no. 1).

396 For more information and more details about that, see Piet Hein P.H.M.C. van Kempen & Masha I. Fedorova, *International Law and Cannabis I*, Cambridge: Intersentia, 2019, sections 2.2.3, 2.3.3, 2.4.3 and 4.2.4.

and to prevent illicit cultivation, production and manufacture of, and illicit trafficking in and use of, drugs.'

It is not possible to achieve both goals with maximum effect if illegal cannabis cultivation and trade and recreational cannabis use are actually more successfully fought with a permissive approach (in which cannabis cultivation and trade is permitted within a regulatory framework and cannabis use is also discouraged at the same time) than with a prohibitive and repressive approach. This conflict between tasks can be avoided by emphasizing the latter task, but at the same time urging states as much as possible to discourage cannabis use because of the former task.

The most important objection against this solution is that while it does offer a solution to the task conflict of the INCB, it has no effect as such on the general obligation for states to limit the availability of narcotic drugs exclusively to medical and scientific purposes.

ii. Solution by Including 'Public Health Purposes' in the Interpretation of Drugs Conventions?

A second angle of approach would be to interpret the concept 'medical and scientific purposes' in such a way that it would cover 'individual and public health purposes' too. In our first book on *International Law and Cannabis I* we explained why such an interpretation – from the internal perspective of the drugs conventions – is not possible in good faith.[397] However, by now the external perspective of positive human rights obligations has established itself, which necessitate a reinterpretation of the drugs conventions. Nevertheless, we believe that there are still various objections against this solution.

First of all, from a linguistic point of view, it is rather forced and far-fetched to stretch the meaning of a specific term such as 'medical' to the extent that it would include all relevant interests of individual health and public health. The fact that it would be a hugely broadened interpretation of the term 'medical' is also clear because the availability of cannabis for the recreational user market is not directly intended for reasons of public health (on the contrary, the availability of cannabis for recreational use in itself does not exactly benefit public health), but is only indirectly relevant to it (regulated permission of cannabis would on balance safeguard public health better, according to the hypothesis). Thus, the term would have to be interpreted so widely that policies that are indirectly relevant to public health could also fall under it.

Secondly, such an increased reinterpretation of the 'medical and scientific purposes' clause would only provide a partial solution. While it is true that this would remove the obstacle that prevents fully meeting the positive obligations

397 Ibid, section 4.2.4.

arising from the right to health, it is a different story for the positive obligations stemming from the rights with respect to life, inhuman treatment and privacy. The above-mentioned broader interpretation in particular does not provide a solution where the latter positive obligations relate to the prevention of fighting crime in connection with cannabis cultivation and trade.

iii. Solution by Including Interests of Public Health and Welfare in the Interpretation of Drugs Conventions?

In view of the priority position of the human rights obligations discussed in Chapter 2, which will have to be given full effect, eventually it all comes down to a choice. The choice is between fully pushing aside the obligation to allow cannabis exclusively for social and medical purposes (which would actually mean a conflict approach) and interpreting the drugs conventions in such a way that the obligations in the convention do not apply to cannabis that is permitted under regulation because of 'interests of public health and welfare' (harmony approach). The latter option can be realized by considerably broadening the interpretation of the concept of 'medical and scientific purposes' or by recognizing an unwritten 'interests of public health and welfare' clause in addition to that.

A sufficiently broad interpretation could be that this should be taken to mean something like 'interests of public health, social well-being and science'. Of course, this interpretation is even more contorted than the one discussed before, so that it is hard to defend from a linguistic point of view. However, the situation looks more promising from a teleological point of view. After all, as we saw before, the preambles to the drugs conventions emphatically put 'health and welfare of mankind' or 'of human beings' centre stage. The above-mentioned interpretation fits in with that.

However, that is also the case with recognition of an unwritten 'interests of public health and welfare' clause. Moreover, the advantage of that is that the drugs conventions can continue to function as much as possible in this way. After all, the 'medical and scientific purposes' clause can then retain its current meaning so that the conventions remain fully intact in that sense. The unwritten clause to be recognized can then be given a suitable expression and its applicability may be made dependent on specific conditions.

One way or another, simply brushing aside obligations and provisions of the convention must be rejected, as this would subvert it. There is yet another advantage to interpreting the conventions in a way that states are required to permit drugs and/or cannabis for recreational use exclusively (at best) insofar as this happens in the 'interests of public health and welfare'. After all, the burden of proof that on balance, regulation benefits public health and/or public well-being still remains with the state in that case. Moreover, the conventions also provide a criterion with this to assess whether the drugs and/or cannabis policy of a state is useful and effective. This then also implies that the actual effectiveness or ineffectiveness of the drug control system can play a greater part in the interpretation and implementation of provisions under the drugs conventions.

In view of these arguments and in view of the necessity to give full effect to positive human rights obligations, we believe that a harmonizing approach is called for. Recognition of an unwritten clause that ties in with the object of protection of public health and the welfare of people would be our preferred option. In saying this, we do not deny that this solution comes with its own objections, in view of the content of the conventions; it implies that application of the conflict approach in our opinion is fraught with even more serious disadvantages.

3.10.5. CONCLUSION

The foregoing shows that a harmonizing interpretation of the relevant drugs conventions makes it possible to achieve a fair degree of systemic integration of positive human rights obligations and obligations under the drugs conventions. It makes way for a regulated admission of cannabis cultivation and trade in accordance with the positive obligations, while at the same time the obligations under the drugs conventions remain in force and therefore do not have to do be pushed aside rigorously. In the final analysis, that is also true for the obligation (a crucial one within the drugs conventions) to permit the use of cannabis exclusively for medical and scientific purposes. This can be harmonized with the positive human rights obligations through a textually very contorted though teleologically fitting interpretation of the convention.

It is not only on the level of specific provisions within the drugs conventions that there are several departure points for a harmonizing approach. They also exist in a more general sense. The departure points can be found in the judgments by various UN institutions, in the partly shared object and purpose of the human rights conventions and the drugs conventions, in the practical focus of the drugs conventions on transnational risks and cooperation, and in the human rights and constitutional clauses in those drugs conventions.

While from the internal perspective of the drugs conventions there is no room to permit the regulated cultivation of and trade in cannabis, the external perspective of positive human rights obligations forces states to create that room. The foregoing shows that this is also possible. That is not to say that the harmonization is optimal. In achieving that harmonization, the obligations in the drugs conventions will see a reduction in their scope, while their applicability also becomes relative rather than absolute. In view of the priority position of the positive human rights obligations, however, it is in the interests of the drugs conventions to realize this harmonization, because the conflict approach has far more damaging consequences for these conventions.

3.11. STATE RESPONSIBILITY UNDER REGULATED PERMISSION?

One question that could be raised by some relates to state responsibility under international law.[398] Since this topic in itself is not relevant to answering the key questions of this book and therefore falls outside its scope, we will not analyse this in any detail. However, we will not ignore this altogether. After all, there is the matter that where a state permits cannabis cultivation and trade for the recreational user market on account of positive human rights obligations, it is not fulfilling its obligations under the drugs conventions. Does this mean that this state thereby creates state responsibility under public international law because such regulation is a violation of the drugs conventions?

Before addressing this question relatively briefly, it is worth noting that international law regarding state responsibility because of a violation of obligations under conventions is not embedded in a convention, is still being developed, and moreover does not provide answers to many questions. That is why no definitive statements can be made about numerous issues. For this reason, we exercise caution, because of the following points, when concluding that it is not likely that a state which permits cannabis cultivation and trade under regulation under the above-mentioned conditions will be held responsible under international law for violating the drugs conventions.

- *Absence of responsibility because human rights are part of the drug control system.* Among other authorities, the UN General Assembly, the INCB, the CND and the Special Rapporteur on the right to health make it clear that the drugs conventions may only be implemented with due regard for human rights. This means that the obligation to respect human rights has at any rate de facto become part of the drug control system, in particular because of the recognition of that obligation of compliance by the two main monitoring bodies within that system: the INCB and the CND. That recognition is also manifest from Article 14(2) of the Illicit Traffic Convention. This implies not only the recognition of human rights, but also that compliance with the obligations prevails over other obligations within the drug control system. The system thereby indicates how a state must act in the case of interference with human rights obligations. It goes without saying, that implementing human rights according to this prioritization can then not lead to state responsibility under the same system.

[398] For information about this, see the Articles on State Responsibility, as included in: ILC, 'Articles on Responsibility of States for Internationally Wrongful Acts, with commentaries', 2001, and by now also in: United Nations, *Materials on the Responsibility of States for Internationally Wrongful Acts, United Nations Legislative Series, ST/LEG/SER.B/25*, New York: United Nations, 2012.

- *Absence of responsibility because of Article 103 of the UN Charter.* Insofar as it concerns an obligation in the sense of this provision, it is plausible that fulfilment of this obligation in view of Article 59 Articles on State Responsibility cannot lead to international state responsibility. This also applies if that fulfilment entails violation of another obligation under international law.[399,400] We concluded in section 3.7.8.v that one can argue convincingly that the positive obligations arising from the four rights that may be relevant for regulated permission of cannabis cultivation and trade, qualify as obligations in the sense of Article 103 UN Charter. Thus, fulfilling those obligations – on the basis of Article 59 of Articles on State Responsibility – cannot lead to state responsibility for a state that implements a regulated permission of such cultivation and trade in accordance with those obligations. However, that state will need to ensure that the regulatory system does not turn out to be more harmful for other states than a system which is compatible with the drugs conventions. After all, it is difficult to argue that the positive human rights obligations constitute a barrier to the prevention of such harm or disadvantage.
- *Absence of responsibility because of harmonizing interpretation.* Article 103 UN Charter is only applicable if the interference between norms is resolved via the conflict approach. If the interfering norms are resolved through harmonizing interpretation resulting in systemic integration, there is no further conflict and therefore no violation of one of the norms.[401] In the absence of a violation, there is likewise no ground for state responsibility. That means that in applying the harmony approach mentioned before, state responsibility does not enter into it in principle.

---

399 It would be different if a *jus cogens* rule were involved, but that is not the case with the obligations under the drugs conventions, see section 3.7.7.iii.

400 Article 59 Articles on State Responsibility reads: 'These articles are without prejudice to the Charter of the United Nations.' See ILC, 'Articles on Responsibility of States for Internationally Wrongful Acts, with commentaries', 2001, comm. Article 59 (para. 1–2), which explicitly refers to Article 103 UN Charter; ILC, *Articles on State Responsibility with Commentaries Thereto Adopted by the International Law Commission on First Reading*, January 1997, p. 96 (para. 23), 128 (para. 55), 350 (para. 3), which explains why acting in accordance with an obligation in the sense of Article 103 UN Charter cannot lead to state responsibility; Marko Milanović, 'Norm Conflict in International Law: Whither Human Rights?', *Duke Journal of Comparative and International Law* 2009, vol. 20, no. 1, pp. 69–131 on pp. 76–77. For a different opinion based on an *a contrario* argument, which does not clarify which meaning should then be accorded to Article 59 of Articles and why Article 103 of the UN Charter should be excluded from that effect, see Antonios Tzanakopoulos, 'Collective Security and Human Rights', in: Erika De Wet & Jure Vidmar (eds.), *Hierarchy in International Law: The Place of Human Rights*, Oxford: Oxford University Press 2012, pp. 42–70 on pp. 64–66. See also section 3.7.8.i.

401 See also section 3.2.

- *Absence of responsibility by preventing harm or disadvantage for other states.* As far as human rights are concerned, a state that violates these in principle is not only liable to another state party which has been affected by it, but the liability also exists in principle to all other states parties at the same time and to the individual that is affected by the violation.[402] It must be assumed that a violation of the drugs conventions does not lead to similar liabilities. The reason for that is, as we saw in section 3.7.9.xii, that the drugs conventions do not have *erga omnes* effect while it is plausible that they do not constitute 'integral obligations' either. That means that a state that does not carry out obligations under the drugs conventions can in principle only be held liable to states that consequently suffered injury in the sense of damage.[403] In other words, there has to be an 'injured state'.[404]

  The consequence of this is that if regulated permission of cannabis cultivation and trade (despite the foregoing) were still considered a violation of the convention, it would only lead to liability under the Articles on State Responsibility if other states parties genuinely and actually suffered injury as a consequence. In this respect too, it is important to ensure that regulation does not manoeuvre states into a more disadvantageous position than the one they were in while conducting a prohibitive policy that is in full accordance with the drugs conventions. In our opinion, this means that regulated permission of cannabis cultivation and trade for the national recreational user market must not in any case lead to an increase of illegal cannabis export to other countries.

  Incidentally, pursuant to the Articles on State Responsibility, this is not materially different if one assumes – unlike we do – that there is a violation and – wrongly, in our opinion – qualified the obligations under the drugs conventions as 'integral obligations'. In itself, each of the states parties could in that situation invoke the liability of the violating state party and demand cessation of the violation and perhaps demand 'assurances and guarantees of

402 ILC, 'Articles on Responsibility of States for Internationally Wrongful Acts, with commentaries', 2001, comm. Article 33 (para. 3), comm. Article 36 (para. 19), comm. Article 48 (para. 7, 12), comm. Ch. II, Countermeasures (para. 5); ILC, 'Fragmentation of International Law', 2006, para. 400. See also for example Christian Dominice, 'The international responsibility of states for breach of multilateral obligations', *European Journal of International Law* 1999, pp. 353–363 on p. 355, pp. 362–363.

403 See Article 31(2) Articles on State Responsibility: '2. Injury includes any damage, whether material or moral, caused by the internationally wrongful act of a State.', and see on this ILC, 'Articles on Responsibility of States for Internationally Wrongful Acts, with commentaries', 2001, comm. Article 31 (para. 5): 'This formulation is intended both as inclusive, covering both material and moral damage broadly understood, and as limitative, excluding merely abstract concerns or general interests of a State which is individually unaffected by the breach.'; also see comm. Article 42 (para. 12).

404 Article 42 Articles on State Responsibility.

non-repetition'. However, the question is whether any of those states parties would wish to go down that avenue. Moreover, the violating party would at best be required to provide for reparation of the violation in favour of the states or individuals affected by the violation.[405] If the violation does not lead to concrete disadvantage for states or individuals, reparation – including financial compensation – is not applicable.

- *Conclusion.* We conclude primarily that a state which permits the cultivation of and trade in cannabis under regulation so as to fulfil its positive human rights obligations does not create state responsibility in principle. Although such regulation does not meet the obligations of the drugs conventions, there does not seem to be a convention violation in a formal sense, at least when taking into account the priority position that human rights have within the drug control system. The same applies when one uses harmonizing interpretation to arrive at the systemic integration of the human rights obligations and obligations under the drugs conventions. On the other hand, if one applies the conflict approach, then there is a violation but then it is plausible that responsibility is ruled out on the grounds of Article 103 UN Charter. Should one reject the validity of this argument as well, for which we believe there is no justification, then there is a violation for which the state can be held responsible. As long as the regulatory system does not lead to any harmful consequences for other countries, then in principle there will be no ground for financial compensation among other things.

3.12. CONCLUSION

In essence, the conclusion is that if the decision by a state to permit a regulated regime of cannabis cultivation and trade is based on positive human rights obligations from the ICESCR, the ICPPR, the ECHR and the ESC, these obligations can provide national governments with enough room under international law to derogate from the UN drug control system. Consequently, this book leads to another conclusion than the one we arrived at in our first book on *International Law and Cannabis I*. In that book, being based on an internal perspective of the drugs conventions, we concluded that these conventions do not leave any room to permit regulated cannabis cultivation or trade for the recreational

405 See Article 48(2)(b) Articles on State Responsibility: '2. Any State entitled to invoke responsibility under paragraph 1 may claim from the responsible State: (a) cessation of the internationally wrongful act, and assurances and guarantees of non-repetition in accordance with article 30; and (b) performance of the obligation of reparation in accordance with the preceding articles, in the interest of the injured State or of the beneficiaries of the obligation breached'.

user market. Because of the pressure of an external perspective of the positive human rights obligations that are relevant here, the drugs conventions will have to allow that room after all under certain conditions. More specifically, this conclusion, which implies that in the interference between the positive human rights obligations and the drugs conventions the former have priority, is based on the following. Incidentally, none of the arguments presented is in any way crucial or indispensable for that conclusion, so if one or several of these were to fall by the wayside, the conclusion will still be supported by the remaining arguments.

3.12.1. FORMAL PRIORITY POSITION OF POSITIVE HUMAN RIGHTS OBLIGATIONS

The classic rules of precedence – so: the *lex specialis* rule (speciality), the *lex posterior* and *prior* rules (temporality) and the *lex superior* rule (the importance of the interest at stake) – are only useful up to a point for the interfering human rights and drugs conventions in the cannabis issue. The interference cannot be resolved formally by means of the *lex specialis* rule. The same is true for the *lex posteriori* and *prior* rules as expressed in Article 30 of the Vienna Convention on the Law of Treaties. If, however, this provision is applied to the cannabis issue analogically, then the human rights conventions have priority over the UN drugs conventions. With regard to the *lex superior* rule, the *jus cogens* concept is of paramount importance. Unfortunately, that does not provide a clear solution for the interference between human rights obligations and the obligations under drugs conventions. After all, there is insufficient ground to assume that positive human rights obligations have *jus cogens* status, even if these obligations stem from negative human rights which do have that status. Such a status is definitely not accorded to – obligations in – the drugs conventions.

However, Article 103 UN Charter is important: this provision constitutes a special implementation of the *lex superior* rule. Obligations in the sense of that provision have precedence over obligations conflicting with them. Whereas obligations from the drugs conventions do not fall within the scope of Article 103, that is the case for the negative obligations to respect the rights regarding health, life, inhuman treatment and privacy from the UDHR, the ICESCR and the ICCPR. It is also possible to argue convincingly that this also applies to the positive obligations arising from these rights that may be relevant for the regulated permission of cannabis cultivation and trade. Those obligations then unconditionally prevail over obligations from drugs conventions pursuant to Article 103 of the UN Charter. It follows from the case law of the ECtHR that human rights obligations under the ECHR have a similar absolute validity. It is plausible that this also applies to the ESC.

3.12.2. POSITIVE HUMAN RIGHTS OBLIGATIONS CARRY MORE WEIGHT IN A SUBSTANTIVE SENSE

According to both international law in general and more specifically the UN drug control system, the drugs conventions can only be implemented within the frameworks that are delineated by human rights and fundamental freedoms.

From a more substantive approach of the *lex superior* rule – which acts not so much as a formal rule of priority but rather as a principle for interpretation and consideration – the thing that matters most is that human rights, unlike the drugs conventions, have a special substantive status. The special weight of human rights is reflected in the rationale and the main purposes of the great public international law organizations (such as the UN and the CoE), the system of international law (among other things *jus cogens*, *erga omnes*, customary law and 'integral obligations'), in specific provisions in general agreements as well as in international case law. That special status at any rate extends indirectly to positive human rights obligations and to a large extent applies also directly to them.

It is also important that authorities such as the UN General Assembly, the INCB, the CND and the Special Rapporteur on the right to health as well as the Special Rapporteurs on globalization and its impact on the full enjoyment of all human rights are all of the opinion that the drugs conventions may only be implemented with due regard for human rights. Insofar as this specifically concerns measures to prevent and eradicate, among other things, illicit cannabis cultivation, this also follows from Article 14(2) of the Single Convention. The Special Rapporteur on the right to health makes it clear that in the event of a conflict between human rights obligations and obligations under drugs conventions, the former take precedence. There is no reason to assume that this would not also apply for the positive obligations which are relevant to the cannabis issue. On the contrary. These positive obligations happen to have found permanent recognition under the general human rights conventions and therefore belong to these convention systems, in other words 'human rights and fundamental freedoms'.

3.12.3. STATE RESPONSIBILITY UNDER INTERNATIONAL LAW

Given the recognition of human rights from within the drug control system, human rights norms may by now be considered part and parcel of the system. Because of that, and also because of the effect of Article 103 UN Charter, a state which permits the cultivation of and trade in cannabis under regulation so as to fulfil its positive human rights obligations does not create state responsibility in principle. That applies in particular if the interference between norms is solved by harmonizing interpretation. One of the things that is important for this conclusion is that the state must prevent that regulated permission from becoming more harmful to other countries than a cannabis policy that is in accordance with the drugs conventions.

3.12.4. REJECTION OF THE CONFLICT APPROACH TO SOLVE THE INTERFERENCE

If the interference between human rights obligations and obligations under the drugs conventions were subjected to the so-called conflict approach, this would mean that the obligations under the drugs conventions would be swept aside rigorously. This approach flies in the face of the principles of international law. Consequently, the primacy of the principle of systemic integration, the presumption of compatibility and the presumption against conflict apply. In the event of interference between norms, international law calls for harmonizing the norms as much as possible by way of interpretation. On top of that, a conflict approach does not exactly benefit the drugs conventions, since it would affect the obligations it contains more than is strictly necessary. Moreover, it must be borne in mind that human rights are not the be-all and end-all, (reonly a means to an end. That is why one must continually evaluate how the values they intend to protect can best be implemented. Solving the interference between norms within the cannabis issue by simply basing one's position on the absolute validity and formal prevalence of human rights obligations will not do.

3.12.5. AXIOMS IN HARMONIZATION

When applying the harmonization approach, a few important axioms apply. The first basic rule is that the interpretation must take place from within current international law. They include at any rate the relevant positive obligations regarding the rights to health, life, the right not to be subjected to inhuman treatment and the right to a private life, all of which are relevant to the cannabis issue. In addition to this, in our opinion the first axiom implies that if there are clear data that obligations under the drugs conventions are less effective than is assumed, this must play a part in the interpretation of the drugs conventions pursuant to international law.

The second axiom means that to arrive at systemic integration through harmonizing interpretation, one must look for common objectives ('object and purpose') and values in the interfering norm systems. These objectives and values can be found in the drug control system on three levels. Extensive commonality with the human rights can be seen on the first level: both the subsystem of the human rights and that of the drug control system seek to promote the well-being of people and public health. On the second level, there is a less perfect commonality, but it is by no means absent. For example, both subsystems require discouragement of drug and/or cannabis use and fighting serious drug and/or cannabis related crime (by definition, these concern illicit acts taking place outside any regulatory framework). On the third level, the subsystems are diametrically opposed: both a fundamental assumption of this purpose level (the risks of recreational drugs for public health are best combated by a prohibitive and repressive approach) and the core of this purpose level (complete eradication of recreational drugs), is completely at odds with regulated permission of cannabis cultivation and trade because of positive human rights obligations. So there is a great deal of commonality on the first level, while there are important departure points for harmonizing interpretation on the second level. They need to be used to help bridge the strong interference on the third level.

The third axiom is very important: an interpretation of the interfering norms where both systems retain optimal effect is preferred. This is particularly important because the harmonization cannot be perfect. This is because first of all full effect must be given to human rights obligations. The harmonization will therefore have to take place through reinterpretation of the drugs conventions, and some compromises will have to be made in the application of the drugs conventions. This will lead to a situation where certain obligations in the drugs conventions will see a reduction in their scope, while their applicability also becomes relative rather than absolute. Secondly, the harmonization will be less than optimal, because the human rights obligations and the obligations under the drugs conventions belong to different international subsystems. The different nature, design and content of these subsystems impedes further harmonization. This is why it is important to see how much justice can be done to the obligations under the drugs conventions in addition to and under regulated permission of cannabis cultivation and trade.

3.12.6. OBLIGATIONS UNDER DRUGS CONVENTIONS THAT CAN AND MUST BE MAINTAINED

It is possible and therefore necessary to keep the drug control system fully operational with respect to a number of crucial points. First, a state's decision to permit cannabis cultivation and trade for the recreational user market under regulation must not have any effects on other countries that prove to be more harmful – indeed, they must preferably prove to be more beneficial – than a prohibitive policy that is fully compliant with the drugs conventions. This requires a closed system and/or chain for cultivation, trade and perhaps even use of cannabis for recreational purposes, thus a system without leaks to national or foreign illegal markets. Furthermore, any cannabis cultivation and trade that is not part of the regulatory framework will have to be deemed illicit and must therefore be combated pursuant to the drug control system (by criminalization, prosecution, administrative prohibitions and seizure). Thirdly, recreational cannabis use – pursuant to Article 38 of the Single Convention and also pursuant to the right to health – will have to be discouraged. Finally, the regulatory framework will need to comprise, among other things, a licensing system (for cultivation, production, distribution and trade of cannabis), as well as an effective system of supervision and inspection of persons and organizations which are involved in the cultivation, distribution and trade, among other things. The system of estimates may well play a part in this.

3.12.7. HARMONIZING INTERPRETATION OF DRUGS CONVENTIONS WITH A VIEW TO REGULATED PERMISSION

Following the example of the UN General Assembly, the drug problem according to the INCB requires 'comprehensive, integrated and balanced approaches' and 'the health and welfare of mankind [must be] at the core of drug policies'. To some extent, this position suggests a harmonizing approach in which human rights obligations can be given priority. With these considerations, the INCB also gives the object and purpose of the drugs conventions pride of place on the first level mentioned above.

In doing so, the INCB provides legitimacy to a harmonizing interpretation in which public health and the well-being of people serve as a primary departure point for a solution of the interference between the subsystems of human rights and drug control. As we observed above, other departure points can be found on the second level in terms of objectives and values: discouragement of drug and/or cannabis use and combating serious drugs and/or cannabis related crime tie in with both subsystems.

Furthermore, there are various departure points in the drugs conventions to interpret the drug control system primarily from the angle of transnational and international interests and objectives. The consequence of that is that the obligations that states have with regard to their own territory lose some significance. They can then be more easily interpreted and applied in such a manner that the regulated permission of cannabis cultivation and trade within the own territory of a state party becomes possible. This is not allowed to lead to reduced protection for other states, and at the same time that regulation will have to protect public health and the well-being of people in their own territory better than a prohibitive approach.

Currently, the drug control system with the so-called human rights clause in Article 14(2) of the Single Convention and various constitutional clauses in both the Single Convention and the Illicit Traffic Convention offer concrete possibilities to give full effect to positive human rights obligations in the drugs conventions. However, a certain reinterpretation of these clauses will be necessary for that. For example, it will be necessary – and incidentally also possible and desirable to achieve harmonization – to interpret the terms 'constitution' and 'constitutional' no longer strictly nationally, but to include European and international constitutional law as well.

Additionally, there are all sorts of provisions in the drugs conventions concerning 'illegal' or 'illicit' acts or 'illicit traffic'. These terms can be interpreted in such a way that they include acts that have not been legalized and therefore take place outside the regulatory framework. The opposite applies where the convention talks about 'legal', such as legal authority for possession of drugs in Article 33 of the Single Convention. It must then be assumed – also in view of the axiom of maximum retention of norms – that the acts can only be qualified as non-illegal or legal if the legalization takes place in the framework of implementing human rights obligations.

With the foregoing, it is also possible to arrive at a solution with regard the obligation in the drugs conventions to limit the circulation of narcotic drugs to 'exclusively' drugs that serve 'medical and scientific purposes'. Of all the various options, recognition of an unwritten clause on 'interests of public health and welfare' deserves to be preferred in our opinion. To the extent that this clause is applicable, states do not need to prohibit narcotic substances. That option has various advantages. It fits in with the first level of object and purpose of the drugs conventions. Furthermore, it leaves the content and effect of the drugs conventions intact as much as possible. The option also makes it possible to impose specific further conditions on the applicability of the clause. And the burden of proof that regulation on balance benefits public health and/or public well-being remains with the state in that case. Nevertheless, the actual effectiveness and ineffectiveness of the drug control system can have a stronger bearing on the interpretation and application of the provisions in the drugs conventions. In view of these arguments and in view of the necessity to give full effect to positive human rights obligations, we conclude that this harmonizing approach must be chosen, even though it does not achieve perfect harmonization.

3.12.8. CONCLUSION: ONCE MORE, THE HYPOTHESIS

With interference between positive human rights obligations and obligations arising from the drug control system, the former have priority. This means that if regulated permission of cannabis cultivation and trade is based on positive obligations, the drugs conventions system will need to be interpreted and applied according to international law in such a way that a state can proceed to introduce that regulation. This conclusion is based on an important hypothesis. The hypothesis is that regulated permission will achieve better protection – of individual health and public health and against crime – required by positive obligations than a prohibitive drugs policy in accordance with the drugs conventions. As we saw in Chapter 2, the state is responsible for furnishing evidence to substantiate the hypothesis, should it decide in favour of regulation. The next chapter is an analysis of this responsibility on the part of the state.

CHAPTER 4
SYNTHESIS AND CONCLUSIONS

4.1. INTRODUCTION

Regulated permission of cannabis cultivation and trade for recreational use in the interest of individual and public health, security and crime control can be based on positive human rights obligations that arise from international human rights conventions. Under international law, states must give priority to those positive obligations over and above any obligations under the UN drugs conventions if they interfere with each other. If the above-mentioned basis is there, states have the possibility under international law to regulate cannabis despite their obligations under the UN drugs conventions.

This is the gist of the answers to the two main questions in this book, which have been explored at length in the preceding chapters. Together, they provide a qualified – in other words: subject to conditions – positive answer to the cannabis issue. We will therefore not summarize the nuances and corresponding analyses that apply to these conclusions again; please refer to sections 2.5 and 3.12. Instead, we will discuss the steps, assumptions and conditions that are relevant if a state were to decide, on the basis of the incumbent positive human rights obligations, to permit cannabis cultivation and trade for the recreational user market under regulation.

4.2. RELEVANT ARGUMENTS IN FAVOUR OF REGULATED PERMISSION

All four human rights discussed – to wit, the rights regarding health, life, inhuman treatment and privacy – give rise to positive obligations that can support regulated permission of cannabis cultivation and trade for the purpose of recreational cannabis use. This essentially concerns positive obligations incumbent on the state to protect individuals from the harmful effects – on life, health, physical and psychological integrity and privacy – of unregulated cannabis cultivation and trade. However, not all arguments with regard to individual and public health, safety and fighting crime that are presented to support permission under regulation are relevant for these positive obligations.[1]

4.2.1. ARGUMENTS THAT ARE DIRECTLY RELEVANT FROM THE PERSPECTIVE OF POSITIVE OBLIGATIONS

First of all, the arguments involved in this research to support regulation that do have a basis in one or more of those positive human rights obligations. They concern the arguments implying that regulated permission is desirable, because such regulation would serve the following interests better:[2] safeguarding the quality of cannabis; monitoring the cannabis chain; reducing peripheral crime (murder, manslaughter, causing death by negligence, abuse and assault and threats); protection of health, life and the physical and mental integrity of local residents (e.g. against fire or seriously harmful infections, such as legionella contamination, that result from illegal and unsafe installations for illicit cannabis plantations); protection of health of juveniles; reducing substantial nuisance and damage that directly affects the enjoyment of people's private lives (due to, for example, stench, noise, flooding, fire and seriously harmful infections) and the separation of the soft drugs market and the hard drugs market (which would divide the simultaneous availability of and access to soft drugs and hard drugs).

This list is not exhaustive. These arguments – presented in political and academic discourses in various countries – form the backbone of our first book, *International Law and Cannabis I*.[3] For that reason, these have been at the heart of this book as well. That does not alter the fact that, particularly in foreign and international literature, many other arguments in favour of regulation can be found. Some of these are also relevant from the perspective of positive human rights obligations. This seems to be the case for arguments that, for example, the prohibition and repression of cannabis is primarily detrimental to minorities and/or the social underclass and leads to a good deal of judicial documentation and detention with considerable consequences for those involved, their family and society.[4] To prevent such consequences of a prohibitive policy, the state would have to take all manner of positive measures, for example measures on a social level, regarding the education of law-enforcers and regarding the drugs and/or cannabis policy.

---

1 See the overviews of arguments in sections 2.3.1 and 2.4.1.

2 For more information, see the overview in section 2.5.

3 Piet Hein P.H.M.C. van Kempen & Masha I. Fedorova, *International Law and Cannabis I*, Cambridge: Intersentia, 2019.

4 See for example Steve Rolles et al., *The Alternative World Drug Report. Counting the Costs of the War on Drugs*, United Kingdom: Count the Costs, 2012 and 2016 (2nd edition).

4.2.2. ARGUMENTS THAT ARE NOT DIRECTLY RELEVANT FROM THE PERSPECTIVE OF POSITIVE OBLIGATIONS

Besides, there are various other arguments in favour of – and as it happens, also against – regulated permission that are not directly relevant for the positive obligations arising from the four human rights we have discussed. Since such arguments are not supported by human rights and/or positive obligations, in principle these cannot enable member states to wriggle out of their obligations under the drugs conventions. Arguments that belong to this category and are reviewed in this book are that with regulated permission of cannabis: there will be a fall in organized crime as such; cannabis export will decrease; the corruption of the upper world will be countered.

The fact that strictly speaking, these and other arguments are not relevant with regard to the interference between human rights obligations and obligations under the drugs conventions does not mean though that they are also without meaning once there is room for regulated permission under international law. For example, it is interesting that the argument about corrupting the upper world ties in with the preamble to the Illicit Traffic Convention. It shows that it is an objective of this Convention to stop 'the steadily increasing inroads into various social groups' made by illicit traffic. Such arguments may very well play a part in deciding how the regulation of cannabis cultivation and trade should be shaped and in the considerations of a state in this respect.

4.3. SUBSTANTIATION FOR THE CLAIM THAT REGULATED PERMISSION IS MORE EFFECTIVE

The conclusion that regulated permission of cannabis cultivation and trade for recreational use can be based on positive human rights obligations does not mean that such regulation is automatically permissible. After all, it is important that the conclusions in previous chapters are based on a hypothesis that has been used throughout this book. That hypothesis is that regulated permission of cannabis cultivation and trade would better fulfil the relevant positive human rights obligations (derived from the rights to health, life, physical and mental integrity and privacy) than an approach in which the cultivation and trade of cannabis is prohibited and combated. The hypothesis is therefore also that the validity of the arguments discussed in favour of regulation suffices to ensure the applicability of the positive obligations. This legal research is not about determining whether these arguments are actually valid. However, a state that wishes to proceed with regulated permission, will have to make a case that these arguments are valid. Otherwise, it would not be possible to base such regulation on positive human rights obligations and the state would be obliged to fully honour its obligations under the drugs conventions. In respect of the substantiation required, the following is of paramount importance.

4.3.1. REQUIREMENT OF GREATER EFFECTIVITY

Positive human rights obligations will only justify regulated permission of cannabis cultivation and trade at the expense of the drugs conventions if that permission leads to a more effective human rights protection than a cannabis policy in line with the drugs conventions. If that protection under regulated permission is only equal to the protection provided by a prohibitive cannabis policy, it makes no difference which policy is implemented from the point of view of the positive obligation to protect health. In that case, that positive obligation will no longer oppose the obligations arising from the drugs conventions. There is no longer any interference between obligations in that case. Both the positive human rights obligations and the obligations under the drugs conventions can then be fully met. If a prohibitive drugs policy provided an even more effective positive protection of human rights, it goes without saying that there is no longer any reason to pit positive human rights obligations against the drugs conventions.

Whether regulated permission leads to a more effective protection of human rights than a prohibitive approach is determined first and foremost by the question to what extent positive human rights obligations are fulfilled by it. However, we take the view that this does not mean that negative human rights obligations are irrelevant here.[5] After all, it is obvious that an approach of regulated permission leads to many fewer infringements of human rights than is the case with a prohibitive and repressive policy. Moreover, the latter policy in principle implies more frequent criminal proceedings against individuals. This is also problematic in relation to the principle of subsidiarity (in the sense of necessity) that follows from the human rights conventions. After all, that principle entails that infringements of human rights can only be tolerated if a less onerous means with which the same objective can be achieved is not available. That means that if a policy of regulated permission and prohibitive policy led to the same level of fulfilment of positive human rights obligations, the first policy is more attractive from the human rights perspective. This is because it would better meet the negative obligation to respect human rights. That makes the policy of regulated permission more effective in the area of human rights protection.

5 See section 2.4.12.ii. For the concepts of negative and positive obligations, see sections 1.3 and 2.2.

Meanwhile, if we are looking at the question which approach – regulated permission or prohibition and fighting cannabis cultivation and trade – results in more effective human rights protection, it will not do to take only the advantages of regulated permission into account. One will also have to consider the disadvantages, if any, of reduced repression and whether those disadvantages can be avoided. For example, will regulated permission lead to an increase or decrease in cannabis use? What are the consequences of this vis-à-vis the use of other drugs and addictive stimulants? Can any harmful consequences be prevented? In this context, it will also be relevant to what extent the use of cannabis is fraught with risks and what the actual scope and seriousness of any risk is.[6]

4.3.2. REQUIREMENT OF PLAUSIBILITY

The crucial question therefore is in what way and to what degree of certainty a state must substantiate that regulated permission of cannabis results de facto in a more effective protection of human rights than a prohibitive and repressive approach. At any rate, this will not have to be proven absolutely and definitively in a scientific way. Such a requirement would undermine the workings of positive human rights. If the obligation only applied subject to availability of such proof, there would be no incentive to look for more innovative solutions with a view to fulfilling the human rights obligations in the best possible way. The fact that states are required to do exactly that is illustrated most clearly by the general obligation, which is relevant to the right to health, to achieve progressively 'the full realization' of the convention rights.[7] That obligation would be considerably weakened if states were not obliged to take steps to this end that are expected – but not guaranteed – to be effective.

The positive obligations with regard to the right to health provide more clarity about the requirements for substantiation.[8] Insofar as regulated permission of cannabis cultivation and trade takes place to realize this right, the state will have to support this with a strategy and plan of action. It would appear that epidemiological data must play a part in this and that holds true at any rate for 'up-to-date statistics or information on trends in the consumption' of cannabis. To this end, methods must be used such as indicators and criteria related to the right to health, by which progress can be closely monitored. In any case, a political belief that regulation is desirable will surely fail to make the grade for substantiation.

---

6 See section 3.10.1.i.

7 See section 2.3.7.iii.

8 See sections 2.3.7.viii, 2.3.7.x, 2.3.10.i, 2.3.10.ii and 2.3.12.iii.

It boils down to the fact that a package of policies and measures regarding cannabis cultivation and trade based on arguments of individual and public health will need to be backed up by relevant available scientific and other data, arguments and considerations. That substantiation must justify the expectation that regulated permission will lead to better protection of individual and public health. In a nutshell: the state will have to make it plausible that regulation realizes the right to health more effectively than a prohibitive cannabis policy and that the arguments used to underpin the decision are therefore actually valid. In the absence of directly relevant figures about the regulation policy, the state may in first instance rely on genuine analyses, arguments and considerations that are convincing and that are backed up as far as possible with indirect relevant figures and scientific research.

The case law on positive obligations about the right to life, the right not to be subjected to inhuman treatment and the right to a private life does not show clearly in what way and to what degree of certainty states will need to demonstrate the effectiveness of measures. The Human Rights Committee and the ECtHR do not impose specific requirements in this respect, as far as we know. It goes without saying that, at any rate, states are required to implement conventions in good faith.[9] This means that they will have to be able to argue truthfully and convincingly that they are fulfilling their positive obligations (in good faith with respect to human rights conventions) and that therefore they are not able to fulfil the obligations under the drugs conventions in each and every aspect (in good faith with respect to the drugs conventions). Thus, in our opinion, states – in accordance with the principles outlined above – will at least have to make a convincing case that the measures of regulation taken lead to a more effective protection of life, the physical and psychological integrity of their subjects and the right to a private life than a prohibitive policy in accordance with the drugs conventions.

As the policy of regulated permission remains in force for ever longer periods of time, the volume of data about its effects increases. These can then be compared with data about the previous policy. In addition to this, academic research into the consequences of the policy may be carried out. As time goes by, the state will therefore have to submit genuine data that will show whether or not the change in policy on balance led to an improved protection of the rights regarding health, life, inhuman treatment and/or privacy. Therefore, the requirements imposed on the substantiation of the efficacy of regulated permission may well be tightened in the course of time. A convincing argument will therefore have to be augmented with hard data and robust research results. Otherwise, it seems difficult to us to keep relying on positive human rights

9 See Article 26 of the Vienna Convention on the Law of Treaties.

obligations so as to justify non-compliance with obligations under the drugs conventions that states voluntarily entered into.

4.3.3. PILOTS

Another question is whether a state that intends to permit cannabis cultivation and trade subject to regulation because of its positive human rights obligations should first collect data on the effects of such regulation through pilot studies rather than introduce nation-wide regulation without any further ado. For example, this would involve projects where cannabis cultivation and trade is permitted under regulation for a certain period of time for a specific municipality or region or between certain producers, dealers and buyers. The idea would be to analyse and monitor the effects of the project carefully (such as a study to ascertain whether the objectives have been met, a process study and impact study).

There are various ways of looking at the legal necessity of such pilots. From the perspective of the drugs conventions, the utmost caution is called for in permitting recreational cannabis under regulation. In that sense, pilots appear to offer the opportunity to review whether regulated permission is desirable and effective with every step of the way. However, the question is whether this is really possible.

Several of the arguments depend in principle on national implementation. This is the case, for example, for monitoring the chain for cannabis for recreational use and the separation of the soft drugs and the hard drugs markets. Pilots may not be entirely suitable for demonstrating to what extent such arguments are valid. To require that pilots are used first to see what the effects are could lead to the situation where effective national implementation is precluded, because due to their methodological limitations, pilots cannot lead to the conclusion that such implementation will be effective. That may eventually be detrimental from the perspective of positive human rights obligations, as the conclusions drawn about the effectiveness of regulation are not adequate.

The same applies with regard to corollary arguments, such as undermining organized crime and the argument of preventing the corruption of the upper world. It is the more detailed implementation of the regulation policy where they can play a role. We are of the opinion, also taking into account the so-called primarity principle,[10] that it is up to the state to make a considered and substantiated decision on whether pilots can be meaningful and whether their deployment is desirable all in all.

---

10 See sections 2.3.7.ix and 2.4.7.viii.

4.4. SOCIETAL SUPPORT AND NATIONAL DEMOCRATIC DECISION-MAKING

If there are intrinsically valid arguments in favour of regulation of cannabis cultivation and trade that are supported by positive human rights obligations, that too does not yet mean that the state is required to permit that trade and cultivation under regulation. The obligation to do that will only manifest itself for real if the state and/or the national government, on the basis of public support and democratic decision-making, genuinely and convincingly comes to the conclusion that regulated permission results in a more effective implementation of positive human rights obligations than a prohibitive cannabis policy in accordance with the drugs conventions.

That is the case partly because states and their societies have their own idiosyncrasies, peculiarities and constellations, so that an approach that is effective in one state does not necessarily work in another state. It is partly for this reason that every state – because of the so-called principle of primarity – in order to fulfil its treaty obligations is first and foremost responsible for determining which measures are most adequate, in the light of the specific circumstances of the relevant state and for subsequently taking those measures.[11] It is exactly with a view to being able to take that responsibility fully given the circumstances that the state has a so-called margin of appreciation at its disposal.[12] If a state therefore takes a well-reasoned and substantiated position, in good faith, that positive human rights protection is most adequately realized through regulated permission, it must be assumed that this is indeed the case, unless it can be demonstrated that there is insufficient ground for this position.

Additionally, in the context of positive obligations regarding the right to health, the importance of participation of the public in the decision-making process concerning health-related issues is emphasized.[13] This also concerns a guarantee for the quality and effectiveness of policy. If the state takes measures that implement positive human rights obligations and these are legitimized through democratic decision-making, public support and citizen participation, these are important indications that the measures are well suited to the circumstances in the relevant state. Therefore, with such legitimization of regulated permission of cannabis, the assumption will have to be that this most adequately realizes the positive obligations to protect health, unless again this assumption can be shown to be insufficiently substantiated.

Even when regulated permission of cannabis cultivation and trade for recreational use in itself can qualify as a suitable and to that extent required

---

11 Ibid.

12 See sections 2.3.7.x and 2.4.7.ix.

13 See section 2.3.9.

implementation of the right to health, this does not yet mean that this is true for all countries. There may be all sorts of circumstances that explain why regulated permission may work well in one country while it is hard to achieve in another country. If, for example, there is democratic and social aversion to taking certain measures in a country, this, in principle, is an indication that those measures are less adequate for that state. Without public support, a measure will in many instances also prove to be less effective than in a case where such support does exist.

This means that one cannot simply assume that positive obligations for human rights protection are most adequately ensured by permitting cannabis cultivation and trade under regulation, if the state itself happens to be in favour of a cannabis policy in accordance with the drugs conventions.

4.5. POSITION OF DECENTRALISED AUTHORITIES ON REGULATED PERMISSION

In view of the observation above, the question arises whether decentralised authorities or individuals and private organizations can resort to treaty law to force the national government (administration and legislator) to implement regulated permission if the national government refuses to do so. We think that an affirmative answer to this question is not easy to defend.

First of all, it is the state and/or the national government (and not, for example, local authorities) that are primarily responsible for deciding for which purpose positive obligations must be fulfilled, and with which means. If the state is against regulation under permission, in principle one must assume that such permission is a less effective solution for the country in view of the primarity principle. It is then fairly easy for the state to take the view that there is no interference between positive human rights obligations and obligations under the drugs conventions.

This becomes even more pertinent if there is no democratic majority or public support for regulated permission in the state that is opposed to regulation. But even if that majority and that public support do exist, that state will, in principle, be able to rely on its margin of appreciation to avoid having to introduce such regulation. This applies, in particular, to states that make a sufficiently strong case for an alternative approach. The fact that the drugs conventions still command considerable international support certainly makes life easier for that state. After all, from a legal point of view (although this does not automatically mean from an empirical point of view as well), the choice of the state is supported by the conventions.

Only if there are hard, fairly incontestable data that regulated permission actually leads to significantly more effective human rights protection than a prohibitive policy will it be difficult for the state to persist in pursuing that prohibitive policy. After all, in that scenario the state will have to explain – in good faith – why it settles for a fundamentally less effective positive protection of the rights regarding health, life, inhuman treatment and privacy than that which can be realized within that state.

That situation, however, appears to be rather hypothetical for the time being. If there is no regulated permission in a country as yet, there will not be any hard data about the positive effects that regulated permission will have in that country either. It remains to be seen whether the experiences of other states – that usually have different circumstances and conditions – can be a decisive factor in this respect.

Moreover, if the effectivity of regulation does not markedly outstrip that of prohibition according to the hard data, it is more acceptable if the national government continues its prohibitive policy of choice. In the final analysis, choices about measures to be taken not only depend on their effectiveness, but other factors may also play a part, such as costs, moral judgements, the operational possibilities in the relevant state to enforce a regulatory framework and the state's relation with other states.

Finally, if the national government is actually in favour of regulated permission, it will also be important for the required level of social support as to how local authorities that are involved in or have experience with drug policies feel about this. If these local authorities favour regulated permission on account of the protection of individual and public health, life, the physical and psychological integrity of people as well as their privacy, the national government can more easily adopt the position that such regulation is suitable in their own country because of the positive human rights obligations.

4.6. NO HARM ABROAD: A CLOSED SYSTEM

When a state proceeds with regulated permission of cannabis cultivation and trade for recreational use, it should make sure to monitor the regulation to such a degree that other states are not confronted with negative consequences. In our opinion, it is important in this respect how regulation affects the export from the regulating state to other countries. The protection offered to other countries should not be less – and preferably be even more effective – than that offered under the prohibitive approach that fully accords with the drugs conventions. Therefore, a closed national system and/or chain for cultivation, trade and possibly also use of cannabis will have to be provided, i.e., closed in the sense that cannabis cannot leak away to illegal markets. Moreover, a closed national system does not have to exclude the possibility of legal export to and import from other jurisdictions that do allow this. Such a closed system is necessary because of the following.

The practical foundation for the creation of the drugs conventions appears to be primarily the will of the parties to the convention to combat the transnational effects of illicit drug trafficking.[14] An important prerequisite for this is effective national drugs monitoring. Exactly because positive human rights obligations do not constitute a barrier for preventing cross-border harmful effects, these conventions must be fully implemented in this respect. That implies an adequate strategy for fighting cultivation, trade and export of illegal cannabis (i.e., cannabis outside the regulatory framework) and cooperation with other states parties (including international legal assistance) in accordance with the drugs conventions. After all, there is no interference between norms in this respect. Therefore, these obligations will have to be fulfilled completely. This is necessitated, among other things, by the obligation to implement conventions in good faith (*pacta sunt servanda*),[15] the axiom of maximum retention of norms[16] and the right to health,[17] while at the same time it is called for because of state responsibility under international law.[18]

Regulated permission of cannabis will therefore not be allowed to prove more harmful to other countries than a prohibitive policy in accordance with the drugs conventions. It would be even better if the protection of other countries would actually improve as a consequence. In that case, the state would achieve better results in realizing the practical foundation and object and purpose of the drugs conventions, to combat the transnational effects of illicit drug trafficking. That will make the introduction of a national closed regulatory system easier to defend, also from the perspective of the drugs conventions.

4.7. REQUIREMENT OF A POLICY THAT DISCOURAGES CANNABIS USE

The human rights conventions we have discussed (the ICESCR, ESC, ICCPR and the ECHR) do not require states to ban alcohol, tobacco, recreational drugs or other harmful stimulants, at any rate not with respect to adults. Nor does the right to health require anything like that.[19] A 'zero tolerance' drug policy is even problematic from the point of view of human rights and is rejected by the Human Rights Committee and the Special Rapporteur on the right to health.

---

[14] See section 3.10.2.iii.

[15] See Article 26 of the Vienna Convention on the Law of Treaties.

[16] See section 3.10.1.iii.

[17] See sections 2.3.7.xi, 2.3.12.iii, 2.4.7.x and 2.4.12.iii.

[18] See section 3.11.

[19] For human rights related requirements for drug policy see sections 2.3.10, 2.3.11, 2.3.12.iii and 2.4.11.

With regard to human rights, what matters is that states pursue that policy which best realizes the highest attainable standard of health and other human rights interests.

In principle, the human rights conventions leave room for a moderately prohibitive approach as well as legalization, decriminalization and/or policy-based tolerance, depending on which approach produces the best results. When a state proceeds with regulated permission of cannabis cultivation and trade for recreational use, it should create an adequate policy to ensure discouragement and limitation of recreational use of cannabis and to raise public awareness of the risks associated with that use. Without this, a policy of regulated permission would soon run the risk of being less effective than a prohibitive drug policy and in that case the policy would not implement positive obligations in the most effective manner. That itself is problematic from the point of view of positive human rights obligations, which after all were used to justify regulated permission.

That is particularly the case in relation to the right to health. If addictive stimulants are permitted, the positive obligations ensuing from this right dictate that states must provide policies that focus heavily on preventing the consumption of these stimulants. This is true for cannabis use among adults and even more so with regard to minors and children. The obligation to discourage use covers a huge number of subsidiary obligations. The most important of these are the obligation to provide for effective restrictions on and control of production, distribution and trade of or in cannabis; the obligation to inform the public effectively about and making them aware of the risks associated with cannabis; the obligation to combat illegal cannabis trade with due regard for human rights; the obligation to levy high taxes (excise duties) on cannabis; the obligation to ban advertising and promoting cannabis; the obligation to ban smoking cannabis in public indoor spaces. It is highly desirable to include health warnings on packs/units of cannabis and to impose legal limits on the THC content of cannabis for example. Also in view of the obligation of states to strive for the highest attainable standard of health, in implementing all these sub-obligations the state will have to establish which strategy is ultimately the most effective one. Obligations do not need to and must not be implemented in such a way that they have the opposite effect.

The regulation of cannabis cultivation and trade for the recreational user market must therefore be informed by the interests of protecting health. The WHO Framework Convention on Tobacco Control (2003) could be the model for establishing an adequate policy of discouragement according to the UN Special Rapporteur on the right to health.[20] Results from scientific research may

[20] See section 2.3.11.

also play an important part in this.[21] At any rate, it goes without saying that the obligations under Article 38 of the Single Convention must be heeded in full.[22] This means that the drug and/or cannabis policy will need to contain measures aimed at the early identification, treatment, education, after-care, rehabilitation and social reintegration of problem drug users, on the training of personnel working in these areas, and to promote an understanding among the relevant professions and the public of the problems of drugs with a view to preventing these problems.

4.8. OTHER DEPARTURE POINTS FOR REGULATION

Even if cannabis cultivation and trade could be permitted under regulation on account of positive human rights obligations, there are still various obligations in the drugs conventions that may be – and therefore must be – taken into consideration. In fact, the positive human rights themselves impose requirements on any regulatory framework and policy. One important requirement featuring in both human rights and the drugs conventions was already mentioned above: serious discouragement of cannabis use. However, there are other requirements too.

First of all,[23] the regulatory framework must comprise a licensing system, which will need to cover cultivators, producers, distributors, dealers (see also section 4.10.1 below) and also points-of-sale for cannabis for the recreational user market. Then there is the requirement that persons who obtain licences and persons who are employed by them are not allowed to have a criminal record with regard to drugs regulations. Furthermore, there must also be an effective system of supervision and inspection regarding persons and institutions involved with that cultivation, distribution and trade. This regulatory framework could well be designed along the lines of the UN narcotic drugs conventions' system of estimates.[24]

Secondly, cannabis cultivation and trade that do not take place within the regulatory framework must needs be qualified as illegal. This will have

---

21 See, for example, the many recommendations in Joanne Csete et al., 'Public health and international drug policy', *The Lancet* 2016, vol. 387, pp. 1427–1480; American Public Health Association, 'Regulating Commercially Legalized Marijuana as a Public Health Priority', APHA, 2015, on: www.apha.org. See also, for a much wider perspective than merely that of health, Jonathan P. Caulkins, Angela Hawken, Beau Kilmer & Mark A.R. Kleiman, *Marijuana Legalization. What Everyone Needs to Know*, Oxford: Oxford University Press, 2016.

22 See section 3.10.3.iii.

23 For more information, see section 3.10.3.iv.

24 See Articles 12–12bis Single Convention.

to be combated in accordance with the drug control system (for example by criminalization, prosecution, administrative prohibitions and seizure). Incidentally, that is also important in view of the interests of other countries, as we discussed before.

Thirdly, the fight against illegal cannabis cultivation and trade (in other words, cannabis outside the regulatory framework) must of course conform to the pertinent human rights and fundamental freedoms.[25]

Fourthly, regulated permission of cannabis may not lead to discrimination of certain individuals or groups in the state. Nor may there be a disproportionate impact on certain vulnerable groups. Insofar as regulated permission would increase the risks of cannabis for certain groups, sufficient compensatory protective measures will have to be taken.[26] This requirement ties in with the necessity of discouraging cannabis use that was discussed earlier.

4.9. LEGALIZATION, DECRIMINALIZATION OR POLICY-BASED TOLERANCE

Human rights conventions and international case law about them do not indicate how drug and/or cannabis policy must be fleshed out. Nor do they state explicitly whether regulated permission of cannabis cultivation and trade for the recreational user market must take place via regulated legalization, decriminalization or policy-based tolerance. In a general sense, the human rights conventions require states to take those measures that best implement and protect those human rights. Therefore, it remains to be seen whether the best results are to be expected from legalization, decriminalization or policy-based tolerance. This also necessitates considerations that the state will have to take into account within its margin of appreciation. Yet, this does not alter the fact that legalization from the point of view of human rights and – curiously enough – the drugs conventions as well seems to offer the most suitable solution if a state decides to proceed with regulated permission.

It follows from the foregoing that far-reaching regulation is necessary to achieve optimum implementation of the positive human rights obligations arising from the rights regarding health, life, inhuman treatment and privacy through regulated permission of cannabis cultivation and trade. Relevant areas include a system of licences and supervision (for cultivators, producers, distributors, dealers and points of sale), quality control with regard to the manufacture of cannabis products and the composition of these products (many requirements),

---

25 See also section 1.4.i.

26 See section 2.3.12.iii.

the manner in which products may be sold (for example regarding quantities, labelling, warnings, restrictions on advertising), a policy to discourage cannabis use (all manner of measures for this) and optimizing the separation between the soft drugs market and the hard drugs market (which also necessitates various measures).

Decriminalization of cannabis cultivation and trade as such is not suitable for achieving this regulation.[27] After all, decriminalization means that conduct which is prohibited under criminal law is removed from the criminal code and will no longer lead to criminal proceedings. However, this does not yet allow the conduct, since the product will still be prohibited under administrative law and may be combated in administrative proceedings (if that is not the case either, then we are dealing with legalization instead of decriminalization). Moreover, decriminalization as such does not constitute further regulation. Decriminalization of cannabis cultivation and trade would only be relevant for regulated permission thereof if a regulatory policy was also provided.

This leads us to the second form: policy-based tolerance. The question is whether a policy of tolerance (whether or not as a complement to decriminalization) will help provide the regulation that is necessary to justify regulated permission with an appeal to positive human rights obligations. From a legal perspective, it is not inconceivable per se to impose all sorts of quality requirements for a product and its production when that product as such is prohibited under criminal and/or administrative law. The question though is whether such a policy of tolerance can work effectively in practice. After all, that would mean that the government will actually have to define detailed quality requirements for prohibited products and production and subsequently will have to monitor whether those products and that production meet those requirements. In addition to this, the question is whether such a system could truly distance itself far enough from the criminal circuit in which cultivation and trade usually take place.

In a situation of regulated legalization of cannabis cultivation and trade, this would all be less problematic. In that case, there could be clear and hard separation between legal and illegal cultivation and trade. This may be attractive for the legal certainty of citizens and the government. Illegal cultivation may then be combated normally just like other crimes, whereas legal cultivation and trade can be subjected to detailed quality requirements, a licensing system and checks and may thus be maintained. A clear division between legal and illegal cultivation and trade may also be relevant in preventing the corruption of the upper world, because it will also be really clear to the citizens what is prohibited and what is permitted.

[27] Section 1.3 offers an explanation of the concept.

Finally, it is also germane to the subject that both the human rights conventions and the drugs conventions in certain respects aim to protect individual health and public health and to combat drug-related crime. To that end, as we have seen in the sections 4.7 and 4.8 above, both subsystems require various measures that would benefit from a clear systematic specification and implementation. Therefore, it is perfectly conceivable that both the protection of human rights and the interests vested in drugs conventions that function as best as possible, ultimately make the case for regulated legalization of cannabis cultivation and trade if a state decides to switch to regulated permission.

4.10. CANNABIS CULTIVATION AND TRADE: VIA THE STATE, COMPANIES OR CANNABIS SOCIAL CLUBS?

Where legal narcotic substances are concerned, the UN drugs conventions allow states the possibility to let commercial parties take care of production, distribution and trade. With respect to cannabis, though, the possibilities are more stringent, at least when interpreting the text of the conventions, although it is a different matter with a teleological interpretation as we will see below.

4.10.1. GOVERNMENTS AND/OR (NON) COMMERCIAL ACTIVITIES IN PRIVATE SECTOR

It follows from Article 28(1) in conjunction with Article 23(2) of the Single Convention that cannabis cultivation may be left to private cultivators.[28] Nevertheless, Article 28(1) in conjunction with Article 23(2)(c) and (d) of the Single Convention also stipulate that all cultivators of cannabis are required to sell their entire crop to a national government agency for cannabis in good time. That agency has a monopoly of import, export and wholesale trading. This monopoly will not have to be enforced in the case of medicinal opium and cannabis preparations.

In the light of the foregoing, the cultivation of cannabis for recreational use although not its distribution or wholesale trading could be left to private persons. Moreover, retail trading (and therefore the sale to consumers) could take place through private entities. The shortest chain allowed in which private persons are involved would have to be as follows: private entity (cannabis cultivation) → government entity (stocking and selling) → private entity (consumer sales).

28 United Nations, *Commentary on the Single Convention on Narcotic Drugs*, 1961, New York: 1973, pp. 281 (no. 1) 282 (no. 3) 283 (no. 1). See also Piet Hein P.H.M.C. van Kempen & Masha I. Fedorova, *International Law and Cannabis I*, Cambridge: Intersentia, 2019.

The rationale of the stricter system laid down in Article 28(1) in conjunction with Article 23(2) of the Single Convention is to ensure from an operational point of view that the circulation of cannabis for recreational use is entirely prevented and eradicated. In the official UN Commentary to the Single Convention, the period in which the drug is in the hands of individual cultivators is seen as the most critical period from the point of view of the drug control system. This is why stocks must be physically placed under government supervision in a short period of time.[29] These provisions thereby emphasize the importance of a national closed system and/or chain, without leaks to national or foreign illegal markets. The question is whether the government (in the form of a national government agency for cannabis) should automatically be included in that chain as well. It seems defensible to us that this is not necessary once a policy of regulated permission of cannabis cultivation and trade has been implemented on the grounds of positive human rights obligations.

In this respect, it is important to note that the strict system of the drugs conventions no longer applies with regard to cannabis under regulated permission. This significantly qualifies the practical use – which is the rationale of Article 28(1) in conjunction with Article 23(2) of the Single Convention – and therefore the importance of stocking and selling cannabis through a national government agency. In addition to this, it follows from Articles 29 and 30 for example that the production, distribution and trade in (other) narcotic substances (including substances considered to be far more serious than cannabis) is allowed to take place through entities other than state-owned companies.[30] This may involve private persons, companies and cooperatives The fact that it is not important as a matter of principle from the point of view of the drug control system whether entities are commercial in nature or not, also shows from the fact that this does not feature in criminal and administrative prohibitions, as well as the many other obligations to fight cannabis cultivation and trade under the drugs conventions.[31]

We think it can be argued that if regulated permission of recreational cannabis is possible on the grounds of positive human rights obligations, taking in stocks and wholesale trading may then also be left to entities that may or may not be commercial and private, provided there are sufficient guarantees that there is indeed a genuine closed system and/or chain. Of course, this still leaves the state room to place cultivation, wholesale trading, distribution and/or retail trading in the hands of a state-owned and state-run organization. In the final

29 United Nations, *Commentary on the Single Convention on Narcotic Drugs*, 1961, New York: 1973, pp. 283 (no. 1).

30 Ibid, p. 317–318 (nos. 3–5) 329 (no. 4).

31 See Piet Hein P.H.M.C. van Kempen & Masha I. Fedorova, *International Law and Cannabis I*, Cambridge: Intersentia, 2019, section 5.3.3.iii.

analysis, that choice is the state's prerogative. If the state, however, preferred an entirely private cannabis chain (in which private cultivators supply retail shops, for example), this appears to be possible provided that the chain is subject to a clearly defined regulatory framework.

4.10.2. CANNABIS SOCIAL CLUBS

If one assumes, in accordance with the foregoing, that private entities could take care of the entire cannabis chain, that also leaves room for allowing so-called Cannabis Social Clubs (CSCs). These are private, 'members only' clubs where individuals grow and consume cannabis together in a communal area ('shared consumption'), where each of the club members has a few cannabis plants of their own within the club.[32]

In answering the question whether regulated permission of cannabis cultivation and trade could actually take place in a system of CSCs, the main consideration is whether such a system is the best way to implement the positive human rights obligations that are relevant to the cannabis issue. Specifically, it is important whether it is possible to ensure the quality of cannabis and the production with CSC's at least as well as with any other regulatory system in respect of individual and public health, to guarantee that there is a closed system and to prevent and fight crime related to cannabis trade and cultivation.

To the extent that CSCs are less useful for realizing these objectives, positive human rights obligations will be less effective in justifying derogations from the obligations under the drugs conventions. In our view, it is not evident that CSCs would function sufficiently adequately in this respect, so this would have to be given careful consideration by a state planning to go down this avenue. Meanwhile, this is yet another illustration of the fact that in shaping and implementing the regulatory system, the first priority will need to be the most adequate implementation of the relevant positive human rights obligations. Those obligations after all form the justification for regulated permission.

4.11. CONCLUSION

This legal research shows that in spite of the Single Convention and the Illicit Traffic Convention, it is possible for states to regulate cannabis cultivation and trade for recreational use by legalization in accordance with current positive international law. To this end, the state should then, in good faith, on the basis

---

[32] See for more information ibid, section 4.4.2 and 5.3.3.ii.

of societal support and democratic legitimacy, demonstrate the plausibility that regulated permission would constitute a better protection of human rights than a prohibitive approach in accordance with the drugs conventions. These human rights first and foremost concern positive obligations deriving from the rights regarding health, life, inhuman treatment and privacy, to the extent that these obligations serve to ensure individual and public health, security and crime control. The regulation, however, will have to satisfy several requirements and must be accompanied by a policy that discourages cannabis use. If the state is able to satisfy these conditions, under current international law it can legitimately prioritize the human rights obligations over and above any conflicting obligations arising from the UN narcotic drugs conventions.

BIBLIOGRAPHY

INTERNATIONAL DOCUMENTS

UNITED NATIONS SECURITY COUNCIL

Security Council Resolution 1456 (2003), *UN Doc.* S/RES/1456, 20 January 2003.
Security Council Resolution 1483 (2003), *UN Doc.* S/RES/1483, 22 May 2003.
Security Council Resolution 2170 (2014), *UN Doc.* S/RES/2170, 15 August 2014.

UNITED NATIONS GENERAL ASSEMBLY

UN General Assembly Resolution 1248 (XIII), 'Question of race conflict in South Africa resulting from the policies of apartheid in the Government of the Union of South Africa', adopted 13th plenary meeting on 30 October 1958, *UN Doc.* A/3962.

Declaration on the Use of Scientific and Technological Progress in the Interests of Peace and for the Benefit of Mankind, *UN Doc.* A/RES/3384(XXX), 10 November 1975.

UN General Assembly Resolution 66/183, 'International cooperation against the world drug problem', adopted 66nd plenary meeting on 19 December 2011, *UN Doc.* A/RES/66/183, 3 April 2012.

UN General Assembly Resolution 67/193, 'International cooperation against the world drug problem', adopted 67th plenary meeting on 20 December 2012, *UN Doc.* A/RES/67/193, 23 April 2013.

UN General Assembly, Resolution 69/201, 'International cooperation against the world drug problem', adopted 69th plenary meeting on 18 December 2014, *UN Doc.* A/RES/69/201, 12 February 2015.

UNITED NATIONS SECRETARY-GENERAL

Report of the Secretary-General, Compilation of Guidelines on the Form and Content of reports to be submitted by State Parties to the International Human Rights Treaties, 3 June 2009, *UN Doc.* HRI/GEN/2/Rev.6.

UN Secretary-General, Ban Ki-Moon, 'Message on International Day Against Drug Abuse and Illicit Trafficking', *UN Doc.* UNIS/SGSM/645, 26 June 2015.

UNITED NATIONS HUMAN RIGHTS COUNCIL

Human Rights Council Resolution 6/29, 14 December 2007.
Human Rights Council Resolution 24/6, 20 September 2013.

UNITED NATIONS HUMAN RIGHTS COMMISSION

Commission on Human Rights resolution 2002/31, 22 April 2002.

COMMISSION ON NARCOTIC DRUGS

CND Resolution 56/16, 'Enhancing international cooperation to strengthen efforts in West Africa to counter illicit drug trafficking', *UN Doc.* E/CN.7/2013/14.
CND, 'Joint Ministerial Statement of the 2014 High-Level Review by the Commission on Narcotic Drugs of the Implementation by Member States of the Political Declaration and Plan of Action on International Cooperation towards an Integrated and Balanced Strategy to Counter the World Drug Problem', CND 57th session, Vienna, 13 and 14 March 2014.
CND Resolution 58/4, 'Promoting the implementation of the United Nations Guiding Principles on Alternative Development', *UN Doc.* E/CN.7/2015/15.

UNITED NATIONS HIGH COMMISSIONER FOR HUMAN RIGHTS

Office of the United Nations High Commissioner for Human Rights, *Economic, Social and Cultural Rights. Handbook for National Human Rights Institutions*, UN/OHCHR: New York/Geneva, 2005.
Report of the United Nations High Commissioner for Human Rights, *UN Doc.* E/2007/82, 25 June 2007.
——, Study on the impact of the world drug problem on the enjoyment of human rights, *UN Doc.* A/HRC/30/65, 4 September 2015.

UNITED NATIONS SPECIAL RAPPORTEURS

Report of the Special Rapporteur on the right of everyone to the enjoyment of the highest attainable standard of physical and mental health, Paul Hunt, Addendum (mission to Sweden), *UN Doc.* A/HRC/4/28/Add.2, 28 February 2007.
Report of the Special Rapporteur on the right of everyone to the enjoyment of the highest attainable standard of physical and mental health, Anand Grover, *UN Doc.* A/65/255, 6 August 2010.
Special Rapporteur on the right of everyone to the enjoyment of the highest attainable standard of physical and mental health, Anand Grover, Submission to the Committee against Torture regarding drug control laws, 19 October 2012.

Report of the Special Rapporteur on the right of everyone to the enjoyment of the highest attainable standard of physical and mental health, Anand Grover, on access to medicines, *UN Doc.* A/HRC/23/42, 1 May 2013.
Report of the Special Rapporteur on the right of everyone to the enjoyment of the highest attainable standard of physical and mental health, Anand Grover, *UN Doc.* A/HRC/26/31, 1 April 2014.
Report of the Special Rapporteur on the right of everyone to the enjoyment of the highest attainable standard of physical and mental health, Anand Grover, *UN Doc.* A/69/299, 11 August 2014.
Report of the Special Rapporteur on the right of everyone to the enjoyment of the highest attainable standard of physical and mental health, Dainius Pūras, *UN Doc.* A/HRC/29/33, 2 April 2015.
Open Letter by the Special Rapporteur on the right of everyone to the highest attainable standard of mental and physical health, Dainius Pūras, in the context of the preparations for the UN General Assembly Special Session on the Drug Problem (UNGASS), which will take place in New York in April 2016, 7 December 2015.
Progress report of the Special Rapporteurs on globalization and its impact on the full enjoyment of all human rights, J. Oloka-Onyango and Deepika Udagama, *UN Doc.* E/CN.4/Sub.2/2001/10, 2 August 2001.
Final report of the Special Rapporteurs on globalization and its impact on the full enjoyment of all human rights, J. Oloka-Onyango and Deepika Udagama, *UN Doc.* E/CN.4/Sub.2/2003/14, 25 June 2003.
Report of the Special Rapporteur in the field of cultural rights, Farida Shaheed, The right to enjoy the benefits of scientific progress and its applications, *UN Doc.* A/HRC/20/26, 14 May 2012.

UNITED NATIONS OFFICE ON DRUGS AND CRIME

UNODC, 'Drug control, crime prevention and criminal justice: A Human Rights perspective', Note by the Executive Director, *UN Doc.* E/CN.7/2010/CRP.6, E/CN.15/2010/CRP.1 3 March 2010.

INTERNATIONAL NARCOTICS CONTROL BOARD

INCB, *Report of the International Narcotics Control Board for 1996*, New York: United Nations, 1997.
——, *Report of the International Narcotics Control Board for 2007*, New York: United Nations, 2008.
——, *Report of the International Narcotics Control Board for 2008*, New York: United Nations, 2009.
——, *Report of the International Narcotics Control Board for 2010*, New York: United Nations, 2011.
——, *Report of the International Narcotics Control Board for 2012*, New York: United Nations, 2013.

——, *Report of the International Narcotics Control Board for 2013*, New York: United Nations, 2014.
——, *Report of the International Narcotics Control Board for 2014*, New York: United Nations, 2015.
——, *Availability of Internationally Controlled Drugs: Ensuring Adequate Access for Medical and Scientific Purposes*, New York: United Nations, 2016.
——, *Report of the International Narcotics Control Board for 2015*, New York: United Nations, 2016.
——, *Report of the International Narcotics Control Board for 2016*, New York: United Nations, 2017.
——, *Report of the International Narcotics Control Board for 2017*, New York: United Nations, 2018.

CONFERENCES UN HUMAN RIGHTS AND DRUGS CONVENTIONS

United Nations, 'Conference for the adoption of a Single Convention on Narcotic Drugs. New York - 24 January–25 March 1961, Official Records, Volume I', *UN Doc.* E/CONF. 34/24.
——, 'United Nations Conference to consider amendments to the Single Convention on Narcotic Drugs, 1961. Geneva - 6–24 March 1972, Official Records, Volume I', New York, 1974, *UN Doc.* E/CONF. 63/10.
——, 'Conference for the Adoption of a Convention against Illicit Traffic in Narcotic Drugs and Psychotropic Substances. Vienna, 25 November–20 December 1988, Official Records, Volume I', *UN Doc.* E/CONF. 82/16.
UN World Conference on Human Rights, Vienna, 14–25 June 1993, 'Vienna Declaration and Programme of Action', *UN Doc.* A/CONF.157/24, 12 July 1993.

OFFICIAL COMMENTARY ON UN COVENANTS AND CONVENTIONS

Annotations on the Text of the Draft International Covenants on Human Rights, *UN Doc.* A/2929, 1 July 1955.
United Nations, *Commentary on the Single Convention on Narcotic Drugs*, 1961, New York: 1973.
——, *Commentary on the United Nations Convention Against Illicit Traffic in Narcotic Drugs and Psychotropic Substances*, Vienna: 1988.

INTERNATIONAL LAW COMMISSION

ILC, Draft Articles on the Law of Treaties with commentaries 1966, *Yearbook of the International Law Commission* 1966, vol. II.

——, *Yearbook of the International Law Commission, 1971*, vol. II, part two (1973), *UN Doc.* A/CN.4/SERJV/1971/Add.l (Part 2).
International Law Commission, 'Draft articles on Responsibility of States for Internationally Wrongful Acts, with commentaries', *UN Doc.* A/56/10, 2001.
ILC, Report of the Study Group finalized by Martti Koskenniemi, 'Fragmentation of International Law: Difficulties arising from the Diversification and Expansion of International Law', 13 April 2006, *UN Doc.* A/CN.4/L/682, 13 April 2006, A/CN.4/L/682.
——, 'Report 58th Session. Chapter XII. Work of the Study Group on the Fragmentation of International Law: Difficulties arising from the Diversification and Expansion of International Law', 2006, *UN Doc.* A/61/10.
Report of the ILC on the Work of its 63rd session, General Assembly, Official Records, 66th Session, Supplement n° 10, Addendum 1, *UN Doc.* A/66/10/ Add.1. (2011).
UN, *Materials on the Responsibility of States for Internationally Wrongful Acts, United Nations Legislative Series, ST/LEG/SER.B/25*, New York: United Nations, 2012.

OTHERS

UN Sub-Commission for the Prevention of Discrimination and the Protection of Minorities, Resolution 1998/12 on 'Human rights as the primary objective of trade, investment, and financial policy', UN Doc. E/CN.4/Sub.2/RES/1998/12, 20 August 1998.
United Nations Environment Programme, *UNEP Compendium on Human Rights and the Environment. Selected international legal materials and cases*, UNEP 2014.
——, *Perspectives on the Development Dimensions of Drug Control Policy*, UNDP 2015.

COUNCIL OF THE EUROPEAN UNION

Council Decision 90/611/EEC of 22 October 1990 concerning the conclusion, on behalf of the European Economic Community, of the United Nations Convention against illicit traffic in narcotic drugs and psychotropic substances, *OJ* 1990 L 326/56.
Council Decision 64/732/EEC of 23 December 1963, *OJ* 1964, 217, p. 3685.

COUNCIL OF EUROPE

Council of Europe Parliamentary Assembly, Resolution 1576 (2007) For a European convention on promoting public health policy in drug control, 3 October 2007.
Explanations to the Charter of Fundamental Rights, *OJ* 303/17, 14 December 2007.
Council of Europe, *Digest of the Case Law of the European Committee of Social Rights*, 1 September 2008.
Committee on Social Affairs, Health and Sustainable Development of the Parliamentary Assembly of the Council of Europe, Statement: Committee calls for a public-health-oriented drug policy, 23 November 2015.

NATIONAL DOCUMENTS

NETHERLANDS

Kamerstukken II 2013–2014, 29 911, nr. 92 (Brief minister van Veiligheid en Justitie over Bestrijding georganiseerde criminaliteit) (i.e., Letter of the Minister of Security and Justice about fighting organized crime).

'Declaration Recognizing the Jurisdiction of the Court as Compulsory' of the Netherlands of 1 August 1956, *Trb.* 1956/119.

LITERATURE

M. Akehurst, 'The Hierarchy of the Sources of International Law', *British Yearbook of International Law*, vol. 47, 1974–1975, pp. 273–285.

J. E. Alvarez, 'How Not to Link: Institutional Conundrums of an Expanded Trade Regime', *Widener Law Symposium Journal* 2001, vol. 7, no. 1, pp. 1–19.

All Party Parliamentary Group for Drug Policy Reform (APPG), *Guidance on Drug Policy. Interpreting the UN Drug Conventions*, 2015.

P. Alston, 'Out of the Abyss: The Challenges Confronting the New U. N. Committee on Economic, Social and Cultural Rights', *Human Rights Quarterly* 1987, vol. 9, no. 3, pp. 332–381.

P. Alston & G. Quinn, 'The Nature and Scope of States Parties' Obligations under the International Covenant on Economic, Social and Cultural Rights, *Human Rights Quarterly* 1987, vol. 9, pp. 156–229.

Y. Arai-Takahashi, *The Margin of Appreciation Doctrine and the Principle of Proportionality in the Jurisprudence of the ECHR*, Antwerp/Oxford/New York: Intersentia, 2001.

M. Baderin & R. McCorquodale, *Economic, Social, and Cultural Rights in Action*, Oxford: Oxford University Press, 2007.

R. Baker & V. Taylor, 'The Right To Health: A Right On The Rise?', *The Journal Jurisprudence* 2013, pp. 275–303.

T. Barkhuysen, 'Het EVRM als integraal onderdeel van het Nederlandse materiële bestuursrecht', in: T. Barkhuysen, A.B. Blomberg, M.K. Bulterman & J.M. Verschuuren, *De betekenis van het EVRM voor het materiële bestuursrecht* (Preadviezen VAR), Den Haag: Boom Juridische uitgeverij, 2004.

D. Barrett, *'Unique in International Relations'? A Comparison of the International Narcotics Control Board and the UN Human Rights Treaty Bodies*, London: International Harm Reduction Association 2008.

D. Barrett et.al, *Recalibrating the Regime. The Need for a Human Rights-Based Approach to International Drug Policy*, The Beckley Foundation Drug Policy Programme, Report Thirteen, March 2008.

D. Barrett, 'Drug Use and the Right of Everyone to the Highest Attainable Standard of Health', in: Sven Hessle (ed.), *Human Rights and Social Equality: Challenges for Social Work*, Farnham, UK/Burlington, USA: Ashgate, 2014.

D. Barrett & Manfred Nowak, 'The United Nations and Drug Policy: Towards a Human Rights-Based Approach', in: A. Constantinides & N. Zaikos (eds.), *The Diversity of International Law: Essays in Honour of Professor Kalliopi K. Koufa*, Amsterdam: Brill & Martinus Nijhoff, 2009.

L. Bartels, 'Human rights and sustainable development through regional trade agreements', in: J. Wouters, A. Marx, D. Geraets & B. Natens (eds.), *Global Governance through Trade: EU Policies and Approaches*, Cheltenham, UK/ Northampton, USA: Edward Elgar, 2015.

F.F. Basch, 'The Doctrine of the Inter-American Court of Human Rights Regarding States' Duty to Punish Human Rights Violations and Its Dangers', *American University International Law Review* 2007, vol. 23, pp. 195–229.

R. Bayer, 'The continuing tensions between individual rights and public health. Talking Point on public health versus civil liberties', *EMBO reports* 2007, vol. 8, no. 12, pp. 1099–1103.

M. Beijer, 'Active Guidance of Fundamental Rights Protection by the Court of Justice of the European Union: Exploring the Possibilities of a Positive Obligations Doctrine', *Review of European Administrative Law* 2015, vol. 8, no. 2, pp. 127–150.

M.-L. Bemelmans-Videc, 'Guaranteeing the authority and effectiveness of the European Convention on Human Rights. Explanatory memorandum', Council of Europe Parliamentary Assembly, 4 November 2011, *AS/Jur* (2011) 44.

E. Benvenisti, 'Margin of Appreciation, Consensus, and Universal Standards', *International Law and Politics* 1999, vol. 31, pp. 843–854.

D. Bilchitz, *Poverty and Fundamnetal Rights: The Justification and Enforcement of Socio-Economic Rights*, Oxford: Oxford University Press, 2007.

T. Blom, *Opiumwetgeving en drugsbeleid*, Deventer: Kluwer, 2015.

G. Boas, *Public International Law: Contemporary Principles and Perspectives*, Cheltenham, UK/Northampton, USA: Edward Elgar, 2012.

I. Boerefijn, 'Impact on the Law on Treaty Reservations', in: M.T. Kamminga & M. Scheinin, *The Impact of Human Rights Law on General International Law*, Oxford: Oxford University Press, 2009.

T. Bogdanoski, 'A dose of human rights: An antidote to the criminal prohibition of cannabis for medical use?', *Criminal Law Journal* 2009, vol. 33, pp. 251–262.

N. Boister, *The Suppression of Illicit Drugs Through International Law*, Nottingham: University of Nottingham, 1998.

——, '"Transnational Criminal Law"?', *European Journal of International Law* 2003, vol. 14, 953–976.

——, *An Introduction to Transnational Criminal Law*, Oxford: Oxford University Press, 2012.

——, *An Introduction to Transnational Criminal Law*, Oxford: Oxford University Press, 2018.

N. Boister & Martin Jelsma, '*Inter se* Modification of the UN Drug Control Conventions, *International Community Law Review*, vol. 20, 2018, pp. 456–492.

M. Bone & T. Seddon, 'Human rights, public health and medicinal cannabis use', *Critical Public Health* 2016, vol. 26, no. 1, pp. 51–61.

K.E. Boon, A. Huq & D.C. Lovelace (eds.), *Terrorism. Commentary on Security Documents vol. 107, U.N. Response to Al-Qaeda*, Oxford: Oxford University Press, 2010.

C.J. Borgen, 'Resolving Treaty Conflicts', *The George Washington International Law Review* 2005, vol. 37, pp. 573–648.

——, 'Treaty Conflicts and Normative Fragmentation', in: D.B. Hollis (ed.), *The Oxford Guide to Treaties*, Oxford: Oxford University Press, 2012.

M. Bothe, 'Conflict Settlement in the Field of International Drug Control', in: D. Bardonnet (ed.), *Le Règlement Pacifique Des Différends Internationaux en Europe: Perspectives D'avenir*, Dordrecht/Boston/Londen: Martinus Nijhoff Publishers, 1991.

C. Brölmann, 'Law-Making Treaties: Form and Function in International Law', *Nordic Journal of International Law* 2005, vol. 74, pp. 383–404.

T. Buergenthal, 'The Normative and Institutional Evolution of International Human Rights', *Human Rights Quarterly* 1997, vol. 19, no. 4, pp. 703–723.

M. Byers, 'Conceptualising the Relationship between Jus Cogens and Erga Omnes Rules', *Nordic Journal of International Law* 1997, vol. 66, pp. 211–239.

P.G. Carozza, 'Subsidiarity as a Structural Principle of International Human Rights Law', *American Journal of International Law* 2003, vol. 97, pp. 38–79.

A. Cassese, *International Law*, Oxford: Oxford University Press, 2005.

J.P. Caulkins, Angela Hawken, Beau Kilmer & Mark A.R. Kleiman, *Marijuana Legalization. What Everyone Needs to Know*, Oxford: Oxford University Press, 2016.

A.R. Chapman, 'A "Violations Approach" for Monitoring the International Covenant on Economic, Social and Cultural Rights', *Human Rights Quarterly* 1996, vol. 18, no. 1, pp. 23–66.

——, 'Towards an Understanding of the Right to Enjoy the Benefits of Scientific Progress and Its Applications, *Journal of Human Rights* 2009, vol. 8, pp. 1–36.

J.I. Charney, 'Universal International Law', *The American Journal of International Law* 1993, vol. 87, pp. 529–551.

S.K. Chatterjee, *Legal Aspects of International Drug Control*, The Hague/ Boston/London: Martinus Nijhoff Publishers, 1981.

S. Hwan Choi, '"Human Dignity" as an Indispensable Requirement for Sustainable Regional Economic Integration', *Journal of East Asia and International Law (J. E. Asia & Int'l L)* 2013, vol. 6, pp. 81–105.

J. Christoffersen, *Fair Balance: Proportionality, Subsidiarity and Primarity in the European Convention on Human Rights*, Leiden/Boston: Martinus Nijhoff Publishers, 2009.

M. Craven, 'Legal differentiation and the concept of the human rights treaty in international law', *European Journal of International Law* 2000, vol. 11, pp. 489–519.

J. Crawford, *Brownlie's Principles of Public International Law*, Oxford: Oxford University Press, 2012.

J. Csete et al. 'Public health and international drug policy', *The Lancet* 2016, vol. 387, pp. 1427–1480.

H. Cullen, 'The Collective Complaints System of the European Social Charter: Interpretative Methods of the European Committee of Social Rights', *Human Rights Law Review* 2009, vol. 9, no. 1, pp. 61–93.

W. Czapliński & G. Danilenko, 'Conflict of Norms in International Law', *Netherlands Yearbook of International Law* 1990, vol. 21, pp. 3–42.

A. D'Amato, 'Good Faith', in: Rudolf Bernhardt (ed.), *Encyclopedia of Public International Law*, 1992, p. 600.

D. Davison-Vecchione, 'Beyond the Forms of Faith: Pacta Sunt Servanda and Loyalty', *German Law Journal* 2015, vol. 16, no. 5, pp. 1163–1190.

C. Dominice, 'The international responsibility of states for breach of multilateral obligations', *European Journal of International Law* 1999, pp. 353–363.

V. Đuro Degan, *Sources of International Law*, The Hague/Boston/London: Martinus Nijhoff Publishers, 1997.

K. Dzehtsiarou, *European Consensus and the Legitimacy of the European Court of Human Rights*, Cambridge: Cambridge University Press, 2015.

N. Eastwood, E. Fox & A. Rosmarin, *A Quiet Revolution: drug decriminalization across the globe*, Release Publication, 2016.

A. Eide, *Food as a Human Right*, A. Eide et al. (eds.), Tokyo: United Nations University, 1984.

M. Evans (ed.), *International Law*, Oxford: Oxford University Press, 2014.

B. Fassbender, *The United Nations Charter as the Constitution of the International Community*, Leiden/Boston: Martinus Nijhoff Publishers, 2009.

A.X. Fellmeth & M. Horwitz, *Guide to Latin in International Law*, Oxford: Oxford University Press, 2009.

C. Fijnaut & B. De Ruyver, *De derde weg. Een pleidooi voor een evenwichtig cannabisbeleid*, Antwerpen/Cambridge: Intersentia, 2014.

J. Finke, 'Regime-collisions: Tensions between treaties (and how to solve them)', in: C.J. Tams, A. Tzanakopoulos & A. Zimmermann (eds.), *Research Handbook on the Law of Treaties*, Cheltenham, UK/Northampton, USA: Edward Elgar, 2014.

A. Fischer-Lescarno & G. Teubner, 'Regime-Collision: The Vain Search for Legal Unity in the Fragmentation of Global Law', *Michigan Journal of International Law*, 1999, vol. 25, pp. 999–1046.

G. Fitzmaurice, 'The Law and Procedure of the International Court of Justice 1951–1954: Treaty Interpretation and other Treaty Points', *British Yearbook of International Law* 1957, vol. 33, pp. 203–293.

C.-A. Fleischhauer & B. Simma, 'Article 13', in: B. Simma, D.E. Khan, G. Nolte & A. Paulus (eds.), *The Charter of the United Nations*, Oxford: Oxford University Press, 2012.

A. Follesdal, 'The Principle of Subsidiarity as a Constitutional Principle in International law', *Global Constitutionalism* 2013, vol. 2, pp. 37–62.

M. Forowicz, *The Reception of International Law in the European Court of Human Rights*, Oxford: Oxford University Press, 2010.

J.C. Garzón & Luciana Pol, 'The Elephant in the Room: Drugs and Human Rights in Latin America', *SUR International Journal on Human Rights* 2015, vol. 12, no. 21, pp. 1–7.

A.A. Ghouri, 'Determining Hierarchy Between Conflicting Treaties: Are There Vertical Rules in the Horizontal System?', *Asian Journal of International Law* 2012, vol. 2, no. 2, pp. 235–266.

——, 'Is Characterization of Treaties a Solution to Treaty Conflicts?', *Chinese Journal of International Law* 2012, vol. 11, pp. 247–280.

Th. Giegerich, 'Article 60', in: O. Dörr & K. Schmalenbach (eds.), *Vienna Convention on the Law of Treaties*, Berlin/Heidelberg: Springer-Verlag, 2012.

T.D. Gill, 'Legal Aspects of the Transfer of Authority in UN Peace Operations', *Netherlands Yearbook of International Law* 2011, vol. 42 pp. 37–70.

M.E.C. Gispen, 'A human rights view on access to controlled substances for medical purposes under the international drug control framework', *European Journal of Pharmacology* 2013, pp. 16–24.

——, *Human Rights and Drug Control: Access to Controlled Essential Medicines in Resource-Constrained Countries*, Antwerp: Intersentia, 2017.

M. Haden & B. Emerson, 'A vision for cannabis regulation: a public health approach based on lessons learned from the regulation of alcohol and tobacco', *Open Medicine* 2014, vol. 8(2), pp. 3–80.

D.J. Harris, M. O'Boyle, E.P. Bates & C.M. Buckley (eds.), *Harris, O'Boyle & Warbrick, Law of the European Convention on Human Rights*, Oxford: Oxford University Press, 2014.

Harm Reduction International, 'What is harm reduction?', op: http://www.ihra.net/what-is-harm-reduction.

D. Heilmann, 'The International Control of Illegal Drugs and the U.N. Treaty Regime: Preventing or Causing Human Rights Violations?', *Cardozo Journal of International & Comparitive Law* 2011, vol. 19, pp. 237–290.

A. Hendriks, 'Het recht op gezondheid en het IVESCR-Comité', *NJCM-bul.* 1994, pp. 171–180.

M. Hirsch, 'Interactions between Investment and Non-investment Obligations', in: P. Muchlinski, F. Ortino & C. Schreuer (eds.), *The Oxford Handbook of International Investment Law*, Oxford: Oxford University Press, 2008.

R. Hodgkin & P. Newell, *Implementation Handbook for the Convention on the Rights of the Child*, Geneva: UNISEF, 2007.

D.B. Hollis, 'Treaty clauses', in: D.B. Hollis (ed.), *The Oxford Guide to Treaties*, Oxford: Oxford University Press, 2012.

M.O. Hudson, 'Integrity of International Instruments', *American Journal of International Law* 1948, vol. 42, no. 1, pp. 105–108.

M. Jacob, 'Precedents: Lawmaking Through International Adjudication', in: A. von Bogdandy & I. Venzke (eds.), *International Judicial Lawmaking*, Heidelberg: Springer, 2012.

M. Jelsma, N. Boister, D. Bewley-Taylor, M. Fitzmaurice & J. Walsh, *Balancing Treaty Stability and Change: Inter se modification of the UN drug control conventions to facilitate cannabis regulation* (GDPO Policy Report 7, March 2018) pp. 1–43.

C.W. Jenks, 'The Conflict of Law-Making Treaties', *British Yearbook of International Law* 1953, vol. 30, pp. 401–453.

D.S. Jonas & T.N. Saunders, 'The Object and Purpose of a Treaty: Three Interpretive Methods', *Vanderbilt Journal of Transnational Law* 2010, vol. 43, no. 3, pp. 565–609.

S. Joseph, *Blame it on the WTO?: A Human Rights Critique*, Oxford: Oxford University Press, 2011.

S. Joseph & M. Castan, *The International Covenant on Civil and Political Rights*, Oxford: Oxford University Press, 2014.

W. Karl, 'Conflicts between Treaties', in: R. Bernhardt (ed.), *Encyclopedia of Public International Law*, 1984.

R.D. Kearney & R.E. Dalton, 'The Treaty on Treaties', *American Journal of International Law* 1970, vol. 64, pp. 495–561.

H. Kelsen, *The Law of the United Nations*, London: The London Institute of World Affairs, 1950.

——, 'Derogation', in: Ralph A. Newman (ed.), *Essays in Jurisprudence in honour of Roscoe Pound*, Indianapolis: Bobbs-Merrill Publication, 1962.

——, *General Theory of Norms*, Oxford: Oxford University Press, 1991.

R. Kicker & M. Möstl, *Standard-setting through monitoring? The role of Council of Europe expert bodies in the development of human rights*, Strasbourg: Council of Europe Publishing, 2012.

B. Kilmer, K. Kruithof, M. Pardal, J. P. Caulkins & J. Rubin, *Multinational overview of cannabis production regimes*, RAND Europe/WODC, 2013.

E. D. Kinney, 'The International Human Right to Health: What Does this Mean for Our Nation and World?', *Indiana Law Review* 2001, vol. 34, pp. 1457–1475.

Jan Klabbers, 'Beyond the Vienna Convention: Conflicting Treaty Provisions', in: Enzo Cannizzaro (ed.), *The Law of Treaties Beyond the Vienna Convention*, Oxford: Oxford University Press, 2011.

J. Klabbers, *International Law*, Cambridge: Cambridge University Press, 2013.

J. Klabbers, A. Peters & G. Ulfstein (eds.), *The Constitutionalisation of International Law*, Oxford: Oxford University Press 2010.

T. Koji, 'Emerging Hierarchy in International Human Rights and Beyond: From the Perspective of Non-derogable Rights', *European Journal of International Law* 2001, vol. 12, no. 5, pp. 917–941.

R. Kolb, 'Does Article 103 of the Charter of the United Nations Apply Only to Decisions or Also to Authorizations Adopted by the Security Council?', *Zeitschrift für ausländisches öffentliches recht und Völkerrecht* 2004, vol. 64, no. 1, pp. 21–35.

M. Koskenniemi, 'Hierarchy in International Law: A Sketch', *European Journal of International Law* 1997, vol. 8, pp. 566–582.

M. Koskenniemi & P. Leino, 'Fragmentation of International Law? Postmodern Anxieties', *Leiden Journal of International Law* 2002, vol. 15, no. 3, pp. 553–579.

M. Kotzur, 'Good Faith (Bona fide)', in: *Max Planck Encyclopedia of Public International Law*, Oxford: Oxford University Press (online; last updated: Jan. 2009).

S.D. Krasner, 'Structural Causes and Regime Consequences: Regimes as Intervening Variables', in: Stephen D. Krasner (red), *International Regimes*, Ithaca/London: Cornell University Press, 1983.

M. Langford (ed.), *Social Rights Jurisprudence: Emerging Trends in International and Comparative Law*, Cambridge: Cambridge University Press, 2008.

D. Lapas, 'Some remarks on fragmentation of international law: disintegration or transformation?', *Comparative and International Law Journal of Southern Africa (Comp. & Int'l L.J. S. Afr.)* 2007, vol. 40, pp. 1–29.

Kjetil Mujezinovic Larsen, *The Human Rights Treaty Obligations of Peacekeepers*, Cambridge: Cambridge University Press, 2012.

H. Lauterpacht, 'Restrictive Interpretation and the Principle of Effectiveness in the Interpretation of Treaties', *British Yearbook of International Law* 1949, vol. 26, pp. 48–85.

——, *International Law and Human Rights*, Archon Books, 1968 (1950).

V.A. Leary, 'The Right to Health in International Human Rights Law', *Health and Human Rights* 1994, vol. 1, no. 1, pp. 24–56.

A. Legg, *The Margin of Appreciation in International Human Rights Law. Deference and Proportionality*, Oxford: Oxford University Press, 2012.
A.E.M. Leijten, *Core Rights and the Protection of Socio-Economic Interests by the European Court of Human Rights* (diss. Leiden), Leiden, 2015.
M.A. Leinwand, 'The International Law of Treaties and United States Legalization of Marijuana', *Columbia Journal of Transnational Law* 1971, vol. 10, no. 2, pp. 413–441.
R. Liivoja, 'The Scope of the Supremacy Clause of The United Nations Charter', *International and Comparative Law Quarterly* 2008, vol. 57, pp. 58–612.
R.B. Lillich, 'The Growing Importance of Customary International Human Rights Law, *Georgia Journal of International and Comparative Law* 1995–1996, vol. 25, pp. 1–30.
U. Linderfalk, *On the Interpretation of Treaties*, Dordrecht: Springer, 2007.
——, 'International Legal Hierarchy Revisited – The Status of Obligations *Erga Omnes*', *Nordic Journal of International Law*, 2011, vol. 80, pp. 1–23.
A. Lindroos, 'Addressing Norm Conflicts in a Fragmented Legal System: The Doctrine of *Lex Specialis*', *Nordic Journal of International Law* 2005, vol. 74, pp. 27–66.
R. Lines, *International Human Rights Jurisprudence on Issues relating to Drug Use and Harm Reduction*, New York: Open Society Institute, 2007.
——, *Drug Control and Human Rights in International* Law, Cambridge: Cambridge University Press, 2017.
R. Lines & D. Barrett, 'Cannabis Reform, 'Medical and Scientific Purposes' and the Vienna Convention on the Law of Treaties', *International Community Law Review*, vol. 20, 2018, pp. 436–455.
R. Lines & R. Elliott, 'Injecting drugs into human rights advocacy', International Journal of Drug Policy 2007, vol. 18, pp. 453–457.
P. Lynch (ed.), *Human Rights Law Resource Manual*, Melbourne: Human Rights Law Resource Centre Ltd, 2006.
Maastricht Guidelines on Violations of Economic, Social and Cultural Rights, Maastricht, January 22–26, 1997.
K. Månsson, 'Reviving the 'Spirit of San Francisco': The Lost Proposals on Human Rights, Justice and International Law to the UN Charter', *Nordic Journal of International Law* 2007, vol. 76, pp. 217–239.
G. Marceau, 'Conflict of Norms and Conflict of Jurisdictions: The Relationship between the WTO Agreement and MEAs and Other Treaties', *Journal of World Trade* 2001, vol. 35, pp. 1081–1131.
M. Marochini, Council of Europe and the Right to Healthcare – Is the European Convention on Human Rights Appropriate Instrument for Protecting the Right to Healthcare?, *Zbornik Pravnog fakulteta Sveučilista u Rijeci* 2013, pp. 729–760.
A. Marschik, 'Too Much Order? The Impact of Special Secondary Norms on the Unity and Efficacy of the International Legal System', *European Journal of International law* 1998, vol. 9, pp. 212–239.
F.F. Martin, 'Delineating a Hierarchical Outline of International Law Sources and Norms', *Saskatchewan Law Review* 2002, vol. 65, pp. 333–368.
B.M. Mayer & Larisa M. Mori, 'The Highest Attainable Standard: Advancing a Collective Human Right to Public Health', *Columbia Human Rights Law Review* 2005, pp. 101–147.

N. Matz-Lück, 'Harmonization, Systemic Integration, and 'Mutual Supportiveness' as Conflict-Solution Techniques: Different Modes of Interpretation as a Challenge to Negative Effects of Fragmentation?', *Finnish Yearbook of International Law* 2006, vol. 17, pp. 39–53.

M. McFarland Sánchez-Moreno, 'The Human Rights Case for Drug Reform. How Drug Criminalization Destroys Lives, Feeds Abuses, and Subverts the Rule of Law', in: Human Rights Watch World Report 2014, New York: HRW 2014.

C. McLachlan, 'The Principle of Systemic Integration and Article 31 (3) (c) of the Vienna Convention', *International and Comparative Law Quarterly* 2005, vol. 54, pp. 279–320.

T. Meron, 'On a Hierarchy of International Human Rights', *American Journal of International Law* 1986, vol. 80, pp. 1–23.

——, *Human Rights and Humanitarian Norms as Customary Law*, Oxford: Oxford University Press, 1991.

R. Michaels & J. Pauwelyn, 'Conflict of Norms or Conflict of Laws?: Different Techniques in the Fragmentation of Public International Law', *Duke Journal of Comparative & International Law* 2012, vol. 22, pp. 349–376.

M. Milanović, 'Norm Conflict in International Law: Whither Human Rights?', *Duke Journal of Comparative and International Law* 2009, vol. 20, no. 1, pp. 69–131.

D. Moeckli, 'The Emergence of Terrorism as a Distinct Category of International Law', *Texas International Law Journal* 2008, vol. 44, pp. 157–183.

M. de Mol, *De directe werking van de grondrechten van de Europese Unie* (diss. Maastricht), Oisterwijk: Wolf Legal Publishers, 2014.

L. Mola, *The margin of appreciation accorded to States in times of economic crisis. An analysis of the decision by the European Committee on Social Rights and by the European Court of Human Rights on national austerity measures, Lex Social* 2015, vol. 5, no. 1, pp. 174–194.

J.S. Morton, *The International Law Commission of the United Nations*, Columbia, South Carolina: University of South Carolina Press, 2000.

J.B. Mus, 'Conflicts between Treaties in International Law', *Netherlands International Law Review* 1998, vol. 45, pp. 208–232.

E. Myjer & P. Kempees, 'Thoughts on the Positive Impact of Negative Case-Law', in: Luis López Guerra, Carmen Morte Gómez, Anna Maria Mengual I Mallol & Guillen Cano Palomares (eds.), *El Tribunal Europeo de Derechos Humanos. Una visión desde dentro. En homenaje al Juez Josep Casadevall*, Valencia: Tirant lo Blanch, 2015.

G. Nolte, 'Article 2 (7)', in: B. Simma, D.E. Khan, G. Nolte & A. Paulus (eds.), *The Charter of the United Nations*, Oxford: Oxford University Press, 2012.

M.E. O'Connell, J. Paust & R. Pauks (panel), in: 'The Second Major General John L. Fugh Symposium', *Military Law Review* 2015, vol. 223, p. 440.

K. Odendahl, 'Application of successive treaties relating to the same subject matter', in: O. Dörr & K. Schmalenbach (eds.), *Vienna Convention on the Law of Treaties, A Commentary*, Heidelberg/Dordrecht/London/New York: Springer, 2012.

J. Ondrovičová, Book review of: P. Šturma, S. Hýbnerová, J. Ondřej, V. Balaš, V. Bílková & V. Honusková: *Competing Jurisdiction of International Judicial Bodies* (Prague: Charles University in Prague, Faculty of Law, 2009, 117 p.), *Czech Yearbook of International Law* 2010, pp. 255–258.

A. Orakhelashvili, *Peremptory Norms in International Law*, Oxford: Oxford University Press, 2008.

——, 'Article 30', in: Olivier Corten & Pierre Klein, *The Vienna Convention on the Law of Treaties, A Commentary*, Oxford: Oxford University Press, 2011, vol. I, pp. 764–800.

A. Paulus & J.R. Leiß, 'Article 103', in: B. Simma, D.E. Khan, G. Nolte & A. Paulus (eds.), *The Charter of the United Nations*, Oxford: Oxford University Press, 2012.

J.J. Paust, 'The Bush-Cheney Legacy: Serial Torture and Forced Disappearance in Manifest Violation of Global Human Rights Law', *Barry Law Review* 2012, vol. 18, no. 1, pp. 61–85.

——, 'Human Rights on the Battlefield', *The George Washington International Law Review* 2015, vol. 47, pp. 509–561.

J. Pauwelyn, 'A Typology of Multilateral Treaty Obligations: Are WTO Obligations Bilateral or Collective in Nature?', *European Journal of International Law* 2003, vol. 14, no. 5, pp. 907–951.

——, *Conflict of Norms in Public International Law: How WTO Law relates to Other Rules of International Law*, Cambridge: Cambridge University Press, 2003.

S. Peers & S. Prechal, 'Article 52 – Scope and Interpretation of Rights and Principles', in: S. Peers et al. (eds.), *The EU Charter of fundamental rights: a commentary*, Oxford: Hart Publishing 2014.

A. Pellet, '"Human Rightism" and International Law' (Lecture delivered on 18 July 2000 at Geneva), in: *Gilberto Amado: Memorial Lectures*, Brasília, FUNAG, 2012, pp. 267–284.

A. Peters, 'Article 25', in: B. Simma, D.E. Khan, G. Nolte & A. Paulus (eds.), *The Charter of the United Nations*, Oxford: Oxford University Press, 2012.

P. Picone, 'The Distinction between Jus Cogens and Obligations Erga Omnes', in: E. Cannizzaro (ed.), *The Law of Treaties Beyond the Vienna Convention*, Oxford: Oxford University Press, 2011.

N. Quénivet, 'Binding the United Nations to Human Rights Norms by Way of the Laws of Treaties', *The George Washington International Law Review* 2010, vol. 42, pp. 587–621.

M. Ragazzi, *The Concept of International Obligations Erga Omnes*, Oxford: Oxford University Press, 2000.

M. Rama-Montaldo, 'Universalism and Particularisms in the Creation Process of International Law', in: Sienho Yee & Jacques-Yvan Morin, *Multiculturalism and International Law. Essays in Honour of Edward McWhinney*, Leiden/Boston: Martinus Nijhoff Publishers, 2009.

S. Reinhold, 'Good Faith in International Law', UCL *Journal of Law and Jurisprudence* 2013, vol. 2, pp. 40–63.

A. Rengel, 'Privacy as an International Human Right and the Right to Obscurity in Cyberspace', *Groningen Journal of International Law* 2014, vol 2, no. 2, pp. 33–54.

E.H. Riedel & J.-M. Arend, 'Article 55 (c)', in: B. Simma, D.E. Khan, G. Nolte & A. Paulus (eds.), *The Charter of the United Nations*, Oxford: Oxford University Press, 2012.

S. Rolles et al. *The Alternative World Drug Report. Counting the Costs of the War on Drugs*, United Kingdom: Count the Costs, 2012.

R. Room & P. Reuter, 'How well do international drug conventions protect public health?', 379 *The Lancet* 2012 (January 7), pp. 84–91.

C. Rousseau, 'De la Compatibilité des Norms Juridique Contradictoires dans l'Ordre International', *Revue générale de droit international public* 1932, vol. 39, pp. 133–192.

K. Sachariew, 'State Responsibility for Multilateral Treaty Violations: Identifying the "Injured State" and its Legal Status', *Netherlands International Law Review* 1988, vol. 35, no. 3, p 273–289.

S.A. Sadat-Akhavi, *Methods of Resolving Conflicts between Treaties*, Leiden/Boston: Martinus Nijhoff, 2003.

J.C. Sainz-Borgo, 'The International Criminal Court, Drug Trafficking and Crimes against Humanity: A local Interpretation of the Rome Statute', *The Journal Jurisprudence* 2012, pp. 373–388.

J.A.C. Salcedo, 'Reflections on the Existence of a Hierarchy of Norms in International Law', *European Journal of International Law* 1997, pp. 583–595.

B. Saul, D. Kinley and J. Mowbray, *The International Covenant on Economic, Social and Cultural Rights*, Oxford: Oxford University Press, 2014.

E. Schmid, *Taking Economic, Social and Cultural Rights Seriously in International Criminal Law*, Cambridge: Cambridge University Press, 2015.

O. De Schutter, *International Human Rights Law: Cases, Materials, Commentary*, Cambridge: Cambridge University Press, 2014.

G. Schwarzenberger, *International Law as Applied by International Courts and Tribunals*, vol. I, London: Stevens & Sons Ltd, 1957.

E. Schwelb, 'The International Court of Justice and the Human Rights Clauses of the Charter', *American Journal of International Law* 1972, vol. 66, pp. 337–351.

I.D. Seiderman, *Hierarchy in International Law*, Antwerpen/Groningen/Oxford: Intersentia/Hart, 2001.

M. Sepúlveda, T. van Banning, G.D. Gudmundsdóttir, C. Chamoun & W.J.M. van Genugten, *Human Rights Reference Handbook*, Ciudad Colon, Costa Rica: University for Peace, 2004.

D. Shelton, 'Hierarchy of Norms and Human Rights: Of Trumps and Winners', *Saskatchewan Law Review* 2002, vol. 65, pp. 301–331.

——, 'Normative Hierarchy in International Law', *American Journal of International Law*, 2006, vol. 100, pp. 291–323.

D.L. Shelton, *Advanced Introduction to International Human Rights Law*, Cheltenham, UK/Northampton, USA: Edward Elgar, 2014.

D. Shelton, *Remedies in International Human Rights Law*, Oxford: Oxford University Press, 2015.

H. Shue, *Basic Rights: subsistence, affluence and U.S. foreign policy*, New Jersey: Princeton University Press, 1996.

B. Simma, 'International Crimes: Injury and Countermeasures. Comments on Part 2 of the ILC Work on State Responsibility', in: J.H.H. Weiler, A. Cassese & M. Spinedi (eds.), International Crimes of State, Berlin/New York: Walter de Gruyter, 1989.

B. Simma & P. Alston, 'The Sources of Human Rights Law: Custom, Jus Cogens, and General Principles', *Australian Year Book of International Law* 1988–1989, vol. 12, pp. 82–108.

B. Simma, D.E. Khan, G. Nolte & A. Paulus (eds.), *The Charter of the United Nations*, Oxford: Oxford University Press, 2012.

B. Simma & A.L. Paulus, 'The "International Community": Facing the Challenge of Globalization', *European Journal of International Law* 1998, vol. 9, pp. 266–277.

B. Simma & D. Pulkowski, 'Of Planets and the Universe: Self-contained Regimes in International Law', *Europeans Journal of International Law* 2006, vol. 17, no. 3, pp. 483–529.

I. Sinclair, *The Vienna Convention on the Law of Treaties*, Manchester: Manchester University Press, 1984.

M. Singer, 'Jurisdictional Immunity of International Organizations: Human Rights and Functional Necessity Concerns', *Virginia Journal of International Law* 1953, vol. 36, pp. 53–165.

S. Smis, C. Janssens, S. Mirgaux & K. Van Laethem, *Handboek mensenrechten. De internationale bescherming van de rechten van de mens*, Antwerpen: Intersentia, 2011.

L.B. Sohn, 'The Human Rights Law of the Charter', *Texas International Law Journal* 1992, vol. 12, pp. 129–140.

H.J. Steiner & P. Alston, *International Human Rights in Context: Law, Politics, Morals*, Oxford: Oxford University Press, 2000.

T. Stoll, 'Article 55 (a) and (b)', in: B. Simma, D.E. Khan, G. Nolte & A. Paulus (eds.), *The Charter of the United Nations*, Oxford: Oxford University Press, 2012.

A.S. Sweet & J. Mathews, 'Proportionality Balancing and Global Constitutionalism', *Columbia Journal of Transnational Law* 2008, vol. 47, pp. 72–164.

S.P. Subedi, 'Protection of Human Rights through the Mechanism of UN Special Rapporteurs', *Human Rights Quarterly* 2011, vol. 33, pp. 201–228.

A. Tahvanainen, 'Hierarchy of Norms in International and Human Rights Law', *Nordisk Tidsskrift For Menneskerettigheter* 2006, vol. 24, no 3, pp. 191–205.

S. Takahashi, 'Drug Control, Human Rights, and the Right to the Highest Attainable Standard of Health: by no means straightforward issues', *Human Rights Quarterly* 2009, vol. 31, no. 3, pp. 748–776.

J. Tobin, *The Right to Health in International Law*, Oxford: Oxford University Press, 2012.

B. Toebes, 'Het recht op gezondheid: geen recht om gezond te zijn', *Ars Aequi* 1999, pp. 912–915.

——, *The Right to Health as a Human Right in International Law*, Antwerpen: Intersentia, 1999.

Trimbos Instituut, 'Harm reduction bij drugsverslaving', op: https://www.trimbos.nl/themas/infectieziekten-en-harm-reduction-bij-drugsgebruik/harm-reduction-bij-drugsverslaving.

A. Tzanakopoulos, 'Collective Security and Human Rights', in: E. De Wet & J. Vidmar (eds.), *Hierarchy in International Law: The Place of Human Rights*, Oxford: Oxford University Press, 2012.

UN Office of the High Commissioner on Human Rights: http://www.ohchr.org/EN/HRBodies/CCPR/Pages/GC36-Article6Righttolife.aspx.

G.J.H. Van Hoof, Legal nature of economic, social and cultural rights: a rebuttal of some traditional views, in: P. Alston & K. Tomaševski (eds.), *The Right to Food*, Utrecht: Martinus Nijhoff Publishers, 1984.

H. Van Houtte, 'Treaty Protection against Economic Sanctions', *Revue belge de droit international* 1984–1985, vol. 18, pp. 34–56.

P.H.P.H.M.C. van Kempen, *Heropening van procedures na veroordelingen door het EHRM* (diss. Tilburg), Nijmegen: Wolf Legal Publishers, 2003.

——, *Repressie door mensenrechten. Over positieve verplichtingen tot aanwending van strafrecht ter bescherming van fundamentele rechten* (oratie Nijmegen), Nijmegen: Wolf Legal Publishers, 2008.

—— (ed.), *International and Regional Human Rights Documents* (with a foreword by ECtHR Judge E. Myjer), Nijmegen: Wolf Legal Publishers, 2010.

——, 'The Recognition of Legal Persons in International Human Rights Instruments: Protection Against and Through Criminal Justice?', in: M. Pieth & R. Ivory (eds.), *Corporate Criminal Liability. Emergence, Convergence, and Risk*, New York/Dordrecht/Heidelberg/London: Springer 2011.

——, 'Four Concepts of Security – A Human Rights Perspective', *Human Rights Law Review* 2013, vol. 13, no. 1, pp. 1–23.

P.H.P.H.M.C. van Kempen & J. Bemelmans, 'Over de betekenis van het EU-Handvest voor het materiële strafrecht. Onder- en overontwikkeling van fundamentele strafrechtelijke beginselen in unierechtelijke context', in: J. Gerards, H. de Waele & K. Zwaan (eds.), *Vijf jaar bindend EU-Grondrechtenhandvest. Doorwerking, consequenties, perspectieven*, Deventer: Wolters Kluwer, 2015.

——, 'EU protection of the substantive criminal law principles of guilt and ne bis in idem under the Charter of Fundamental Rights: Underdevelopment and overdevelopment in an incomplete criminal justice framework', *New Journal of European Criminal Law* 2018, vol. 9(2) pp. 247–264.

P.H.P.H.M.C. van Kempen & M.I. Fedorova, *Internationaal recht en cannabis. Een beoordeling op basis van VN-drugsverdragen en EU-drugsregelgeving van gemeentelijke en buitenlandse opvattingen pro regulering van cannabisteelt voor recreatief gebruik*, Deventer: Kluwer, 2014.

——, 'Regulated Legalization of Cannabis through Positive Human Rights Obligations and *Inter se* Treaty Modification, *International Community Law Review*, vol. 20, 2018, pp. 493–526.

——, *International Law and Cannabis I. Regulation of Cannabis Cultivation for Recreational Use under the UN Narcotic Drugs Conventions and the EU Legal Instruments in Anti-Drugs Policy*, Cambridge: Intersentia, 2019.

M. van Ooyen-Houben & E. Kleemans, 'Drug Policy: The "Dutch Model"', *Crime & Justice* 2015, vol. 44, pp. 165–226.

E. van Ree, 'Drugs as a human right', International Journal of Drug Policy 1999, vol. 10, pp. 89–98.

F. Vellinga-Schootstra & W.H. Vellinga, 'Positive obligations' en het Nederlandse straf(proces)recht (Oratie Groningen), Deventer: Kluwer, 2008.

S.K. Verma, *An Introduction to Public International Law*, Delhi: Prentice-Hall, 1998.

E. Vetere, 'Opening statement', in: *The Application of the United Nations Standards and Norms in Crime Prevention and Criminal Justice*, Papers of Expert Group Meeting, Vienna: UNODC, 2003.

E.W. Vierdag, 'The Time of "Conclusion" of a Multilateral Treaty: Article 30 of the Vienna Convention on the Law of Treaties and Related Provisions', *British Yearbook of International Law* 1988, vol. 20, pp. 74–111.

E. Vranes, 'The Definition of "Norm Conflict" in International Law and Legal Theory', *European Journal of International Law* 2006, vol. 17, pp. 395–418.

J. Walsh & G. Ramsey, *Uruguay's Drug Policy: Major Innovations, Major Challenges*, Washington: Brookings, 2015.

T. Weatherall, 'The Status of the Prohibition of Terrorism in International Law: Recent Developments', *Georgetown Journal of International Law* 2015, vol. 46, pp. 589–627.

C.K. Webster, 'The Making of the Charter of the United Nations', *History* 1947, vol. 32, no. 115, pp. 16–38.

P. Weil, 'Towards Relative Normativity in International Law?', *The American Journal of International Law* 1983, vol. 77, pp. 413–442.

E. de Wet, 'The International Constitutional Order', International and Comparative Law Quarterly 2006, vol. 55, pp. 51–76.

——, 'From Kadi to Nada: Judicial Techniques Favouring Human Rights over United Nations Security Council Sanctions, *Chinese Journal of International Law* 2013, vol. 12, pp. 787–807.

E. de Wet & J. Vidmar (eds.), *Hierarchy in International Law: The Place of Human Rights*, Oxford: Oxford University Press 2012.

J. Wouters, 'Bronnen van het internationaal recht', in: Nathalie Horbach, Rene Lefeber & Olivier Ribbelink (eds.), *Handboek Internationaal Recht*, Den Haag: T.M.C. Asser Press, 2007.

D.A. Yigzaw, 'Hierarchy of Norms: The Case for the Primacy of Human Rights over WTO Law', *Suffolk Transnational Law Review* 2015, vol. 38, pp. 33–68.

K.G. Young, 'The Minimum Core of Economic and Social Rights: A Concept in Search of Content', *The Yale Journal of International Law* 2008, pp. 113–175.

S. Yun, 'Breaking Imaginary Barriers. Obligations of Armed Non-State Actors Under General Human Rights Law – the Case of the Optional Protocol to the Convention on the Rights of the Child', *Journal of International Humanitarian Legal Studies* 2014, vol. 5, pp. 213–257.

G.O. Zabalza, *The Principle of Systemic Integration*, Wien: Lit Verlag GmbH & Co, 2012.

K. Zemanek, 'New Trends in the Enforcement of Erga Omnes Obligations', *Max Planck Yearbook of United Nations Law* 2000, 1–52.

A.R. Ziegler & B. Boie, 'The Relationship between International Trade Law and International Human Rights Law', in: E. de Wet & J. Vidmar (eds.), *Hierarchy in International Law: The Place of Human Rights*, Oxford: Oxford University Press, 2012, pp. 272–299.

S. Zorzetto, 'The Lex Specialis Principle and its Uses in Legal Argumentation. An Analytical Inquire', *Eunomía. Revista en Cultura de la Legalidad*, Sept. 2012–Febr. 2013, no. 3, pp. 61–87.

EXECUTIVE SUMMARY INTERNATIONAL LAW AND CANNABIS I

How authorities should deal with the cultivation and trade of cannabis for recreational use is a difficult but relevant question from a legal, social and political perspective. The same holds true for new phenomena that are currently developing such as joint cultivation and consumption in so-called Cannabis Social Clubs. Against this background, the central question of this research is whether legalization, decriminalization, policy-based tolerance and/or other forms of regulating cannabis cultivation for recreational use is permissible under international law. The assessment expressly focuses on the question to what extent arguments and initiatives in and outside the Netherlands to regulate cannabis cultivation for recreational use, relate to prevailing international law. More particularly, this concerns the UN 1961 Single Convention on Narcotic Drugs as amended by the 1972 Protocol, the UN 1988 Illicit Traffic Convention, the so-called EU Schengenacquis, the EU 1996 Joint Action Illegal Drug Trafficking and the EU 2004 Framework Decision Illicit Drug Trafficking. In order to provide a substantiated answer to the research question, this book offers an extensive and detailed account and analysis of these international legal instruments. The findings and views of the international bodies designated to supervise such instruments will also be considered. Within the ensuing framework under international law, the municipal arguments and plans, and initiatives in other jurisdictions are scrutinized from a purely legal perspective. To this end, these arguments, plans and initiatives are first inventoried and categorized.

The UN narcotic drugs conventions are of primary importance to the international legal framework. The UN drug control system aims at limiting the use of narcotics, such as cannabis, for purely medical and scientific purposes. In view of the Preamble, the body of text, the system and the history of deliberations of the UN Drugs Conventions, eradicating cannabis for recreational use is the 'object and purpose' of these conventions. This eradication target is based on the assumption that realisation thereof most effectively serves the interests of public health and crime control in particular. For this research, it is of importance that next to coca and poppy products, cannabis products are the main object of these conventions. Allowing cannabis cultivation for recreational use by legalisation, decriminalization, policy-based tolerance and/or other forms of regulation would contravene the aim of eradicating cannabis products for purposes other than medical and scientific. This applies to both cannabis cultivation for supply to retail shops and cultivation within the framework of a Cannabis Social Club. We find the same irreconcilability with respect to European law. The EU drugs instruments aim at cracking down on the illicit drug trade and they confirm and build on the existing obligations for the member states ensuing from the UN drugs conventions.

In order to achieve the stated eradication target, the UN drugs conventions provide for a prohibitive, repressive and multi-layered enforcement system, which imposes a wide spectrum of various criminal, administrative and other obligations on the parties to the convention. These include obligations to cooperate in an estimate system (which serves to ensure the availability of a sufficient amount of narcotic drugs only for medical and scientific purposes), general obligations to combat cannabis cultivation for recreational purposes e.g., the obligation to realize a total ban on cannabis cultivation for recreational use among others through criminalization, obligations to prosecute for cannabis cultivation that is not small-scale and not intended for personal use, a total ban on the possession of cannabis intended for personal recreational use, obligations to also seize cannabis intended for recreational use, and the obligation to implement and participate in a system of international cooperation in criminal matters. Implementation of all these obligations should result in a zero circulation of narcotics – including cannabis – for recreational use. The obligations pertaining to European law are in line with this. These include obligations to criminalize cannabis cultivation for recreational use by third parties and to take the most appropriate measures against that cultivation in order to combat it.

In light of these obligations, legalization or decriminalization of the cultivation of cannabis is not an option under these international instruments. In view of the various prosecution obligations ensuing from the UN drugs conventions and European law with respect to, in principle, serious criminal offences, it is hard to defend criminal policy-based non-prosecution (penal tolerance) of cannabis cultivation for the supply of retail shops as legally permissible on the basis of the prosecutorial expediency principle. The reservation formulated by the Netherlands concerning Article 3 sub 6 of the Illicit Traffic Convention – and therefore not with reference to the Single Convention as well as other obligations ensuing from the Illicit Traffic Convention and the European law framework – does not offer the Netherlands sufficient room for policy-based or any other form of tolerance of cannabis cultivation for recreational use by third parties. This conclusion is based on the content and background of the reservation, international public law according to which reservations are fixed with respect to the law applicable at the time that they are formulated, the 'object and purpose' of the Illicit Traffic Convention, and the view of the International Narcotics Control Board (INCB) that general policy-based penal tolerance of cannabis cultivation for recreational consumption – not designated for personal use – is contrary to the drugs conventions. Moreover, the criminal law expediency principle does not affect the obligations of criminalization or the non-criminal obligations for states ensuing from the UN drugs conventions. Furthermore, it seems reasonable to assume that in view of the considerations of the European Court of Justice, for example, the EU Framework Decision in principle also demands prosecution of the large-scale cultivation or cultivation aimed at illicit trade of cannabis for recreational use. The obligations to prosecute for joint cultivation and consumption in Cannabis Social Clubs, however, is less clear-cut. Although such cultivation cannot be equated with cultivation for private personal use, the connection is such that states are at liberty to refrain from prosecution based on expediency considerations. However, this does not discharge those states from applying the other, mostly non-criminal obligations to combat the cultivation and possession of cannabis.

From a legal perspective, there is no room for a positive answer to the question whether cannabis cultivation intended for recreational use may be placed under the general exception of 'medical and scientific purposes' under the UN drugs conventions. The scope of the exception is far too limited. The exception, therefore, does not comprise public health in a broad sense so that arguments for legalization, decriminalization or regulation of the cannabis market for recreational use meet public health interests, fail against the UN drugs conventions and European law built on these conventions. The fact that this demonstrates the conventions' limited, unilateral and rigid approach to public health interests, does not negate this conclusion. For that matter, the INCB also opposes stretching the exception of medical purposes in order to enable access to cannabis for recreational use.

The assessment of the municipal arguments and foreign jurisdictions' initiatives for regulating cannabis cultivation for recreational use consists of three parts. The first part presents an account and evaluation of the legal arguments. Next, in the same manner, factual, social and/or political arguments are discussed. The third part concerns a discussion and evaluation of the various regulating modalities proposed in the Netherlands and applied in other jurisdictions. The legal arguments mainly aim at amending the conventions, amending the lists of the Single Convention, leaving the convention and consequently re-acceding with formulation of a reservation, allowing for the application of the exception 'medical and scientific' use based on public health interests, and the application of the prosecutorial expediency principle relative to criminal prosecution policy. The conclusion is that permitting cannabis cultivation for the supply of retail shops cannot be implemented on the grounds of the legal arguments provided by Dutch municipalities with due observance of the UN drugs conventions and the EU legal instruments. The factual, social and/or political arguments advance public health and crime control as the most important interests that regulated cannabis cultivation should serve. Many of these arguments reflect the problems that municipalities face relative to the cultivation, distribution, trade, sale, purchase and use of cannabis. Nevertheless, the arguments with regard to public health, crime control and other social interests cannot constitute a legitimacy under international law for permitting cannabis cultivation for recreational use and for the supply of retail shops or other distribution points. The various regulating modalities in the final part of the evaluation include regulated legalization (Uruguay and the US federal states Colorado and Washington), joint cultivation in Cannabis Social Clubs (Belgium, Spain and Uruguay), cannabis cultivation by non-profit growers, cannabis cultivation by licensed commercial parties, and cannabis cultivation for recreational use under the veil of medical or scientific programmes. The conclusion with respect to all these modalities is that the fight-against-drugs framework under international law leaves no room for legalization, decriminalization, policy-based tolerance and/or any other regulating approaches. Only with respect to Cannabis Social Clubs, however, would a state be less likely to be in conflict with the obligations pursuant the UN drugs conventions and European law whenever that state would in fact just leave those Clubs untouched (thus without applying regulating measures or any explicit policy thereto).

The final conclusion is that legalization, decriminalization, policy-based tolerance and/or other forms of regulating cannabis cultivation for the recreational user market is not permissible under the UN narcotic drugs conventions or European law. This also implies that, in view of the international obligations concerning the fight against drugs, there is no room for regulating cannabis cultivation for the supply of retail shops, in relation to Cannabis Social Clubs or through other modalities that serve recreational use by third parties.

ABOUT THE AUTHORS

Piet Hein van Kempen is Full Professor of Criminal Law and Criminal Procedure Law and Dean (since 2018) of the Faculty of Law of Radboud University, Nijmegen, the Netherlands. Van Kempen is also Secretary-General of the International Penal and Penitentiary Foundation (IPPF). Furthermore, he has been a Justice (judge) *ad litem* for fifteen years, and as of 2008, in the Court of Appeals, criminal chamber, 's-Hertogenbosch, the Netherlands. Van Kempen has been a member of various editorial boards, including that of *Delikt en Delinkwent*, the major Dutch Journal on criminal law, criminal procedure law and criminology. He is also a member of the Committee Modernization of the Code of Criminal Procedure, established by the Minister of Justice and Security to advise the legislator. Van Kempen (co)authored, amongst others, numerous books and articles, commentaries and case notes in the field of (national, international, European, transnational and comparative) criminal law and criminal procedural law, penitentiary law and human rights law. More specifically, his research and teaching cover themes such as the effect of European, international and transnational criminal law on national criminal justice systems and the interaction between international and national criminal law and procedure; various substantive and procedural criminal law topics, including legality, *mens rea*, justifications and excuses; the basic principles of the criminal justice system; human rights issues, including positive obligations, fair trial, deprivation of liberty, religion, the rights of prisoners, the position of legal persons; transnational criminal law, including terrorism, corruption and trafficking in human beings, drugs and cultural goods; and fundamental legal questions and the dogmatics, foundations and principles of legal regimes and their systemic quality.

Masha Fedorova is Full Professor of Criminal Law and Criminal Procedure Law and Head of the Department of Criminal Law and Criminology at the Faculty of Law of Radboud University, Nijmegen, the Netherlands. Fedorova is also a part-time judge in the criminal law section of the District Court in 's-Hertogenbosch, the Netherlands. Furthermore, she is a member of the Legal Experts Advisory Panel (LEAP) of Fair Trials International and a member of the editorial board of *Nederlands Tijdschrift voor de Mensenrechten (NTM/NJCM Bulletin)*, one of the leading academic journals on human rights in the Netherlands. Fedorova specializes in Dutch substantive criminal law and criminal procedure law; international, transnational and EU criminal law;

and human rights law (with an emphasis on the UN, EU and ECHR framework). Her principal research interest is the interaction between and mutual influence of these different areas of law. Alongside her research on the international drug control system, she conducted research, amongst others, on the appropriateness of certain legislative initiatives in the Netherlands in the fight against the so-called 'foreign terrorist fighters' from the perspective of fundamental principles of substantive criminal law, human rights law and public international law; on the concepts of fairness and equality of arms in international criminal proceedings; on appeal proceedings in Dutch criminal law and on the fair trial concept and the rights of the defense in Article 6 of the European Convention of Human Rights.

www.ingramcontent.com/pod-product-compliance
Ingram Content Group UK Ltd.
Pitfield, Milton Keynes, MK11 3LW, UK
UKHW051920100926
8556IPUK00021B/1282

9 781780 68871